Accounting Information Systems

Principles, Applications, and Future Directions

MAWDUDUR RAHMAN
Suffolk University

MAURICE HALLADAY
Suffolk University

Prentice Hall, Englewood Cliffs, New Jersey 07632

Library of Congress Cataloging-in-Publication Data

Rahman, Mawdudur.
Accounting information systems : principles, applications, and future directions / Mawdudur Rahman, Maurice Halladay.
p. cm.
Includes bibliographies and index.
ISBN 0-13-001851-1
1. Information storage and retrieval systems—Accounting.
2. Accounting—Data processing. I. Halladay, Maurice (date).
II. Title.
HF5657.R33 1988
657'.028'5—dc19 87-28440
CIP

Editorial/production supervision and interior design: Barbara Grasso
Cover design: Wanda Lubelska
Manufacturing buyer: Ed O'Dougherty

Printed in the United States of America

10 9 8 7 6 5 4 3 2 1

ISBN 0-13-001851-1 01

Prentice-Hall International (UK) Limited, *London*
Prentice-Hall of Australia Pty. Limited, *Sydney*
Prentice-Hall Canada Inc., *Toronto*
Prentice-Hall Hispanoamericana, S.A., *Mexico*
Prentice-Hall of India Private Limited, *New Delhi*
Prentice-Hall of Japan, Inc., *Tokyo*
Simon & Schuster Asia Pte. Ltd., *Singapore*
Editora Prentice-Hall do Brasil, Ltda., *Rio de Janeiro*

To Rashida, Mahmhood, and Sarah

To Janet, John, and Mary

Contents

part three
THE DYNAMICS OF THE AIS

part four
THE AIS AT WORK

Preface

This book provides an introduction to accounting information from the accountant's perspective. In our search for an AIS text to use in undergraduate and MBA courses, we discovered a number of excellent books on the subject that emphasize computerized information systems and use accounting applications liberally. However, these texts are more appropriate for a course in systems analysis than for accounting. They provide a background in systems analysis and design equal to the best texts in the computer information systems curriculum. Our goal is not to compete with these texts, but to emphasize the use of the computer as a *tool* for accountants. This text is designed to assist students in understanding the rationales for developing different forms and types of accounting information; the relationships between and among accounting departments, information services departments, operating departments, and staff agencies of private and public sector organizations; and the several support modes available via emerging computer technologies, along with their capabilities, limitations, and liabilities.

The text is divided into four parts. Part I consists of three introductory chapters. Chapter 1 covers the uses of accounting information. This chapter is particularly useful in broadening the perspective of undergraduate students. Beginning accounting students tend to compartmentalize learning according to the content of courses offered in the different branches of accounting. Chapter 2 provides an overview of the systems approach to analyzing organizations. We find that the systems view clearly represents both the static and dynamic elements of organizations. Chapter 2 uses systems concepts to define the AIS, to provide a distinction between the AIS and its computerized components, and to examine those environmental factors that facilitate AIS success or constrain its development. Chapter 3 briefly reviews basic accounting principles. We have found this to be especially useful for our in-service MBA students, who have relatively weak accounting preparation or who have been away from academia for some time. It is not intended to be a comprehensive accounting review, but rather emphasizes fundamentals. The chapter establishes the basic procedures followed in a manual accounting system and illustrates how these are accomplished via automated procedures available to large and small organizations.

Part II identifies and discusses the essential components of an AIS and the interfaces among them. This section focuses on the static features of the AIS. Chapter 4 deals with the primacy of the accountant in the human-machine relationship. Chapter 5 provides an overview of the hardware available to support accounting requirements. Chapter 6 reviews the levels of software and the generation of software that activates the hardware. Chapter 7 investigates the capabilities and limitations of different data storage configurations.

Part III turns to the more dynamic aspects of the AIS. Chapter 8 considers the relative merits of batch and on-line processing techniques. This is the dynamic of the AIS in the short run—the use of existing capabilities. Chapters 9 and 10 outline the alternatives open to the accountant faced with the need to acquire additional capabilities, given the reality that accounting information requirements change over time. Chapter 9 describes the traditional application development life cycle. Chapter 10 is devoted to more innovative methods of developing or procuring the necessary software for accounting support.

Part IV deals with the practical day-to-day considerations in using AIS to support the needs of management. This section provides an in-depth understanding of the roles of the AIS in supporting management's requirements and objectives at all levels in the organizational hierarchy. The issue of control is emphasized throughout these chapters.

Chapter 11 describes control perspectives in an organization and deals with different operating control frameworks. Chapter 12 is devoted to highlighting the AIS role in management control. Chapter 13 introduces new materials to the AIS subject areas and provides guidance for future directions. Chapter 14 is devoted to internal accounting controls and systems controls.

ACKNOWLEDGMENTS

We wish to extend sincere thanks to our students, who have critically reviewed the materials in this text as we developed them and tested them in the classroom environment. Special thanks go to our graduate assistants Andrea Demetroulakos, Laurie Reichwein, and Mary Ann Ida, who have actively contributed their artistic and editorial talents to this project; to Sara Leefman, manager of the Suffolk University Faculty Resource Unit, who has provided essential secretarial support; to Myra Lerman, who has corrected our sometimes tortured syntax; and to Dean Richard McDowell of the Suffolk University School of Management for making the necessary time and resources available to us to complete this work. Our special thanks are also due to Julie Warner, Barbara Grasso, and their editorial staffs, whose careful attention made this publication possible.

Permission has been received from the Institute of Management Accounting of the National Association of Accountants to use questions and/or unofficial answers from past CMA examinations.

part one

Introduction

A course in accounting information systems deals with the multiple facets of accounting, and integrates organizational aspects relevant to the design, operation, and use of accounting information. Students of accounting learn the technical aspects of the profession from various accounting courses. For example, financial accounting deals with the manipulation of financial transactions that must satisfy relevant accounting principles; cost accounting deals with the process of assigning costs to individual product units, and tax accounting deals with the technicalities of tax computation. The scope of any one of these individual subjects does not include the manipulation of information from an overall systems perspective.

A course in accounting information systems is an evolving subject. It is not solely a data processing course, nor is it limited to computer-assisted functions. It requires a multidisciplinary perspective on the design, implementation, and use of machine-processed information.

An accounting information system integrates accounting techniques with data processing hardware and software, managerial decision-making processes, and human behavior and motivation. Thus the subject matter of the course relies on tools, techniques, and theories from other subjects in a business curriculum. The study of AIS helps students to relate different accounting functions to a common base and to use the knowledge acquired from other subject areas. More specifically, it helps them to:

1. Identify effective ways to report and communicate financial information
2. Identify efficient techniques of data manipulation
3. Satisfy organizational needs and environmental constraints in accounting reporting
4. Understand the distinction between data processing and an accounting information system
5. Relate more effectively to other people, departments, and functions
6. Develop a broader organizational outlook

chapter one

Accounting Information Systems—An Overview

CHAPTER OUTLINE

INTRODUCTION

Accounting is a service function. It provides financial information to people inside and outside the organization who need and are authorized to have such information. A *system,* in the most general sense of the word, is a group of interrelated components that processes inputs into outputs to meet some objective. An accounting information system (AIS), then, is a group of components that processes raw data into financial information to meet the purposes of these internal and external users. In this general sense, accounting is and always has been an information system; however, when we speak of accounting information systems today, we invariably refer to computer-assisted techniques.

The accounting profession has evolved slowly, over a long period of time. Control and auditability have been the hallmarks of this evolution. Automated information systems have burgeoned in modern society at a rate unparalleled by any comparable technological development in history. Rapid change, technological obsolescence, and exponential expansion have been the hallmarks of this revolution. The study of AIS is an exercise in understanding how these two apparently conflicting disciplines complement each other in the service of an organization's objectives.

This book focuses on the uses and production of accounting information in an organization and its environment. Chapter 1 discusses the uses of accounting information and defines the characteristics accounting information must possess if it is to be usable. It also lays the foundation for considering the AIS in systems terms.

We lack a uniform, accepted systems definition of AIS, and opinions differ about the proper scope of its subject matter. We will develop a systems definition of the AIS in Chapter 2; here an AIS can be viewed as a measurement, manipulation, and communications system.[1] Its task is to assign quantitative values to past, present, and future economic events. The accounting process measures economic events for an entity and relates them to different time periods. It combines these elements into a usable form by applying commonly agreed upon rules and principles.

To get a clear picture of the scope of AIS activity, we need to look at how accounting data are used. Two useful classifications of accounting have been proposed:

[1] Committee on Foundations of Accounting Measurement. *Accounting Review,* supplement, XLVI, AAA, 1971, p. 3. The Committee stated that "... accounting measurement is an assignment of numerals to an entity's past, present or future economic phenomena, on the basis of observation and according to rules."

1. Operational accounting
2. Equity accounting[2]

Operational accounting is concerned with the use of accounting information for decision making by managers and investors. It is oriented toward the future, because decisions made by managers and investors relate to future goals and expectations.

Equity accounting focuses on the safeguarding and settlement of the economic rights and obligations of different groups of interests. It is used to establish social, organizational, and individual equity, and to support custodial functions. A manager uses equity accounting when performing custodial functions, and operational accounting when making resource allocation decisions. An investor performs no custodial functions; his or her interests revolve around resource allocation. The investor uses operational accounting information, such as dividends per share, net income, and price-earnings ratio, for decision making. Managerial accounting and externally reported financial reporting fall within the category of operational accounting.

OBJECTIVES OF FINANCIAL ACCOUNTING

The objectives of financial accounting are embodied in the question: "What is accounting?" Accounting is an information system. The objective of financial accounting, then, is to provide useful information for making economic decisions. The process of recording, aggregating, and summarizing the effects of historical transactions in financial statements under a specified set of rules constitutes the bulk of financial accounting. Financial accounting serves its users through a well-defined and closely controlled process.

Financial accounting reports primarily serve external users. Some external users, such as government agencies, have the authority to prescribe their information needs. Others lack such authority and use the accounting information available through general purpose reports. Investors and creditors are the major users in this latter category. If general purpose reports are to be useful to these groups, the reports should

[2] For further discussion of operational accounting and equity accounting, see the Committee on Foundations of Accounting Measurement, op. cit., p. 6. Other sources are Yuji Ijiri, *The Foundations of Accounting Measurement* (Englewood Cliffs, N.J.: Prentice-Hall, 1967), and Gjesdal Fraystein, "Accounting for Stewardship," *Journal of Accounting Research,* 19 (1981), pp. 208–231.

1. Support investment and credit decisions
2. Provide cash flow information
3. Provide information on the quality and changes in the enterprise's resources and claims

In using financial accounting information in investment and loan decisions, investors and creditors evaluate these aspects of a business:

1. Profitability: Will the enterprise make a profit in the future?
2. Liquidity: Will the enterprise be able to pay current obligations from current assets?
3. Solvency: Does the enterprise have enough resources to pay off its debts?
4. Stability: Does the enterprise have control over its debt, and do sales revenues confirm market demand for its products?
5. Growth: What is the growth potential? This potential is demonstrated by sales growth, new product development, and introduction of new technology.

To satisfy the needs of these users, general purpose accounting reports contain nonaccounting information. However, the reports do not provide an evaluation of an enterprise or of managerial performance. Users must make their own evaluations, estimates, and predictions. Even the best accounting information cannot replace users' judgment.

OBJECTIVES OF MANAGERIAL ACCOUNTING

Managerial accounting is concerned with accounting information useful for decision making. The managerial accounting process includes identifying the managerial decisions where accounting information is needed, developing the essential information, analyzing that information by applying appropriate techniques, and reporting the results of the analysis. Managerial accounting assists in planning and control decisions through measurement and feedback of financial and nonfinancial information. The National Association of Accountants (NAA) defines managerial accounting as "the process of identification, measurement, accumulation, analysis, preparation, interpretation, and communication of financial information used by management to plan, evaluate and control within an organization and to assure appropriate use of and accountability for its resources. Management accounting also comprises the preparation of financial reports for nonmanagement groups such as shareholders, creditors, regulatory agencies and tax authorities."[3] Figure 1–1 illustrates the objectives, activities, and processes of managerial accounting.

[3] NAA Statement Number 113, June 19, 1983, "Objectives of Management Accounting."

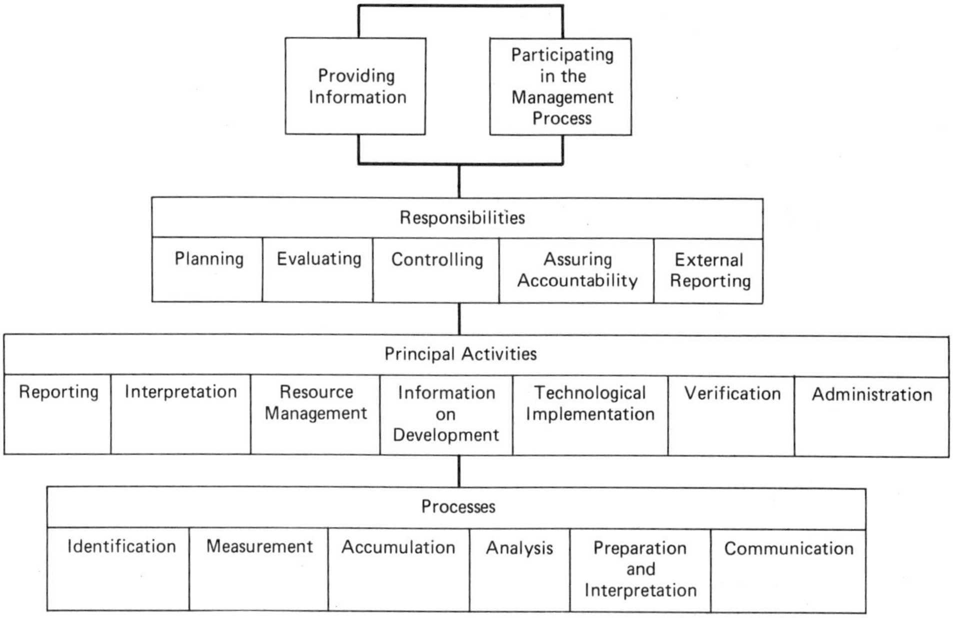

FIGURE 1–1 Objectives of Management Accounting
Source: NAA Statement No. 113, *Objectives of Management Accounting,* June 17, 1982.

Management accountants may have different titles, organizational positions, and functions. However, in most cases their functions involve two tasks:

1. Providing information
2. Participating in the decision-making process

In varying degrees, management accountants are responsible for (1) planning, (2) evaluating, (3) controlling, (4) establishing accountability, and (5) external reporting. These responsibilities are met by performing the activities of (1) reporting, (2) interpreting, (3) managing resources, (4) developing information systems, (5) implementing new technology, (6) verifying accuracy of data and information, and (7) administering their segment of the organization.

AIS AND MIS

AIS and Management Information Systems (MIS) have developed somewhat in parallel in business organizations. The considerable controversy that exists in regard to the boundaries and relationships between these support activities is illustrated in the following three views:

1. AIS is a subset of MIS. Those who hold this position consider AIS a measurement system for external parties. The primary tasks of AIS are considered to be the production of income statements, balance sheets, and statements of changes in financial position. AIS is considered a subset of MIS, fulfilling the external reporting needs of financial accounting data. This view stems from the traditional role of financial accounting.

2. MIS is a subset of AIS. This opposite view is held by certain accounting educators and professionals who argue that accounting has a much broader scope and is not limited to external reporting. Accounting data play significant roles in internal planning and control purposes. For example, budgets are used in planning and control decisions at different levels of an organization. A big part of management information is financial in nature, and all managerial decisions, in the end, culminate in accounting numbers. Thus, management can best be served by developing MIS as a subset of AIS. This view often stems from the fact that computers were first introduced into organizations via the Accounting Department.

3. The third view is that AIS and MIS are interdependent systems with significant overlap. AIS is not a subsystem of MIS, nor is MIS a subset of AIS. Both must work together to meet the information needs of management and external users. This is the view of this book. We shall emphasize the role of AIS, but we will repeatedly caution that AIS exists to serve a large number of internal and external interests and that it is affected and constrained by these interests.

ATTRIBUTES AND PRINCIPLES OF ACCOUNTING INFORMATION

The *attributes* of accounting information refer to the qualities necessary to satisfy users' needs. Two essential qualities for general purpose accounting reports supplied to external users are (a) relevance and (b) reliability.

To be useful, information must be relevant. Relevance of accounting information is judged in relation to the users' situation. For example, a comparative balance sheet giving data for two consecutive years provides relevant information for the average user. However, comparative data for more years may not be relevant unless one is willing to evaluate trends, adjust for price level changes, and do extensive research into company, industry, and economic factors.

If one is evaluating the liquidity position of an enterprise, the relevant accounting information includes data on current assets and current liabilities, and qualitative information about them. Annual accounting reports provide relevant information for liquidity evaluation. Note that a great deal of other accounting information is available—for example, net income or earnings per share (EPS). EPS is a measure of return on stockholders' investment. If one is interested in profitability, net income data and EPS data are relevant accounting information. However, they are not relevant for liquidity evaluation. Historical accounting information supplied by general purpose accounting reports is relevant for assessing past performance only; to predict future profitability or liquidity, one has to use forecasts that are not usually included in accounting reports.

Accounting information must also be reliable. Reliability in accounting information signifies faithfulness, constancy, and trustworthiness. One way of ensuring reliability in accounting information is to ensure adherence to accounting principles. An independent audit of accounting reports checks on the reliability of the information provided in these reports. For example, in income reporting, only relevant and reliable revenue and expense items are included. Relevant revenue items are those that belong to the period of reporting and are earned through the transfer of goods or services. Reliable revenue items are those that have supporting documents, such as sales invoices, as verifiable objective evidence.

The Hierarchy of Accounting Attributes

Figure 1–2 shows the hierarchy of accounting attributes as presented in FASB Concept No. 2 and further breaks down the accounting qualities. Relevance is subdivided into (a) predictive value, (b) feedback value, and (c) timeliness. Relevant accounting information assists users in predicting the future, provides feedback on past decisions, and is available when needed.

An example will be useful in explaining these qualities. Investors use EPS data to assess the future earnings potential of an enterprise because EPS data have predictive value. Investors can assess the quality of their past decisions by looking at present EPS data. And, needless to add, the EPS data must be available at the appropriate time to be used for either of these functions.

The reliability quality has been subdivided into (a) verifiability, (b) representational faithfulness, and (c) neutrality. Earlier, we noted that one virtue of accounting information is that it is verifiable; it has some form of verifiable, objective evidence to support it. We shall see that automation of accounting functions significantly alters what constitutes verifiable, objective evidence. Accounting information must faithfully represent the financial position of an enterprise. Thus, accounting information has to be a close approximation of the state of the entity to satisfy the reliability test. Neutrality refers to the

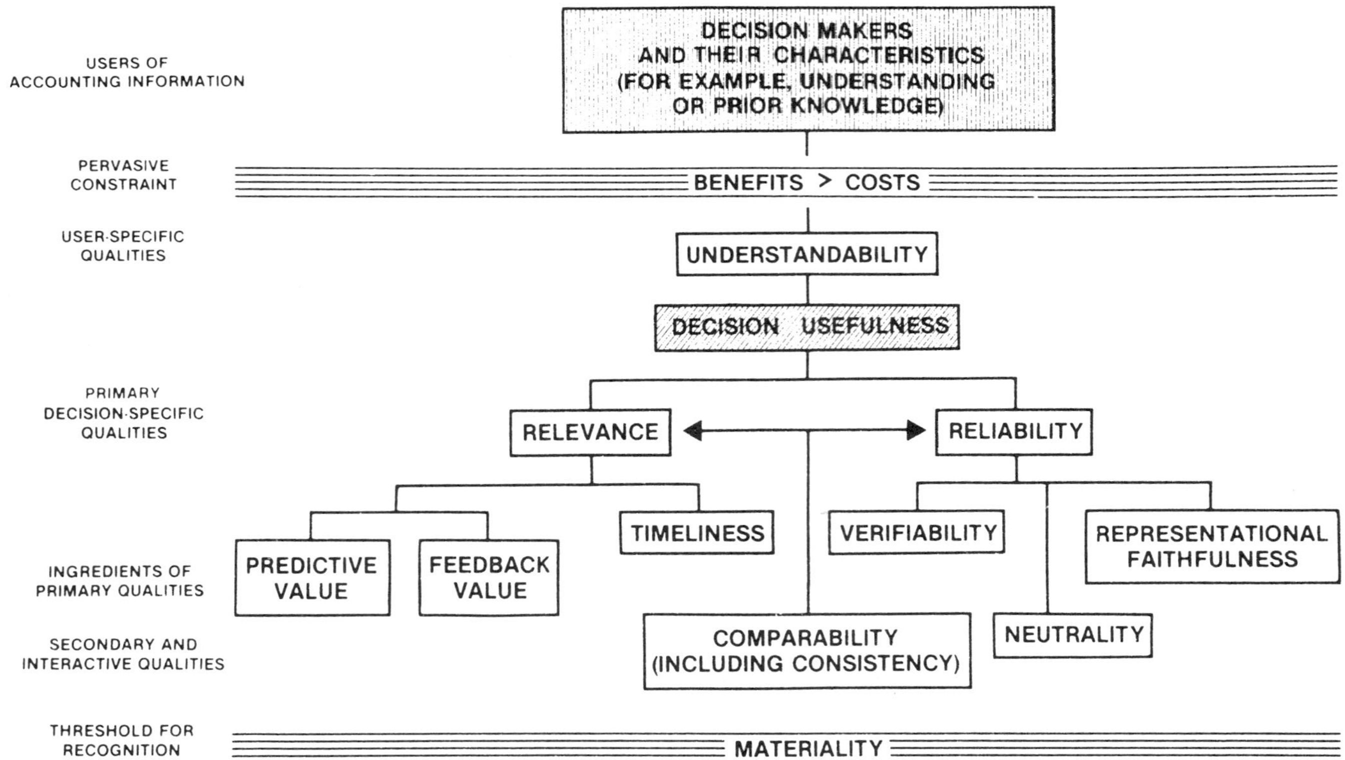

FIGURE 1–2 A Hierarchy of Accounting Qualities

Source: Reproduced from FASB Concepts Statement No. 2, *Qualitative Characteristics of Accounting Information.* Copyright 1980 by Financial Accounting Standards Board, High Ridge Park, Stamford, Connecticut 06905, U.S.A. Reprinted with permission. Copies of the complete document are available from the FASB.

unbiased estimation of facts. For example, when an income statement is prepared, the result may be a profit or a loss. An income statement should not be prepared with the objective of showing a profit. Any statement prepared with such an objective would not present an unbiased estimate of the facts—it would fail the neutrality test and be useless.

Level of Detail

Determining the appropriate level of accounting detail is always a problem. The task of processing accounting information has costs attached to it. An increase in accounting detail results in an increase in costs which may or may not result in a corresponding increase in benefits. If one is not careful, the benefits derived from additional accounting information may not be worth the costs. For example, to reduce accounting work and other processing costs, many companies record small items, like nails and glue used in production, as *indirect costs*. These costs, though directly traceable to production, are not recorded and treated as direct costs because the additional effort required to do so is not justified by the benefits derived. Other examples are material-related costs, fringe benefits for labor, and personnel-related costs. These costs are treated as indirect costs in many situations to avoid the considerable recordkeeping required to trace them directly to production. Benefit-cost considerations thus set limits on the level of detail in recordkeeping tasks.

At the other end, the principle of materiality sets limits on the units of records. Accounting units of records are *material facts*. Material facts have been defined in FASB Concept No. 2 as:

> The magnitude of an omission or misstatement of accounting information that in the light of surrounding circumstances makes it probable that the judgment of a reasonable person relying on the information would have been changed or influenced by the omission or misstatement.

The statement indicates that materiality is a judgment factor. Sometimes a small dollar amount is material, and sometimes figures may be rounded to the nearest thousand without affecting materiality. What is a material fact depends on the surrounding factors and the situation.

Conservatism

Conservatism is another significant principle in accounting. Conservatism stems from uncertainty about future events. Most accounting statements include some estimates, such as allowances for uncollectible accounts receivable or lower of cost or market inventory valuation. Prudent accountants know that all accounts receivable are not collectible—some will eventually become bad debts. These amounts need to be estimated and shown as a necessary reduction from revenue before net profits are derived and distributed to guard against future losses from current credit sales. Selection of lower of cost or market method is also based on the principle of conservatism. In the past, the rule was: "Anticipate no profit and provide for all possible loss." This has changed. Today, conservatism means cautious optimism, not deliberate understatement. The conservatism principle is difficult to describe and evaluate because of the dependence on individual judgment. What it means in practice is that the prudent accountant must exercise care and not underestimate or overestimate accounting numbers deliberately.

Accounting Data as Surrogates

Accounting measures are estimates of economic events; it is not possible to provide an actual representation of events through accounting measures. Thus accounting measures are not treated as actual measures—they are taken as substitutes for actual measures. There are reasons for this. For example, subjective judgment is often necessary in accounting measures. In addition, accounting measures consider only monetary value. But other criteria of measurement are necessary for complete understanding. Therefore, we substitute what we can measure for what we would like ideally to measure. A substitute measure is called a *surrogate*. Since accounting measures are substitute measures, we refer to them as accounting surrogates.

Need for Detailed and Aggregated Data

The multiple uses of accounting require data to be provided as both detailed and aggregate measures. Accounting data as detailed measures are most often used at the level of data generation. For example, production cost data like material use, waste, and labor hours are detailed measures used at the shop floor, where they are generated. Accounting data as aggregate measures are available at various levels to meet the needs of multiple users. For example, production cost data may be aggregated at an immediate level for use in production cost control and inventory valuation. It may be further aggregated for use in product pricing and internal rate of return determinations. Finally, it may be aggregated into a single value for reports to external users.

Time Period of Accounting Information

Conventional accounting deals with historical data. Accounting information systems, in providing data for economic decisions, deal with past, present, and future events. The need for future data has been stressed by the Trueblood Committee: "In other words, accountability requires that information be provided about potential as well as actual results. Quite apart from any need to predict, users are better served when they have information about the present and future as well as the past" (The Trueblood Committee, AICPA, 1973).

Thus, a user-oriented accounting information system covers past, present, and future events in order to serve users' information needs.

The Value of Accounting Information

The value of any information depends on two factors: (a) its accuracy, and (b) its ability to reduce uncertainty.[4]

Accuracy is defined as the degree of mapping from the events to the data. When accounting data closely represent the measured events, the data are said to have high accuracy and the value of information based on the data increases. On the other hand, data that do not represent the measured events closely cannot be used to develop valuable information.

Uncertainty is a characteristic of any decision situation. One major objective of information is to reduce uncertainty. Thus, initial uncertainty in a decision situation increases the value of information. Accounting data are useful and of value when they have the potential to reduce uncertainty in a decision situation. The costs of collecting additional information must always be balanced against the value expected.

USERS OF ACCOUNTING INFORMATION SYSTEMS

A wide variety of people within and outside the organization use accounting information for decision making. Accounting information is useful in all types of organizations: a business organization, a not-for-profit organization, or a government agency. The survival and growth of an organization depend, to a large extent, on supplying effective accounting information to internal and external users. The size of an organization determines the appropriate volume and complexity of accounting information for managerial decisions in such areas as purchasing, production, hiring, borrowing, and investment.

[4] R. W. Hilton and R. J. Swieringa, "Perceptions of Initial Uncertainty as a Determinant of Information Value," *Journal of Accounting Research,* 19 (1981), pp. 109–119. For further discussion of accounting and uncertainty, see Charles T. Horngren, *Cost Accounting—A Managerial Emphasis,* 5th ed. (Englewood Cliffs, N.J.: Prentice-Hall, 1982), pp. 720–730.

TABLE 1–1 Cost Statement: The Machine Shop of XYZ Company

	Machine Shop No. XT203	*Supervisor R. M. Wise, Week 10/Mar. 15, 1982*	
		Actual	*Actual Month*
No.	*Account*	*This Period*	*to Date*
1000	Direct labor		
1010	Lathe operator	$ 565	$1020
1020	Punch press operator	620	1115
1030	Grinding machine operator	120	250
	Total direct labor	$1305	$2385

This report usually includes budgets and various statistics which have been deleted to keep the report simple at this stage.

Outsiders who use accounting information include creditors, shareholders, regulatory agencies, government data-gathering agencies, economists, trade unions, customers, industry analysts, and potential investors. Most accounting systems tend to concentrate on meeting the needs of managers, creditors, and shareholders and to ignore the remaining users.

Internal Users

Internal users of accounting information work for the organization. They usually have some managerial or supervisory responsibilities in a line or staff function. Production or marketing are typical line functions. Staff functions include activities such as accounting, data processing, and planning. A production foreman, a line supervisor, a plant manager, a division manager, and a production vice president are examples of internal users. The types of information used by people in an organization vary according to the function and level of the user. For example, the production foreman will be interested in daily and weekly cost reports showing details such as those presented in Table 1–1; the production vice president will be interested in corporation-wide reports of budget and performance data such as those shown in Table 1–2.

TABLE 1–2 Factory Cost Summary: Vice President, Production, XYZ Company

	This Month	*Year to Date*
Departments	*Amount*	*Amount*
Administrative expenses	$10,000	$ 30,000
Machining department	52,000	150,000
Finishing department	12,000	40,000
Assembly department	6,000	20,000
	$80,000	$240,000

To avoid complexity, budget items and other conceptual elements were excluded at this stage.

External Users

Organizations supply accounting information to outsiders to meet regulatory needs, business needs and to inform others interested in the affairs of the organization. External users are interested in the accounting information of a firm for a variety of reasons. External users include present and potential stockholders, government agencies, banks, trade unions, and professional institutions. Government agencies commonly include the Internal Revenue Service (IRS), the Federal Trade Commission (FTC), and the Securities and Exchange Commission (SEC). Accounting information needs of government agencies are met by supplying information on special forms for each agency. The needs of other users are normally met by the corporation's routine published reports.

Privately held companies, nonprofit organizations, and government agencies do not face the same external reporting requirements as publicly owned companies. However, they do encounter varying reporting requirements and have to consider external users' needs. The accounting information systems of these organizations have goals similar to those of the publicly owned companies, but they may have significantly different output requirements.

THE ROLES OF ACCOUNTANTS IN THE AIS

Accountants perform a wide variety of roles relating to accounting, financial, and information systems functions within an organization. The position designations of accountants depend on the functional roles they perform (a list of typical position descriptions is given in Chapter 4). An accountant may specialize in any branch of accounting—financial, cost, governmental, tax, investment. He or she will be concerned with specific tasks within these branches, such as fixed assets, cash, payroll, inventory, billing, general ledger. At the lower end of the hierarchy, accounting clerks, supervisors, and managers perform these and related subtasks. Upper-level managers and controllers work in broader areas such as financial accounting, cost accounting, or managerial accounting. Many large organizations have a systems branch that specializes in translating accounting needs into data processing specifications and performing other liaison tasks with the information systems group.

An AIS covers accounting functions at all levels from data entry to control and reporting. An accountant working in any specific accounting function needs expertise to manipulate the system effectively. Depending on the nature of the work, an accountant should be able to recognize valid data, make required inputs, perform functional manipulations, generate reports, and interpret results.

To be an accountant today requires:

1. Expertise in functional area accounting
2. Computer competence and understanding of applications software
3. A clear understanding of how the accounting system works
4. An awareness of the business as a whole

The modern AIS has expanded the roles of accountants in many ways. Accountants not only manipulate larger volumes of data and generate more timely reports in a wider variety of formats, but also share greater responsibility for personal interactions, data processing, hardware and software acquisitions, and for coordination inside and outside the accounting domain.

The development of accounting information systems has increased the importance of accounting functions and the responsibilities of accountants. This, in turn, has contributed to the prestige of the profession.

SYSTEMS CONCEPTS AND THE AIS

The systems approach to studying organizations has proved to be an excellent method of gaining insight into organizational structures and processes. *Systems* may be viewed as static structures consisting of a number of components that interact in pursuit of some goal, or they may be viewed as dynamic entities that accept inputs from the environment, process these inputs in some manner, and return the modified product as an output to the environment. Another key concept of the systems view is that every system exists in a hierarchy of systems. We will use the static property of systems to examine the components of the AIS, the dynamic property to examine the interactions of the AIS with its environment, and the hierarchical property to determine how the goals of the AIS must be in consonance with the goals of its organizational suprasystem. We will be particularly concerned with the computer-assisted components and subsystems of the more broadly defined AIS.

Functional Departments and the Systems View

The traditional organization chart divides the organization neatly into functional departments. Titles and tasks depend upon the type of organization. For example, marketing, manufacturing, engineering, personnel, and planning departments are typical of production organizations, and we are all familiar with the admissions, student aid, bursar, registrar, and academic departments typical of universities.

The systems approach deliberately minimizes references to these functional departments. This approach is particularly useful in the study of information flows, as data and information, especially in the financial field, should be viewed as resources belonging to the organization as a whole. Effective development and use of information systems generally transcends traditional boundaries. Nevertheless, history, technology, and economics have conspired to produce information systems along departmental lines in many organizations, and we would be doing the reader a disservice if we failed to address this issue. Most organizations today have an information system for each department. We find, among others, marketing information systems, materials requirements planning information systems, human resources information systems, and, of course, accounting information systems. This development is a consequence of viewing organizations as they are shown in the organizational chart.

The tendency to follow functional lines has been further reinforced by technological and economic factors. Early computer technology was constrained by the storage capabilities of magnetic tape. This type of storage encouraged, and in many cases dictated, establishing an individual file for each application. Applications were often viewed in a narrow functional sense; for example, it was common to automate a particular desk procedure, with little thought to its broader context. A marketing application might thus have a set of marketing files, a production application a set of production files, and each of the accounting functions its own set of files. The manager or systems analyst who wished to retrieve information scattered about in the resulting maze of files faced a formidable task. Excessive fragmentation of data persists in many organizations despite a widespread move to magnetic disk storage, a medium that facilitates wider views of data.

Compartmentalization of data is also promoted by the internal budgeting process. Most organizations charge back the cost of information systems development and operations to their users. This is an effective means of controlling computer costs; however, it promotes a departmental, or even a branch level, sense of ownership of data, applications programs, and the resulting information. This pattern of development tends to obscure the need for lateral flow of information within an organization and often results in a less than optimal use of information resources.

To be effective, accountants must maintain a broad view of organizational capabilities. Throughout this text we will maintain the systems view of the organization, which emphasizes the flow of data and information necessary to support organizational effectiveness and efficiency. We recognize the reality of departmental information systems, but emphasize the need for interfaces between and among the various information system components. We strongly believe this to be the way to improved organizational use of information resources. A review of current trends in information systems suggests that there is a strong tide running in this direction in most modern organizations. This tide was temporarily stemmed in the early 1980s with the introduction of stand-alone microcomputers; however, users soon found that they needed to use more data and information than they could economically gather singlehandedly, and they then sought access to centralized databases.

Managerial Levels and the Systems View

Anthony[5] has proposed a systems framework based on the organizational level of planning and control activities in large human organizations. This framework has proved useful in the analysis of organizations, and we have adopted it as part of the basic framework of this text. Three levels of activity are identified in Anthony's scheme: strategic planning, management control, and operational control. Although there is some overlap between the levels, and some activities span the boundaries between them, the levels are sufficiently distinct to merit definition and analytic use.

Strategic Planning. Strategic planning is defined as "the process of deciding on objectives of the organization, on changes in these objectives, on the resources used to attain these objectives, and on the policies that are to govern the acquisition, use, and disposition of these resources."[6]

The strategic planning process uses external and internal sources of information. It develops answers to such general questions as "What are the needs of society that this organization can fulfill effectively with the resources at its command?" In the business world, the answer to this type of question is determined, in large part, by market forces. The general question resolves into more specific ones, such as "What product lines should we continue/expand/delete?" "Should we expand capacity by building a new plant or acquiring an existing company?" "Should we finance new growth by debt or equity?" In the nonprofit sector, strategic planning depends upon a political process. For example, the board of governors of a university may establish goals and objectives based on the recommendations of the university faculty and administration and upon independent assessments of economic and demographic conditions. Strategic questions might include these:

[5] Robert N. Anthony, *Planning and Control Systems: A Framework for Analysis* (Cambridge, MA: Harvard University Press, 1965).

[6] Ibid.

"What rates of growth in student population should we target for the next five years?" "What should the university policy be in regard to acquiring information systems hardware?"

In the government sector, strategic planning, if it is to be effective, must transcend party politics. This can often be achieved at the goal-setting level, but legitimate differences of opinion, policy selection, and priorities often produce vacillation that would be fatal in the other sectors. For example, at the national level, both parties can agree that two of the long-term goals should be to maintain an adequate national defense and to eliminate poverty. The means selected and the resources committed to reach these goals will vary widely, depending on the administration. A similar problem can be identified at virtually all levels of government.

The common element in strategic planning in all sectors is that it depends on elements over which the organization has little control. Strategic planning is an effort to adapt. Many of the inputs to the strategic planning process originate in the environment of the system under consideration. Nevertheless, if the strategic plan is to be viable, it must also have inputs based on the history of the organization, the current status of the assets and capabilities of the organization, and the trends in operations of the organization. The AIS plays a significant role in providing these internally generated inputs.

Management Control. Management control is defined as "the process by which managers assure that resources are obtained and used effectively and efficiently in the accomplishment of the organization's objectives."[7] Note that at this level, the organization's objectives are a given. Management control involves the selection and definition of processes, but it does not involve the selection of objectives or the determination of policy. Management control includes a large planning element; however, this planning determines how fast an objective should be achieved, not what the objective should be. Management, in general, involves making progress toward objectives via the effective use of resources. Typical questions at the management control level are these: "Are sales in the western territory ahead of budget?" "Do current cost data support our standard costing estimates?" "Are our personnel policies consistent with equal opportunity requirements?"

Almost all the information used in management control is generated internally. Planning at this level is frequently translated into budget terms, and the budget is usually based on some projection of historical data. Control is exercised in the form of analyzing and correcting deviations from the plan. All this activity is heavily dependent on the AIS.

[7] Ibid.

Operational Control. We may define operational control as the process of assuring that specific tasks are carried out efficiently. At this level, goals have been specified and methods of attaining these goals determined. What remains is to use the available resources in the most productive manner. Some discretion may remain, particularly in those organizations that define tasks broadly and encourage some form of participative management; nevertheless, the operational controller is concerned primarily with executing tasks with the minimum expenditure of resources. Typically, computers were introduced into organizations to support the efficiency concerns of operational control. Even the earliest machines were faster, less error-prone, and less costly than a battery of bookkeepers working with electromechanical tabulators. In most modern organizations, operational control of financial resources is totally dependent upon automated support. Operational control of other resources has tended to lag behind developments in the financial sector, but recent improvements in the automation of human resource management, material resources planning, production planning, and computer-assisted design are rapidly narrowing this gap.

THE COMPUTER AND ACCOUNTING INFORMATION IN HISTORICAL PERSPECTIVE

The computer was initially introduced into most organizations to satisfy the efficiency concerns of processing vast amounts of accounting transaction data at the operational control level. It has proved so effective in this role that virtually no sizable organization can survive competitive pressures without using this tool. Throughout the 1970s, computer technology limited the production of accounting information to predetermined formats. These standard reports were usually adequate to support the needs of external users and many of the internal functions of management control. The introduction of microcomputers in the early 1980s brought a rapid rise in the computer literacy of all levels of management and contributed to the development of a new class of programs aimed specifically at meeting the needs of strategic management. Many of these programs are based on accounting information processed by the AIS. Figure 1–3 is a graphic depiction of the growth of the AIS in a typical business organization.

The scope of today's AIS is influenced by two factors: (1) the rapid growth of information processing technology, and (2) the increased complexity of business in general. The AIS of the foreseeable future must establish and maintain the capability for complex manipulation of vast volumes of financial and nonfinancial data with higher speed and greater accuracy than ever before.

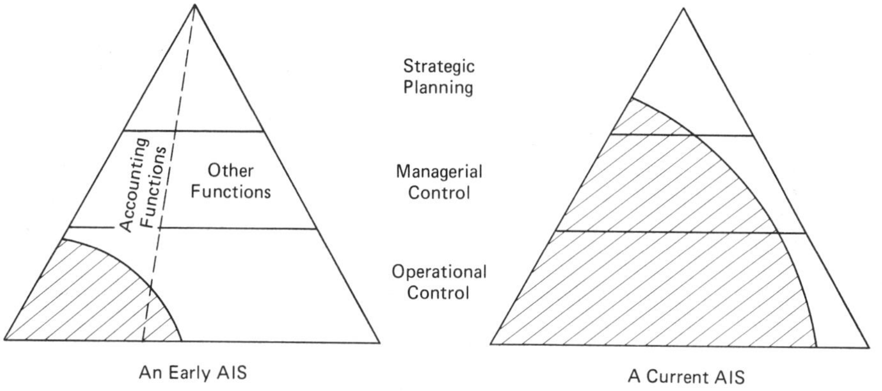

FIGURE 1–3 The Growth of the AIS

The enhanced power of data handling in a complex environment has altered the character of the AIS. The AIS of the past was little more than bookkeeping which relied on electronic devices of limited capability and required a great deal of human involvement at almost every step of the process. Such an AIS was not able to cope with the dynamic challenges of business complexity. Its products were unable to satisfy users' needs for planning and control information. The primary concern of the AIS was to manipulate historical data, satisfy audit needs, produce after-the-fact financial statements, and provide preformatted reports for managerial use.

Today's AIS deals with future events as well as historical data. It must produce projected financial statements as well as historical ones. It must support unanticipated managerial needs for financial information for decision making, in addition to satisfying the needs of auditors. It must develop new and efficient controls, reporting techniques, and audit trails in response to the trends toward increasing public access to accounting data and reports. As a simple example, consider the monthly statements provided to bank customers. These must incorporate detailed information about numerous transactions performed in a variety of ways from a number of locations. A bank cannot survive today without providing this level of service; yet the capability to do so did not exist even a few years ago.

SUMMARY

This chapter has introduced you to the uses of accounting information. We have seen that there are two general classes of accounting information, equity accounting and operational accounting. Our primary focus will be operational accounting. Operational accounting includes financial accounting and managerial accounting. Financial accounting has both internal and external uses. It is used internally to track progress at the micro level. It is used externally for a wide variety of purposes. These vary from government use to ensure compliance with regulations to investor use to determine the desirability of the company's stock. Not-for-profit organizations also maintain financial and managerial accounting systems; however, their reporting requirements vary from those of publicly held companies. Managerial accounting is used exclusively for internal planning and control purposes.

Two essential qualities of accounting information are relevance and reliability. Relevance can be subdivided into predictive value, feedback value, and timeliness. Reliability can be subdivided into verifiability, representational faithfulness, and neutrality. In addition, accounting information must meet tests of its benefits-to-costs ratio, materiality, and conservatism.

Accounting data are surrogate measures in that they cannot capture the full reality of the events they represent. The data may be highly detailed or aggregated at various levels according to its intended use. It may deal with past, present, and future events. The value of accounting information depends upon its accuracy and its ability to reduce uncertainty.

Although the information systems of many organizations developed along functional lines, a systems view of information needs and information systems is gaining popularity. The uses of accounting information and the applicability of computer-assisted processing can be related to three levels of organizational control. The computer is indispensable to operational control; it has a lengthy history of assistance in decision making at the managerial control level; and it has recently become an effective aid to strategic management.

REVIEW QUESTIONS, DISCUSSION QUESTIONS, AND PROBLEMS AND CASES

A. Review Questions

A1.1 Why is accounting called a service function? What is the task of an accounting system?

A1.2 What is an accounting information system? What type of information does an accounting information system deal with?

A1.3 Why is accounting information used? Define (a) operational accounting, and (b) equity accounting.

A1.4 What are the three views of the relationship between an AIS and an MIS?

A1.5 "AIS is a subset of MIS." Do you agree? Give your reasons.

A1.6 "MIS is a subset of AIS." Do you agree? Why or why not?

A1.7 "AIS and MIS are independent." Do you agree? Why or why not?

A1.8 What does an accounting system measure? Why are accounting data called surrogates?

A1.9 What accounting data are detail and aggregate measures? Give some examples where aggregate accounting data are used.

A1.10 What is the need for future accounting data?

A1.11 "The value of information depends on (1) accuracy and (2) uncertainty." Define "accuracy" and "uncertainty" in this context.

A1.12 Who are the outside users of accounting information? Why does an organization supply information to outsiders?

A1.13 (a) Who are the internal users of accounting information? (b) Define and provide examples of line managers and staff managers.

A1.14 Why are external users interested in the accounting information of a firm? Of a nonprofit organization? Of a government agency?

A1.15 What are the essential attributes of accounting information?

A1.16 What are the two essential qualities that influence general purpose accounting reports?

A1.17 Define (1) relevance and (2) reliability in relation to accounting information.

A1.18 What are the three ingredients of the relevance quality of accounting information?

A1.19 What are the three ingredients of the reliability quality of accounting information?

A1.20 What is materiality? Why is it important?

A1.21 Classify the accounting qualities as (a) user-specific and (b) decision-specific.

A1.22 Explain benefit-cost and materiality considerations for accounting.

A1.23 Define three broad concepts that apply to using the systems approach to study organizations.

A1.24 What is meant by a hierarchy of systems?

A1.25 What is the static view of a system?

A1.26 What is the dynamic view of a system?

A1.27 Name three factors that have contributed to the development of information systems along functional lines.

A1.28 What is the functional view of organizations?

A1.29 What are Anthony's three managerial levels? Explain each briefly.

A1.30 Why were computers initially very successful at the operational control level? Has this changed with advancing technology?

A1.31 How did the role of the computer in the AIS change between the mid-1970s and the late 1980s? What factors permitted this change? What factors caused it?

B. Discussion Questions

B1.1 "A manager uses operational accounting when he or she makes resource allocation decisions and uses equity accounting when he or she performs custodial functions." Discuss.

B1.2 "AIS and MIS have considerable overlap between them." Identify areas of overlap and discuss their relevance.

B1.3 Conventional accounting data are historical, but decision makers need past, present, and future data. Discuss the scope of the AIS with reference to the time period of accounting information.

B1.4 "External and internal users of accounting information have different information needs. Sometimes it is difficult to meet all of them." Discuss. How would you establish priorities in those cases where all needs cannot be met?

B1.5 In spite of the significant and extensive overlap among financial, cost, and managerial accounting, organizations usually maintain these three subsystems. Why do you think this is done?

B1.6 What is relevant information? How is the relevance of accounting information judged? Why is relevance so important for accounting information?

B1.7 What does the hierarchy of accounting qualities explain? Does it serve any integrative purpose?

B1.8 Why is benefit-cost a "constraint" and materiality a "threshold point" for accounting information?

B1.9 Is it important to have a clear understanding of the foundations of accounting to appreciate accounting information fully? Why or why not?

B1.10 Discuss the interaction between technological developments in information processing and the complexity of business needs for information. Do these factors tend to reinforce one another?

C. Problems and Cases

C1.1 Assume you are the controller of a mid-sized manufacturing firm that has an information system supporting each of several departments. What arguments would you make for and against integrating these into a single system? Which, if any, managerial levels would you recommend for integration? What reaction would you expect from your counterparts in manufacturing and marketing if you propose a move toward integration?

SUGGESTED READINGS

AICPA. *Objectives of Financial Statements. Report of the Study Group on the Objectives of Financial Statements.* Vol. 1. New York: AICPA, 1973.

Concepts, statements, and technical bulletins. Published by The Financial Accounting Standards Board, Stamford, CT.

DAVIS, G. B., and M. OLSON. *Management Information Systems,* 2nd ed. New York: McGraw-Hill, 1984.

GRADY, PAUL. *Inventory of Generally Accepted Accounting Principles for Business Enterprises.* New York: AICPA, 1965.

JENSEN, DANIEL L. (Ed.). *Information Systems in Accounting Education.* Columbus: The Ohio State University, 1985.

chapter two

The AIS and Its Environment

CHAPTER OUTLINE

INTRODUCTION

This chapter provides an operational definition of the AIS in systems terms and examines the aspects of the AIS's internal and external environment that most affect AIS development and operations. In defining the AIS, we will make a distinction between the AIS and its major subsystem, the computer-assisted accounting information system (CAAIS) to emphasize that the computer is a tool to be used in furthering the much broader purposes of the AIS. We will then expand our view to examine how accounting information is affected by factors within its parent organization, by the actions of regulatory agencies, and by the march of technology in the world beyond the organization. Internally, we will see that organizational structure and individual and group behavior have significant effects on the growth and structure of the AIS. Externally, we will see that the AIS is constrained by a number of formal and informal agencies, and that to be successful, the AIS must be adjusted to technological advances.

ELEMENTS OF A SYSTEMS DEFINITION

The systems approach to studying organizations has proved to be an excellent method of gaining insight into organizational structure and processes. If we are to use systems concepts effectively in discussing the AIS, it is essential that we develop a common understanding of systems terms. In this section, we discuss six elements of a systems definition.[1]

Goal Orientation

The goal-seeking nature of systems is an essential feature in reducing the complexities of organizations to a level that can reasonably be subjected to analysis. The number of possible interactions between and among components become astronomical in any but the smallest of organizations. Determining which interactions are significant can be done only if we know what goals the system is to accomplish. Only when goals are specified can the analyst determine which patterns are essential to understanding the problem at hand, which may have peripheral effects, and which may be safely ignored. There is danger in prematurely simplifying the goal-seeking dimension. If we assume, as is often done in a business environment, that the goal of the business

[1] For further information on the elements of systems concepts, see Fremont E. Kast and James E. Rosenzwieg, "General Systems Theory: Applications for Organization and Management." *Academy of Management Journal,* December 1972, pp. 447–465.

is profit maximization, we may be led into an erroneous definition of the system of interest and into neglecting important components and processes.

Any complex organization will have multiple goals. For example, one leading firm in the computing industry has long held that there is a compelling need for executives in the business sector to take the initiative and provide the leadership in addressing major societal needs as an integral part of their businesses. An analyst in this firm who addresses problems in narrow terms of profit maximization will fail to define a system or to provide a solution to the satisfaction of top management.

Interrelated Components

The components of a system may be conceptual, physical, or a mixture of both. The components of a conceptual system might include facts, ideas, hypotheses, and theories. The components of a physical system might include raw materials, people, machines, and products. Organizations and their information-processing components are invariably a mixture of conceptual and physical elements. The objectives and policies are conceptual in nature; the implementation of these concepts requires physical components. Such terms as social systems and man-machine systems, common in the study of organizations and information processing, imply such a mixture of elements. It is fundamental to the definition of a system that there are at least two interacting components. Note that the components of one system may constitute a system (more properly, a subsystem) in their own right. The interrelationship between and among the components is the key factor in this feature of the systems definition. Components may be related serially; that is, one component may have to complete its process before a second component may start. The action of one component may be conditionally dependent upon the action of another; that is, either process B or process C may take place, depending upon the result achieved in process A; or components may be related such that two or more components must complete their processing before a third can begin. The most complex cases can be described in terms of these relationships. Figure 2–1 is a representation of these basic forms of interaction.

Consider a greatly simplified business example. The communications center of a wholesale firm receives an order for $2000 worth of merchandise. The order is acknowledged and sent to the credit office. This is a simple serial process; the communications center exercises no discretion—all orders are sent to the same location. The credit office cannot begin its processing until it has received the order. Next, the credit office determines if the customer is known and in good standing.

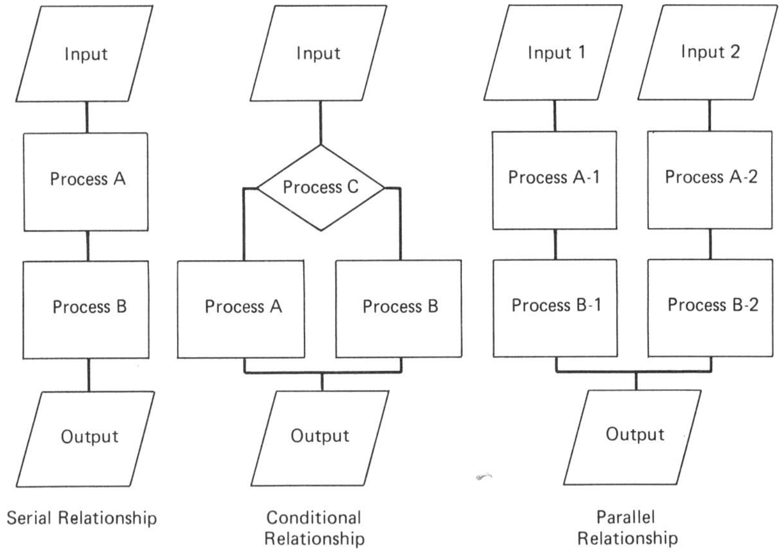

FIGURE 2–1 Three Basic Interrelationships among Processes

If so, and the order is within the customer's credit limit, the order is forwarded to the operations department for further processing; if not, a further credit check may be initiated or the order may be refused. This is an example of conditional dependence. Assume the order is accepted for further processing. The original is now sent to the billing office, and a copy is sent to the warehouse for use in selecting the merchandise. When the packaged goods arrive at the shipping office, they will not be sent until a matching document is received from billing to ensure that all goods ordered have been supplied and properly charged. This is an example of parallel processing.

Hierarchy of Systems

The hierarchical nature of the systems approach is another key to understanding organizations. We have noted that the components of any given system may themselves be subsystems. In turn, we will find that the level of system which is of primary interest to us is a component of one or more larger systems. These are commonly called *suprasystems.* At first it may appear that we can fully understand a firm or public agency by a careful examination of its goals, structures, and processes. However, we will soon find it necessary to divide the organization into a number of suborganizations and study each of these in some detail to see how they operate as self-contained entities, and how they are reassembled to form the organizational whole. No matter how well we accomplish these tasks, we will still find our understanding of the organization incomplete until we know something about the larger systems in which it exists. A firm will be part of many suprasystems. It is part of an industry; it is part of the community in which it is located; and it is part of the community of states and nations. The effects of these larger systems may be obvious, or they may be quite subtle. An applicable ruling of the Securities and Exchange Commission leaves little ambiguity about its impact, whereas the woes of a small subcontractor to General Motors in the early 1980s may have been the result of a strategic marketing decision made in Tokyo decades ago. The developer of an AIS must be aware that each of a firm's superior systems may require quite different accounting procedures and outputs.

The hierarchical nature of the systems approach introduces an unfortunate ambiguity into the use of the systems model. It is essential to define the level of system being examined and to indicate whenever the analysis moves from one level to another. Failure to do so can result in invalid comparisons among organizational units.

Clearly, the system of primary interest in understanding how an organization uses information is the organization itself. Properly, then, we should speak of the accounting information *sub*system. As we progress through the text, we will encounter data processing systems, management information systems, accounts receivable systems, systems ad infinitum. Each of these has a legitimate claim to be considered a system. Each will meet all the requirements of the definition we are now developing. However, each does not have the same significance to the organization as a whole. If we fail to place the system being defined at its appropriate level in the hierarchy of systems, we will be unable to maintain a holistic view of the organization. As we write this book, we take special care to keep the level of the system under review in its proper hierarchical perspective. We encourage readers to establish the habit of doing so whenever they consider complex systems. Figure 2–2 depicts three levels of hierarchy.

Synergy

The property of *synergy* simply suggests that the whole is greater than the sum of its parts. It is axiomatic that people organize to accomplish in concert that which they cannot achieve acting as individuals. The results that we note from observing components interacting in pursuit of the system's goals are greater than we would expect from observing each component acting alone. The concept of synergy is not new to the world of enterprise. It dates at least to the time of Adam Smith's observation that the division of labor in a pin factory resulted in a much greater output of higher quality pins than could be obtained from a similar number of workers each manufacturing the entire pin on his own.

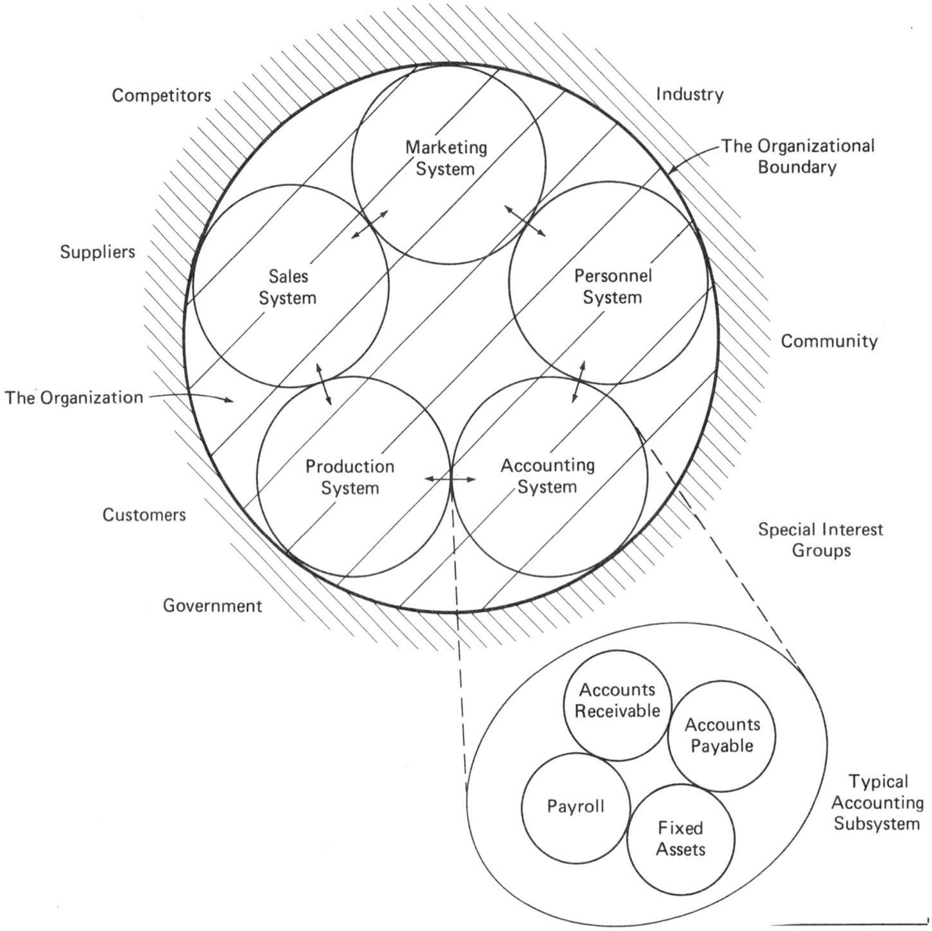

FIGURE 2–2 A Hierarchy of Systems

Defined Boundary

The precise definition of a system's boundary is another major element that separates the analytic use of the systems approach from the popular use of the term "system." For instance, in everyday use we speak of the inadequacy of the public transportation system, or the strengths and weaknesses of a particular political or economic system. These terms have little real meaning until we define them with some precision. We can debate an issue through the night, only to find that no two people in the discussion are talking about the same set of entities. Defining the boundary permits us to identify exactly which elements are part of the system under review and which are part of that system's environment. This simple statement should not lead us to believe that establishing a boundary is an easy or trivial matter.

Several issues complicate boundary definition. First, a component may be a member of more than one system. Perhaps this is most clearly seen in the physical world. In the human system, is the heart a member of the circulatory subsystem or the muscular subsystem? The answer is that it is a member of both. Similarly, we will find it necessary to include the central processing unit (CPU), auxiliary storage devices, and system software in our description of the AIS. These components are equally a part of the management information system, the marketing information system, and such other information subsystems as may share the resources of a centralized computer system. Figure 2–3 illustrates this relationship.

A second factor that makes boundary definition difficult is related to the open-closed dimension we discuss more thoroughly in the following section. A relatively open system is characterized by a high level of interaction with its environment. But interaction between components is characteristic of the system itself. How does one draw the line? The best approach is to determine if a component or interaction is essential to explain how the system functions to meet its objectives. If it is essential, then include that component or interaction within the system's boundary. An iterative procedure to arrive at a system definition is a common feature of the systems approach in practice. Often, elements that were originally considered to be a part of the system prove to be irrelevant and are excluded in the final analysis. Other elements originally considered to be part of the environment may later be found to be essential to the system's functioning. This feature is initially disturbing to many observers, particularly those accustomed to rigid definitions and established standards. However, it is the main feature of the systems approach, since it provides the flexibility to address a wide variety of problems.

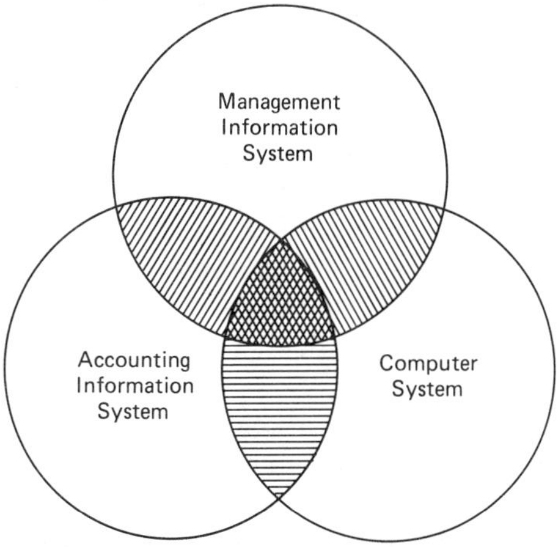

FIGURE 2–3 Overlapping Subsystems

Time factors are a third issue that complicate boundary decisions. An element that is essential to our analysis today may be irrelevant in some future time period. Nowhere is this more critical than in the field of data processing. A very few years ago, the computer processing system could be clearly defined by physical boundaries. The computer and its peripheral equipment were in a totally enclosed, tightly controlled, air-conditioned space. The only physical entry was via an air-lock set of doors; the only conceptual entry was via a job request at a production control desk. The march of technology—remote terminals, distributed data processing, networks of microcomputers—has rendered such a system concept useless in today's environment.

Interaction with Environment

This element of the systems definition refers to the open-closed dimension of systems analysis. A *closed* system is one that has no interaction with its environment. Totally closed systems are difficult to visualize, and if the effort to define a closed system were successful, the system would be of little interest in the study of organizations. An *open* system is one that has no control over the boundary between itself and its environment. Again, there appears to be little utility in defining a system at this pole of the dimension. The area of interest, then, lies between the conceptual extremes.

Relatively closed systems are those that have a small amount of interaction with their environment, and that have a level and type of interaction which is subject to a high degree of control by the system or by the suprasystem within which the system operates. A timed traffic signal is an everyday example of a relatively closed system. If it is set to provide a green light to traffic on Main Street for 3 minutes followed by a green light on Cross Street for 2 minutes, it will continue to operate in this mode, regardless of how congested automobile traffic may become. It is operating as a closed system. However, it should not be considered totally closed. If the traffic delays become intolerable, citizens will complain and the light will be reset.

Relatively open systems are those that sense changes in their environment and make some sort of adaptation to those changes. We can continue the example of the traffic light. If instead of merely adjusting the timing mechanism, the traffic bureau elects to install a traffic counting device in the roadway, the light system can now react to its environment. As traffic alternately becomes heavier on one street or the other, the light adjusts its timing cycle to improve traffic flow. We have changed our traffic signal from a relatively closed to a relatively open mode of operation.

The open-closed dimension of systems is an important feature of the systems model. It embodies the organization's need for stability and protection from uncertainty, as represented by relatively closed systems, and the organization's need to adapt to a changing world, as represented by relatively open systems. Our need, then, is not to make a decision as to which type of system best describes an AIS, but rather to take advantage of the features of both approaches to enhance our understanding of how the AIS operates to support its parent organization.

To summarize, the essential elements of a functional definition of a system are these:

1. A system is goal oriented.
2. A system is composed of two or more interrelated components.
3. Every level of a system exists in a hierarchy of systems.
4. A system is synergistic.
5. A system has a boundary.
6. A system interacts with its environment.

SYSTEMS IN ACTION

Inputs, Processes, and Outputs

We have now provided a definition of a system, but this is a static view. The principal value of the systems approach is that it provides greater insights into the dynamics of an organization than do other organizational models. The basic dynamics are usually expressed in terms of inputs, processes or transformations, and outputs. If a system is to be subject to control, then an additional dynamic feature, feedback, becomes of concern.

A system receives inputs from its environment, processes or transforms these inputs in some manner, and then returns the transformed product back to the environment as output. The resources involved may be physical—a manufacturing system transforms raw materials into finished goods, or a power generating system transforms coal into electrical energy. Or they may be conceptual—a scientist transforms observations into theories, an automated system transforms data into information, or more relevant to our interest, an accounting system transforms financial transactions into accounting information.

Consider a physical example first. The human respiratory system will serve to illustrate a number of points. (We leave development of a systems definition of the respiratory system as an exercise for the student. Surely, a first step will be to note that it is a subsystem in the hierarchy of human systems.) A careful observer will note certain characteristics of the input to this system. Let us say that it is air of a particular temperature, humidity, and gaseous content. When the same characteristics are measured in the output, we note that some transformations have taken place. Typically, we would expect to find an increase in temperature and humidity, a relative increase in carbon dioxide content, and a relative decrease in oxygen content. Note that in this case we have discovered quite a bit about the human respiratory system without knowing anything about the internal processes of the system. This is known as a *black box* observation. It has wide application in developing a quick understanding of how complex systems operate and in segmenting problems for analysis and design.

To continue the example, suppose we are interested in studying the earth's ecosystem rather than human breathing. We observe that plant life uses the carbon dioxide of the air as an input and returns oxygen to the air as an output. This increases our macro-level understanding of one major facet of atmospheric equilibrium, with no micro-level knowledge of any internal process. Note further how the outputs from one system become inputs to another. This is as typical in man-made accounting operations as it is in nature. For example, the outputs from the accounts receivable section become inputs to the general ledger. In turn, the outputs from the general ledger become inputs to balance sheets and earnings statements. Establishing and maintaining compatibility among cooperating subsystems is a major design consideration in either manual or automated accounting systems.

Feedback and Control[2]

Most systems with which we will be concerned in our study of AIS will involve elements of control, one of the fundamental principles of management in general and of particular concern to the accountant. If a system is to be controlled, then the output from that system must be measured and compared to some expected value. If there is a variance between the measured and expected values, then the system's inputs, processes, or objectives must be altered to eliminate the variance. *Feedback* is the general term used in systems analysis to denote the process of measuring, comparing, and adjusting systems operations. Figure 2–4 illustrates the input-process-output operations of a system with a provision for feedback control.

Feedback is universal in controlled systems. The field of cybernetics, for example, is devoted to the study of this phenomenon. A detailed review is beyond our scope, but a brief outline of the subject, together with a few examples, will provide insight into this important area.

[2] This discussion of feedback is based on Hare Van Court, Jr., *Systems Analysis—A Diagnostic Approach* (New York: Harcourt, Brace & World), 1967.

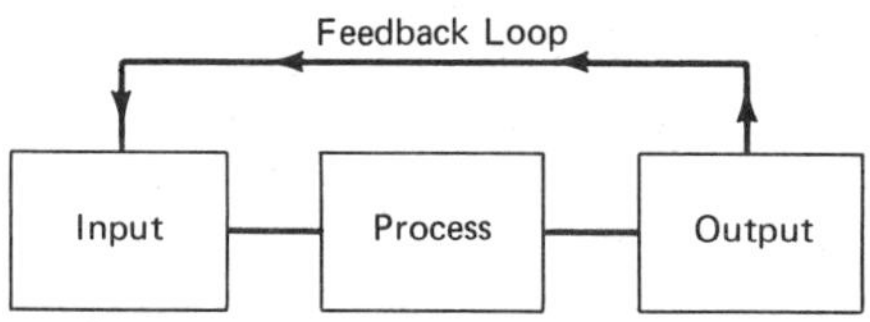

FIGURE 2–4 The Principles of Feedback

First Order Feedback. This feedback is concerned with correcting deviations from expected output. The simplest case is *negative feedback* with a zero time delay. As an example, most modern automobiles have a cruise control capability. The driver simply selects a desired speed and engages the control mechanism. If the automobile starts to go uphill, the speed tends to decrease. This change will be measured by the control device and compared to the established standard. This will initiate an offsetting increase in fuel flow, and the desired speed will be maintained within a narrow range. If the automobile starts to go downhill, the opposite process will occur—the speed will tend to increase, this tendency will be sensed, and the fuel flow will be decreased. Note that the adjusting action is taken to reverse the output tendency—hence the term negative feedback.

Negative feedback controls may operate in a totally automated mode, or they may require human intervention. Although fully automated controls are widely used in continuous process operations such as oil refining, a human-made machine mode is more common to the AIS. Perhaps the most common accounting application is the organization's operating budget. Typically, in the budgetary process a manager negotiates expected revenue and expense targets with his or her superiors at the outset of a fiscal year. The automated portion of the AIS provides periodic reports of actual values which the manager compares with the target values, initiating corrective action as required.

Note that budgetary control, while essentially a first order feedback process, introduces several possibilities not included in the simple speed control example. First, the deviation from the standard may be desirable: Revenues may be higher than planned or expenses may be lower. This introduces the idea of *positive feedback*. Instead of counteracting this tendency, the manager will wish to identify the cause and, if possible, reinforce it. Second, the manager receives periodic rather than continuous feedback. This introduces the notion of *delay*, or *lag*, in feedback systems. Consideration of lag effects leads to much of the complexity of feedback controls. Suffice it to say that if the disturbances causing deviation from the standard are cyclical or discontinuous, then the selection of appropriate adjustment measures is seriously affected. Consider the case of a company that sets its July production schedule based on a rapidly rising sales trend in the months of January through April. If the May and June data reverse this trend, the company will have a severe excess of inventory on the first of August. Finally, the introduction of the human element into the feedback loop raises the possibility of altering system operation rather than simply adjusting input values.

Second Order Feedback. This feedback is concerned with predicting probable changes in output values as a result of monitoring systems inputs. It is sometimes called *feedforward control*. The object of second order feedback is to prevent deviations from the standard before they occur, rather than waiting to take corrective action. Second order systems generally require more sophisticated sensors than do first order systems; in addition, they require a memory function. To continue the example of automobile speed control: If we replace the automatic unit with a highly skilled driver, we will find that we can obtain more precise control. The driver can detect changes in terrain and initiate necessary corrective action before the automobile starts to change speed.

Second order feedback can be successfully automated if the variety of actions required can be completely specified, and if criteria can be established to select the best action. The U.S. Weather Bureau's prediction system is an example. A particular set of atmospheric conditions is compared to a memory bank of previous conditions. The computerized system then selects the closest match between the current state of the atmosphere and a stored pattern and predicts, with a specified probability, that the future weather will correspond to that which followed the stored pattern. Second order feedback systems exist in the AIS. Inventory control models are often of this nature. In a properly constructed model, the rate of inventory depletion is monitored and corrective action is taken before inventory reaches a high or low limit. It is technologically possible to automate highly complex functions, but one soon approaches an economic limit where increasing complexity is best handled by human intervention. This is particularly true in situations where changing conditions may require frequent modification of corrective actions or appropriate selection criteria.

Third Order Feedback. This feedback involves the use of systems output to alter systems processes. In essence, it is a result of learning better ways to accomplish the system's goals. At this time, few third order feedback systems are fully operational in the AIS. Researchers in artificial intelligence continue to address this type of system, but for the immediate future the role of the computer in regard to third order feedback will be to provide input to the human element of the AIS. Third order feedback is most often associated with managerial control, a subject discussed in Chapter 1.

Fourth Order Feedback. This feedback involves using a system's output to evaluate and modify the system's goals. Feedback from AIS operations is one of the major inputs to strategic planning. The use of accounting information in decision support systems and simulation models falls in this category. Again, fourth order feedback in the AIS requires human use of automated products.

A SYSTEMS DEFINITION OF THE AIS

We can now define and analyze the accounting information system in terms of the elements of our functional systems definition:

> The AIS is a relatively open system of personnel, data, software, and hardware which provides internal and external users timely, accurate, and relevant information regarding an organization's financial activities in a cost-effective manner.

Goals

The goals of the AIS are to provide timely, accurate, and relevant information to internal and external users. As we saw in Chapter 1, internal users are primarily concerned with accounting information which will assist them in setting realistic objectives and tracking progress toward these objectives. External users require information which will enable them to make informed decisions regarding the organization. In the case of publicly held corporations, these decisions include whether or not to invest in the system, whether management is acting in the best interests of the shareholders, and whether the system is acting in accordance with sound managerial and accounting practices. For nonprofit institutions, external users need to know if the organization is acting in accordance with its charter; tax authorities need to determine that the institution is complying with exemption regulations. For governmental agencies, taxpayers are entitled to know that the agency is expending funds in an authorized and cost-effective manner.

Components

The components of an AIS include people, data, software, and hardware. The human element is by far the most important of these. Accountants, accounting technicians, systems analysts, programmers, and data entry personnel make up the people component of the AIS. It is this element that permits us to classify the AIS as a relatively open system. In particular, the accountants and systems analysts sense changes in the operational and technological environments, respectively, and set the adaptive process in motion. Our discussion of the AIS will focus on the role people play in the adaptive processes of the system, and the interactions between the human component, the environment, and changes to the internal software and hardware elements. At the AIS level, we are concerned with modifications to the existing configurations that are essential if the organization is to survive and grow. The remaining components of interest include the data, software and hardware that are necessary for the automated production of accounting information. The existing data structures, software and hardware compose a subsystem of the AIS with which we shall deal in the following section.

Hierarchy of Systems

The position of the AIS in the hierarchy of systems is implied in the definition. The AIS is a service function providing information to users who include line and staff managers of the organization and numerous external groups. In the business sector, the hierarchy extends upward to the general public, as represented by governmental agencies and special interest groups. In the case of multinational corporations, this hierarchy must include foreign as well as domestic governments. A similar hierarchy exists in the nonprofit sector. In the governmental sector, the hierarchy extends upward through senior agencies, again culminating with the general public, as represented by the executive, legislative, and judicial branches of government. A distinguishing feature of public sector management is continuous scrutiny of administrative actions by numerous groups. The public's right to know how it is being served by government officials demands the highest quality of AIS.

Looking downward in the order of systems, the most significant subsystem of the AIS in terms of the objectives of this book is the computer-assisted accounting information subsystem (CAAIS). This system, in turn, is composed of still lower-level subsystems.

Synergy

The AIS is synergistic. The components of the AIS, acting in concert, must produce useful information in a more cost-effective manner than would be possible by expending an equivalent amount of resources in some other manner. This quality of the AIS cannot be taken for granted; it is the result of sound conceptualization and design. Each component of the system must be subjected to initial rigorous cost justification and then to periodic review. The widespread introduction of microcomputers in the early 1980s provided an excellent test of this quality. In those organizations where the AIS components were ineffectively coordinated and did not provide management with timely and useful information at reasonable cost, microcomputers flourished in a stand-alone mode of operation. Where the AIS was effectively designed, the micros were quickly coordinated with the mainstream of accounting information processing.

Boundary

The AIS has a boundary. We have already seen that the AIS includes people, data, software, and hardware. These components and the relationships among them define the limits of the AIS. A relationship between any component of the AIS and an element of the environment is a *boundary-spanning activity.* A discussion between a firm's accountant and a member of its information services department takes place within the boundary of the AIS. A discussion between an accountant and a member of the planning staff crosses that boundary, as does a discussion between an accountant and a member of the Internal Revenue Service. A special word is in order in regard to the data component. Data pertinent to accounting operations exist outside the AIS boundary. If the AIS is to meet its objective, such data must be captured and become an input to the system. Once entered into the system, data may be retained for an indefinite period. However, data in the system are copies of data outside the system—that is, the same data are part of the environment and part of the system.

Open-Closed Dimension

The AIS is a relatively open system. Any particular AIS is tuned to provide a variety of accounting information to its established users. In addition to these routine demands, the AIS has frequent, unpredictable, and loosely structured contacts with its environment. In general, the AIS has little control over such contacts. For instance, in the case of a corporation, the contacts might include requests for ad hoc reports from top management, a need to interpret a new government regulation and provide the appropriate response, or a demand for historical information in a new format to assist in making decisions regarding alternate investment opportunities. In the case of a government activity, the AIS may have to respond to such events as a change in tax collection procedures, a request for ad hoc information from a legislative committee or an executive agency, or the projection of revenues and expenses in support of budgeting activites.

The common characteristic of all these contacts is that their timing and content cannot be predicted in advance, and they require a departure from standard operating procedures. The ability of the AIS to respond effectively to such demands is a determining factor in the ability of its parent organization to adapt successfully to a changing environment. In our discussion of the AIS, we will concentrate on this type of activity. The more mundane, but equally essential, demand for routine information will be discussed as a function of the CAAIS, which we now examine.

DEFINING THE COMPUTER-ASSISTED ACCOUNTING INFORMATION SUBSYSTEM (CAAIS)

Certain functions that must be performed to achieve the objectives of the AIS are particularly well suited to automation. Historically, the computer was introduced into most organizations by the accounting department as a very high speed calculating machine. From this modest foothold it has steadily grown to have a role in virtually every department and activity of its host organization. No end to the expansion of the computer's role is currently in view. No organization can continuously update its investment in computer hardware and software to keep pace with the latest technology. The role of the CAAIS must be viewed in this dynamic and expanding environment.

Any specific AIS may fall along a continuum from the introductory to the highly developed state. We view the CAAIS as that subsystem of the AIS which meets user demands for routine and predictable accounting information; the CAAIS provides information to end user personnel without the need for programming assistance from the organization's information services department:

> The CAAIS is a relatively closed subsystem of the AIS. It consists of the data, software, hardware, and personnel necessary to meet existing and defined needs of internal and external users for timely, accurate, and relevant information regarding an organization's financial activities in a cost-effective manner.

The similarity of this definition to that of the AIS is apparent. As a subsystem of the AIS, the CAAIS shares common objectives and is composed entirely of elements of its parent system. Note that the order of the elements has been changed to emphasize the relative importance of the human and nonhuman components. In the AIS, people predominate. In the CAAIS, the creative work has already been accomplished. People are still essential to functioning at the CAAIS level, but their role has been reduced to housekeeping chores in connection with the input, processing, and output cycles of the system.

The major distinction we wish to make between the AIS and the CAAIS is that the former is a relatively open system that interacts with and adapts to a widely varied environment, whereas the latter is a relatively closed system protected from the general environment by other elements of the AIS. While the overall AIS provides flexibility, the CAAIS provides stability. Changes in the CAAIS are executed only as the result of planned action in the AIS. The CAAIS accepts properly formatted input and produces highly predictable output with little or no further human intervention. It frees the human element of the AIS for more creative work, including improvements in the CAAIS.

The CAAIS includes a number of subsystems, including the software subsystem. What actions must accountants take to ensure that the correct software is developed or acquired? What procedures must be modified to make most effective use of existing software capabilities? What are the tradeoffs between in-house development and package procurement? What tools are available and cost-effective for improving service to management? These are reasonable questions that we will prepare readers to address.

We will also be concerned with the hardware system, particularly as it provides opportunities and imposes constraints in relation to accomplishing overall AIS objectives. The accounting professional is not expected to be a hardware expert, but he or she must be fully aware of the impact of hardware configurations on the use, development, and control of accounting aids, and he or she must be knowledgeable in the control and evaluation of hardware use. The data subsystem plays a major part in determining the CAAIS's capabilities and limitations. Are data stored to facilitate ad hoc retrieval? Is each application supported by its own file system, or do several applications draw data from a common database? Can a user originate data on a trial basis without disturbing the integrity of the production database? Is there access to databases external to the user's organization?

The foregoing discussion has provided operational definitions of the AIS and its subsystems. We now turn to considering the environmental factors that affect the AIS and its processes.

THE INTERNAL ENVIRONMENT

Organizational functions, purposes, structures, control strategies, resources, and constraints, together with individual and group values, norms, and culture, all contribute to the internal environment of the AIS. Theoretically, there are an infinite number of ways an organization can combine its resources, employ available technology, and group its members to accomplish its tasks. A successful AIS is carefully created, developed, and maintained in harmony with a given configuration of variables.

Some factors within the organizational context are more relevant than others to the success of an information system. Ein-Dor and Segev have identified 10 contextual variables that relate to the success of an information system:[3]

1. Size of the organization
2. Organizational time frame and planning horizon
3. Organizational structure
4. Extra-organizational situation
5. Resources
6. Maturity—degree of formalization
7. Psychological climate
8. Rank of the responsible executive
9. Location of the responsible executive
10. Steering committee

Nine of the ten factors relate directly to the internal environment. Although Ein-Dor and Segev were looking at information systems in general, their findings apply equally as well to the AIS.

Size of the Organization. The size of an organization influences the complexity and sophistication of the AIS. A large organization has more complex information flows than a small organization. Consequently, if it is to compete successfully, it must have a more complex information system.

Organizational Time Frame and Planning Horizon. An organization's decision time frame depends on the rate and complexity of the changes in its environment. In a stable environment, decisions tend to be routine and predictable. The AIS can easily be structured to respond to predetermined needs for information. In a more dynamic environment, the decision time frame becomes shorter and the needs of the decision makers cannot be well specified in advance. The AIS is under great pressure to produce the required information and may be unable to respond in a timely manner.

Organizational Structure. The structure of the organization influences the AIS. There are several measures and dimensions of organizational structure. Two that have been found to be closely related to the design and operation of an AIS are (1) the degree of centralization, and (2) the degree to which the organization maintains unity of command.

[3] P. Ein-Dor and E. Segev, "Organizational Context and the Success of Information Systems." *Management Science,* 24 (1978), pp. 1064–1077.

An administrative organization is *centralized* to the extent that decisions are made at relatively high levels in the organization, *decentralized* to the extent that discretion and authority to make important decisions are delegated to lower levels of management. Decentralization provides the opportunity for lower-level executives to participate effectively in the decision-making process; however, it does complicate the task of implementing an AIS.

Many large organizations use divisional decentralization. This is a vehicle to manage growth, diversity, and geographic dispersion. Under divisional decentralization, an enterprise may have several product divisions, service divisions, or territorial divisions. These divisions operate independently, with the goal of maximizing divisional income. A highly decentralized organization operates each division as an independent company that makes its own purchase, production, and sales decisions. In this type of enterprise, each division would have an independent AIS, but these would have to interact with the corporate AIS. In most instances, this works as an application of the black box principle: The internal workings of the divisional AISs are of little concern to the corporate AIS, but their outputs must be acceptable as inputs at the corporate level.

The unity of command principle states that each employee should report to one superior. This is embodied in the functional form of organizational structure. Most manufacturing, service, and public enterprises are organized in this manner. This type of organization provides clear lines of responsibility and promotes functional specialization; however, it creates problems of integration and coordination among the different functional groups. In this situation, the AIS is usually centralized as a staff function, although there may be some decentralization to functional areas.

The matrix organization superimposes a product or project structure on the functional organization. Personnel are still assigned to functional areas for administrative accountability, but they are assigned to product or project managers for operational accountability. In these organizations, the functional structure provides stability and the product or project structure provides flexibility. In addition to its flexibility, the matrix organization provides a broader experience base and additional career potential for its personnel; however, it is often difficult to implement and it may induce ambiguity, anxiety, and stress among individuals assigned to more than one supervisor. The matrix structure increases the demands on the AIS.

Resources. An organization must be prepared to invest an adequate amount of resources in its AIS. In cases where resources are unduly limited and AIS growth is constrained, a high rate of turnover is experienced and technological obsolescence curtails effectiveness of the system.

Organizational Maturity. Three stages of the organizational life cycle are relevant to AIS effectiveness: growth, maturity, and decline. The *growth* stage is characterized by rapid change, relatively ineffective controls, and an abundance of resources. The AIS benefits from the availability of up-to-date technology, but is hard pressed to keep abreast of expanding and changing demands for information. The *mature* stage is characterized by increasing managerial control and a greater degree of stability. The AIS benefits from the more stable environment, but must expend additional effort to justify personnel, software, and hardware requests. The *declining* stage is characterized by internal competition for resources and the need to reduce costs. The AIS may suffer the loss of key personnel and technological obsolescence.

Psychological Climate. Psychological climate is a complex phenomenon discussed at greater length in Chapter 4. Briefly, the success of an AIS will depend on the attitude of users. Personnel need to be educated in the capabilities and limitations of their AIS to bring about realistic expectations and positive experiences.

Rank of the Responsible Executive. The rank of the responsible executive is of concern both within the AIS and its counterpart in the Information Services Department. The senior AIS executive must be high enough in the accounting hierarchy to ensure that automated methods are used wherever the cost is justified. The senior Information Services Department executive must have sufficient influence to obtain the necessary hardware and software capabilities for the entire organization.

Location of the Responsible Executive. The responsibility for information services may reside at several locations in an organization. As we noted, the computer is often introduced to organizations via the Accounting Department. In those organizations where the senior accounting executive still controls the computer resources, the AIS retains the highest priority for enhancement. However, this placement results in less than optimal use of the computer for the organization as a whole. Most large organizations have established an Information Services Department and provide the senior manager for computer resources a position equal to that of the controller or treasurer. This results in an improved use of automated products by the organization, but requires the AIS to compete more vigorously for its necessary share of the computer resources.

Information Systems Steering Committee. The presence of an Information Systems steering committee has been found to have a beneficial effect on the overall growth of the use of computers in organizations. This committee is composed of the divisional or department heads of the organization, and, when used effectively, tends to promote balanced growth of computer utilization across functional and product areas.

THE EXTERNAL ENVIRONMENT

Regulatory Aspects

In Chapter 1, we noted that the financial accounting system operates within a clearly defined domain. The financial accounting process is guided by certain principles and conventions known as Generally Accepted Accounting Principles (GAAP), which are directly influenced by the pronouncements of regulatory agencies, government legislation, and voluntary acceptance of practicing accountants.

In this section we will briefly introduce the roles of two principal agencies that influence accounting principles and reporting practices: The American Institute of Certified Public Accountants (AICPA) and the Securities and Exchange Commission (SEC). Of these, the AICPA exerts moral and voluntary authority and the SEC exerts legal and regulatory power to influence, monitor, and control accounting and reporting practices in business organizations. The AICPA acts as the catalyst in advancing and disseminating the accounting principles followed by accountants and auditors.

Historically, the AICPA played a significant role in shaping the accounting and reporting practices followed by business and nonbusiness organizations. Over the past several decades, the AICPA has established a series of boards and committees to develop and disseminate accounting principles. These include:

1. The Committee on Accounting Procedure (CAP)
2. The Accounting Principles Board (APB)
3. The Financial Accounting Standards Board (FASB)

The CAP was the earliest of these committees (1938). It produced a number of pronouncements on significant issues which were later consolidated in 1953 as Accounting Terminology Bulletin No. 1, "Review and Resume," and Accounting Research Bulletin No. 43 (ARB-43). The ARB series was continued through 1959 with Bulletins 44–51.

Although the CAP was disestablished in 1953, many of these bulletins are still considered part of the GAAP. Some of their recommendations have been superseded by later pronouncements.

The Accounting Principles Board

The Accounting Principles Board (APB) was formed in 1953 to overcome the weaknesses in the CAP. The APB included members from the profession, and from industry, government, and academia.

The APB's pronouncements are called the APB Opinions. It circulated as many as 31 opinions. Support for most of the APB Opinions was voluntary. By 1960, the need to review the APB was apparent, and in 1972 it was replaced by the FASB.

The Financial Accounting Standards Board

The Wheat Committee (1972) of the AICPA recommended abolition of the APB and establishment of the FASB. The FASB was entrusted with issuing accounting standards. The FASB has an 11-member Board of Trustees who serve full time and represent a cross section of interests. The Financial Accounting Foundation (FAF) has the responsibility for raising funds to operate the FASB and appointing its members.

The FASB's pronouncements are classified into four groups:

1. Statements of Financial Accounting Concepts
2. Statements of Financial Accounting Standards
3. Interpretations
4. Technical Bulletins

The Statements of Financial Accounting Concepts provide the foundation on which the financial accounting standards are based. The Statements of Financial Accounting Standards include accounting procedures and methods for handling specific accounting issues. Interpretations extend or modify previously issued statements. Technical bulletins give guidance on accounting and reporting problems.

To date, the FASB has issued 4 statements of concepts, 47 statements of standards, 35 interpretations, and 26 technical bulletins. The designer or user of an AIS in the corporate sector must be aware of the content and impact of these pronouncements.

The Securities and Exchange Commission (SEC)

Since the enactment of the Securities Act of 1933, the SEC has played an important role in monitoring the accounting and reporting practices of publicly held corporations.

The AICPA and its committees and boards do not have any legal authority; compliance with their pronouncements is voluntary. The SEC, however, has the legal authority to prescribe accounting methods under specified circumstances. The SEC pronouncements are published in the form of Accounting Series Releases. Corporations that are legally required to submit financial statements to the SEC must comply with SEC requirements.

National Council of Governmental Accounting

The accounting and reporting practices of governmental units are monitored by the National Council of Governmental Accounting (NCGA). The NCGA is expected to be replaced by the Governmental Accounting Standards Board (GASB). The GASB will perform functions relating to accounting and reporting practices in governmental units similar to those performed by the FASB in business. The basic principles of governmental accounting and reporting practices are outlined in Statement No. 1, "Governmental Accounting and Financial Reporting Principles." Twelve principles published in 1979 by NCGA cover the following areas:

1. Accounting and reporting capabilities
2. Fund accounting systems
3. Types of funds
4. Number of funds
5. Accounting for fixed assets and long-term liabilities
6. Valuation of fixed assets
7. Depreciation of fixed assets
8. Accrual basis in governmental accounting
9. Budgeting and budgeting control
10. Transfer, revenue, expenditure, and expense account classification
11. Common terminology classification
12. Interim and annual financial reports

Other Organizations

The AICPA and the SEC in the private sector and the NCGA in the governmental sector provide leadership in promulgating accounting principles and reporting practices. However, many other agencies and associations influence the AIS environment directly and indirectly. Principal among these are the following:

1. The American Accounting Association (AAA)
2. The Federal Trade Commission (FTC)
3. The Institute of Management Accountants (IMA)

4. The Interstate Commerce Commission (ICC)
5. The Internal Revenue Service (IRS)

Technological Aspects

A major part of this book is devoted to the technological environment of the AIS. The chapters on hardware, software, data components, and applications development are all about the CAAIS's technological environment. Here we provide an overview of general trends in this segment of the environment.

The AIS student or practitioner is faced with one of the most dynamic and demanding technological environments encountered in any field. The rapid development of hardware devices, software technologies, and processing concepts is unparalleled in business or industrial experience. In less than three decades of widespread use of computers in business data processing, we have progressed from entering data on punched cards to using a wide variety of keyboard and nonkeyboard devices, from processing a single job at a time in the batch mode to processing dozens of on-line and batch jobs simultaneously, from a computer sealed into a virtually impregnable air-conditioned sanctuary to a terminal or desktop computer in virtually every office, from programming in machine language to generating applications in a screen-driven mode, from serial access to data on punched cards or magnetic tape to direct access to millions of items of information stored on magnetic or optical disks. The list could go on for pages, but the point is clear—data processing technology has progressed at an extremely rapid rate. Experts agree that there is no perceptible slowing in the technological pace: Machines of the future will process data still more rapidly, will require less space, will be less expensive for a given capacity, will provide greater flexibility of information retrieval, and may embody the rudimentary elements of intelligence.

The rapid march of technology leads to two organizationally dysfunctional courses of action. An aggressive data processing manager will press to keep the data processing facility at the forefront of technology. This often leads to introducing equipment and software packages that have little or no use in supporting the organization's goals. At the other extreme, a conservative manager may be reluctant to commit resources to today's technology, secure in the knowledge that the same capabilities will be available at a lower cost some months in the future. This leads to procrastination, technological obsolescence, and the need for massive updates in the future.

The accounting profession has two concerns in regard to evolving information systems technology. First, as financial managers, accountants must have a major input in decisions regarding the overall allocation of the organization's resources. Funds spent on data processing equipment are not available for other use. Second, as principal users of information systems services, accountants must ensure that the automated support necessary to develop accounting information is readily available.

The two concerns are clearly complementary. A sound decision to invest in the correct amount of information systems support in period 1 results in the production of the essential amount of accounting information to continue to make sound decisions in period 2. Underinvestment in information systems technology will result in less than optimal information flow; overinvestment will deprive the organization of the opportunity to achieve other objectives. The best approach to determining the correct level is as follows:

1. Conduct an assessment of current needs
2. Project requirements based on the organization's long-range plan
3. Translate these requirements into the hardware, software, facilities, and personnel necessary to meet information demands

A needs-based approach permits the organization to maintain a steady course between the Charybdis of procuring unnecessary equipment and the Scylla of becoming technologically obsolete.

SUMMARY

Six elements of a systems definition are essential to using the system concept effectively. These are: (1) A system is goal oriented; (2) a system is composed of two or more interrelated components; (3) every level of system exists in a hierarchy of systems; (4) a system is synergistic; (5) a system has a boundary; and (6) a system interacts with its environment. These static characteristics of systems are supplemented by four dynamic characteristics: (1) input, (2) processing or transformation, (3) output, and (4) feedback.

These system characteristics can be used to define the AIS and its major subsystem of interest in this text, the CAAIS. The important distinction between these two systems is that the AIS is relatively open to its environment, whereas the CAAIS is relatively closed. The AIS is able to adjust to changing environmental conditions because of the dominance of the human component. In contrast, the CAAIS provides the stability necessary for routine processing of data into accounting information.

The AIS is strongly influenced by both internal and external environmental factors. The internal factors relate to organizational structure and human behavioral characteristics, and the external factors relate to regulatory bodies and information processing technology.

REVIEW QUESTIONS, DISCUSSION QUESTIONS, AND PROBLEMS AND CASES

A. Review Questions

A2.1 List the six key elements of a systems definition as used in this text.

A2.2 Why is the goal-seeking nature of systems important to the study of AIS?

A2.3 What are three ways in which system components may interact?

A2.4 What is synergy?

A2.5 What three issues complicate defining a system's boundary?

A2.6 Define a relatively open system.

A2.7 Define a relatively closed system.

A2.8 Name four characteristics of systems dynamics.

A2.9 What is a "black box" observation? Is it ever useful?

A2.10 What is first order feedback? Give an example of negative and positive first order feedback?

A2.11 Define the AIS in systems terms.

A2.12 What are the components of an AIS?

A2.13 Contrast the AIS and the CAAIS in terms of the open-closed dimension of the systems approach.

A2.14 Define the CAAIS. What is its relationship to the AIS?

A2.15 Why does the environment of the AIS encompass such a wide area?

A2.16 How is an AIS related to its parent organization?

A2.17 List the contextual variables relevant to AIS success.

A2.18 Define organizational structure. What are the characteristics of organizational structure?

A2.19 What is meant by centralization and decentralization of decision-making authority in an organization?

A2.20 Define and give an example of functional organization.

A2.21 Define divisional decentralization.

A2.22 What is a matrix structure? How does it relate to functional structure?

A2.23 What are the two principal agencies that influence accounting in business organizations?

A2.24 Discuss the historical role of the AICPA in shaping accounting practice.

A2.25 What are:

1. GAAP.
2. CAP.
3. APB.
4. FASB.
5. SEC.

A2.26 What are the four classifications of FASB pronouncements?

A2.27 What are the similarities and differences among the AICPA, FASB, and the SEC? Which of these have legal authority, and which do not?

A2.28 What is the GASB? Discuss the role of the National Council on Governmental Accounting in monitoring government agencies.

A2.29 What principles are published by the NCGA?

A2.30 List the names of associations and agencies that may directly influence the AIS.

A2.31 What single feature dominates the technological environment of the AIS?

B. Discussion Questions

B2.1 Define your class in AIS in terms of the six elements of a systems definition. How does this compare with a functional definition? What are the advantages and disadvantages of each approach?

B2.2 Most colleges and universities require or encourage students to evaluate their classes and their instructors. Describe how these evaluations relate to the concept of feedback. What is/are the major limitation(s) in these programs? How could these be overcome?

B2.3 AIS is a widely used acronym. In contrast, the term CAAIS is unique to this text. Why do you suppose this subsystem was introduced? Do you find it useful in clarifying the subject?

B2.4 What is the environment of the AIS? Can you relate the contextual variables of an organization to the probability of a successful AIS?

B2.5 There is no one ideal or best form of organizational structure; different structures are suitable for different organizations. Discuss (1) functional structure, (2) divisional decentralization, and (3) matrix organization. Give examples of situations where each might be appropriate.

B2.6 How does decentralization affect information needs? Describe a highly decentralized marketing department. Will the AIS be processing more information in this department than in one which is more highly centralized?

B2.7 Discuss the roles of the AICPA and the FASB in formulating accounting principles.

B2.8 "AICPA and FASB provide a rigid boundary for an AIS." Discuss.

B2.9 How does an AIS in an organization cope with rapid changes in its technological environment?

B2.10 Technological considerations of an AIS involve accountants in at least two roles. Describe these roles.

C. Problems and Cases

C2.1 A medium-sized manufacturing organization wants to develop a financial reporting system for its marketing, production, and research departments.

a. Comment on the AIS needs with respect to:
- **(1)** Frequency of reports
- **(2)** Coverage of detail
- **(3)** Nature of data
- **(4)** Use of estimates

b. What types of external constraints will be important to consider?

C2.2 To satisfy SEC regulations and AICPA principles, an organization must maintain an efficient accounting system. However, the AIS may lack many useful qualities if it only satisfies AICPA and SEC requirements. Discuss the influence of external agencies on the AIS.

C2.3 The internal environment of an organization can be analyzed and classified in a number of ways. The most common is the degree of centralization of decision making. For a highly centralized organization, discuss the roles of the AIS at the lower, middle, and upper levels of the organizational structure.

C2.4 As an AIS specialist in a CPA firm, James Howell has the responsibility to inform the partners and system designers of any new development or subject he thinks may influence the direction of future design strategy and systems review. Assume you are working for Mr. Howell.

a. What parts of this chapter would you bring to his notice?

b. Prepare a one-page summary report regarding critical environmental factors for Mr. Howell to present at the partners' meeting.

c. Review the last four weeks of *Computerworld* or a similar trade publication to determine if there are any current changes in technology that may be relevant.

SUGGESTED READINGS

ASHBY, H. R. *Introduction to Cybernetics*. New York: John Wiley, 1963.

CHURCHMAN, C. WEST. *The Systems Approach*. New York: Dell Publishing, 1968.

DELANEY, PATRICK R., JAMES R., JAMES R. ADLER et al. *GAAP Interpretation and Application*. New York: John Wiley, 1986.

HARE, VAN COURT, JR. *Systems Analysis: A Diagnostic Approach*. New York: Harcourt, Brace & World, 1967.

chapter three

The Accounting System

CHAPTER OUTLINE

INTRODUCTION

In spite of the differences among financial, managerial, and cost accounting, the governing principles of financial accounting dominate the accounting universe. The accounting principles are mainly concerned with financial accounting priorities. In this chapter we discuss the relevant aspects of financial accounting which are useful to users of AIS. The principal sources of financial accounting principles are FASB pronouncements and concepts.[1]

THE STRUCTURE OF THE ACCOUNTING SYSTEM

In any enterprise, the financial accounting system maintains the database that generates financial statements. Financial statements prepared by a profit-making entity serve the needs of various interest groups. Often these reports are called *general purpose external statements*. (Readers may consult any text on financial accounting to review illustrations of classified income statements, balance sheets, and statements of changes in financial position). The elements of an accounting system are structured by the requirements of financial statements. Ledger accounts and journals are the main building blocks of the process that produces financial statements. In fact, the general ledger system functions as the primary database for any accounting system, manual or computerized. The journal system operates as a check to the data entry in the ledger system.

Table 3–1 shows the structure of an accounting system hierarchically and includes financial statements, ledger accounts, journals, and transactions.

Journal and ledger systems play vital roles in the accounting process. They not only produce and provide the database for financial statements, but also facilitate financial and operating controls. The accounting subsystems used for operating and financial controls are developed around the journal and ledger systems. For example, the subsystem used for inventory control is related to the purchase journal, sales journal, inventory ledger card (bin card), and inventory ledger account. We will discuss the details of specific controls and their relation to ledger and journal systems in Chapter 11.

[1] FASB = Financial Accounting Standards Board. The main authoritative body in promulgating accounting concepts and principles. The FASB Concepts that were used in developing parts of this chapter are as follows: FASB Concept No. 1: Objectives of Financial Reporting by Business Enterprises; FASB Concept No. 2: Qualitative Characteristics of Accounting Information; and FASB Concept No. 3: Elements of Financial Statements of Business Enterprises.

TABLE 3–1 The Structure of the Accounting System

Accounting Statements and Reports Periodic financial statements prepared at the end of each accounting period, summarize accounting transaction data, and provide information on performance and financial position	*Balance sheet* *Income statement* *SCFP* (Statement of Changes in Financial Position)
Ledger Accounts A database for accounting transactions data, classifying data into common categories, and providing input to periodic summary statements	*Assets Accounts* Cash, property, plant, inventory, receivables *Liabilities Accounts* Accounts payable, expenses payable, bonds payable *Owner's Equity* Capital, retained earnings *Revenues* Sales, fees, commissions *Expenses* Cost of goods sold, operating expenses, utilities expenses
Journals Place of first recording of exchange-priced transactions, identification of debits and credits, and posting to the ledger accounts	Sales journal and/or accounts receivable Purchases journal and/or accounts payable journal Cash receipt journal Cash payment (disbursement) journal General journal
Transactions Exchange-priced transactions recognized on the basis of verifiable objective evidence	Economic transactions involving exchanges of money or money's worth

The Journal

Journal entries are the first steps in recognizing and recording accounting transactions. Journals are called books of original entry because they are where accounting transactions are first recorded. The journal contains necessary transaction information—namely (a) the date of transaction recognition, (b) the value attached (exchange price) to the transaction, and (c) the accounts classification. Questions about these bits of information are related to different aspects of measurement in accounting, and are resolved through generally accepted accounting principles (GAAP). For example, when is a transaction considered recognized? What is to be recorded as depreciation? How are intangible assets to be amortized?

The Ledger

Accounting transactions are classified and summarized in the ledger accounts. In modern accounting systems, ledger accounts are the master files of accounting data. Transaction entries are posted to the debit and credit columns of appropriate ledger accounts, and the account balances adjusted accordingly. Periodic account balances are used to prepare the income statement and the balance sheet. Specific ledger account balances are useful for financial control, audit purposes, and planning. For example, if the inventory account balance of a particular date is below the required level, inventory ordering activity starts. Inventory comparison helps in financial control. The audit function involves taking inventory balances and verifying the receipts and issues of inventory items.

The ledger accounts are organized on two levels, subsidiary ledgers and general ledgers. Subsidiary ledger accounts provide details of each balance sheet account, while the general ledger summarizes the entries in the subsidiary accounts.

For example, accounts payable is a general ledger account (sometimes called the general ledger control account), while the subsidiary ledger accounts are the individual accounts kept for each vendor or creditor. Here is a sample:

General Ledger Account	*Subsidiary Ledger Accounts*
	Trade creditors' accounts by name
Accounts payable	Accounts Payable—Jones
	Accounts Payable—Smith
	Accounts Payable—Ray
	Trade debtors' accounts by name
Accounts receivable	Accounts Receivable—Meyers
	Accounts Receivable—Jim
	Accounts Receivable—Brigg

The core of an accounting system is the general ledger system and the financial reporting system. The general ledger system is usually coordinated with the other control subsystems to establish a complete system useful for financial control and reporting purposes. The other control subsystems usually include those shown in Table 3–2.

THE ACCOUNTING CYCLE

To understand the functioning of an accounting system that operates through journals and ledger systems, you need to know the accounting cycle.

An accounting cycle involves six steps or sets of actions:

1. Recognizing and analyzing the transactions
2. Recording the transactions in the journal

TABLE 3–2 The General Ledger and Control Subsystem

General Ledger System (GLS)	*Control Subsystems*
The general ledger	Cash management system Accounts payable system Accounts receivable system Cash accounting system Fixed assets system Purchasing and inventory system Financial reporting system Budgeting system Strategic planning system

3. Posting the entries to the ledger
4. Making adjusting entries
5. Preparing the financial statements
6. Closing the ledger accounts and preparing for the beginning of the new accounting period

These steps describe the sequence of activities that take place in an accounting process during an *accounting period.* The frequency and time periods of steps 1 through 3 may vary from system to system within an accounting period. However, steps 4 through 6 always happen at the end of an accounting period.

COMPUTERIZED ACCOUNTING SYSTEMS

An accounting system can be designed for manual or computerized operation. In either case, the basic structure remains the same. Nowadays, except in a very small business or a nonbusiness organization, accounting systems are computerized. Some organizations will have their important subsystems computerized and the total system will have manual coordination. Payroll systems, point of sale systems, cash receipts, and disbursement systems can be separately computerized without having a complete computerized accounting system.

In this section we briefly discuss the features of computerized accounting systems, using as an example Software International's Accounting System. This system is useful for large organizations with diversified operations. There are also advantages to using a computerized accounting system in small organizations. Our second example is from MAS, Inc.'s Client Accounting System, which is designed for smaller organizations.

A computerized accounting system uses the general ledger as the master file. The general ledger master file is the cluster of ledger accounts stored in internal or external computer storage media. A computerized system uses software programs to manipulate data entry, editing, updating records and files, and periodic closing electronically. It has many advantages, such as on-line data entry and inquiry, faster manipulation, timely report preparation, and greater analytical ability.

A computerized accounting system can satisfy a wide range of user needs. Software International identified the following user needs for its accounting systems. Any good accounting system should address these needs.

- *Faster closing of books,* substantially decreasing the closing cycle from weeks to days, and sometimes hours
- *Increased speed and accuracy* of reports to all managers, concomitantly more time for analysis
- *On-line data entry and inquiry,* for faster processing and reporting—more control
- *Flexibility* in the chart of accounts structure, imposing no restrictions on how users define their numbering systems
- *Complete audit trails* for close tracking that are always current
- *Account summary and control balances* that are always current
- *Complete allocation capability* to more accurately distribute costs
- *Multicompany processing* and reporting capability
- *Automatic consolidations* and eliminations for wholly or partially owned subsidiaries
- *Foreign currency conversions* with an unlimited number of currencies
- *Complete budgeting facility,* utilizing both fixed and variable budgeting
- *Financial management* (statistical) information always available for complete statistical and management reporting
- *Clerical efficiency,* with easy-to-use input techniques

Software International's Accounting System [2]

This section outlines the general ledger and reporting systems of the accounting system developed by Software International, Inc.

The salient features of Software International's accounting system include these:

1. *Database design.* Provides the operating programs, and manipulation files relating to all accounting information which are readily accessible.
2. *Account master file.* Incorporates all ledger accounts arranged in hierarchical levels; relationships with accounts at different levels can be easily established.
3. *Variable report writer.* Reports for senior management review, regula-

[2] Materials in this section are taken from Software International publications, with permission. See Software International®, *General Ledger and Financial Reporting Systems* (Andover, MA: 1978).

tory reports, and financial statements can be prepared according to user needs.

The following sections provide an introduction to the database design, files, chart of accounts and relationships with accounts, and sample financial statements of the Software International Accounting System.

Database Design. Fundamental to the system is the concept of an easily accessible location for all financial information. This database design, rather than requiring slow, sequential access to information, allows for rapid and precise data retrieval.

The user advantages of a database approach are substantial. At period end, or any time during the cycle, financial information is immediately available for updating and reporting. Accounts are kept current throughout the accounting period.

Account Master File. This system has been developed around the Account Master File, shown in Figure 3–1. Flexibility is provided to accommodate up to 24-character account numbers using any combination of numbers, letters, or special characters desired by the user.

Functioning in a manner similar to the general ledger card in a manual system, the standard account record stores amounts for both current and last year's actuals (including beginning balance) and two groups of budget fields, current year and a revision to current.

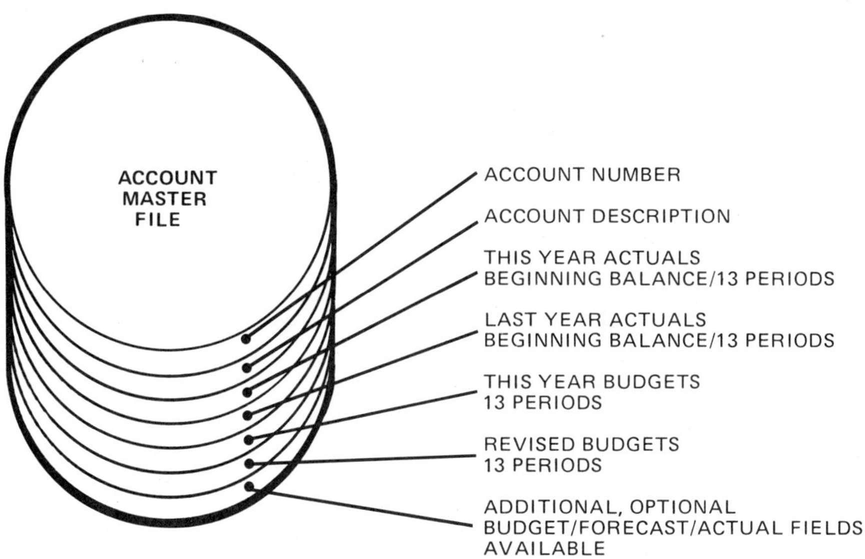

FIGURE 3–1 Account Master

Source: Software International, *General Ledger and Financial Reporting Systems* (Andover, MA: 1978). Reprinted by permission.

Optional sets of fields are available for other time periods. All sets can handle 13 periods of information. For users with a 12-period cycle, the 13th period space is frequently used for year-end adjustments.

Account records mirror the chart of accounts. The detail level (posting) accounts are subordinate to higher-level (summary) accounts. These summary accounts, in effect parents to detail accounts, may in turn be subordinate to higher-level summary accounts throughout an unlimited number of reporting levels.

During an accounting period, monetary amounts are posted to the detail accounts and then automatically rolled up, or summarized, into their parent accounts. These are rolled into higher level accounts, level by level, finally reaching division or corporate accounts at still higher levels of consolidation. Parent accounts always contain the net amounts resulting from transactions processed against their posting accounts.

Chart of Accounts/Relationships. Automatic summarization, the backbone of the system, provides an additional dimension to the chart of accounts structure. The summarizations are controlled by a unique feature, the *relationship file,* which contains all the user-determined paths among accounts. These paths do not depend on a logically structured chart of accounts or numbering system.

The relationships can follow the chart of accounts numbering structure, but the system also provides the option of expanding on this framework, of establishing relationships as needed among various accounts to create a fully responsive database. The proper definition and development of this file gives users total control over any desired monetary and statistical summarizations.

The general ledger and financial reporting system uses the parent-subordinate structure of the chart of accounts and the interaction of the relationship file to give users constant access to current information. Net amounts, as well as year-to-date balances at any level, are always ready to be retrieved. As a result, users have a flexible, need-responsive tool for control and reporting.

A typical example demonstrating the flexibility provided by the interaction of the chart of accounts with the relationship capability is shown in considering the needs of the controller of the Breton Company,[3] who also reviews the foreign and domestic direct labor expenses of the company.

Figure 3–2 represents the accounting relationships in the Breton Company's Direct Labor–Consumer Division account; the blocks connected by solid lines in Figure 3–3 illustrate these relationships.

[3] All company names and figures in examples for this and subsequent sections have been changed, but they portray actual business situations.

Account Name	*Account Number*
Direct Labor—Consumer Division	05-200-000
Direct Labor—U.S. Sites	05-230-000
Direct Labor—New York City	05-230-010
Direct Labor—Los Angeles	05-230-020
Direct Labor—Houston	05-230-030
Direct Labor—Atlanta	05-230-040
Direct Labor—Non–U.S. Sites	05-270-000
Direct Labor—Mexico City	05-270-010
Direct Labor—Hong Kong	05-270-020
Direct Labor—Paris	05-270-030

FIGURE 3–2 Direct Labor Expenses

The direct labor accounts for New York City, Los Angeles, Houston, and Atlanta are subordinate to *Direct Labor—U.S. Sites,* which is their parent account. *Direct Labor—Non–U.S. Sites* is the parent account of the direct labor accounts for Mexico City, Hong Kong, and Paris. Similarly, *Direct Labor—Consumer Division* is the parent account for both Direct Labor—U.S. Sites and Direct Labor—Non–U.S. Sites.

When the Breton Company's financial and statistical information was arranged according to the system database, the parent-subordinate relationships described in Figure 3–2 were identified to the system simply by filling out the form in Figure 3–4. Each time an expense amount is posted to the New York City account, the system automatically rolls up and nets the amount into both parent accounts, Direct Labor—U.S. Sites and Direct Labor—Consumer Division. Ac-

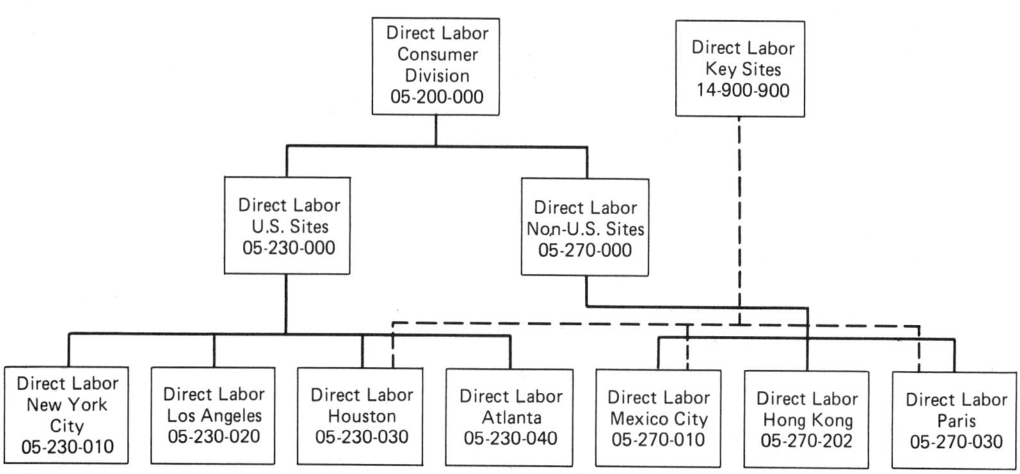

FIGURE 3–3 Chart of Accounts for Direct Labor Expenses

Relationship File

Trans Code (1–2)	Parent Account (3–26)	Subordinate Account (27–50)
32	05200000	05230000
32	05230000	05230010
32	05230000	05230020
32	05230000	05230030
32	05230000	05230040
32	05200000	05270000
32	05270000	05270010
32	05270000	05270020
32	05270000	05270030

FIGURE 3–4 Relationship File Input

curate and current balances are immediately accessible for review and reporting.

In addition, the controller of the Breton Company needs constantly to review the direct labor summary figure of the sum of Breton's most labor-intensive sites—Houston, Mexico City, and Paris—to alert management when this amount exceeds a predetermined labor to sales ratio. The controller can use the existing database to develop this information: He simply establishes a new control account, Direct Labor—Key Sites (see Figure 3–5) as a parent to the appropriate posting level (subordinate) accounts. This is accomplished using the coding form shown in Figure 3–6. When the transactions are processed, three new relationships are created (see the dotted lines in Figure 3–3). Direct labor posted to any of the Houston, Mexico City, or Paris accounts will not only be rolled up into the chart of account parents (account numbers 05-230-000 and 05-270-000), but also into the new parent account, Direct Labor—Key Sites.

Thus, one posting to Direct Labor—Houston updates four different accounts: Direct Labor—Houston, Direct Labor—U.S. Sites, Direct Labor—Consumer Division, Direct Labor—Key Sites, in two different directions. The Direct Labor—Key Sites account always contains a current balance reflecting labor transactions at all key sites worldwide.

The general ledger and financial reporting system also supplies auxiliary reports to assist accounting and financial personnel in developing and managing basic accounts and relationships. There are several types of relationships reports: They show all account relation-

Account Master File

Trans Code (1–2)	Account Number (3–26)	Account Description (27–50)
12	14900900	DIRECT-KEY SITES

FIGURE 3–5 Account Master File Input

Relationship File

Trans Code (1–2)	Parent Account (3–26)	Subordinate Account (27–50)
32	14900900	05230030
32	14900900	05270010
32	14900900	05270030

FIGURE 3–6 Relationship File Input

ships, selected account relationships, or unrelated accounts. These reports can be used as audit and maintenance trails to aid in managing the account master records and monitoring the relationships between them. The interaction of the Chart of Accounts and the Relationship file gives users a basis for producing financial and analytical reports tailored to the needs of each organization or reporting unit.

By using a well-defined Chart of Accounts and a Relationship file that supports all the supplementary roll-ups, coupled with the system's report writer feature, financial managers have a comprehensive, computer-aided system of account management.

Financial Statements and Regulatory Reporting. The Software International General Ledger and Financial Reporting System satisfies all basic financial reporting requirements for both large and small companies (balance sheets, income statements, and supporting schedules). The format library contains a variety of report types developed by the company through years of experience with users in a wide cross section of business environments.

For custom-designed reports needed for additional reporting, the Variable Report Writer is available. All data constantly reside on the system database and can be retrieved easily and displayed in any format the user chooses—all by means of simple input instructions. This means that accountants and financial managers can tailor financial reports to fit a wide range of reporting requirements (see Figure 3–7).

The financial reporting feature of the general ledger system is a complete management control tool: comprehensive, accurate, and easy-to-use. To give you a firsthand look at some of the ways this feature is used, we include some report samples. Figure 3–8 shows the system's ability to deliver snapshot reports for senior management review. Figure 3–9 displays the asset portion of a comparative balance check for a typical manufacturing company. Figure 3–10 shows a portion of the bankwide income report for a commercial bank.

In addition to the many internal management reports necessary for the smooth operation of a business, there are frequent external reporting requirements, such as reports for state and federal regulatory agencies. Often these regulatory reports require unique information and layout.

```
                                   BRETON COMPANY

                      SINGLE LEVEL ACCOUNT WHERE USED ALL FILES

                                  EASTERN DIVISION

**************************************************************************************************

ACCOUNT REQUEST 01 22 213 860 060    DESCRIPTION TRAVEL ## ENTERTAINMENT         ACCOUNT CODE 4

**************************************************************************************************

PARENT ACCOUNT            ACCOUNT NUMBER              DESCRIPTION             ACCOUNT CODE    ALLOC FROM#NO
                          01 22 213 801 000        TOTAL OTHER EXPENSES       D
                          01 22 999 860 060        TRAVEL ## ENTERTAINMENT    D
                          01 99 013 860 060        TRAVEL ## ENTERTAINMENT    D

SUBORDINATE ACCOUNTS      ACCOUNT NUMBER              DESCRIPTION             ACCOUNT CODE
                          NONE
REPORT USED IN            REPORT NUMBER            REPORT FRMT                REPORT LINE
                          42000                    D2                         1310

**************************************************************************************************

ACCOUNT REQUEST 01 22 213 600 000    DESCRIPTION-TOTAL EXPENSES                  ACCOUNT CODE D

**************************************************************************************************

PARENT ACCOUNT            ACCOUNT NUMBER              DESCRIPTION             ACCOUNT CODE    ALLOC FROM#NO
                          01 22 213 600            NET EXPENSES               D

SUBORDINATE ACCOUNTS      ACCOUNT NUMBER              DESCRIPTION             ACCOUNT CODE
                          01 22 213 601 000        TOTAL DIRECT COSTS         D
                          01 22 213 701 000        TOTAL PAYROLL EXPENSES     D
                          01 22 213 801 000        TOTAL OTHER EXPENSES       D

REPORT USED IN            REPORT NUMBER            REPORT FRMT                REPORT LINE
                          41000                    D1                         1100
                          20000                    A2                         3200
```

FIGURE 3–7 "Where Used" Report

Arrow Engineering Quarterly Income Analysis September 1977						
Revenues	Act—	4,953,700	5,328,800	4,876,450	5,101,720	20,260,670
	Bud—	5,100,000	5,200,000	4,950,000	5,000,000	20,250,000
	Var—	146,300-	128,800	73,550-	101,720	10,670
Cost of Services	Act—	2,784,900	2,932,850	2,832,490	2,805,300	11,355,540
	Bud—	2,805,000	2,860,000	2,722,500	2,750,000	11,137,500
	Var—	20,100	72,850-	109,990-	55,300-	218,040-

FIGURE 3–8 Quarterly Income Analysis

The database design, updating techniques, and flexible report writing capabilities of the General Ledger and Financial Reporting System combine to support all types of regulatory reporting requirements. Users of the system can respond to the requirements of such government agencies as the Securities and Exchange Commission, the Federal Communication Commission, the Department of Public Utilities, and the Civil Aeronautics Board. In addition, with advanced training in the use of the Variable Report Writer, report generation of this type can become an automatic system function. Figure 3–11 shows an example of a utility reporting to the Department of Public Utilities.

The Client Accounting System of MAS, Inc.

The Client Accounting System is an example of a computerized accounting system for small or medium-sized companies. The Client Accounting System of MAS, Incorporated, operates with three sets of files:

1. General Ledger Transaction Master File
2. General Ledger Transaction Work File
3. Year-to-Date General Ledger Transaction File

Utilizing these files, the Client Accounting System generates the following reports:

1. General ledger account list
2. General ledger transaction register
3. Financial statements
4. Departmental statements
5. Schedules to balance sheet and income statements
6. Sources and application of funds
7. Cash flow statements
8. Comparative reporting
9. Trial balance
10. Accumulative ledger
11. 941-A and W-2 reporting
12. Source cross reference for general ledger

UNITED MANUFACTURING
BALANCE SHEET
FOR PERIOD ENDING: SEPT, 1977

REPORT #06172

	CURRENT MONTH	CUMULATIVE YEAR-TO-DATE
ASSETS:		
CURRENT ASSETS:		
CASH	$ 153,249.15	$ 261,760.83
RECEIVABLES:		
TRADE ACCOUNTS	614,015.77	5,384,147.84
LESS: ALLOWANCE BAD DEBTS	7,957.77	55,822.63-
INTERCOMPANY	208,570.76	13,481,647.26
TOTAL RECEIVABLES	$ 814,629.28	$ 18,809,972.47
REFUNDABLE TAXES	.00	.00
DEFERRED INCOME TAXES	.00	1,240.00
INVENTORIES:		
UNFINISHED	$ 535,468.68	$ 10,422,140.37
FINISHED	58,060.22	3,453,616.39
CUSTOM PRODUCTS	252,384.18	765,616.38
SERVICE	17,800.53	684,331.43
INTER-DIVISIONAL	58,098.71	58,098.71
RESALE	.00	.00
CHICAGO INVENTORY	48,265.93	48,265.93
TOTAL INVENTORIES	$ 970,078.25	$ 15,432,069.21
PREPAID EXPENSES	8,103.42	133,479.58
TOTAL CURRENT ASSETS	$1,946,060.10	$ 34,639,282.09
PROPERTY PLANT EQUIPMENT:		
LAND IMPROVEMENTS	$ .00	$ 205,100.61
BLDG/LEASEHOLD IMPROVEMENT	1,536.15	6,126,529.86
MACHINERY/EQUIPMENT	45,574.06	2,240,090.28
OTHER FIXED ASSETS	25,325.92	1,540,352.05
LESS: ACCUM DEPRECIATION	48,734.83-	5,802,202.42-
TOTAL FIXED ASSETS	$ 23,701.30	$ 4,309,870.38
OTHER ASSETS:		
NET INVEST/AD TO SUBS	$ .00	$ 4,185,545.94
PATENTS/OTHER INTANGIBLES	4,901.77	57,053.54
OTHER RECEIVABLES	12,880.33	54,283.83
MISCELLANEOUS ASSETS	5,584.45	249,994.02
TOTAL OTHER ASSETS	$ 23,366.55	$ 4,546,877.33
TOTAL ASSETS	$1,993,127.95	$ 43,494,029.80

FIGURE 3–9 Balance Sheet

RIVER VALLEY BANK

INCOME REPORT BANK LEVEL
AS OF MAY 01, 1977

ACCOUNT NAME	INCOME
INT & DISC ON LOANS	812,239.59
INTEREST ON REAL ESTATE LOANS	
FINANCIAL INSTITUTIONS	
PURCHASE/CARRYING SECURITIES	
TO FARMERS	3,170.13
COMMERCIAL & INDUSTRIAL	705,672.84
ACCOUNTS RECEIVABLE	1,900.11
INSTALLMENT LOANS	654,096.39
INDIVIDUALS-SINGLE PAYMENT	79,021.60
PARTICIPATIONS	
COMMERCIAL PAPER	
BANKERS ACCEPTANCES	
ADVANCE CHECKING	
NON-ACCRUAL LOANS	
OTHER LOANS	19,272.35
TOTAL INT & DISC ON LNS	2,275,373.01
FDS FDS SOLD & REPOS	
FEDERAL FUNDS SOLD	69,444.59
SECURITIES PURCHASE U/R/A	
TOTAL IN FDS & REP	69,444.59
FEES & COMMS ON LOANS	
FEES & COMM ON REAL ESTATE LNS	21.91
FEES & COMM ON ACCTS REC LOANS	
FEES & COMM ON INSTALL LOANS	19,688.55
FEES & COMM ON ADVANCE CHECKING	
FEES & COMM ON OTHER LOANS	
TOTAL FEES & COMM ON LOAN	35.31
	19,745.77
INT ON DEP WITH BANKS	
DOMESTIC BANKS	17,249.00
FOREIGN BANKS	124,218.82
TOTAL INT ON DEP W/BKS	141,467.82
IN & DIV SECURITIES	
US GOVERNMENT OBLIGATIONS	502,143.01
US AGENCIES/CORPORATIONS	23,864.34
OBLIG OF STATE/POL SUBDIVIS	381,707.02
OTHER SECURITIES	7,550.00
CORPORATE STOCK	
TOTAL INT & DIV ON SECUR	915,264.37
TRUST FEES	
TRUST FEES-CORPORATE TRUST	
TRUST FEES-PERS SEC SERV	3,170.53
TRUST FEES-EMPLOYEE BENEFITS	
TRUST FEES-ESTIMATES	28,873.93
TRUST FEES-PERS INVEST MANAG	
TRUST FEES-ANNUAL TRUSTS	
TRUST FEES-TRUST TERMINATIONS	32,044.46
TOTAL TRUST FEES	

FIGURE 3–10 Income Report

Most of the standard accounting entries are done easily and, where possible, automatically, like analyzing entries, reversing entries, closing entries, preparation of work sheet, trial balance, and the periodic and special purpose financial reports.

Figures 3–12 and 3–13 are CRT displays of a standard journal entry and an adjustment journal entry. Figure 3–14 shows an example of a comparative income statement produced by the Client Accounting System.

T.E.C. COMPANY
D.P.U. INCOME STATEMENT

		YEAR TO DATE		PROJECTED YEAR	
1.	OPERATING INCOME				
2.	OPERATING REVENUES	178,745,047	$	238,989,199	$
3.	OPERATING EXPENSES:				
4.	OPERATION EXPENSES	130,676,840		176,633,896	
5.	MAINTENANCE EXPENSES	5,248,306		6,829,806	
6.	DEPRECIATION EXPENSE	5,357,956		6,985,600	
7.	AMORT. OF UTILITY PLANT	257,280		345.682	
8.	AMORT. OF PROPERTY LOSS	355,905		474,540	
9.	AMORT. OF INVEST CREDIT	(120,726)		(160,968)	
10	TAXES OTHER THAN INC TAX	16,526,433		21,353,720	
11.	INCOME TAXES	5,960,880		7,757,142	
12.	PROV FOR DEF FED INC TAX	1,173,429		1,521,056	
13.	FED INC TAX DEF-PRIOR YR				
14.	TOTAL OPERATING EXPS	165,436,313	$	221,740,474	$
15.	NET OPERATING REVENUES	13,308,734	$	17,248,645	$
16.	INC FROM UTIL PLT-LEASD OTH				
17.	OTHER UTIL OPER INCOME				
18.	TOTAL UTIL OPER INCOME	13,308,734	$	17,248,645	$
19.	OTHER INCOME				
20.	INCOME FROM MERCH&JOBBING	(23,385)		(29,595)	
21.	INCOME FROM NON UTIL OPER	14,159		14,159	
22.	NONOPERATING RENTAL INCOME	0		0	
23.	INTEREST & DIVIDEND INCOME	151,047		175,047	
24.	MISC NONOPERATING INCOME	176,407		176,407	
25.	TOTAL OTHER INCOME	318,228	$	336,018	$
26.	TOTAL INCOME	13,626,962	$	17,584,663	$
27.	MISC INCOME DEDUCTIONS:				
28.	MISC AMORTIZATION				
29.	TOTAL INCOME DEDUCTIONS	0	$	0	$
30.	INCOME BEFORE INT. CHARGES	13,626,962	$	17,584,663	$
31.	INTEREST CHARGES				
32.	INTEREST ON LONG TERM DEBT	5,296,905		7,008,608	
33.	AMORT OF DEBT DISC & EXP.	92,769		135,859	
34.	AMORT OF PREM ON DEBT-CR				
35.	INT ON DEBT TO ASSOC. CO'S				
36.	OTHER INTEREST EXPENSE	389,483		565,507	
37.	INT CHGED TO CONSTR-CREDIT	(3,228)		(8,828)	
38.	TOTAL INTEREST CHARGES	5,775,929	$	7,701,146	$
39.	NET INCOME	7,851,033	$	9,883,517	$
40.	EARNED SURPLUS				
41.	BALANCE BEGINNING OF YEAR	28,983,255		28,983,255	
42.	BALANCE TRANSF FROM INCOME	0		0	
43.	MISC CREDITS TO SURPLUS	336,689		336,689	
44.	MISC DEBITS TO SURPLUS	172,991		172,991	
45.	NET ADDS TO EARNED SURPLUS	36,997,986	$	39,030,470	$
46.	DIVIDENDS	8,406,908		10,283,908	
47.	BALANCE END OF YEAR	28,591,078		28,746,562	

FIGURE 3–11 D.P.U. Income Statement

Client Accounting
CRT Display—3

"M.A.S." Client Accounting Sample

Standard Journal TRX Entry
Add

1.	G/L Account #	1208-000	Acc. Depreciation Motor Vehicle
2.	TRX Date	01/31/82	
3.	Debit Amount	.00	
4.	Credit Amount	$221.00	
5.	Source	STD1	
6.	TRX Reference	Book Monthly Depreciation	

Accumulated Cash = 120800 Accumulated Balance = $221.61
Any Change?

FIGURE 3–12 Standard Journal Entry

Client Accounting
CRT Display—3

"M.A.S." Client Accounting Sample

Adjustment Journal TRX Entry

1.	G/L Account #	4680-100	Inventory Ending
2.	TRX Date	04/19/82	
3.	Debit Amount	.00	
4.	Credit Amount	$150.00	
5.	Source	REO3	
6.	TRX Reference	Year End Adjustment	

Accumulated Cash = 15493100 Accumulated Balance = $150.00-

FIGURE 3–13 Adjustment Journal Entry

'M.A.S.' ACCOUNTING SAMPLE
LEXINGTON, MASSACHUSETTS 02173

COMPARATIVE STATEMENT - INCOME
FOR THE PERIOD 11/01/81 TO 03/31/82

	NOV.	DEC.	JAN.	FEB.	MAR.	APR.	TOTAL
INCOME							
SALES - BOATS	$72,757.10	$35,534.28	$43,315.21	$231,396.33	$481,991.00	$0.00	$864,993.92
SALES-ACCESORIES & SUPPLIES	0.00	0.00	432.00	17,538.00	41,196.40	0.00	59,166.40
CASH SALES EXCHANGE	0.00	0.00	0.00	0.00	0.00	0.00	0.00
	72,757.10	35,534.28	43,747.21	248,934.33	523,187.40	0.00	924,160.32
RETURNS & ALLOWANCES	948.65	637.78	2,657.85	924.93	4,376.10	0.00	9,545.31
RETURNS & ALLOWANCES - A	0.00	0.00	0.00	0.00	0.00	0.00	0.00
TRADE DISCOUNTS	1,430.48	1,270.44	960.73	4,269.52	9,925.80	0.00	17,856.97
	2,379.13	1,908.22	3,618.58	5,194.45	14,301.90	0.00	27,402.28
NET SALES	70,377.97	33,626.06	40,128.63	243,739.88	508,885.50	0.00	896,758.04
COST OF SALES							
INVENTORY, BEGINNING	(22,487.68)	(9,873.69)	(234,864.26)	(155,689.71)	825,986.48	0.00	403,071.14
PURCHASES - BOATS	73,597.41	37,124.02	205,247.39	329,779.03	599,782.13	0.00	1,245,529.98
PURCHASES - A & S	0.00	0.00	55,596.75	11,645.22	112,811.13	0.00	180,053.10
PURCHASES - AFFILIATES	0.00	0.00	0.00	0.00	0.00	0.00	0.00
FREIGHT & TRUCKING	6,322.63	719.40	5,977.84	10,405.73	15,336.45	0.00	38,762.05
SALES AT COST	1,129.99	1,068.88	294.84	5,293.00	32,301.71	0.00	40,088.42
PAYROLL - A & S DEPARTMENT	0.00	0.00	440.03	4,144.63	7,627.49	0.00	12,212.15
	56,302.37	26,900.85	32,102.91	194,991.90	1,529,241.97	0.00	1,839,540.00
INVENTORY, ENDING	0.00	0.00	0.00	0.00	1,122,133.57	0.00	1,122,133.57
TOTAL COST OF SALES	56,302.37	26,900.85	32,102.91	194,991.90	407,108.40	0.00	717,406.43
GROSS PROFIT	14,075.60	6,725.21	8,025.72	48,747.98	101,777.10	0.00	179,351.61
EXPENSES							
WAREHOUSE EXPENSES	3,146.56	11,948.11	15,886.52	9,120.20	13,825.88	0.00	53,927.27
SELLING EXPENSES	4,895.33	5,602.63	6,410.12	12,640.19	11,714.32	0.00	41,262.59
GENERAL & ADM. EXPENSES	10,051.78	14,764.53	19,471.29	9,981.94	9,482.06	0.00	63,751.60
A & S DEPARTMENTAL EXPENSES	7,081.13	17,728.82	21,164.47	11,467.54	11,313.27	0.00	68,755.23
TAXES	559.72	1,615.08	1,496.52	1,249.23	1,575.33	0.00	6,495.88
TOTAL EXPENSE - SCHEDULE	25,734.52	51,659.17	64,428.92	44,459.10	47,910.86	0.00	234,192.57
OPERATING INCOME	(11,658.92)	(44,933.96)	(56,403.20)	4,288.88	53,866.24	0.00	(54,840.96)
OTHER INCOME & EXPENSES	(79.78)	(2,160.85)	(75.32)	(4,526.82)	(1,690.94)	0.00	(8,533.71)
INCOME BEFORE TAXES	(11,579.14)	(42,773.11)	(56,327.88)	8,815.70	55,557.18	0.00	(46,307.25)
PROVISION FOR INCOME TAXES	0.00	0.00	0.00	0.00	0.00	0.00	0.00
NET INCOME OR (LOSS)	(11,579.14)	(42,773.11)	(56,327.88)	8,815.70	55,557.18	0.00	(46,307.25)

FIGURE 3–14 Comparative Income Statement

SUMMARY

Certain aspects of financial accounting are useful to users of AIS. The elements of most accounting systems are structured to provide the information needed to generate financial statements. The structure of an accounting system includes financial statements, ledger accounts, journals, and financial transactions, organized in a hierarchical order.

The journal and ledger systems play vital roles. They provide the accounting database and the mechanism for financial control. Journals provide the initial record of a business transaction and are called books of original entry. The ledger accounts summarize the transaction data and are used as master files in a computerized system. Ledger accounts have two levels: the general ledger system, and the subsidiary ledger system.

The accounting cycle runs over an accounting period; when the ledger accounts are closed, adjustment entries are given, and the account balances are drawn to prepare the financial statements. The six steps of the accounting cycle start with the affirmation of an accounting transaction and end with the closing of the ledger accounts.

A computerized accounting system uses software programs to manipulate accounting functions through the computer. It can satisfy a wide range of user needs. Computerized accounting systems are available to small as well as large organizations.

REVIEW QUESTIONS, DISCUSSION QUESTIONS, AND PROBLEMS AND CASES

A. Review Questions

A3.1 What is the primary database for an AIS?

A3.2 Outline the structure of an AIS.

A3.3 Give examples of ledger accounts and journals.

A3.4 State the purpose of ledger accounts and journals.

A3.5 Explain the difference between general ledger accounts and subsidiary ledger accounts, using examples.

A3.6 Draw an interface between a general ledger system and control subsystems.

A3.7 Outline the steps in an accounting cycle.

A3.8 What conditions must be satisfied to record a purchase transaction?

A3.9 Atlas Corporation purchased 1000 items of computer diskettes from Elektron, Inc., on January 20, 19XX, at $9.25 each, terms 2/10 n/30. Enter the transaction in a purchase journal in good form.

A3.10 Post the same transaction in the appropriate ledger accounts.

A3.11 What is a chart of accounts? Why is it helpful in AIS?

A3.12 Why is an appropriate database design important to an AIS?

A3.13 What is an Account Master File (see Software International).

A3.14 What is a Relationship file in Software International's AIS? How does it work?

B. Discussion Questions

B3.1 Give examples of the data files a computerized accounting system can use. How are these data files used?

B3.2 Discuss briefly the capabilities of a computerized accounting system.

B3.3 List functional capabilities that are not possible using a manual system.

B3.4 What user needs can be satisfied by a computerized accounting system?

B3.5 Discuss the advantages and disadvantages of Software International's Chart of Accounts.

C. Problems and Cases

C3.1 The Haloid Company manufactured and marketed photographic products for office and industrial applications, including photocopying machines and paper, photocopy chemicals, photographic papers, and negative materials for the graphic arts. In 19X2, the company purchased xerography patents and patent applications from the Battelle Development Corporation, a wholly owned subsidiary of Battelle Memorial Institute. Products based on these patents became so successful that the company changed its name to Xerox a few years later. Exhibits 3–1 and 3–2 present Haloid's comparative consolidated balance sheets and income statements for 19X1 and 19X2.

a. Accounting terminology is not uniform across firms, and it is particularly subject to change over time. Identify unfamiliar terms in these statements and speculate as to the current description of the item.

b. Compute Haloid's working capital at the end of 19X1 and 19X2.

c. During 19X2, the company retired fully depreciated plant and equipment that had originally cost $277,125.61. What amount of property, plant, and equipment did Haloid purchase in 19X2?

d. Haloid follows the standard practice of including among current liabilities that portion of long-term debt that is due to be repaid within one year. Given that there is no additional long-term borrowing during the year, compute the amount of long-term debt repaid in 19X2.

e. Compute the amount of dividends paid in cash in 19X2.

EXHIBIT 3–1 The Haloid Company Comparative Consolidated Balance Sheet

	December 31 1955	1954
Assets		
Current Assets:		
Cash on hand and demand deposits	$ 1,971,120.97	$ 2,585,311.43
Notes and accounts receivable: Trade (less provision for doubtful notes and accounts: 1955—$106,693.87; 1954—$88,212.80)	2,723,128.53	2,247,203.18
Inventories:		
Finished goods, work in process, raw materials and supplies (Note 1)	3,911,119.49	3,292,699.69
Other current assets	65,099.68	72,200.51
Total current assets (Note 6)	$ 8,670,468.67	$ 8,197,414.81
Investment:		
Mortgage receivable	$ 6,138.02	$ 6,954.38
Property, Plant and Equipment (Note 2):		
At cost	$ 8,594,424.29	$ 6,960,629.65
Less: Reserves for depreciation and amortization	2,728,887.29	2,123,318.31
Net property, plant and equipment	$ 5,865,537.00	$ 4,837,311.34
Intangibles:		
Patents (nominal cost) Note 12	$ 1.00	$ 1.00
Formulae (nominal cost)	1.00	1.00
Total intangibles	$ 2.00	$ 2.00
Deferred Charges:		
Unexpired insurance premiums and deposits	$ 56,226.06	$ 56,517.54
Research development costs largely recoverable upon completion of military and other contracts	162,376.11	70,832.87
Other deferred charges	58,591.88	63,666.57
Total deferred charges	$ 277,194.05	$ 191,016.98
Total Assets	$14,819,339.74	$13,232,699.51
Liabilities and Capital		
Current Liabilities:		
Accounts payable:	$ 884,748.54	$ 690,120.62
Accrued liabilities:		
Salaries, wages and commissions	126,451.21	91,866.09
Estimated provision for taxes based on income (Note 3)	1,461,000.83	1,199,191.11
Miscellaneous	282,002.88	149,914.68
Other current liabilities:		
Dividends payable	115,682.85	102,826.40
Payment due within one year on long-term debt (below)	5,474.64	5,234.18
Employees' pension and profit-sharing trust funds (Note 4)	445,025.18	291,853.26
Miscellaneous	153,623.53	154,892.56
Total current liabilities (Note 6)	$ 3,474,009.66	$ 2,685,898.90
Executive Compensation Earned, Payment Deferred (Note 5)	203,470.58	84,547.28
Long-Term Debt:		
Notes payable (Note 6)	3,000,000.00	3,000,000.00

EXHIBIT 3–1 (continued)

	December 31	
	1955	1954
Mortgage payable (less amount payable within one year: 1955–$5,474.64; 1954—$5,234.18) (Note 2)	2,353.08	7,827.72
Commitments and Contingent Liabilities (Notes 7, 8, 10 and 12)	—	—
Total Liabilities	$ 6,679,833.32	$ 5,778,273.90
Rental Income Prepaid: Less Expenses Applicable Thereto (Note 9)	$ 180,832.05	$ 208,287.69
Capital and Surplus:		
Common stock: Par value of $5.00 each share (Notes 6, 11 and 12):		
Authorized 1955—1,500,000 shares; 1954—600,000 shares		
Issued and outstanding 1955—771,222 shares; 1954—257,074 shares	$ 3,856,110.00	$ 1,285,370.00
Unallocated capital:		
Excess of par value of preferred stock converted over par value of common stock issued (Note 11)	—	2,014,895.00
Surplus:		
Paid-In (Notes 11 and 12)	900,166.05	1,456,011.05
Earned (Note 6)	3,202,398.32	2,489,861.87
Total Capital and Surplus	$ 7,958,674.37	$ 7,246,137.92
Total Liabilities and Capital (Notes 7, 8, 10 and 12)	$14,819,339.74	$13,232,699.51

EXHIBIT 3–2 The Haloid Company Comparative Consolidated Income Profit and Loss Statement

	Year Ended December 31	
	1955	1954
Net Sales, Equipment Rentals and Royalties	$21,390,653.22	$17,318,403.21
Cost of Sales (Notes 1 and 2)	13,213,335.69	10,860,796.38
Gross Profit from Sales	$ 8,177,317.53	$ 6,457,606.83
Shipping, Selling, and Administrative and General Expenses	$ 5,082,098.25	$ 4,059,901.92
Profit-Sharing and Pension Plans	520,922.42	361,652.73
Total	$ 5,603,020.67	$ 4,421,554.65
Net Operating Income	$ 2,574,296.86	$ 2,036,052.18
Other Income Less Other Income Charges	68,115.64	43,429.49
Net Income Before Provision for Taxes	$ 2,642,412.50	$ 2,079,481.67
Provision for Taxes		
Federal and Canadian taxes	$ 1,375,000.00	$ 1,090,000.00
State taxes	105,000.00	105,000.00
Total	$ 1,480,000.00	$ 1,195,000.00
Net Income to Surplus (Notes 2, 9, and 10)	$ 1,162,412.50	$ 884,481.67

SUGGESTED READINGS

CEREPAK, JOHN R., and DONALD H. TAYLOR. *Principles of Accounting*. Englewood Cliffs, New Jersey: Prentice Hall, 1987.

HORNGREN, CHARLES T., and GARY L. SUNDEM. *Introduction to Financial Accounting,* 3rd ed. Englewood Cliffs, New Jersey: Prentice Hall, 1987.

HORNGREN, CHARLES T., and GARY L. SUNDEM. *Introduction to Management Accounting,* 7th ed. Englewood Cliffs, New Jersey: Prentice Hall, 1987.

part two

The AIS: Components and Interfaces

In Part II we examine the AIS as a relatively static collection of components. Before we can grasp the dynamics of the system in interaction with its environment, we must first understand the nature of each component and its relationship to other elements of the system.

No matter what the level of automation within an organization, the first and most important component of any human-machine system is the human element. So we open this section with Chapter 4, a discussion of the role accountants play in supporting the organization's need for and use of information and in adapting information systems technology to these needs.

Chapter 5 follows with a discussion of information systems hardware, viewed from a managerial perspective. We have tried to avoid the hardware approach usually found in introductory texts. Concerns about hardware are presented *as they appear to managers,* rather than as technical problems to be solved.

The discussion then shifts to software (Chapter 6). We have chosen to view software in three categories: operating systems, general purpose programs, and application programs. Again, we maintain a user's perspective. We have emphasized those components of general purpose software essential to support the increasing information requirements of modern competitive firms and those application programs that directly support accounting functions.

The data component of the AIS is often given little attention in many AIS texts. But as users become more directly involved with retrieving information from automated media, they must have a greater understanding of the nature of data and how it can be stored in order to provide the information support needed. Chapter 7, "The Data Component: Characteristics, Storage, and Retrieval" therefore treats this subject in detail.

chapter four

The Human Component of the AIS

CHAPTER OUTLINE

INTRODUCTION

In line with our perception that people are the most important component of an AIS, we start our discussion of the system components with the human element. Hardware does not appear magically, application programs do not materialize on their own, optimal file structures do not jump out at a passive information system user. These and other data processing components become an integral and productive part of an AIS as a result of detailed requirements planning, system design, and implementation strategies based upon interchange of information among the people in an organization.

The involvement of people as monitors, operators, and users of an AIS has far-reaching managerial implications that influence the success of an enterprise in many ways. People working with an AIS should be able to understand some of the broad issues in the human side of the system.

In our examination of human elements of the AIS, we first consider several levels of data processing personnel and the corresponding levels of financial managers and accounting support personnel; then we briefly outline the managerial and behavioral issues arising from human involvement.

HUMAN INVOLVEMENT IN AN AIS

Within an organization, the AIS involves people as both *providers* and *users* of information. The providers of information include two groups of technical people: the data processing people, and the financial and managerial accounting people. The internal users of AIS include those in supervisory managerial positions in various functional and service areas of the organization. Human involvement in the information processing task depends on many factors, of which the nature of the technology employed is an important one. A system relying on manual and mechanical means will employ many people in data recognition, data gathering, input preparation, and processing to provide output information; a technically advanced system using electronic devices frees people from repetitive jobs and allows them more time for innovative and judgment-based tasks. Advanced technology, effectively employed, increases people's capacity to work faster and handle more complex problems.

Data Processing Personnel

Figure 4–1 shows the functions that must be performed if an information systems department is to support its parent organization ade-

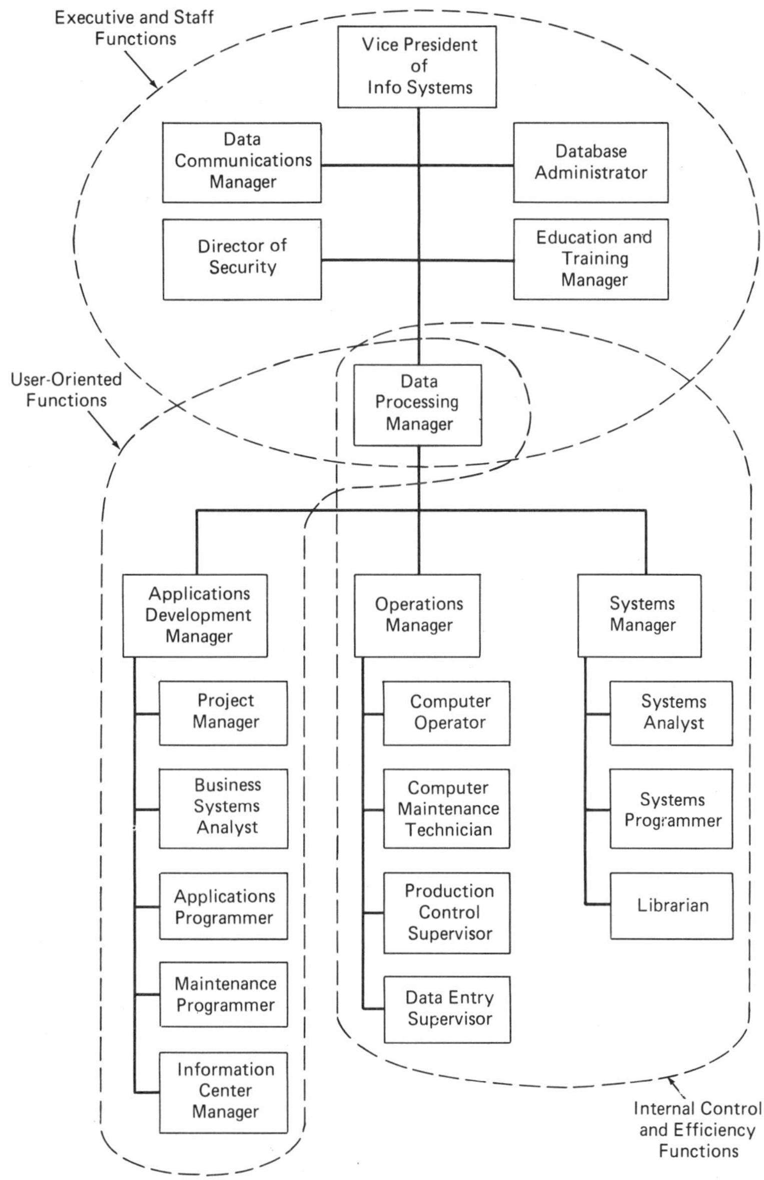

FIGURE 4–1 Line and Staff Representation of Information Systems Functions

quately. For convenience, we represent the functions as positions in a conventional line and staff organization chart. Actual structure will vary among organizations, and some functions shown as individual positions in the figure are likely to be combined, particularly in smaller organizations. We will consider information systems department functions vis-à-vis the AIS in the three categories indicated by the dashed lines in the figure. Detailed functions for each position may be found in standard information systems texts.

The Executive and Staff Group. The positions of vice president for information systems and the supporting staff exist, literally, only in large corporate organizations. Nevertheless, the effectiveness of the information systems department in supporting the goals of the overall organization depends upon successful performance of these executive-level tasks. The vice president for information systems is the executive in charge of all information systems, including data communications, office automation, and conventional data processing. The responsibilities of this official include ensuring that there is adequate long-range planning for information systems to support the goals of the organization, establishing and controlling budgets for information systems, and setting organizational policy for the use of information systems. He or she plays a major role in establishing priorities for application developments. The staff positions in this group represent functions that apply to all users of information systems.

The *data communications manager* is responsible for ensuring that there are adequate telecommunications facilities to serve the organization's needs for exchanging data over long-haul and local area networks. A particularly important responsibility of this position is to ensure that equipment procured to solve the problems of any one department is, or can be made, compatible with other data processing equipment with which it may need to exchange information.

The *database administrator* is responsible for maintaining the integrity of the organization's data, controlling redundancy of data, and in a distributed processing environment, determining at which locations data should be kept. The position combines the conceptual requirement to view and model the organization's data as a major resource with the detailed requirement to control the size and structure of each data element in the shared database. The position becomes increasingly important as an organization converts from using individual files to support each application to shared databases that support wider functional areas.

The *director of security* is responsible for protecting the organization's resources from accidental loss and preventing unauthorized access to data. The sensitive nature of accounting data requires particularly close liaison between the AIS and the director of security.

The *education and training manager* is responsible for ensuring that both information systems and user personnel are kept current in the use of evolving technology. This position becomes increasingly significant to accounting and other end-user departments as end-user application development tools are introduced into the information processing system.

The Data Processing Manager. In Figure 4–1, the data processing manager is shown as belonging to all three functional groups. Indeed, in a small organization, the holder of this position may fulfill all the executive and staff functions noted above. In any event, it is the DP manager who has line responsibility for implementing hardware and software acquisitions, for developing new applications programs and maintaining the old ones, and for the efficient use of available processing resources. In addition, the DP manager will have major input into planning and budgeting concerning information systems. Close coordination between the DP manager and the controller or treasurer is essential to the success of the AIS.

User-Oriented Functions. The *applications development manager* has line responsibility for the development and maintenance of applications programs. Priorities for major development efforts are usually established by higher management; however, the applications development manager will have some flexibility in assigning resources to small development projects and maintenance programming. A *project manager* will be in charge of analysis and programming for each approved major project. The team working under the project manager will include one or more business systems analysts, one or more applications programmers, and liaison personnel from the department requesting the application. (In some organizations, the manager in overall charge of an applications development may come from the primary user department involved; however, the DP project manager will be in charge of detailed analysis and programming.)

The *business systems analyst* is responsible for analysis of business problems and for designing suitable automated solutions. This is the primary point of contact between the user and the information systems department. The need for positive interaction between knowledgeable accounting department personnel and the project manager/business systems analyst assigned to work on an AIS development is vital. The *applications programmer* is responsible for encoding an approved problem solution into a suitable programming language. This has traditionally been done in COBOL in the business community; however, more powerful languages are beginning to make inroads in this area (see the discussion of very high-level languages in Chapter 6). The *maintenance programmer* is responsible for correcting errors discovered in operational programs and for keeping these programs current as the needs of management and the external environment change.

The *information center manager* is responsible for training and assisting end users who wish to develop their own application programs. Such programs may be one-time information retrievals to meet an immediate need, or they may be prototypes for entirely new applications. Information centers may utilize very high-level languages in connection with the organization's central computer, microcomputers in either a stand-alone or network configuration, or a combination of the two technologies.

Internal Control and Efficiency Functions. The positions that support these functions are generally of little direct interest to AIS personnel, though they are the very heart of the data processing department. The *operations manager* is responsible for the efficient day-to-day use of computers. In a batch-oriented system, the AIS user will most likely interact with production control and data entry personnel. The *production control supervisor* is responsible for scheduling input and output to the computer in accordance with established priorities. The *data entry supervisor* is responsible for keying and verifying data from source document to computer-sensible media. *The systems manager* is responsible for implementing and maintaining the operating system and other systems-level software.

Accounting Personnel

Typically an accounting organization within an enterprise includes managerial, financial, and cost accounting functions. However, the structuring of these functions varies, depending on such factors as management style, the technology employed, and the nature of products and services.

Usually the head of accounting and finance functions is among the top executives of an enterprise. In most organizations, the accounting functions are grouped into two major subdivisions, such as treasurer functions and controller functions.

Figure 4–2 shows the relationship between the accounting functions and other corporate functions and provides two lists of functions usually assigned to a controller and a treasurer.

The Treasurer's Position and Responsibilities.[1] Here is a typical statement of the treasurer's duties and responsibilities:

> The Treasurer shall be the custodian of the company's funds and securities and shall keep, or cause to be kept, full and accurate records of receipts and disbursements in books belonging to the company. He shall

[1] This is an example from a real company (Paul E. Olsen, a Suffolk MBA, supplied materials for this section).

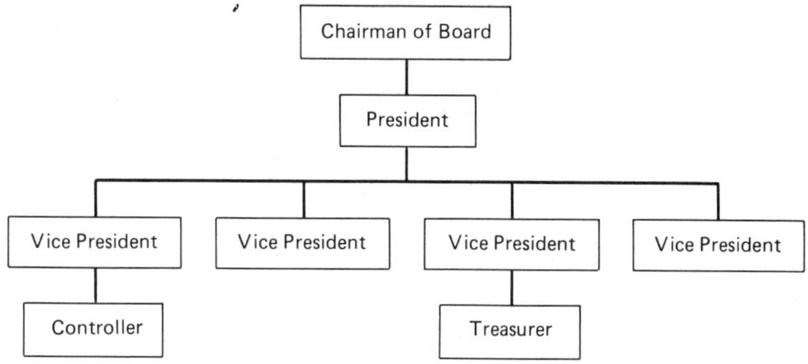

Functions (Controller)

1. Short-and long-term planning
2. Reporting, interpreting, evaluating, consulting
3. Corporate tax
4. Operational accounting
5. Systems review and design
6. Operational and management controls
7. Special studies
8. Cost accounting

Functions (Treasurer)

1. Investment management
2. Financing, short-term and long term
3. Cash flow management
4. Insurance and securities management
5. Credits and collections
6. Banking and custodianship

FIGURE 4–2 Controller and Treasurer Functions

> deposit or cause to be deposited all monies and valuable assets in the name and to the credit of the company in such depositaries as may be designated by the Board of Directors. He shall render to the President and Board of Directors whenever they may require it, an account of all his transactions as Treasurer. In general, he shall perform or cause to be performed, all the duties incident to the Office of Treasurer, and such other duties as may from time to time be assigned to him by the Board of Directors. The Treasurer shall furnish such bond as the Board of Directors might direct.

These duties are performed within the following functional areas of responsibility:

- Management of company debt
- Management of company investments
- Management of foreign exchange
- Management of company cash flow
- Management of company securities
- Management of company insurance program
- Supervision of treasurer's office staff
- Procurement of funds to meet long- and short-term financial obligations
- Forecasting of company financial needs and requirements

Specific duties performed by the treasurer within these functional areas include:

- Assists the senior vice president for finance in the development of financial plans and policies that will provide for the long- and short-term capital requirements of the company
- Selects sources and negotiates loans and administers the repayment of said loans as funds become available and terms of the loan agreements stipulate
- Provides direct supervision of all personnel within the treasurer's office
- Maintains close working relationships with bank officials
- Directs and administers the employees' option and deferred compensation plans
- Develops and administers an insurance program that will provide adequate protection for company assets against insurable risks

Depending upon the size of the firm, the treasurer may supervise a number of staff members. The staff personnel are organized into departments that closely correspond to the functional responsibilities assigned to the treasurer. Typically, these departments are:

- Payroll and expense reporting
- International finance
- Treasury and tax services
- Accounts payable
- Credit

Each of these departments is headed by a manager who reports directly to the treasurer who, in turn, reports directly to the senior vice president for finance or the president of the firm.

The Controller as the Chief Financial Officer.[2] The role of corporate controller has evolved rapidly over the past few years. The controller function traditionally involved maintenance of the general ledger, preparation of financial statements, and tax planning. In many organizations, this position now has the additional responsibility of monitoring profitability, margin, and prices.

In one large organization, seven departments report to the controller:

1. *Special studies.* This department engages in enterprisewide studies seeking to improve the quality of management and strategic planning. This department works with its own staff and uses outside consultants when needed.
2. *Operations research and planning.* There are three main areas under operations research and planning: Operations research responsible for

[2] A real example from a bank. Bernard J. Crowley, a Suffolk MBA, supplied materials for this section.

systems development of financial control; profit planning department responsible for budget comparison and variance analysis; cost accounting department that deals with cost finding, cost analyzing, and reporting for different functions of the bank. Overhead allocation is an important task of this department.

3. *Administration.* This department oversees the application of the adopted accounting principles by all areas and recommends change, inclusion, or exclusion of principles and procedures.
4. *Corporate tax.* This department has three subareas: (1) Tax compliance (prepares and submits corporate tax returns for city, state, and federal government agencies); (2) foreign planning (concerned with the tax problems of foreign branches); and (3) U.S. planning (concerned with tax problems of U.S. affiliates).
5. *Controllership.* The controllership department supervises two functions: Investor reporting (prepares quarterly and annual reports for the corporate head office, branches, and subsidiaries); and domestic subsidiaries accounting (ensures that the accounting policies of the bank are followed by its subsidiaries).
6. *Productivity and expense control.* This department reviews the productivity of various departments to find ways to improve productivity and reduce operating costs.
7. *Operational accounting.* Operational accounting has five areas of responsibility: (1) Bank accounting operations, which deal with accruals, income, and expenses for all domestic and foreign units; (2) general ledger and payroll (general ledger is the core of operational accounting, and the payroll section compiles the payroll data for 10,000 employees of the bank); (3) operational accounting, which has three sections: (a) reconcilement, which reconciles and balances the books; (b) adjustments, which provides information for all loans, payments, and discrepancies (if any); and (c) trust control, which is concerned with the accounting of the Trust Division; (4) archives, which keeps available all old records of the bank; and (5) adjustment control, which controls balances of checking and savings accounting and reconciles the bank's accounts with the Federal Reserve Bank.

Other Accounting Positions. Most of the AIS functions and responsibilities are included within the treasurer and controller functions. In this section we list several positions commonly found in an accounting organization in order to familiarize you with them. Job descriptions and job titles, of course, may vary from organization to organization.

Different designations and classifications are possible for the accounting and finance personnel of an AIS. The following list gives some accounting and finance positions commonly observed at different levels of an accounting system.

1. *Chief Finance Officer (CFO).* Vice president (VP) finance. In many organizations, the VP of finance or CFO heads different divisions of accounting and finance functions. The vice president is the senior executive responsible for the AIS.

2. *Managerial Accounting Functional Positions.* The positions for managerial accounting functions can be many and varied. The following are usually classified as managerial accounting positions: corporate controller, divisional controller, budget manager, budget analyst, internal auditor, financial analyst, management accountant, staff accountant.
3. *Cost Accounting Positions.* Organizations that separately identify cost accounting functions may have a group of support positions like this: chief cost accountant, manager cost accounting, supervisor cost accounting, inventory analyst, production cost analyst, timekeeper, standard cost manager, materials accountant, cost ledger supervisor, cost clerk. Organizations that do not separately recognize the cost accounting function will include some of these functions within managerial and financial accounting positions.
4. *Financial Accounting Positions.* The corporate financial accounting function is managed through a long list of functional positions. The length of the list tends to vary directly with the size of an organization. Here are some of the more common positions: corporate—treasurer, manager—cash management, accountant—assets and properties, credit manager, accounts payable manager, payroll supervisor, purchasing manager, shipping and receiving supervisor, staff accountant, accounts assistant, cashier.

The Information Systems Department

In most large organizations, the AIS is serviced by the information systems department (ISD), which serves a large number of other departments. This department is responsible for managing the technological and operational features of the AIS. The accounting department is responsible for specifying its information support requirements and taking all the necessary steps to ensure that these requirements are met.

In smaller organizations, and in some large organizations that decentralize their data processing capabilities, the CFO may have full responsibility for all facets of the AIS. In this situation, the data processing function will be more responsive to AIS requirements; however, it may also result in inadequate data processing expertise. The proliferation of microcomputers in organizations compounds this problem. For example, one medium-sized New England stationery supply company has its data processing facilities under the control of the corporate controller. Although the hardware was capable of high on-line direct access capability, the system was so overloaded with the task of producing duplicate records and a large volume of unused hard copies of output daily that its capabilities went unused.

MANAGERIAL AND BEHAVIORAL ASPECTS OF THE HUMAN SIDE OF AN AIS

The different role positions involved in an accounting information system are like positions in any part of an organization. These managers, supervisors, and operators have to deal with effort, performance, satisfaction, and rewards for themselves and those they supervise. Managers expect employees to do their best and to give consistently high performance. Employees expect satisfaction from their jobs. Studies show that there are complex interrelationships among performance, effort, reward, and satisfaction.

Here we will discuss some current motivation and behavior theories because we recognize that the human elements in an accounting system are as important as the technical elements. When we deal with the human elements in an AIS, we must be ready to do it effectively. We need to understand why different people within the system behave differently. The theories discussed briefly here are based on the reality that people are different and must be treated differently. An AIS should be flexible enough to accommodate differences in the expectations, needs, and goals of the people within the system.

This discussion is especially applicable when an AIS is undergoing system design, review, and/or change. A system that takes individual motivational factors into account will be a more profitable system.

The factors that influence human behavior within an organization are classified as internal and external. Let us begin with internal factors.

Internal Factors

The internal factors that stimulate people to work were first presented by the psychologist Abraham Maslow and are widely known as Maslow's needs hierarchy. Maslow proposed that an individual has the following hierarchy of needs:

1. Physiological needs—satisfaction of physical needs such as hunger.
2. Security needs—need for protection against threat and danger.
3. Affiliation needs—need for love and affection and association with others.
4. Esteem needs—need for self-respect and recognition from others.
5. Self-actualization needs—need for self-fulfillment.

Maslow[3] posited that people pursue these needs with varying intensity. The hierarchical arrangement connotes that lower-order needs must be satisfied before one seeks to fulfill a higher-order need. For instance, people seek to fulfill physiological needs first. Once physiological needs are satisfied, they then seek to satisfy their

[3] Abraham H. Maslow, *Motivation and Personality* (New York: Harper, 1954).

security needs, and so forth. Self-actualization needs are unlikely to be effective as motivators unless all the lower-level needs are satisfied.

But although Maslow's need theory is very popular, it has several weaknesses. It has not been fully verified empirically because of some inherent difficulties:

1. The needs are not always separable from one another.
2. The order of the hierarchy is not the same for all people.
3. Individuals have different satisfaction preferences for each need level. One person may have a very high need for security, whereas a second may easily satisfy that need.
4. It is difficult to measure these needs because they overlap, and any classification becomes tenuous.

Another psychologist, David McClelland, has proposed three motives that internally stimulate employee behavior:

1. Affiliation need—the same as Maslow's affiliation need.
2. Power—desire to have control and influence over others.
3. Achievement—desire to achieve worthwhile objectives.

McClelland did not arrange these factors in a hierarchy; he also suggested that more than one need may be active at any time. McClelland developed measures which determine the dominant need at any given time.

J. W. Atkinson addressed the issue of motivation in a different way. According to Atkinson, aroused motivation is a function of (1) basic motive (M), (2) goal attainment expectancy (E), and (3) incentive value of the goal (I). He expressed the relationship as a multiplicative function: aroused motivation $= M \times E \times I$. Atkinson's[4] model was originally based on need for achievement (N Achievement), but was later expanded to include need for power (N Power), and need for affiliation (N Affiliation).

Atkinson's model posits that in order to arouse the desired motivation and ensure certain patterns of behavior, managers should learn to identify different kinds of motives and the effects of incentives on aroused motives.

External Factors

The Two Factor Theory. F. Herzberg, an expert in motivation theory, presented the two-factor theory, which is very popular because it distinguishes between motivators and nonmotivators in work

[4] J. W. Atkinson, *An Introduction to Motivation* (Princeton, N.J.: Van Nostrand, 1964).

situations. His hygiene factors, for example, do not contribute to motivation. They are policies and administration, supervision, work conditions, job security, status, interpersonal relationships. What he considers motivators are achievements, challenge in the job, increases in responsibility, growth and development, and recognition.

Hygiene factors are called *dissatisfiers*. Contributions to dissatisfiers do not provide motivation to employees, whereas contributions to motivators provide job satisfaction and increase output. However, subsequent research has shown that dissatisfiers, when improved, can be viewed as rewards and do motivate people. Managers can use both hygiene factors and motivators to improve employee output. We can draw a parallel with Maslow's need theory: Managers can use hygiene factors to meet employees' physiological, security, and affiliation needs, and the motivators to meet esteem and self-actualization needs.

Equity Theory. Another perspective on motivation at work is the perceived equity in the work situation. Proponents of equity theory argue that perceived equity or inequity in work situations is a major determinant of effort, satisfaction, and performance. The actual set of events is not important; what is important is the perceived equity and inequity. Again, managers of AIS should be aware of the social context in which various managerial actions to motivate people are perceived and interpreted.

Behavior Modification or Reinforcement Theory. Managers are not confined to the given behavior of employees; they may try to modify undesirable behavior and reinforce desirable behavior. The theory behind this approach is called *behavior modification*. It argues that human behavior can be shaped, altered, or engineered. It uses a reward structure to modify and manipulate behavior patterns. The reward for desirable behavior is increased by providing positive reinforcement and establishing a predictable relationship between reward and performance. The employee is expected to repeat the same behavior under similar circumstances. Behavior modification theory requires that managers make explicit which behaviors are rewarded and which are not. Employees should receive regular feedback on their performance and receive rewards accordingly.

There are examples of successful applications of behavior modification theory. For instance, Hamner and Hamner[5] reported that Emery Air Freight, Michigan Bell, Standard Oil of Ohio, General Electric, and B.F. Goodrich were successful in setting up formal reinforcement motivational programs.

[5] W. Clay Hamner and Ellen P. Hamner, "Behavior Modification on the Bottom Line," *Organizational Dynamics* (Spring 1976), pp. 8–21.

Expectancy Theory. Motivation alone is not sufficient to explain performance at work. Three distinct factors appear to account for performance:

1. Motivation
2. Abilities
3. Role clarity

Expectancy theory argues that motivation to work is a function of expectations about the relationships between (1) effort and performance, (2) performance and rewards (outcome), and (3) the value (valence) of outcome to an individual.[6] The theory posits the motivation to behavior sequence depicted in Figure 4–3.

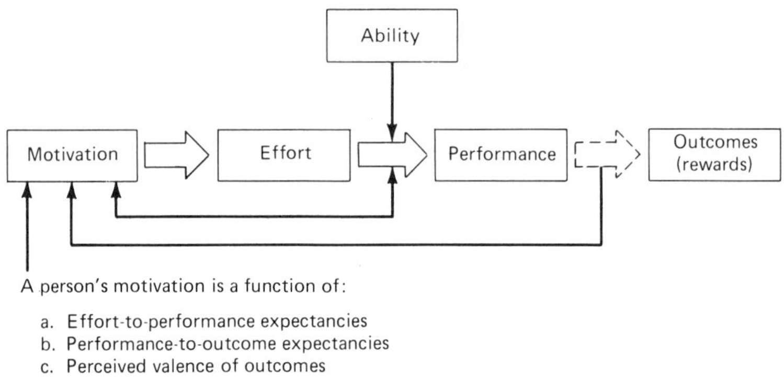

FIGURE 4–3 The Motivation to Behavior Sequence
Source: David A. Nadler and Edward E. Lawler, III, "Motivation: A Diagnostic Approach," in J. Richard Hackman, Edward E. Lawler, III, and L. W. Porter, *Perspectives on Behavior in Organizations* (New York: McGraw-Hill, 1977). Reprinted by permission.

Expectancy theory holds that effort expended by individuals results from the interaction between the actual outcome, expectation about the outcome, and motivation; performance results from the individual effort and ability interaction. This theory has several implications for managers. According to it, managers should:

1. Identify the desirable behavior.
2. Establish a set of attainable performance goals.
3. Link outcome with performance.
4. Determine the outcome valuable to the employee.

At the organizational level, the pay and reward system, tasks, jobs, and roles should be attuned to the expectations of the individual.

[6] David A. Nadler and Edward E. Lawler, III, "Motivation: A Diagnostic Approach," in J. R. Hackman, E. E. Lawler, and L. W. Porter, *Perspectives on Behavior in Organizations* (New York: McGraw-Hill, 1977), pp. 26–36.

This is a powerful theory because it combines forces in the organization and forces in the individual; it provides operational guidance for understanding forces in an individual's motivation to achieve organizational goals.

A well-designed AIS should be able to satisfy many of the needs of an individual. The AIS system designer can design jobs that are challenging, empower individuals, and satisfy their self-actualization needs. Operating control jobs in an AIS are the most difficult to accommodate to the needs of individuals for variety and flexibility. The lower-level cost and financial accounting positions listed previously also fall into this category.

Well-designed jobs provide a favorable work environment and encourage better performance. Jobs that require skill and have task variety provide meaningful experience for the employee. Autonomy in the task provides a sense of responsibility, and feedback provides knowledge about actual performance. Variety, autonomy, and feedback provide work motivation, improve performance, and lower absenteeism and turnover.

DYSFUNCTIONAL BEHAVIOR AND MOTIVATION

The human side of the AIS creates many control problems that may be dysfunctional to the organization. Instances of falsification of data, fraudulent transactions, errors of omission, and errors of commission are abundant. (The control aspects of an AIS will be discussed in detail in the chapters of Part IV.) Apprehension about dysfunctional behavior associated with an AIS is not without validity. Table 4–1 provides a summary of human behavior factors and motivational alternatives influencing dysfunctional behavior within an information system.

AIS User Behavior

There are now research findings supporting the influence of accounting information on organizational behavior. Accounting information may be viewed as a role prescription, role communication, and role perception device within an organization. For example, departmental budgets which are used for planning and control purposes provide role prescriptions and role communications to the incumbent managers and influence their role perceptions. Budgets also help develop performance and reward expectancy relationships.

Chris Argyris, a pioneering researcher in budget and motivation, reported as far back as 1953 that budgets affect people directly. They can be used as a pressure device, or to measure success and failure;

TABLE 4–1 Designing Effective Information Systems That Minimize Dysfunctional Behavior

Work Group	*Human Factors*	*Motivation and Information Systems Strategy*
Operating employees	Resistance to new systems Tendency to believe rumor vs. fact Need for reassurance as to job security Need for good motivation Dislike for more rigid work pace Instinct for self-protection from blame Faith in company promises Tendency to short-range goals Fear of machines Desire for affection, recognition, attention Desire to know reasons for change Influence of key workers	*Extrinsic Motivational Factors* Set achievable goals, standards Pay, as a major incentive Organize into small work groups System of rewards System of punishments System of promotions *Intrinsic Motivational Factors* Do not suppress informal organization *Other Strategies* Prepare and distribute brochures describing intra-company training programs
Operating management and middle management	Fear of replacement by young workers Tendency to concentrate on technical aspects of jobs Need for visible evidence of production Lack of job mobility Desire to air views and participate Worry about ability to learn and supervise new procedures Pride in status symbols of position Fear of becoming mere machine monitors Fatigue and pressure during system change Fear of loss of promotional opportunity	*Extrinsic Motivational Factors* Set achievable goals Participation in systems change System of promoting Pay incentive systems Bonuses *Intrinsic Motivational Factors* Praise from supervisors Interesting work Tenure Status symbols *Other Strategies* Tailor system to meet manager's needs Provide only needed information Intracompany training programs Distribute brochures describing new systems Simplify reporting procedures Avoid information overload Standardize report formats, headings Provide accurate, objective, timely, understandable information
Top management	Status symbols as motives for change Courage to carry through change Isolation of top people Tendency toward secrecy Ability to adjust and learn Impatience with rate of progress	*Extrinsic Motivational Factors* Bonuses Stock options *Intrinsic Motivational Factors* Status symbols *Other Strategies* Promptness in making decisions Concern for human relations Willingness to use new tools and skills

Source: Adapted from M. J. Cerulli, "Information Systems Success Factors," *Journal of Systems Management*, December 1980, p. 12. Reprinted by permission of the Association for Systems Management.

accordingly, inappropriate use of the budgeting process may result in managerial resistance.

Several studies document the different ways in which managers use accounting information. One of the pioneering studies in the use of accounting information by managers was done by Hopwood (1974).[7] Hopwood showed four different ways in which managers use accounting data (budget data):

1. Budget constrained style: People who use accounting information rigidly.
2. Budget profit style: People who try to meet the budget and at the same time remain concerned with cost.
3. Profit conscious style: People who are conscious about cost but not constrained by budget.
4. Nonaccounting style: People who are not primarily concerned with costs or budget.

Rahman (1976)[8] evaluated the differences in the use of accounting information and suggested that care should be taken to supply optimal information to managers. Some of the findings from Rahman's study are given here.

1. Managers differ considerably in their use of accounting data. This difference can be systematically evaluated. To realize the goal of supplying managers with optimal accounting data, systems should be designed to take into account the organizational orientations and personal factors of managers. Managers who need to use extensive accounting data should be supplied with such data. This may help avoid creation of informal systems which are generally inefficient and perhaps inaccurate. Conversely, the supply of accounting data should be kept at a minimum to those who use it the least. It may save devoting scarce resources to the production of unneeded reports and data. Differential access to the information database with a flexible output format may be an answer.

2. Managers who can be expected to make extensive use of accounting data will have some or all of the following characteristics.

a. The high user will have modest interest in items of a long-term character. Awareness of his or her functional area goals will be less clear. This manager is likely to have a task orientation (concern for task performance) and will tend to favor a structured environment. This person may have average supervisory ability and intelligence.

[7] A. J. Hopwood, "Leadership Climate and the Use of Accounting Data in Performance Evaluation," *The Accounting Review* (July 1974), pp. 485–495.

[8] M. Rahman and A. M. McCosh, "Influence of Organizational and Personal Factors on the Use of Accounting Information: An Empirical Study," *Accounting, Organization and Society,* Vol. 1, No. 4, 1976, pp. 339–355.

The accounting system designer must ensure that the accounting information provided to such a user reflects a "true and fair view" of the entity's state of affairs, since these data will be used rather literally.

b. The low user manager has characteristics that are almost entirely opposite to the qualities of the high user. Such a manager has higher concern for people than for tasks. This manager likes an unstructured environment, has a clear view of functional goals, and has a long-term time perspective. He or she tends to rely more on supervisory ability than on the surrogate measures provided by accounting for subordinate evaluation and operational controls.

Distortion in the Accounting Information System

Accounting information is susceptible to distortion by both producers and users. This is not a circumstance peculiar to the AIS; it is true for all information and control systems. As Birnberg et al.[9] suggest: "As long as information is generated for evaluative purposes, users and producers will attempt to manipulate it to suit their own needs." Birnberg et al. classified the dysfunctional use of information into six broad categories:

1. Smoothing—when a message is tempered dealing with past or future events, like income smoothing over periods.
2. Biasing—selecting the most favorable messages to transmit, like reporting sales growth and not the growth in credits and uncollectibles.
3. Focusing—highlighting certain aspects, like achievement of budget or introduction of new product.
4. Gaming—in supervisor-subordinate relationships, the use of surrogate measures that receive highest evaluation.
5. Filtering—messages are filtered through the manager's perspective so that only the more desirable elements are communicated.
6. "Illegal" acts—manager's acts violate a private law (company policy) or a public law. There are many examples of illegal acts on the shop floor and at managerial levels. The most common is concealing budget slack to maintain operating flexibility.

SUMMARY

The human side of an accounting information system is as important as the technical side. A well-designed and technically balanced system may fail to achieve the desired results because of neglect or ignorance of the human side.

[9] J. G. Birnberg, L. Turoplolec, and S. M. Young, "The Organizational Context of Accounting," *Accounting, Organization and Society,* 8, 2/3 (1983), pp. 111–129.

In this chapter we address the issue from two sides. The first is the different functional role positions. AIS-related personnel can be classified in two groups: data processing personnel and accounting personnel. The data processing personnel deal with three major subfunctions: executive and staff function, user-oriented function, and internal control and efficiency function. Accounting personnel also deal with three subfunctions: financial accounting, managerial accounting, and cost accounting. The number of positions, levels, and job descriptions for AIS-related positions depends on many factors. The size of the business is the most important.

People in AIS-related functional positions perform individually and in groups. Empirical research on work behavior and worker motivation has classified the relevant factors as: those internal to the individual and those external to the individual. One approach postulates that people work because they have certain needs to satisfy. For instance, Maslow's needs hierarchy lists five classes of human needs arranged in a hierarchical order with the physiological needs at the bottom, self-actualization needs at the top, and a scheme for individuals' needs preferences. McClelland identified three main needs: affiliation, power, and achievement, without suggesting a hierarchical order. Atkinson's theory proposes that aroused motivation is a function of: (1) basic motivation, (2) goals attainment expectancy, and (3) incentive value of the goal.

Factors external to the individual also satisfy internal needs. Herzberg's two-factor theory identifies motivators and nonmotivators in the work situation. Nonmotivators are called dissatisfiers or hygiene factors, such as work conditions and supervision. Motivators are satisfiers, such as achievement and challenge.

Equity theory provides another perspective on work motivation; perceived equity or inequity in a work situation is the major determinant of worker motivation. Behavior modification or reinforcement theory argues that managers can influence worker behavior in a desired direction by providing feedback and reinforcement.

Expectancy theory suggests that motivation alone is not sufficient to understand work behavior. Abilities, efforts, expected outcome, and performance have interacting relationships that must be considered in understanding the human motivation to work.

Organizational environment and job characteristics are also important in motivation theory.

The human side of AIS evokes many behavioral problems. The dysfunctional behaviors associated with the AIS can be modified through a conscious design effort. There are at least three different types of users of accounting information—rigid users, flexible users, and low users. Different types of users have different organizational and behavioral orientations that are important design considerations.

When accounting information is used for evaluative purposes, it is susceptible to distortion by the interested parties. The nature of such distortion can be smoothing, biasing, focusing, gaming, filtering and "illegal" acts.

REVIEW QUESTIONS, DISCUSSION QUESTIONS, AND PROBLEMS AND CASES

A. Review Questions

A4.1 What do you understand by human elements in AIS?

A4.2 What are the types of functional positions involved in AIS?

A4.3 Briefly describe the functions the following data processing personnel perform:

- **a.** The vice president for information systems
- **b.** The data communications administrator
- **c.** The database administrator
- **d.** The director of security
- **e.** The education and training manager
- **f.** The data processing manager
- **g.** The business systems analyst
- **h.** The applications programmer
- **i.** The maintenance programmer
- **j.** The information center manager
- **k.** The operations manager
- **l.** The production control supervisor
- **m.** The data entry supervisor

A4.4 Divide the functional positions in question 4.3 into three categories:

- **a.** User-oriented function.
- **b.** Data processing manager.
- **c.** Internal control efficiency.

A4.5 List six functional positions in each of the following areas:

- **a.** Managerial accounting.
- **b.** Cost accounting.
- **c.** Financial accounting.

A4.6 What is motivation? List the hierarchy of needs proposed by Maslow.

A4.7 What is aroused motivation according to McClelland?

A4.8 According to the two-factor theory, what external factors contribute to the needs of managers?

A4.9 What does equity theory emphasize?

A4.10 Can behavior be modified? What motivation theory advocates this?

A4.11 What are the variables considered in expectancy theory?

A4.12 Describe dysfunctional behavior at the operating level that may be elicited by an information system, and suggest motivational and information system strategies.

A4.13 Define:

- **a.** Budget constraint style.
- **b.** Budget profit style.

- **c.** Profit conscious style.
- **d.** Nonaccounting style.

A4.14 How can accounting information be distorted? Give some examples.

B. Discussion Questions

B4.1 In this chapter we discussed users and providers of AIS as two groups of people. Can users also be designers of AIS? Under what circumstances is such an option available?

B4.2 There is a large number of functional positions in managerial, cost, and financial accounting.
- **a.** Should all organizations have all the functional positions? Give reasons for your answers.
- **b.** Is it advisable to design a system where cost, managerial, and financial functional positions are not separately identified?

B4.3 Discuss the strengths and weaknesses of Maslow's hierarchy of needs.

B4.4 In the design and operation of an AIS, what lessons can a manager learn from motivation theories?

B4.5 What are some of the adverse behavioral attitudes of top management toward an AIS? Discuss a strategy to neutralize those factors.

B4.6 Sometimes operating management shows negative attitudes toward an AIS. Give some illustrations and discuss what intrinsic and extrinsic motivational factors are available to influence their attitudes.

B4.7 Managers differ considerably in their use of accounting data. In a given situation, do you want the same information for all managers, or different information for different managers? Support your answers with arguments and examples.

B4.8 Distortion of accounting information is motivational. Managers should be aware of motivational factors when using accounting information in controls. Discuss the issues, using examples.

C. Problems and Cases

C4.1 The production manager of a divisionalized corporation made the following remarks while commenting about the budget process: "I suppose for machinery repair this year there is $100,000. I want to spend $120,000. I put it back to the group manager, he has come back to me and said 'No. You can spend one hundred.' I put it to him why I want to spend $120,000, but still the decision is a hundred. I would be thinking in terms of volume loss more than anything else to justify my claim."
- **a.** Would you consider this as a dysfunctional behavior?
- **b.** How would you describe the group manager's behavior as an accounting information user?
- **c.** What would have been the right decision for the group manager?

C4.2 The production manager commented: "There is a fair amount of juggling going on, particularly at the present time (because of high inflation). We are strictly constrained and we build a fair amount of contingency figures into our annual budgeting which enables us to make purchases within reasonable limits of unforeseen items."
- **a.** Would you consider this a distortion of accounting information?
- **b.** Could there be an improvement in accounting information systems to safeguard this type of distortion?

C4.3 The following quotations are taken from an interview with a young graduate manager of a manufacturing firm.

a. "Things that are taken up in the director's meeting are obviously those variances that are going to be excessive. However, there would be explanations required on items which are of interest to a particular director. As for example, canteen expenses. This comes up in every meeting. We give special attention to this item." Discuss the issue in this case and suggest the possible AIS role to modify the situation.

b. "I write nothing into the variance reports. I just sign it. Because if you looked into your production day to day you would have known where things were going wrong. Most controls are of some value, but they either misled you or informed you too late—they tell you lies." What type of AIS user is the manager? What types of AIS report do you recommend for the manager? Give your reasons.

C4.4 "Sometimes I feel that the account system is designed for accountants rather than for managers and in some areas this is worse than others. There are conflicts in the varying needs for the auditors on the one hand and for the management accountancy on the other hand. Accountants could give a little more weight to it from the point of view of it being useful to the managers rather than they do now. [For example] the areas under which we control the stock are not the areas under which accounting wants reports to be made. The stock report splits the information in a financial way rather than in a control way, which does not help me to control it."

"The way the accountant sees his role has a big effect on his usefulness. I believe the accountant's job is to be a watch dog for the company to the shareholders—a means of assisting the management of the company to achieve their objectives, precisely the same position as that of a legal man in the company. I like to see an accountant more as a treasurer than as a controller."

a. Comment on the conflicts between the users and providers of information.

b. Do you agree that the financial accounting bias is a weakness of the accounting system?

C4.5 (CMA) The following statements were made by a corporate financial executive: ". . . The corporate financial officer is first an active member of the management team and is every bit as much involved in the conduct of the business as the other principal members of that team. His loyalties are to the chief executive officer and are directed to making the efforts of the corporation successful. . . ." ". . . The amount of disclosure . . . must then reflect management's best judgment. The corporate financial officer, as a member of the management team, must represent not only the corporation, but also the interests of the investor in such disclosure . . . (including publication of information on) events . . . of real importance to the investor. . . ."

a. Do the statements of the corporate financial officer suggest a conflict of interest? Explain your answer.

b. In light of your answer to (a) and the statements above, how would you, if you were a corporate financial officer, respond to the following requests by the chief executive officer in a year of expected decline in earnings? Support your answer with your reasoning.

(1) The company has prepared a program to offer a substantial amount of slow-moving inventory to a large discount chain. The price to the chain will be below cost. The program will take effect in the next fiscal year. The chief executive officer wants the writedown of inventory to be made in the year when the deliveries are made.

(2) The chief executive officer wants to change the fiscal statement depreciation methods for new acquisitions to straight-line. A declining balance method has been used for book and tax purposes since the 1954 Internal Revenue Code revisions and will continue to be used for tax purposes.

(3) The company has spent a large amount of money in the development of a new product. At the present time it is uncertain whether or not a marketable product will emerge. The research and development group believes there is a 70 percent chance that the project will be successful. You have proposed that the capitalized costs of this project be written off. The chief executive officer and the chief research and development officer argue that the chance of success is high enough to leave the costs capitalized for another year. It is expected that the final determination of the potential for the project can be made at that time.

C4.6 (CMA) The Ajax Division of Gunnco, operating at capacity, has been asked by the Defco of Gauntly Corp. to supply it with electrical fitting No. 1726. Ajax sells this part to its regular customers for $7.50 each. Defco, which is operating at 50 percent capacity, is willing to pay $5 each for the fitting. Defco will put the fitting into a brake unit which it is manufacturing essentially on cost-plus basis for a commercial airplane manufacturer. Ajax has a variable cost of producing fitting No. 1726 for $4.25. The cost of the brake unit built by Defco is as follows:

Purchased parts—outside vendors	$22.50
Ajax fitting—1726	5.00
Other variable costs	14.00
Fixed overhead and administration	$49.50

Defco believes the price concession is necessary to get the job. The company uses return on investment and dollar profits in the measurement of division and division manager performance.

a. Consider that you are the division controller of Ajax. Would you recommend that Ajax supply fitting No. 1726 to Defco (ignore any tax issues)? Why or why not?

b. Would it be to the short-run economic advantage of Gunnco for the Ajax division to supply Defco with fitting No. 1726 at $5 each (ignore any income tax issues)? Explain your answer.

c. Discuss the organizational and managerial/behavior difficulties, if any, inherent in this situation. As the Gunnco controller, what would you advise the Gunnco corporation president to do in this situation?

SUGGESTED READINGS

HACKMAN, J. R., E. E. LAWLER, AND L. W. PORTER. *Perspective on Behavior in Organizations*. New York: McGraw-Hill, 1977, pp. 26–36.

KAST, E. FREMONT, AND JAMES E. ROSENZWEIG. *Organization and Management*. New York: McGraw-Hill, 1985.

KLEINER, BRIAN H. "Integrating Major Motivation Theories," *Journal of Systems Management* (February 1983), pp. 26–29.

MCCOSH, A. M., MAWDUDUR RAHMAN, AND M. J. EARL. *Developing Managerial Information Systems*. New York: John Wiley & Sons, 1981.

PORTER, LYMAN W. AND E. E. LAWLER, III. *Managerial Attitudes and Performance*. Homewood, Ill.: Irwin Dorsey, 1968.

STEERS, RICHARD M., AND LYMAN W. PORTER. *Motivation and Work Behavior*, 2nd ed. New York: McGraw-Hill, 1979.

VROOM, VICTOR H. *Work and Motivation*. New York: John Wiley, 1964.

chapter five

The Hardware Component

CHAPTER OUTLINE

INTRODUCTION

The data processing hardware available to or procured by an organization sets a physical limit on the ability of the CAAIS to meet the information needs of the organization. In most organizations, the accounting applications will share hardware resources with other functional areas. In fact, this is essential if there is to be a high degree of integration among applications, a condition usually considered desirable in large organizations. In smaller organizations, accounting may be the only automated function; in large organizations, there may be processors dedicated to the accounting function for specific purposes. And, of course, there is the ubiquitous microcomputer, which turns up on auditors' and other middle managers' desktops. In our review of hardware we will consider a full range of possibilities, and not limit the discussion to large, integrated systems.

The traditional hardware configuration consists of input devices, a central processing unit (CPU), output devices, and auxiliary storage systems (Figure 5–1). Most present-day systems also include some

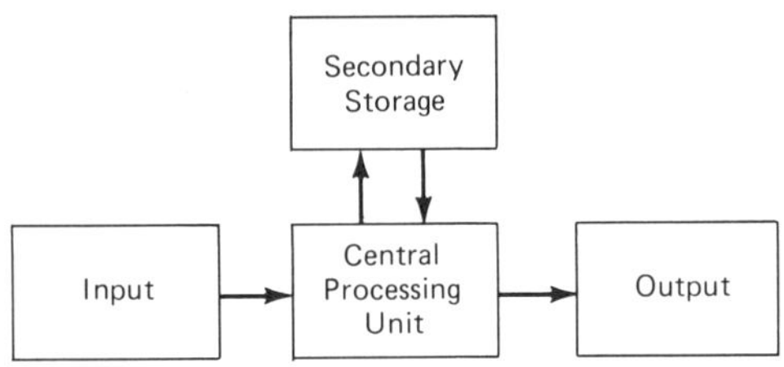

FIGURE 5–1 The Classic Computer Configuration

elements of communications hardware. At some risk of oversimplifying a complex interdependent system, we may say that the input and output devices determine the quality of the human-machine interface, the CPU determines the volume and speed of processing that can be accomplished, and auxiliary storage devices determine the types of processing that can be supported and the total volume of data that can be made available to support operations and analysis. We will see in Chapter 6 that appropriate software is essential to exploit the hardware capabilities, but it is the hardware that provides the ultimate limit for the CAAIS. In this chapter we examine the characteristics of input, output, processing, secondary storage, and communications equipment. Our examination will concentrate on how these components support and/or constrain the needs of the AIS.

INPUT CHARACTERISTICS AND DEVICES

Input devices provide the interface between the CAAIS and the broader AIS. Inputs to the CAAIS must be machine-sensible. This means that all data, whatever their original source and format, must be presented at the CAAIS boundary in a form that can be further reduced to a series of electrical or magnetic impulses. A large and continuously growing number of techniques are available to provide this capability. These techniques can be broadly characterized as off-line devices which prepare data for later batch processing or on-line devices which provide immediate interaction with the CPU. We will examine some of the more widely used methods and some that show promise for the future.

Off-Line Data Preparation

Off-line data preparation refers to the steps and procedures that capture the desired data from business transactions and prepare them for future entry into the computer for processing. Off-line data preparation supports batch processing operations. The devices used are not in direct communication with the main processing programs during the data preparation process.

Punched Card Input. Punched card technology predates the introduction of the electronic computer by over a century; cards were used to control mechanical processes as early as the Jacquard loom in 1801. They were first used in data processing applications to analyze the United States census of 1890. Their use in electromechanical accounting machines was widespread during the 1930s and 1940s. It was a short step to adapt the punched card as a computer input source. Although punched cards have largely disappeared from today's data processing centers, we will review them briefly. There are two reasons for this: First, punched card techniques establish a baseline for comparison of more modern systems; and second, most modern input techniques owe their genesis to the urge to overcome card shortcomings.

The use of punched cards for computer input involves two steps. First the card is punched; then it is verified. A card must be punched from a source document, which is often a form used in the normal business operations in a firm. This form may be specially designed for data processing input, with instructions showing the key punch operator the precise card columns into which each data item must be entered. Alternatively, the source document for key punching may be a worksheet prepared by an accounting clerk in an intermediate step between the business transaction and the key punch operator. The punching operation results in a deck of cards, each of which has a series of holes punched in columns across the card. Each column represents a character, and each card contains a single line of data. In the verification process, a second operator enters the identical data into each of the cards previously punched. No new holes are punched; however, if any character on the card is not identical to the character entered by the verifier, the card is rejected. This process will detect any errors introduced in the punching operation. It cannot, of course, detect any errors that originated on the business form or in the transcription of data to the worksheet.

In card-oriented operations, the data cards submitted for a computer run must be combined with a set of cards which instructs the computer how the data are to be processed. These cards may be few in number, used to call previously established programs from the computer's storage, or they may be the entire program for processing the data.

Advantages and Disadvantages of Punched Cards. Punched card input is generally regarded as an obsolete technology, but some use of cards as an input medium can be expected to continue well into the future. Punched cards provide an excellent *turnaround document.* For example, employee time cards for a given pay period can be prepunched with all identification data. As work is accomplished, it is entered into the card by punching job codes and hours of labor. At the end of the period, the card is ready for immediate processing. Similarly, customer identification and amounts due can be prepunched into billing documents. When the card is returned with payment, only the actual amount of the payment enclosed needs to be punched into the appropriate spaces before the accounts receivable records can be updated. Another reason for the continued existence of cards is that it may not be economical to convert some low-volume operations based on card equipment to more modern systems.

Punched card processing is slow, and the card reader cannot match the input speeds of more modern technology. The card punching process is prone to error; too many steps require human intervention. Punched cards become folded, twisted, and mutilated in spite of all admonitions to handle them with care. They are also sensitive to moisture and high humidity. Processing machinery is subject to jamming and can destroy cards. Card decks can be shuffled inadvertently. Cards are bulky and use up much valuable physical storage space. Finally, cards are limited exclusively to the support of batch processing. Let us look now at some of the more modern techniques that improve data input.

Key-to-Tape and Key-to-Disk. Key-to-tape and key-to-disk input techniques are conceptually similar to the use of punched cards. As in the older technology, a key operator transfers data from a person-readable medium into a machine-sensible medium. As in card processing, the results of the keying operation are accumulated off-line for later entry into the computer. However, the result of the newer data preparation techniques is a coded pattern of magnetic spots on a tape or disk, rather than a series of holes in a stack of cards.

The newer technology incorporates features usually not available for the production of cards. Data are displayed on a cathode ray tube (CRT) for visual checking prior to being entered onto the magnetic medium. This prevents many errors from being recorded. If errors are entered onto the tape or disk, they can easily be corrected during the verification process. The keyboards also have a number of features for tabbing and formatting data.

Key-to-tape and key-to-disk data preparation equipment varies in sophistication. In the simplest configuration, opportunities for editing may be limited. The result of the keying operation is a tape or disk that must be physically removed from the keying station and entered into the computer via a special reader. In more sophisticated installations, data preparation may be conducted in cluster operations under the control of a minicomputer. In this case, a number of keying stations operate under the control of a programmable device. Several keying stations may be preparing input for the same application, and data for several different applications may be prepared simultaneously. The minicomputer can perform a wide range of editing functions and then sort and merge the edited data from several stations to produce a data file which is then read directly by the central processing unit when the user directs that the master files be updated.

Advantages of Key-to-Tape and Key-to-Disk Input. The advantages of key-to-tape and key-to-disk input preparation vis-à-vis key punch input include greater ease of data handling, a more compact data form, and a faster read-in capability. One drawback of the technology is that the capability to use a turnaround document is sacrificed for those applications where this is a consideration. In addition, a switch from key punch to key-to-tape or key-to-disk does not address the procedural problem of introduction of errors in the transcription of a transaction from a source document.

Optical Character Recognition (OCR) and Magnetic Ink Character Recognition (MICR). Use of OCR and MICR documents as input media eliminates the possibility of introducing errors via transcription from a source document by using the source document for input. With either of these approaches, the computer input device reads data directly from the original business document. No intermediate handling steps are required.

OCR is the more versatile of these techniques. A wide variety of capabilities exists. Some OCR readers require a highly stylized set of characters for recognition, whereas others may recognize a variety of standard typewriter and even neatly formed hand-printed characters. OCRs are based on photoelectric cells which scan the printed document and transform the print characters into electronic signals. These signals are transmitted to a memory unit and tested for a match with prestored character patterns. If a match is found, the character is recorded; if not, the document may be rejected.

OCR has found a number of applications. For example, OCR forms have replaced punched cards as a turnaround document in many credit card and billing applications. Many OCR products have the additional capability of physically sorting the input forms. Therefore, the technique is particularly well adapted to applications where it is necessary to maintain a manual file of source documents as well as an automated file for processing. This is often the case when regulations or standard procedures require maintaining a signature on an authorization document. Specific examples include credit card processing and personnel actions in very large organizations.

The ability to process documents without an intermediate step has great cost advantages in high-volume operations. However, OCR has not proved as popular as one might expect. The introduction of OCR techniques frequently involves changes in operating procedures and the use of forms unacceptable to end users. The need for precision in document preparation is critical. Most applications that attempt to convert to OCR initially experience a very high document reject rate. Characters that are malformed or improperly located on an OCR form cannot be recognized and will cause the document to be rejected. The cost of correcting and resubmitting these documents, together with the initial cost of the equipment, are sufficient to discourage many users from expanding OCR usage.

MICR has been highly successful in a limited sphere of applications: It is universally used in clearing checks through the banking system. Every individual check is identified with bank and customer codes preprinted in magnetic ink characters. When a check is processed, the amount of the check is typed in MICR characters in the lower righthand corner of the check. Checks are collected in batches and processed through a reader/sorter which can process approximately 2500 checks per minute. Each character can be read by its magnetic signature in the MICR reader/sorter and by its appearance by any person concerned. The reader/sorter captures the accounting data necessary to maintain current records and at the same time sorts the checks into bank and customer categories for physical processing through the banking system. Additional applications of MICR techniques are unlikely because of the limited nature of the character set used; it consists only of the 10 numerical digits plus four special characters.

Mark-Sense Documents. Although they are not widely used in accounting information systems, mark-sense documents deserve mention as an input source. These documents consist of preformatted forms that require the user to blacken specified areas to indicate a response to designated data items. The mark-sense documents are processed by an optical scanning device onto magnetic tape for further input to the computer. They are familiar to all students who have taken a standardized test administered by the Educational Testing Service and are often used for test scoring in large university classes. States that have lotteries use them to generate tickets and provide interactive input to determine payoffs. They are most likely to be encountered in a business environment as input for some sort of customer or employee survey.

Portable Data Collection Devices. A number of portable data collection devices are now available for off-line data capture. These devices usually employ a magnetic tape cassette as the recording medium. Data may be entered via a keyboard that resembles a hand calculator, or via an optical sensing wand that reads bar-coded identification data. Data recorded on the cassette are later entered into the computer by special tape-reading equipment. Typical uses for portable data collection devices include facilitation of physical inventory count on shelves or in warehouses and the recording of a day's transactions by a salesperson on a trip.

On-Line Data Entry

On-line data entry refers to the use of equipment or devices that are connected to or communicate directly with the central processing unit. They are usually associated with interactive processing. A significant feature in the introduction and spread of terminals as input devices is that they shift the locus of data entry from the data processing center to the user locations. This change has a major impact on the AIS. In systems that used manual processes, virtually all accounting transactions were processed via the accounting department. The approval of some accounting department agent was required before any transaction reached the journal or ledgers. The same held true in punched card and key-to-tape operations. It is no longer the case in a CAAIS that employs terminals. Transactions are captured at their source and are entered into the firm's automated systems and consequently into the files of the CAAIS by nonaccounting personnel.

Controls over data integrity must be maintained by the nonaccounting user and/or by the accounting applications software. The user is primarily concerned with those aspects of a transaction that maintain the integrity of the data as he or she may see it. Accounting considerations are secondary. Therefore, the AIS must ensure that the necessary accounting transactions, edits, and controls are built into the applications software. Figure 5–2 indicates this shift in responsi-

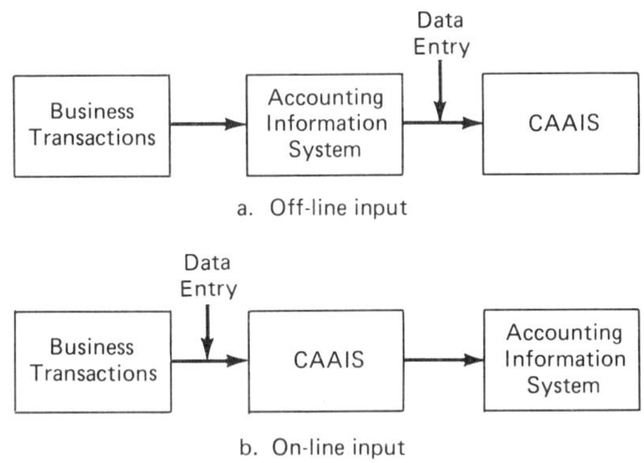

FIGURE 5–2 Impact of Terminal Operations on the AIS

bility. Accounting personnel familiar with traditional procedures may be uncomfortable with this change in control. They may be reassured by the fact that the use of data entry terminals has resulted in reduced error rates and increased efficiency in most applications.

Terminal Systems. In our discussion of off-line data preparation, we have avoided using the word "systems." We have preferred to view these methods and their associated devices as a simple component of the CAAIS. As we consider more recent developments in input technology, we are forced to abandon this simplification. Many input devices available in connection with an up-to-date CAAIS are, in fact, self-contained systems (more properly subsystems) which accomplish many of the editing, sorting, and collating tasks previously performed by the host computer. The previously described key-to-tape and key-to-disk operations, when viewed as a whole rather than as a collection of keying stations, are such subsystems. We turn now to those that bypass the batch mode entirely.

Cathode Ray Tube (CRT) Terminals. The CRT has become ubiquitious in today's business organizations. As a data entry device, the CRT is a marvel of simplicity. Each key on the keyboard creates a coded electrical signal that is directly readable by the computer. In most systems, the characters are held in the terminal's storage until a complete line of data is accumulated. The data are then visually reviewed for accuracy by the operator and, if correct, are made available for transmission to the central processing unit via the host computer's communications processor. CRT terminals may be classified as dumb or intelligent.

A *dumb* terminal is one that has no internal capability to process the data entered into it. The terminal operator may visually inspect the data for accuracy prior to transmission, but any remaining errors can be detected only by programs in the host computer. As with other terminals, a dumb CRT is usually operated by an end user in connection with the business transactions of the firm. (Note that many of the dumb CRT terminals you may observe in business organizations are not input devices. They do not have the necessary data processing authorizations to enter or to alter data that exist in the files, but merely have the capability to display existing data.) One prominent use of dumb terminals as a data entry device occurs in airlines reservations systems. Each airline ticket agent operates a terminal that is directly connected to a central computer. The data entered at the terminal are forwarded to the central computer, which maintains an up-to-the-minute status of reservations, aircraft seat availability, and, of course, customer billing status.

The trend in CRT terminals is toward intelligent systems. An *intelligent* terminal is one that has some capability to edit or otherwise process data. The "intelligence" of a terminal covers a wide range from a few simple accuracy-of-data checks to a full minicomputer capability. At the higher end of the intelligence scale, the terminal concept begins to blend with the distributed data processing concept. Whether dumb or intelligent, the terminal approach permits the user to interact with the computer to make immediate adjustments as required to ensure the accuracy and completeness of input data. When the data are correct to both the user's and the system's satisfaction, they are available for immediate further processing.

Source Data Automation (SDA). Source data automation refers to techniques used to capture data at their source and to move them directly to the central processing unit without further intervention. Most SDA devices depend upon bar codes and optical scanning devices. SDA has found a wide range of applications. For example, in a manufacturing assembly plant, a part may be identified with a suitable code as it is received by the materials department. It is then scanned, added to the inventory, and automatically assigned to its proper bin. When the part is required for assembly, it is scanned again as it leaves the department, and materials inventory is adjusted both in physical count and in terminal value.

Accountability is maintained when the part is scanned entering the assembly process. At this point, the part identification is combined with other identifiable parts in the subassembly, and work-in-process is adjusted. The process is repeated as necessary until the final assembly is completed and aggregate work-in-process is adjusted as the product is moved to completed goods inventory.

SDA has also found applications in such diverse settings as tracking logs from forest to sawmill and tracking freight cars throughout the entire U.S. rail network. One SDA application, point-of-sale terminals, is so widespread as to deserve specific attention.

Point of Sale (POS) Terminals. Point of sale terminals have been developed for a wide range of retail operations. Data are entered into the POS system by keying an electronic cash register or by means of a bar code reader. In either case, the data input consists simply of the product code; the POS system determines the correct price from its memory. Depending upon the sophistication of the particular system, it may then perform an array of additional functions. The use of POS terminals has been brought to its highest form in grocery supermarkets, where the checkout cashier passes any item marked with the Universal Product Code over an optical bar code reader. The system displays the description of each item, together with its cost, for cashier and customer review, updates the sales record and inventory for each item, computes appropriate taxes, totals the customer's order, and records a cash or credit transaction. In addition, it accumulates totals for the store by department and forwards daily totals to management for use in reordering merchandise, updating accounting entries, and monitoring store performance.

New Developments. The development of interactive terminal systems continues. Those having promise for integration into the CAAIS include voice input and touch input systems. Voice input systems find application on jobs where the user literally has his or her hands full. Existing applications are largely experimental. They include control of power in merchant vessels, control of combat aircraft, and sorting of mail. Some material handling jobs that produce accounting-related data may adopt this technology in the near future.

Touch-sensitive screens and data pads have also been developed. Current applications include selection and processing options and computer-assisted design. As terminal use in support of executive decision making becomes more common, this type of input may be used in connection with the AIS database.

CENTRAL PROCESSING UNIT CHARACTERISTICS

Processor Performance

The central processing unit (CPU) is the hardware component that determines the upper limit of the speed of the CAAIS. This can be defined precisely by a number of measures. Those most often encountered are cycle time and MIPS (millions of instructions per second). Two closely related measurements also affect processor speed: word length and size of main memory. We note at the outset that no single measure or any combination of these measures reliably predicts overall performance in an organizational setting; nevertheless, a basic understanding of these terms will increase your understanding of processor capabilities.

Cycle time is defined as the maximum time interval that must elapse between the starts of two successive accesses to any one storage location. In today's computers, it is typically measured in hundreds of nanoseconds (billionths of a second) up to a few microseconds (millionths of a second). A nanosecond is best understood by converting time to distance. An electronic signal can travel approximately 11.78 inches in a nanosecond. Therefore, if a signal is to make a round trip from the processor to a storage location in 1 nanosecond, the physical distance between those two locations cannot be greater than 5.89 inches. In practical terms, nanoseconds are of concern only within the CPU. (Cycle time is the simplest of the performance measures, but it cannot account for variations in system architecture.)

MIPS is the second commonly encountered measure of speed. Theoretically, in a simple computer structure the maximum MIPS would be the reciprocal of the cycle time; however, internal design constraints are such that this limit is not attainable in uniprocessor machines. Conversely, multiple processor configurations, those that have more than one processor operating on a shared memory, can exceed this value. MIPS is a more useful measure than cycle time because it accounts for more features of processor design. Typical mainframe computers used in business applications operate in the range of 1 to 10 MIPS. The instructions counted in this measure are machine-level instructions that will include a multiple, often large, of the more familiar higher-level program instructions such as COBOL or BASIC.

Word length is perhaps the most commonly used performance measure. It refers to the number of *binary digits* (*bits*) which the processor handles at a time. This measure has been popularized by the microcomputer industry, with its moves from 8-bit to 16-bit to 32-bit processors. In general, the greater the word length, the faster the processor will operate. General purpose mainframe and superminicomputers, those most often encountered in large MIS installations, use 32-bit processors. A combination of word length and either cycle time or MIPS begins to give a reasonable sense of overall CPU performance.

Size of main memory is another useful, albeit incomplete, measure of performance. Access times to instructions and data in main memory are measured in nanoseconds or microseconds; access times to instructions and data in secondary storage are measured in milliseconds. Thus, the more often a processor must refer to external storage devices, the slower will be its operations. Memory size varies even more widely than any of the previous measures. The current business microcomputer will have from 256 kilobytes up to 4 megabytes, and 1 to 32 megabytes is typical of mainframes and super-minis.

System Performance

Performance as finally perceived by the user is considerably more complex than the performance of the processor alone. The user is interested in the response time of the overall system. In addition to the characteristics of the processor itself, this will be a function of the type of program he or she is running, the number and types of other programs that may be running concurrently, managerial decisions regarding the priority of operations, the characteristics of the operating system, and the characteristics of the communications network. The best guide to overall performance is provided by *benchmark tests*. These are tests conducted by a number of agencies that provide comparison data for different systems configurations running a standard job or mix of jobs that the test agency believes to be likely in a given environment. Armed with knowledge of the processing requirements and appropriate benchmark tests, data processing professionals can make reasonable estimates of how a particular system will perform in the organizational environment.

Classes of Computers

The wide variety of computer products on the market today provides a continuous range of processing power. Any organization can select a system that will meet its current projected needs. Computers are generally grouped into five categories: micro, mini, super-mini, mainframe, and super. Although the overlap between adjoining categories illustrated in Table 5–1 shows that this distinction is somewhat artificial, we will conform with the general usage. The super computer category has been omitted from Table 5–1 because these are special-purpose machines not used in AIS. The reader is also cautioned that time is an important consideration in these classifications. A vintage 1975 mainframe, many of which are still in operation, would have performance characteristics inferior to a current-year micro.

The Mainframe. The mainframe computer provides the main computing capacity for most mid-size and large organizations. It has the speed and capacity to serve all functional areas and is particularly well

TABLE 5–1 Cost and Performance Data for Classes of Computers

Class	*Cost ($1000)*	*Word Size (Bits)*	*Main Memory (kbytes)*	*Cycle Time (MIPS)*	*Typical AIS Use*
Microcomputer	1–10	8, 16, or 32	128–4,000		Small business accounting, mid-size and large-size organizations for analysis, decision support
Minicomputer	8–100	16	32–4,000		Turnkey accounting systems for mid-size organizations; distributed processing
Super-minicomputer	75–300	32	1000–10,000	.3–5	Fully integrated CAAIS in mid-size to large organizations
Mainframe	250–5000	32 plus	2,000–32,000	.5–20	Fully integrated CAAIS in large organizations

suited to support sophisticated software systems that integrate the operations of several functional areas. Until 1970, all business computing was performed on mainframe computers, although as noted above, the mainframes of earlier years had considerably less processing capability than the microcomputers of today.

The Minicomputer. The minicomputer was the first mutant of the computer species. It was originally marketed in the mid-1960s to provide computational power for scientists and engineers who required more immediate response and more computational power than they could obtain from the organization's mainframe, which was more often than not the property of the accounting department. Members of this user community were technically inclined, and either already knew a computer language or were willing to learn one to get on with their work. Therefore, there was little effort on the part of minicomputer manufacturers to make their machines easy to use. Software entrepreneurs were quick to see a wide variety of uses for the minicomputers. A large number of small firms, referred to as original equipment manufacturers (OEMs), sprang up to customize a minicomputer to support a particular organizational function. An OEM would take delivery of a number of computers from the manufacturer, install operating systems (to be discussed in the next chapter) and/or applications software, and deliver an integrated hardware and software system to the selected user community. Users could operate the system with little or no in-house programming talent.

Accounting was among these functions, and the power of the computer soon became available to accountants in organizations that could not justify the expense of a mainframe. Early minicomputers used a 16-bit processor. This limited the processing speed and main storage capabilities of these machines and precluded their use in support of integrated management information systems. Perhaps their most important contribution to the use of information systems in organizations was to divorce the computer from the control of an in-house data processing staff.

In the chronology of hardware development, the widespread use of the minicomputer coincided with the development of remote terminals for programming and data entry, the extensive use of disk drives for secondary storage, and improvements in data communications. The net result of these changes, together with an ever-growing demand for computer assistance in all functional areas, was to replace the tightly controlled, centralized data processing facility dominant in 1970 with the widely dispersed information systems networks of the 1980s.

The Super-Minicomputer. The super-minicomputer emerged into the business world in the late 1970s. The super-minis replaced the 16-bit architecture of the minicomputer with the 32-bit architecture characteristic of mainframes. There is nearly total overlap between the lower end of mainframe performance and the performance of the super-mini. However, the cost-performance ratio of the super-mini is generally superior to that of the smaller mainframes. This is principally because the former represents the best efforts of the minicomputer manufacturers in a highly competitive market, whereas the latter were incidental products of the mainframe manufacturers. In spite of the lower performance, a firm that anticipates growth might prefer a small mainframe to a super-mini, since these machines are more easily upgraded as processing requirements increase.

The super-mini provided fully integrated processing systems for organizations that could not previously have afforded this capability.

The Microcomputer. The 1980s saw the microcomputer emerge as a serious contender in the business market. The micro completed the trend begun a decade earlier by the mini. It brought the benefits of computer assistance to the smallest organizations; even small partnerships and individual operators could afford a micro. Packaged applications software was readily available to support specific business applications ranging from architectural design to legal research. Of more direct interest to us, a major portion of the software development effort was directed toward accounting functions. It became possible for small organizations to select one or more packaged products to support their basic accounting functions.

In addition to providing computing power to these small organizations, the micro also found a role in larger businesses. It is widely used at all levels of management to facilitate analysis of accounting data, to assist in auditing functions, to examine alternative courses of action and implications of changes in the environment, to access data resident in the organization's central database, and to interrogate databases maintained by external agencies. The rapid development of microcomputer technology has permitted the personal or desktop computer to rival the capabilities of minis and super-minis in some applications. The role of the microcomputer will continue to expand as improved data communications hardware and software facilitate interaction between databases maintained by mainframe computers and microcomputer-based work stations.

A Final Note. We call your attention once again to the extensive overlap among the categories of computers in Table 5–1. There is a level of processor performance to match the AIS requirements of an organization as small as a freelance consultant or a local grocery store or as large as a major international corporation or the largest federal government agency. Deciding on the appropriate computer is based on the current needs of the organization, the projections of growth in these needs, and the availability of resources to support an information system.

SECONDARY STORAGE DEVICES

Data must be located in the computer's main memory if they are to be available for processing. However, the amount of main memory is limited by both physical and economic factors. Even the largest of existing main memories would be inadequate to store all the data relating to a large organization. The cost of a million bytes of main memory in large machines varies from $12,000 to $20,000, whereas the same amount of space on-line in secondary storage is as little as $40 for direct access devices and less than half that for sequential devices. For these reasons, data that are not to be used for immediate processing are placed in secondary storage. Many secondary storage devices have removable units to contain data, thus giving users an essentially unlimited capacity for storage.

Sequential versus Direct Access Storage

The first consideration in selecting an appropriate secondary storage device is the organization's need for immediate access to current data. If this need exists, then direct-access secondary storage is essential.

If it does not exist, then sequential media should be considered for the application. In virtually all installations, magnetic disk is used as the direct-access storage medium and magnetic tape is used as the sequential-access storage medium. We will limit our discussion to these two technologies. In either case, three performance characteristics are of interest: (1) How much data can a single device contain? (2) How rapidly can the desired data be located? (3) At what rate can the data be transferred into main storage for processing? We shall see that magnetic tape is cost-competitive with disk in regard to questions 1 and 3, but that it cannot compare with regard to the speed of locating information. Table 5–2 provides a summary of tape and disk characteristics.

TABLE 5–2 Performance Characteristics of Secondary Storage Media

Storage Device	*Capacity (bytes)*	*Access Time (millisecs)*	*Transfer Rate (kbytes/sec)*
Tape Drives			
Reel-to-reel	3M–150M	NA	200–1250
Cartridge	15M–500M	NA	25–3000
Cassette	600K–45M	NA	3–300
Disk Drives			
Rigid	5M–400M	25–30	1200
Winchester	5M–2500M	20–25	1800–3000
Floppy	250K–16M	60–90	40–250

Note: Values are typical and do not represent extreme range in any category.

Sequential-Access Storage Media

Magnetic Tape Characteristics. Magnetic tape was the principal means of secondary storage for all computer processing until the early 1970s. Since that time it has been replaced by disk for many applications, but we can expect to find magnetic tape in extensive use in most installations well into the future. There are three reasons for this expectation.

1. Magnetic tape is more cost-effective than disk for most batch processing.
2. Most established data processing installations have a large investment in their tape library. A library of 5,000–10,000 tapes is common. The costs of transferring this volume of information to disk are prohibitive.
3. Magnetic tape provides an efficient means of maintaining backup and archival copies of files.

Reel-to-Reel Tape Drives. Reel-to-reel was the original tape technology, and it is still the most widely used. In reel-to-reel operations the computer operator mounts a tape reel on one capstan and threads the tape through a read/write head to a second take-up reel much the way that film is threaded through a motion picture projector. When the tape is no longer needed for processing, it is rewound onto its original reel and delivered to the tape library. Reel-to-reel tapes are highly standardized. They have either seven or nine tracks, which permit a single character of 6 or 8 bits, respectively, plus a parity check bit to be imprinted on one tape position. Tapes usually can record 800 or 1600 bits per inch. (Note that bits per inch equals characters per inch on tape—this is not the case with disk.) This technology has been continually refined, and today's reel-to-reel tapes may hold as many as 150 million characters of information. The data transfer rate between tape drive and main memory may be as great as 1.25 million characters per second.

Tape Cartridges and Cassettes. A major drawback in the use of reel-to-reel tape is the difficulty in handling individual tapes. Careless handling may result in damage to the tape and loss of its data. This factor, combined with the need for effective backup systems for mini and micro computers that do not use the bulky reel-to-reel drives, led to the development of cassettes and cartridges. Both new tape technologies use self-enclosed units that eliminate physical exposure of the recording tape. Cassettes came into use in the 1970s, cartridges in the 1980s. Recall from the previous section that during this time mini, super-mini, and microcomputers were coming into wide organizational use. The proliferation of processors was accompanied by a similar proliferation in secondary storage devices. The standardization of the mainframe era no longer existed. Table 5–2 provides typical performance data for tape drives currently in use. Note that cassettes support the lower end of the processing spectrum. Typically they have 250K to 45M bytes of storage and transfer rates of from 3K to 300K bits per second. The newer cartridge technology serves the higher end of the spectrum. The cartridges typically hold 20M–40M bytes of data and have transfer rates varying from 25K–3000K bits per second. Cassettes are unlikely to be a major concern of AIS practitioners; however, cartridges show considerable promise as a backup media for all sizes of computers.

Direct-Access Storage

Magnetic disk technology was developed in the 1960s but did not come into widespread use until the 1970s. Magnetic disk, or some other direct-access storage device, is essential to support interactive processing, database management systems, end-user applications development, and decision support systems—in short, it is essential for all the features that characterize modern information systems. Disk can be used to support batch processing, but it will not be as cost-effective as tape in most pure batch applications. Management's perceived need for interactive processing, together with steady improvement in disk performance and reliability, has resulted in disk becoming the principal secondary-storage medium in use today. The wide range of processors is supported by a correspondingly wide range of disk capability. Three branches of disk technology have been developed to meet the demands for direct-access storage: rigid, Winchester, and floppy.

Rigid Disks. Rigid disks were the first of the three types to be developed. A single disk is made of aluminum or other nonmagnetic material covered with a thin ferromagnetic film. The film is divided into concentric tracks of magnetizable spots. The bits representing characters are stored sequentially along each track. For ease in addressing data records, each track is usually divided into sectors. Early disks were 14 inches in diameter. This is still the most common size, but smaller rigid disks are also in production. Rigid disks are usually arranged in a stack from 5 to 20 disks on a single spindle. Data are placed on or retrieved from the stack by an actuator consisting of a set of read/write heads mounted on movable arms such that each head is positioned over the same track on its respective recording surface. The set of tracks under the read/write heads at one position is known as a *cylinder*. Data are usually placed on the disk pack by filling a cylinder at a time rather than a surface at a time, as this can be done by electronically switching from head to head without requiring mechanical movement of the read/write assembly. This enhances both speed and reliability.

Disk packs may be fixed or removable. The removable packs permit storing very large amounts of data without the additional cost and complexity of additional on-line drives. Of course, the data in the packs that are not mounted are not immediately accessible. Removable disks may be used for backup and archival storage, but they are considerably more expensive than tape for these purposes. The data stored on fixed disk packs are always available to the central processor. Fixed disk units have higher reliability than removable disks.

Winchester Disk Drives. The rigid disk packs are open to the environment of the computer operations room. In spite of careful controls of temperature, humidity and cleanliness, this environment cannot prevent particles that are many times larger than the distance between a disk surface and its read/write head from contaminating the disk pack. The most common sources of contaminants are human hair, dust, and smoke particles. You are doubtless familiar with the effects of contamination on the performance of stereophonic sound systems. The effect on disk is even more drastic. One small particle can cause errors in the read/write operation and, in the worst case, cause the read/write head to contact the disk surface.

The contamination problem became even more acute when computer operations moved out of the operations room into uncontrolled user spaces. *Winchester disk drives* are an advance in rigid disk technology designed to eliminate the problem. Originally developed in 1973, they are hermetically sealed units that include disks, read/write heads, and a head actuator. Air circulated in the unit is filtered to remove any particles that might interfere with the operation. As a result of controlling the internal environment of the disk, data on Winchester drives may be more tightly packed, data transfer rates may be greater, and a disk of the same diameter can contain a larger amount of data than was previously feasible. For example, a 14-inch Winchester drive can hold up to 2500M bytes of data compared with a typical value of 400M bytes for a rigid disk. Nearly all Winchester drives are fixed installations. A strong argument in favor of the spread of Winchester technology is that the mean time between failures for these systems is in excess of 6000 hours, a figure more than double that of other rigid systems.

Floppy Disks (Diskettes). Floppy disks are usually made of polyester with a ferromagnetic coating. Data are recorded on them much as they are on the rigid disks; however, floppies are smaller in diameter and are used singly rather than in packs. They first came into use as input-output devices for minicomputers, but they are more widely known as the principal secondary storage media for microcomputers. The disk itself is permanently enclosed in a protective cover to prevent damage in handling. The disk rotates freely inside the cover when inserted into the drive. Floppies have proved to be a highly versatile medium. Most packaged programs for microcomputers are sold in this form. Floppies may hold the entire database of a small organization; and they are used as input-output media for key-to-disk operations in off-line data preparation.

Mass Storage Devices

Mass storage devices have been developed to augment the secondary storage provided by tape and disk for organizations that must have extremely large amounts of data readily available for processing. The object of these systems is to eliminate the manual search of tape and disk libraries to locate data on removable storage devices. Such manual searches take minutes of time, an eternity in the data processing domain, and require physical handling of the storage media, a process always prone to error or contamination. Mass storage systems operate on electromechanical principles to locate, retrieve, and mount data stored in an off-line manner for on-line processing under control of the central processing unit. The most straightforward of these systems is essentially an automated tape library. Data are stored on regular reel-to-reel tapes, which are automatically catalogued. Other systems store data on special magnetic strips that must be read onto disk before they can be processed. The operations of all these systems is much like that of a jukebox at a neighborhood restaurant. Most mass storage devices can have data ready for processing in 10 to 30 seconds.

OUTPUT CHARACTERISTICS AND DEVICES

Computer output must provide accurate, timely, and relevant information to its intended users. It must also be easily understood and readily available if it is to be used effectively. Output from the AIS has three distinct uses:

1. It is used by persons and agencies external to the producing organization. The external output of the AIS includes routine documents such as bills, vouchers, and checks; it includes summarized reports for shareholders and investors, such as balance sheets and income statements; and it includes mandated reports for the Securities and Exchange Commission, the Internal Revenue Service, and other regulatory agencies.
2. It is used by internal supervisors, managers, and executives within the accounting department and in all other functional areas of the organization for planning and control.
3. It is used for archival purposes. In many organizations, legal requirements or prudent managerial practice dictate that large amounts of data be retrievable well after the data are no longer needed for routine processing.

Early computer systems had one answer to all output requirements—hard copy from an impact printer. More modern systems provide a variety of capabilities that permit users to tailor output to its intended use. We will consider the three approaches commonly used in the AIS: printers, visual displays, and output to microfilm.

Printers

Hard Copy Printers. Hard copy printers were the original computer output device. They perform the great bulk of output operations today, and they will continue to do so well into the future. Although some industries, notably banking and financial firms, have made considerable progress toward paperless transactions, the vast majority of organizations depend on documents for internal and external exchange of information. There are two basic approaches to producing hard copy output: impact printers and nonimpact printers.

Impact Printers. Impact printers provide a wide range of speed and print quality. In general, the higher the speed, the greater the cost of the printer. Excellent print quality is available at low speeds and at relatively low cost. The print quality of impact printers tends to deteriorate at the higher end of the speed range. Impact printers are most cost-effective for relatively short runs. Perhaps their major drawback is that they tend to be very noisy.

Impact printers operate in either a serial or line printing mode. *Serial printers* are those that print one character at a time, much like a standard typewriter (although most printers can print right to left as well as left to right, a capability rarely found in the typing pool). *Line printers,* as the name suggests, print an entire line at a time. Serial printers are relatively slow and find greatest applicability where a small volume of high-quality output is required. Ball, daisy-wheel and dot-matrix technologies are used in serial printers. The dot-matrix is the most versatile of the serial printers. It can provide a wide variety of type styles simply by changing software controls. Most printers used with microcomputers or at end-user work stations are serial printers.

Line impact printers are the workhorses of the data processing organization. They are orders of magnitude faster than serial printers and are most often used to produce routine reports for both external and internal users. Line printers employ dot-matrix, drum, chain, or band technology. They are used with mini, super-mini, and mainframe computers for high-volume output. They may print on the familiar continuous sheet computer listing paper, on plain paper, or they may be programmed to print in sections of preprinted forms.

Table 5–3 presents representative cost and performance data for several types of printers.

TABLE 5–3 Performance and Cost Characteristics of Printers

Computer Class	*Technology*	*Printer Type*	*Print Speed*	*Print Quality*	*Cost*
Microcomputers	Impact	Dot matrix	50–400 cps	Fair–good	$300–3,000
		Daisy wheel	12–55 cps	Excellent	400–2,000
	Nonimpact	Ink jet	35–240 cps	Excellent	600–6,000
		Laser	300–1000 1pm	Excellent	4,000–20,000
Medium and large systems	Impact	Band	300–2000 1pm	Fair–good	$5,000–25,000
		Chain	300–2000 1pm	Fair–good	10,000–50,000
		Drum	300–2400 1pm	Fair–good	10,000–30,000
	Nonimpact	Laser	5000–25000 1pm	Excellent	20,000–100,000
		Electrostatic	1000–2400 1pm	Good	4,000–6,000

Nonimpact Printers. Nonimpact printers provide very high quality output. Early models were designed to operate at very high speeds on mainframe machines. These printers are extremely versatile; they can print everything from the company's logo to the CEO's signature. They have the further advantage of being quiet. These strong points are offset by higher initial costs and continuing higher maintenance costs than their impact competitors. Laser printers are the most common high-speed nonimpact printers; however, electrostatic, xerographic, and ink-jet technologies are also used. The extensive use of microcomputers has resulted in the adaptation of nonimpact technology for lower-volume output. Ink-jet printers provide high-quality graphics, and laser technology has been adapted to microcomputer applications.

Visual Display Terminals (VDTs)

Presentations on visual display terminals have displaced hard copy for many internal management purposes. If a customer calls to question a bill, it is simpler, faster, and cheaper for a customer service representative to retrieve the necessary information on a VDT than to manually search a preprinted listing. Similarly, an accountant can browse through an electronic file in search of data errors more easily than he or she could shuffle through a pile of hard copy reports. For internal purposes that do not require hard copy for record purposes, the VDT has made broad inroads on the use of printer output in most modern computers. This trend is certain to continue. When the VDT is combined with a printer, we have the best of both approaches. The accountant searches for data of interest using the VDT and then prints the selected data, which can be annotated or otherwise used for managerial or record purposes.

We have discussed the range of VDT capabilities in the input section of this chapter. The versatility of these devices in converting electrical impulses to a form suitable for human understanding is limited primarily by the imagination of the user. Some VDTs can be programmed to have a split-screen capability—a very useful feature in comparing current quarter or fiscal year performance with previous periods. Others have the capability to convert tabular data into line graphs, bar charts, or pie charts at a single keystroke. In fact, some have done away with the keystroke entirely and permit a manager to select a variety of displays or to read through a file by using a mouse or simply pointing to an icon on the screen.

Computer Output Microfilm (COM)

As the needs of external users are met by hard copy output and the needs of the internal users are met by hard copy or VDT presentation, so the need for archival output is met by computer output microfilm. COM is the process of transferring magnetic images to microfilm or microfiche without producing an intermediate paper copy. The resulting images are indexed for retrieval and can be viewed through standard microfilm readers. In high-volume operations, COM is initially less expensive than hard copy, and savings continue to accrue over the lifetime of the COM records in terms of reduced handling and storage costs. COM services are provided by service bureaus for organizations that wish to use this output medium but do not generate enough volume of pages to justify in-house procurement of the necessary equipment.

DATA COMMUNICATIONS CHARACTERISTICS AND DEVICES

The fundamental process involved in communications is that of originating a message in one location, transmitting it through an appropriate medium, and receiving it in its original form at a second location. In its simplest form, communication takes place whenever one person speaks to another in the same room. In this case, the message originates in the vocal cords of the speaker, is transmitted as sound waves through air, and is received at the eardrum of the listener. The situation is only slightly more complicated when we move into the area of telecommunication. To continue the example above, suppose the listener is in an office on the other side of the city rather than in the same room. We now have several stages in the process. As before, the message originates with the speaker. It is now transmitted through air to a microphone in a telephone handset. This transforms the sound wave into an analogous series of electrical voltages. These are imposed on a carrier frequency and transmitted over telephone wires through a switched network to the handset of the listener. There the earpiece transforms the electrical impulses back to sound waves and transmits these to the eardrum of the receiver.

The situation is very similar when we substitute the digital output from a computer terminal for the human voice. As telephone lines are designed to carry analog signals rather than digital signals, we convert computer output into an analog signal at the transmission point and reverse the process at the receiving end. Of course, we must have a device that uses digital input rather than a human ear as a receiver. Although implementations of data communications become highly complex from an engineering viewpoint, they can be understood conceptually as a variation of this simple model.

Data communications is becoming an increasingly vital component of an organization's information system. The ability to transfer information rapidly from one department or location to another in response to organizational needs is a critical element in determining the organization's success in a competitive environment. Communications may take place within a single building or a small cluster of buildings, or they may span continents. Data communications can be understood in terms of: (1) terminal characteristics, devices that originate or receive messages; and (2) transmission characteristics, the medium that carries the electrical message and the devices that facilitate effective use of the medium.

Terminal Characteristics

The communications terminal and its mode of operations define the interface between the user and the communication network. Selection of the type, number, location, and operating mode of these devices is a management concern. Virtually any device that creates or receives digital signals can serve as a data communications terminal. We have examined these in connection with input and output hardware components. Some, such as printers, can act only as communications receivers; some, such as bar code readers, can act only as transmitters; others, such as VDTs, can act as both transmitters and receivers.

The VDT is probably the most familiar communications terminal. Video terminals used in the managerial area are generally limited to the transmission and receipt of alphanumeric characters, although more sophisticated machines may be encountered in some engineering and design applications. These terminals can operate at speeds of up to 1200 characters per second over lines which provide a 2400–9600 bit per second (bps) capability. Video units may be operated singly, or they may be combined with like units to form a cluster which makes more efficient use of transmission facilities. The idea of clustering units at the user's location leads to complex configurations. A first improvement might be to add one or more printers to the VDTs so that permanent copies become available. If the terminals are intelligent, data may be downloaded from the host computer and processed at the user's site. Such operations are often known as work stations. Addition of word processing capability makes the work station essentially self-sufficient. If the cluster of terminals and other peripheral equipment becomes still larger, we may install a minicomputer to control the communications circuitry. Now we have progressed into the realm of a *distributed data processing network.*

Somewhat aside from the mainstream of terminals are the transaction terminals familiar in banking, point-of-sale, and inventory control operations. Although limited to specific functions, these devices may play an important role in generating input to inventory and accounting records. Often they are driven by minicomputers within their particular transaction environment, and information generated within these subsystems must be integrated with the overall information flow of the AIS.

The communications terminal located at the host computer site is known as a *front end processor*. The purpose of this device is to free the host computer from communications processing functions. The front end processor is perhaps the single most important component in a data processing network. It varies from a relatively simple programmable switching unit to a minicomputer designed specifically to enhance overall system efficiency. The front end processor may be limited to control over only the communications aspects of data processing—message addressing, routing, polling. However, it will more often be programmed to perform additional tasks that maximize the efficiency of the host computer on the one hand, and make the best use of the communications channel on the other. These tasks are controlled by software and are discussed further in Chapter 6.

Transmission Characteristics

Three elements of transmission of data need to be considered: the signal itself, the medium through which it travels, and how it is routed through the medium.

As we have noted, computer systems generate and process digital signals—a series of binary pulses that are coded into meaningful characters. Traditional communications networks, such as telephone lines, transmit analog signals—electrical pulses that vary in amplitude or frequency in proportion to the strength of an input message. Therefore, whenever we use traditional communications networks to transmit data, we must convert the digital signal to an analog signal. At the receiving end, we must convert the signal back to digital form for further processing. This is achieved by use of a *modem* (modulator-demodulator). Modems typically operate in the range of 300–1200 characters per second, which is compatible with the data transmission capacity of the telephone lines. Modems are familiar to all microcomputer users who participate in billboard systems or who access data from commercially available databases.

More modern communications networks transmit digital pulses directly, eliminating the need for modems. In fact, the analog voice signals of your telephone conversation may be converted to digital pulses for transmission over microwave or optical fiber networks—a complete reversal of the earlier practice.

A second signal feature which deserves mention is that of synchronous versus asynchronous transmission. Most low-volume transmissions, such as those from a VDT, are transmitted in the *asynchronous* mode. This requires each individual character to have a set of start and stop bits appended to it to enable the receiving terminal to identify the signal correctly. This mode makes relatively inefficient use of the communications channel because approximately 30 percent of the bits transmitted are not part of the message. *Synchronous* transmission is used for higher-volume traffic. In this mode, an initial series of prearranged pulses is sent to alert the receiver that a message will follow. These pulses synchronize the receiver with the transmitter, and the message may be sent without attaching additional bits to individual characters.

The *media* commonly used for data transmission are twisted pairs of telephone wires, coaxial cable, microwave, and fiber optics. The media sets the upper limit on the rate at which data may be transmitted. Choice of media depends on cost as well as volume considerations. In general, the higher-capacity media are more expensive to establish, but they become cost-competitive as volume increases.

Channel capacity depends upon the bandwidth of the media. Telephone, or voiceband, channels have a relatively narrow bandwidth. The transmission rate of data on voice-grade channels is usually in the range of 2400–9600 bits per second (bps), with an upper limit on specially conditioned lines of 19,200 bps. Coaxial cable and microwave have much greater bandwidth and can carry proportionally greater data loads. A rate of 1.54 million bps has become a de facto standard for digital communications on wide-area networks, although rates up to 20 million bps can be achieved. Optical fiber technology promises to extend this capacity still further. A complete data communications network will often combine all three media. The interfaces between lower- and higher-capacity channels are managed by *multiplexors* and *concentrators*. These devices combine the inputs from several low-capacity lines for further transmission along higher-capacity channels.

The final topic to be discussed is that of routing messages through the medium. The simplest case is that of a *direct connection*. If you have used a remote terminal of a mainframe computer, you are familiar with this technique. Whenever the terminal is turned on, it is in direct communication with its host computer. It simply waits its turn to transmit or receive a message. Another familiar form of routing is *circuit switching*. You use this every time you place a telephone call. As you dial a series of numbers, you establish a unique circuit that is totally dedicated to you until you terminate your call. Most microcomputer data communications take place over such circuits. Circuit switching is effective but inefficient. As long as you maintain the connection, you are charged at the same rate whether you are communicating or not, and the line is unavailable for other users. If you plan to use your micro to access a database, you are well advised to plan your actions in advance to avoid useless telephone charges.

Message switching is a method used to increase efficiency. Message switching involves routing the message through the network as time becomes available on a particular communications link. The message is forwarded from its point of origin to the first station in the network, where it is stored until time becomes available for the next leg of its journey. A message sent from New York to California via microwave relay might have in excess of a hundred such legs. This process is referred to as *store and forward* switching. It makes greater use of available communications capacity than circuit switching. One drawback is that one very long message will tie up a segment of the network, causing all other messages to be delayed, thereby reducing overall network efficiency. This problem has been addressed by the development of *packet switching*. A packet switching network is a modification of message switching such that all messages are broken into equal-sized submessages or *packets*. Each packet is routed through the network as an individual message. Packets are then reassembled at the receiving site to reconstruct the original message.

An example will serve to illustrate these ideas. A major international firm needs the ability to exchange data between and among field offices, manufacturing plants, divisional headquarters, and corporate headquarters. Figure 5–3 depicts this organization.

Traffic analysis has shown that there is heavy exchange of computer-to-computer data along the hierarchical paths between corporate and divisional headquarters and between divisional headquarters and plants. The traffic from field office to plant varies widely with the size of the office. In addition, there is sporadic need for exchange of computer-to-computer data among divisional headquarters, and among plants within divisions. Finally, field offices must have the capability to report all customer complaints directly to corporate headquarters via their terminals.

Field Office FO111 is located in a small city. It operates three VDT terminals and has a single printer for incoming traffic. Its needs are met by a conditioned leased line that carries up to 9600 bps. Switching is controlled by software at the plant level.

Field Office FO112 is in a large city. It operates 15 VDTs and has several printers. It utilizes a microwave link to carry its traffic. Since FO112 is located close to Plant II, this is a single link owned and operated by the company under Federal Communications Commission license. It carries all voice telephone communications between the sites, in addition to data. A line concentrator is used at FO112 to control incoming and outgoing traffic.

FO113 is located in a large town. It has only one VDT and a serial printer. Communications are via standard dial-up telephone line, using a built-in modem. Traffic addressed to FO113 is stored at P11 until the terminal is activated.

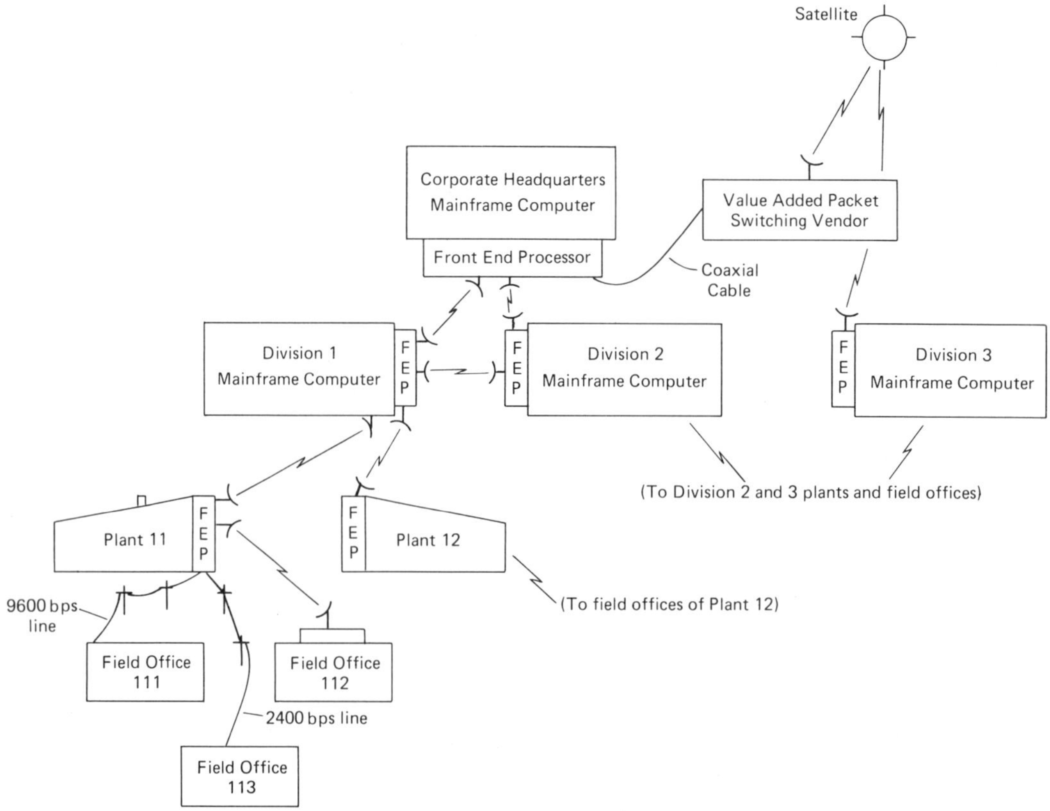

FIGURE 5–3 The Data Communications Network of a Large Manufacturing Firm
Commercial switched services from field offices to corporate headquarters not shown.

Computer-to-computer traffic between corporate headquarters and Divisions 1 and 2 is carried by leased microwave circuits. Division 3 is located overseas. Traffic between it and corporate is via a commercial packet switching service utilizing satellite relay. When required, Divisions 1 and 2 communicate with each other via commercial microwave service. Payment for this service is a flat fee for the first 10 hours per month, with additional charges for time in excess of this value.

SUMMARY

Many hardware options are available to support the AIS and its mission. Technological developments in the areas of input and output have largely overcome early problems that limited the effectiveness of the human-machine interface. For input, keyboard devices have steadily improved and have been augmented by additional devices such as OCR, MICR, and bar code readers. In the output area, paper listings have been improved in content and format and have been augmented by visual display terminals and computer output microfilm in areas where these devices are more appropriate to the needs of the organization.

Central processor technology has evolved so that adequate computing power is available to any organization, regardless of its size, dispersion, and managerial philosophy. Data communications have improved markedly in the past decade and promise continual improvement in the ability to produce the required information when and where it is needed. This chapter does not purport to make you an expert in the selection and evaluation of computer-related hardware—but it does enable you to understand the terms commonly encountered in the field. Mastery of the material will increase your ability to communicate with data processing professionals—an essential element in developing and using effective accounting information systems.

REVIEW QUESTIONS, DISCUSSION QUESTIONS, AND PROBLEMS AND CASES

A. Review Questions

A5.1 Briefly describe the input devices that are applicable to entering data in the batch mode. The interactive mode.

A5.2 Which of the devices you identified in question 5.1 are independent of a keyboard for their operation?

A5.3 Briefly explain the difference(s) between "dumb" and "intelligent" terminals. How does an intelligent terminal differ from a microcomputer?

A5.4 Discuss the use of punched cards as an input medium. Why have they been replaced by other methods in most installations?

A5.5 How do key-to-tape and key-to-disk input devices operate? What are their advantages vis-à-vis punched card technology?

A5.6 What is OCR? When should it be considered as an input device?

A5.7 What is MICR? What is its primary use? Would you expect wider use of the technique in its present form? Explain your answer.

A5.8 What is cycle time? What is MIPS? What are typical values of these measures for a modern mainframe computer?

A5.9 What types of magnetic tape are available? Which type is most likely to be used as a backup for magnetic disk?

A5.10 Name and describe the types of magnetic disk technology. When should disk be used in lieu of tape as a secondary storage medium?

A5.11 What is a head crash? What effect may this malfunction have on the end user?

A5.12 Compare the advantages and disadvantages of direct-access and sequential-access secondary storage devices.

A5.13 What is the most commonly used output device used in batch-oriented computer systems? In interactive systems?

A5.14 What output technology would you recommend for records that are voluminous and must be maintained for a long period of time?

A5.15 What are the essential elements of any communications process?

A5.16 How does a data signal vary from a voice signal?

A5.17 What is the relationship between bits/second and characters/second?

A5.18 What is meant by asynchronous transmission?

A5.19 What are the advantages of coaxial cable and microwave circuits over traditional telephone lines? Why are they not always used?

A5.20 What is the difference between message switching and packet switching?

B. Discussion Questions

B5.1 Consider the evolution of input devices, processing units, secondary storage, and output devices over the last two decades. Has this been a result of a demand for better information? A natural result of scientific inquiry? A result of corporate planning? A result of entrepreneurial competition? A synergistic combination of some or all of the above elements?

B5.2 What criteria should be considered when deciding to convert a function from batch to interactive processing?

B5.3 What performance criteria are of greatest interest to AIS users? Is there any need for non-data-processing personnel to understand such terms as MIPS or "cycles per second"?

B5.4 The microcomputer explosion has been a major factor in information management in the 1980s. Information systems professionals have often been resistant to the introduction of micros, citing loss of data integrity, security problems, weak backup and recovery procedures, and lack of control over programs as their objections. Other managers have embraced the micro enthusiastically, citing the immediate response and flexibility of having their own computing power. They argue that the objections are really based on turf issues. As an accountant, what is your position on this issue?

B5.5 How has the increased variety of output products contributed to the expansion of business computing? Has this been of greater significance to the AIS or to other business functions?

B5.6 Why may ability to communicate data electronically among sites be important to a firm? Cite specific instances where this could be a factor in gaining competitive advantage.

B5.7 How does increased use of data communications affect control and audit issues? What measures would you advocate to protect the firm's financial and information assets when long-haul communications are implemented by your employer?

C. Problems and Cases

C5.1 Labonics, Inc., is a midwestern firm that manufactures control systems used by laboratories, factories, and refineries to monitor and control environmental conditions. The company's 11-year-old minicomputer is overloaded to the point where response times are slow, the system crashes often, and programs must be compiled on a third shift so as not to tie up the system during working hours. Labonics is considering two proposals to replace its current system. The new system must service six major work stations located in its laboratories, continue to provide administrative support, and provide increased response time. The first proposal is to purchase a super-minicomputer from the same manufacturer of its current system. The super-mini can service from 60 to 100 terminals. It has 4 Mbytes of main memory and can handle up to 500 Mbytes of on-line secondary storage. The second proposal is to purchase a microcomputer network composed of four super-micros. Two of these have 512 bytes of main memory and 72 Mbytes of hard disk; the other two have 1 Mbyte of main memory and 220 Mbytes of hard disk. The latter two can each support 4 terminals. There is essentially no difference in the cost of the two proposals. Based on the information available, prepare a recommendation for management's review. What additional data would you like to have before making a final decision?

C5.2 A leading national news service recently established a database service consisting of daily news headlines, up-to-date stock quotations, and the latest betting line on sporting events from horse racing to professional wrestling. After six months of operation, it was losing money at an alarming rate. Market surveys indicated a strong demand for the information, but a reluctance on the part of many users to pay the long distance telephone charges for access to the New York area code. Many early subscribers complained of long delays in getting information even after they had established a telephone connection. Develop a network plan that could bring the service into the black.

SUGGESTED READINGS

"Annual Hardware Review," *Computerworld,* Framingham, MA. (Published in 2–3 consecutive weekly issues, usually in the late fall of each year.)

Datapro Reports, Delran, N.J., Datapro Research Corporation. (A series of reports on hardware and software updated periodically as required.)

ESSICK, EDWARD L. *Business Data Processing,* 5th Ed. Chicago: Science Research Associates, 1986.

SLOAN, M. E. *Computer Hardware and Organization: An Introduction,* 2nd ed. Chicago: Science Research Associates, 1986.

chapter six

The Software Component

CHAPTER OUTLINE

INTRODUCTION

In Chapter 5 we discussed the capabilities and limitations imposed on the AIS by its hardware configuration. The hardware potential cannot be realized without suitable software. It is the software that converts machinery from a collection of digital electronic switches into an information processor. We will consider three categories of software: the operating system, general purpose software, and applications programs.

The operating system is a series of complex programs that governs access to the central processing unit, monitors actions within the CPU, and controls the use of all systems peripherals. General purpose software provides a range of processing and support capabilities likely to be useful to a wide spectrum of programming and user personnel. Applications programs perform one or several related functions in support of a particular business activity. In the case of the CAAIS, these are the programs necessary to support financial, cost, and managerial accounting. Figure 6–1 illustrates the three categories

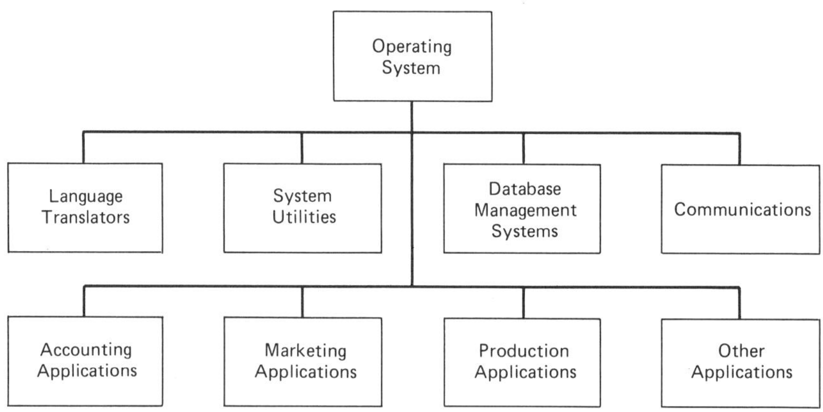

FIGURE 6–1 A Three-Level View of Software

of software. We will investigate the three classes in some detail, relate them to the accounting function, and describe the sources of the various software components.

THE OPERATING SYSTEM

The operating system is the software element that governs the internal activities of the data processing system. The growth of operating systems has paralleled the development of computer hardware. The first operating systems were simply job-loading programs that relieved the human computer operator of the tedium of loading one job, waiting for that job to complete, and then loading the next job to be processed. Current operating systems deal with a multitude of tasks concerned with optimizing and balancing the use of I/O devices, the central processor, and secondary storage. Table 6–1 summarizes the functions performed by a typical mainframe operating system of the 1980s.

TABLE 6–1 Operating System Functions

Hardware-related functions

- Allocation of processor resources
- Allocation of secondary storage space
- Assignment of input/output devices
- Analysis of interrupt signals

Software-related functions

- Scheduling of programs
- Loading of programs
- Interleaving of programs
- Reporting completion
- Dealing with error conditions

Data-related functions

- Support of file creation
- Support of file access methods
- Initiation and control of input/output operations

Personnel-related functions

- Communication with operator
- Recording/reporting of statistics

The operating system is essentially invisible to the AIS user; nevertheless, it is this set of programs which determines the range of capabilities that the computing system will possess. It is pointless to evaluate applications programs without first ensuring that they are compatible with the installed operating system. On all large machines, those classified as minicomputers and larger, the operating system is unique to the supplier of the equipment. This is most often the major hardware manufacturer, but particularly in the case of the minicomputer, it may be an intermediate vendor who purchases the minicomputer and then customizes it for a particular application. The customization often includes an operating system optimized for the designed function. The significance of this to the AIS planner or user is that general-purpose and applications software must be designed to be compatible with the host operating system. The decision to select a particular hardware system is critical not because of the initial costs of the hardware, but rather because of the longer-range investment in associated software. The multitude of applications programs an organization develops over a period of years represents a major investment that is entirely dependent upon continuity of the operating system.

Whenever an organization outgrows the capacity of its current system, it faces a difficult choice. In the best case, it may be able to upgrade to a larger-capacity machine in the same family of computers. Most manufacturers of large systems have one or more families of machines which may have the property of upward compatibility; that is, any program which can be used in one machine of the family can be used on a larger model in the same family with little or no modification. This choice minimizes the difficulty of the transition, but it has the disadvantage of conferring a monopoly position on the computer manufacturer. If the organization is at the high end of a family of computers (or for any other reasons wishes to change computer vendor), it must anticipate a difficult and expensive transition.

Operating systems, like any other set of programs, are subject to periodic review and update. The design and programming of updates is carefully controlled so that changes in the operating system will not adversely affect existing general purpose and applications software. However, the system vendor cannot anticipate all the nuances of programs written by the user organization or other software developers. Frequently, a relatively minor system update will cause disruption of programs that have operated satisfactorily under the old system. To avoid disruption during closing periods, the prudent AIS user will establish procedures with the data processing department to preclude updates to the operating system just before periodic closings.

The lack of a standardized system in the larger machines can be attributed to the developmental history of the computer field. Initially, the costs of purchasing or leasing hardware were perceived to be the major expense in computer operations. Therefore, customers who made the initial commitment to a particular manufacturer were willing to customize their programs to that hardware. The steady decrease of hardware costs relative to software costs is changing this perception, but the large base of installed programming systems precludes the rapid demise of hardware-unique systems in large computers.

The appearance of the microcomputer accelerated the changing perceptions of the cost relationship between hardware and software. No one was willing to spend thousands of dollars developing custom software for a machine that might cost a very small fraction of the software costs. Yet this is precisely what would be required if each of the dozens of microcomputer manufacturers developed a unique operating system. The market response to this potential stumbling block in the introduction of microcomputers has been a high degree of standardization of operating systems among manufacturers. Although standardization is far from achieved, the careful buyer of microcomputer applications software can develop a program library that will run on a variety of computers. There is some indication that the standardization enjoyed in the microcomputer world may soon make inroads in the minicomputer area.

GENERAL PURPOSE SOFTWARE

General purpose software cannot be defined precisely. It occupies the middle ground between the operating systems programs that control the essential functions of the computer system and the applications programs that provide support to users in their pursuit of business objectives. General purpose software programs cover a wide variety of capabilities, but they have the common characteristic of facilitating computer use. Most programs in this category are transparent to the user; nevertheless, knowledge of their existence and their functions is essential to effective use of automated support, systems evaluation, and computer-assisted auditing. We will consider four categories of general purpose software: language translators, database management systems, systems utilities, and communications software.

Language Translators

Recall from your introduction to computer fundamentals that the computer is a symbol-manipulating device which understands only the presence of a high or low voltage at a complex series of logic gates. Recall further that we assemble these high and low voltages into coded packages, or bytes, which represent alphabetic and numeric characters, and that we have input and output devices to convert characters to voltages and vice versa. So far, so good. However, we do not wish to instruct the computer to do our will character by character. We wish to use a language as close as possible to the natural written or spoken language in everyday use. Language translators provide this capability.

The basic instruction set of any computer consists of a number of elementary functions. Each instruction in the set consists of an operation code which tells the computer what function to perform, and one or more operands which tell the computer where to find or place the information to be manipulated. The severely constrained main memory of early machines demanded concise instructions and efficient use of available space. Thus, the earliest language translators used highly abbreviated mnemonic coding techniques. As main memory has expanded, language translators have adopted more complex, natural-language types of phrases. A major research effort in the field of artificial intelligence is aimed at solving the semantic problems associated with interacting with the computer in a fully conversational mode.

Assemblers. Assemblers are language translators closely related to machine code. They provide a programmer with a number of mnemonic phrases and with the capability to use symbolic rather than physical addresses. They were the first of the language translators to emerge and are still widely used. The principal advantage of assembly language vis-à-vis the higher-level languages to be discussed in the following section is that a skilled programmer can code programs in assembly language that will operate more efficiently than those in higher-level languages.

Efficiency of machine operations is particularly important for programs that will be executed frequently—for example, sort or merge routines in a batch environment. These, and many of the other general purpose programs we will discuss, are often written in assembly language. The disadvantages of assembly language are: (1) It requires the highest degree of programmer expertise; (2) it is the most labor-intensive of the language translators; and (3) perhaps most significant, it is unique to the family of machines for which it is written. Assembly languages are sometimes referred to as second-generation languages—first-generation programmers actually wrote strings of 0s and 1s to instruct their machines.

Third-Generation Translators. Third-generation languages have been the workhorses of computers for over a quarter of a century. There are literally hundreds of languages that fall in this category; however, COBOL, FORTRAN, and BASIC are the most widely known and used in the business environment. Two characteristics distinguish third-generation languages: (1) They are procedural—that is, the programmer must specify in a step-by-step manner precisely how the task at hand is to be accomplished; and (2) they have a high degree of machine independence—that is, a program written for one particular computer system can be executed on a second system with little or no modification.

Existing third-generation languages undergo continuous update to keep their capabilities abreast of demands of users and developments in the computer science field. In addition, new languages in this category continue to be developed. Ada, a language sponsored by the United States Department of Defense, may become a significant entry in this area. Third-generation languages are appealing because they strike a balance between ease of programming and efficient use of hardware resources. This fact, coupled with the existence of a massive installed program base, guarantees that third-generation languages will be a mainstay of professionally written programs for the foreseeable future.

Fourth-Generation Languages. Two factors have driven the development of fourth-generation languages: (1) the need to increase the productivity of professional programmers, and (2) the desire to bypass the professional programmer and involve the end user directly in applications development. The category covers a variety of capabilities from full applications generators—systems which may be used to create data files, enter and manipulate data, and provide varying forms of output—to query languages—simplified subsets of a language which permit a relatively unskilled user to develop an ad hoc inquiry and present the results in a system-generated format. Table 6–2

TABLE 6–2 A Sampling of Fourth-Generation Languages

*Language**	*Vendor*	*Hardware Capability*
NOMAD-2	Dun & Bradstreet Computing Services	IBM
MAPPER	Sperry Corporation	Sperry
FOCUS	Information Builders	IBM
RAMIS II	Mathematic Products Group	IBM
DATATRIEVE	Digital Equipment Corporation	DEC
NATURAL	Software AG of North America	IBM
TOTAL	Cincom Systems	IBM/NCR/others
ADS/ON-LINE	Cullinet	IBM
ADF	IBM	IBM
INQUIRE	INFODATA	IBM

* Many of these products include a full DBMS capability using the same name as the fourth-generation language.

provides a sampling of some of the fourth-generation languages currently available. A distinguishing feature of languages in this category is that they are nonprocedural. That is, the programmer or end user simply indicates what actions are to be performed and leaves the details of how to accomplish the result to preprogrammed features built into the software.

The use of fourth-generation languages promises major changes in the development of application programs. The systems specifications, systems analysis, and design stages of application development can be drastically foreshortened by direct user interaction with the computer system. An experienced MIS manager recently noted: "We have a marketing research application that we are about to offer as a commercial product to outside users. It was developed by two end users in two and one-half months using FOCUS™. If we had to go through the traditional justification and development channels, the application, with good luck, would be in the development queue with an expected start date three years down the line."

In addition to being nonprocedural, fourth-generation products differ from third-generation languages in that they are proprietary to a particular vendor.

Decision support system (*DSS*) generators are a special case of fourth-generation languages that deserve mention. These systems are specifically designed to assist higher-level managers in dealing with the less structured types of decisions typical of long-range financial and strategic planning. DSS generators frequently target a specific functional area of an organization. They incorporate a strong model-building capability and a specialized library of computational functions to facilitate analysis and forecasting. (They are discussed at greater length in Chapter 13.)

System Utilities

Systems utilities are a second category of general purpose software. *Systems utilities* are programs that perform functions essential to efficient data processing. For example, in batch processing applications, it is necessary to *sort* transaction file records into the same sequence as the master file records in preparation for file update. Rather than requiring each applications programmer to write a sort routine, the system will maintain one or more standard sort programs that can be called by the application program. Similarly, it is often useful to create a file of records in several parallel segments and then *merge* the partial files into a single large file. There will be a utility program to meet this need.

Figure 6–2 illustrates how a number of work stations may be

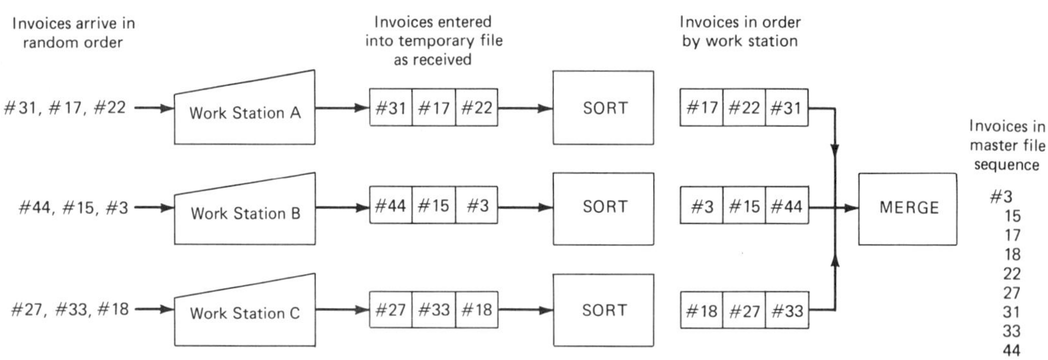

FIGURE 6–2 Multiple Work Stations Create Update File Using SORT and MERGE Utilities

operated in parallel to create a transaction file that will be used subsequently to update a permanent accounts receivable file. Other commonly encountered utilities include Editors that permit a user to establish and modify textual files, Help routines that provide assistance to on-line users when they encounter unanticipated problems, and Copy routines that permit the user to copy files from one account to another or from one medium to another. Numerous other systems utilities will be encountered in specific situations; here we will mention only one more—security programs. Security programs are available to protect an organization's data. They provide password and/or procedural protection at the file, record and, if necessary, data item levels of the data structure. Password protection requires that anyone attempting to access protected data know a specified password. Procedural protection requires the would-be user to follow a specified series of steps.

An additional layer of protection is available to organizations that maintain extremely sensitive data in automated media. Passwords and procedures can be bypassed by a skilled technician. To prevent compromise of information in such a case, the organization may employ encryption software. Data which are encrypted before storage or transmission are unintelligible to anyone who may succeed in accessing them by unauthorized means. Encryption adds a layer of complexity and overhead to information processing, but it should be seriously considered, especially when financial data are transferred via data communications networks.

Systems utilities, like the operating system, are essentially invisible to the AIS user. They are often provided as options by the operating system vendor. However, the user organization may elect to procure one or more of its utilities from software vendors specializing in a particular category, and some utilities are developed in-house. The existence, extent, and prices of systems utilities are important considerations when comparing systems alternatives.

Database Management Systems (DBMS)

A DBMS is a set of programs designed to improve and simplify the use of data stored in automated media. A DBMS facilitates the development of one-time reports and responses to ad hoc queries by management. These features are essential if the AIS is to serve an organization's need for strategic planning and managerial control. As is often true in the data processing field, the term DBMS is subject to a wide range of interpretation. At the lower end of the interpretive scale, a relatively simple utility program that permits a single user to establish a file and retrieve information from that file in accordance with selected criteria is often called a DBMS. Such programs are widely available for use on microcomputers and can be purchased for a few hundred dollars. They can be used effectively to support a variety of activities and require little forethought or planning; however, most do not have the full range of data handling and security capabilities to support a comprehensive AIS. At the other extreme, a DBMS may be a set of extremely complex programs designed to organize the data of a major segment of a very large company. Such a DBMS may cost well over half a million dollars and require detailed planning and data modeling if it is to be used effectively.

For our purposes, we will require a software system to possess the following minimum characteristics to be considered in the DBMS category:

1. It must provide data-structuring features so as to support multiple-user views of a set of data.
2. It must provide independence between the physical storage of data and user application programs.
3. It must provide for ease of information retrieval.

Three types of programs are essential to provide these capabilities—a data description language (DDL) which establishes the structure of the data; a data manipulation language (DML) which provides the capability to enter, change, delete, and retrieve data; and a query language which permits the rapid development of reports and responses to managerial questions. The query language may be a subset of the DML, or it may be a separate element that interfaces with the DBMS. (DBMS are discussed in greater detail in Chapter 7.)

Data Dictionaries

Data dictionaries are programs that enable an organization to monitor and control the use of data items throughout its application programs. A data dictionary may be a passive tool that simply records data about data (sometimes referred to as *metadata*). In such cases, it may operate in a batch or an on-line mode. A passive dictionary can be used to record and display such facts about a data element as:

1. Its English name
2. Mnemonic abbreviation(s) for the item used in files and programs
3. The type of characters allowed
4. Its size
5. The allowable range of values
6. Programs that use it
7. File(s) in which it is maintained
8. The user responsible for maintaining its currency

Passive data dictionaries have been used in large data processing installations for many years, with varying degrees of success. Because they are updated in transactions separate from those required to establish a new file, they may become out of date and fall into disuse.

When maintained effectively, they are a useful aid to analysts, programmers, and end users in developing new applications. They also promote compatibility of data items across files and control of data redundancy.

The evolution of on-line systems has been accompanied by a comparable evolution in data dictionaries. In many modern systems, the data dictionary is an active element. All requests for data are referred first to the dictionary to determine if the data exist, and if so, where and how they may be accessed. Active data dictionaries incorporate the features noted above plus additional metadata regarding the data items' location(s) and, in some cases, a facility to monitor use of the data.

The data dictionary is an important software feature in all data processing operations. It becomes critical when an organization operates in a decentralized mode or when it installs a database management system. In the first case, careful adherence to data standards, as established in the dictionary, may be the only control available to the organization when it wishes to exchange data among its various sites. In the latter case, it is an integral element of automated information handling.

Data Communications Software

The functions required for efficient transfer of data between and among different locations are accomplished by a combination of hardware and software elements. In relatively simple configurations, such as a small number of terminals linked to a single processing unit, all necessary data communications functions may be achieved using hardware devices. Figure 6–3 illustrates a typical configuration. This system may well suffice for its designed purpose, but it will be totally inflexible and cannot be adjusted to meet changing requirements without redesigning the system and replacing the hardware. As systems become more complex, it becomes necessary to include programmable elements to provide flexibility in system use. Figure 6–4 illustrates a data communications network that might be employed by a medium-sized corporation which operates in several locations. Data messages may originate at a terminal, or they may be generated by one of the host computers in the network as part of its ongoing processing. Data communications software may reside in the host computer, the front end processor, or a concentrator located at a site which does not have a general purpose computer. The software provides such capabilities as these:

1. Processing input and output requests from user application programs
2. Converting data from one code to another

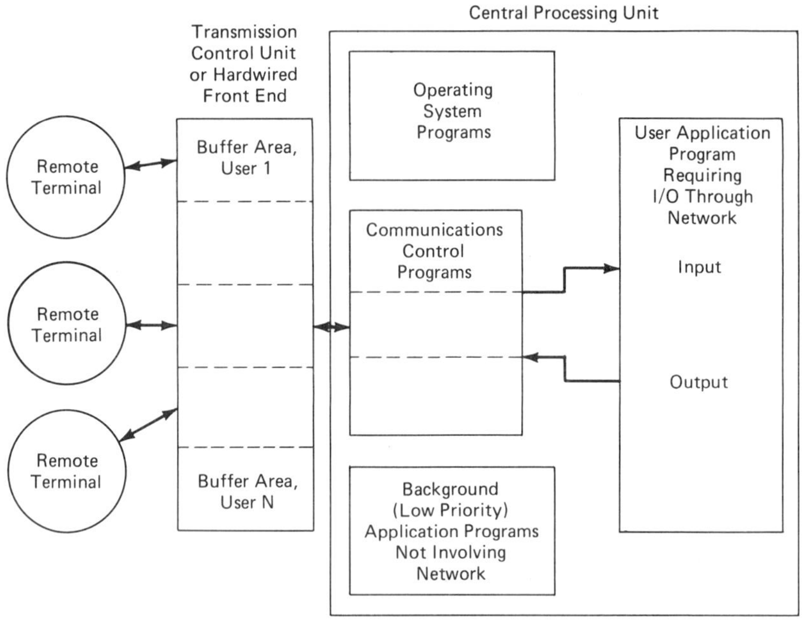

FIGURE 6–3 A Simple Data Communications System
Source: Adapted from Dixon R. Doll, *Data Communications: Facilities, Networks and Systems Design* (New York: John Wiley & Sons, 1978), p. 419. Copyright © 1978 John Wiley & Sons, Inc. Reprinted by permission of John Wiley & Sons, Inc.

3. Formatting data for transmission
4. Storing and forwarding messages
5. Checking for errors in transmission
6. Polling stations in the network to determine if any station has traffic to send
7. Answering incoming calls
8. Generating outgoing calls
9. Establishing priorities for transmission and reception
10. Establishing and terminating circuits
11. Providing multiple addresses for messages

Communications software is available through hardware manufacturers and specialized software vendors. Communications systems are usually divided into two categories: long haul and local area networks.

Long-haul. These capabilities are usually provided by common carriers and/or value-added network vendors. The former provide the physical facilities and the latter reduce costs to individual users by consolidating the requirements of many users to optimize use of circuits.

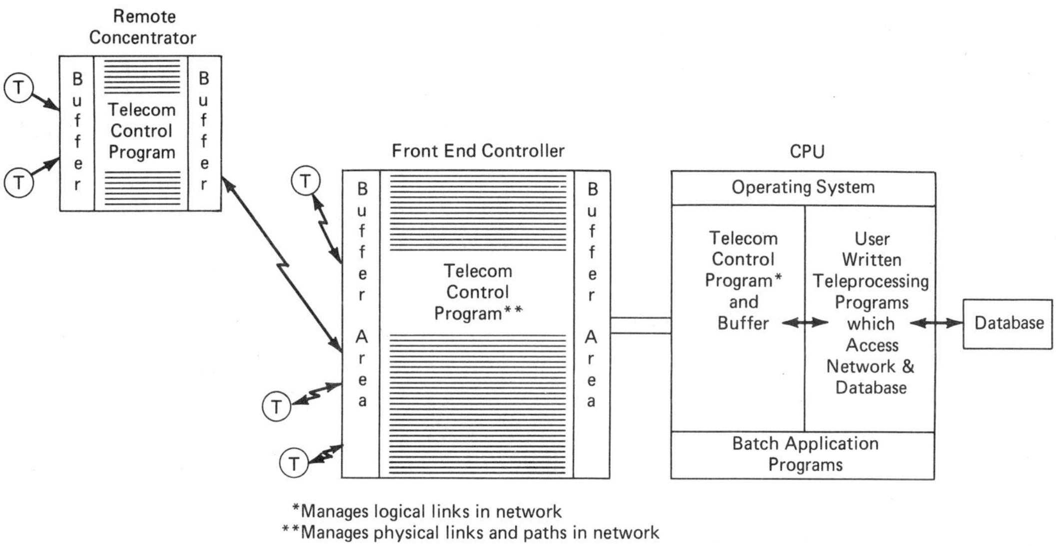

FIGURE 6–4 A Complex Data Communications Network

Source: Adapted from Dixon R. Doll, *Data Communications: Facilities, Networks and Systems Design* (New York: John Wiley & Sons, 1978), p. 422. Copyright © 1978 John Wiley & Sons, Inc. Reprinted by permission of John Wiley & Sons, Inc.

Local Area Networks (LANs). These capabilities are totally under the control of the using organization. The function of a LAN is to connect a number of word and/or data processing devices. As the name implies, a LAN covers a small geographic area, usually a single building or a few buildings in close proximity. A LAN can be integrated into a long-haul network via a software-controlled link referred to as a *gateway*. The AIS practitioner is concerned with communications software in his or her roles as controller, user, and auditor. While the details of communications systems design and implementation are beyond the accountant's range of interest, it is within the purview of the AIS to ensure that all communications software leased or purchased by the organization have these features:

1. It is compatible with all existing software and planned additions.
2. It meets security requirements.
3. It records the statistics necessary to support auditability.

APPLICATIONS SOFTWARE

Operating systems and general purpose software are essential to the efficient operation of computer systems; indeed, without them, computer operations would be so inefficient that they could not support the pace of business operations in our modern economy. Efficiency of operations is a necessary, but not sufficient, condition for information systems support. Effectiveness—the capability to do the right things—is the second required ingredient, and it depends upon the implementation of a correct mix of application programs.

This may be a useful moment to recall several points from our systems discussion in Chapter 2. First, note that the application software is a subsystem of a number of higher-level systems, such as the organization, the information system, and the software system. You may think of other systems levels relevant to your understanding of a particular organization. Second, the applications software subsystem is an element of several functional systems. In this context we may think of personnel systems, marketing systems, materials planning systems, and inevitably, accounting systems. Third, we have defined the AIS as a relatively open system which includes the human element and the CAAIS as the installed hardware and software base. Finally, recall that the objectives of the systems approach determine which elements will be part of our system and which will be part of the system's environment. We use this last feature to concentrate on the AIS elements of the applications software subsystem, somewhat to the detriment of other applications subsystems that are essential to a broader view of a total information system. The bias is introduced as a simplification in pursuing the purposes of this book. Figure 6–5 provides an AIS-centered view of applications software. We will note the potential interfaces between the AIS and other information systems as we discuss the AIS modules, but we will not present non-AIS programs in any detail.

Even with this simplification, the attempt to describe applications software brings to mind the parable of the blind men and the elephant. In the worst case, each observer is likely to sense one particular feature of the beast and reject conflicting views; and even in the best case, a synthesis of views is unlikely to catch all the wrinkles of the subject. We have elected to examine three of the many possible dimensions of accounting applications software in some detail and to note other issues briefly. The three dimensions to be discussed at length are:

1. The nature of the accounting functions supported
2. The types of processing that can be utilized
3. The levels of management to be supported

These dimensions are not mutually exclusive. Figure 6–6 is a depiction of how the three dimensions may be combined to support the objectives of a typical organization.

Financial Accounting Software

In Chapter 1 we noted the primacy of financial accounting in supporting the accounting information needs of an organization. As the

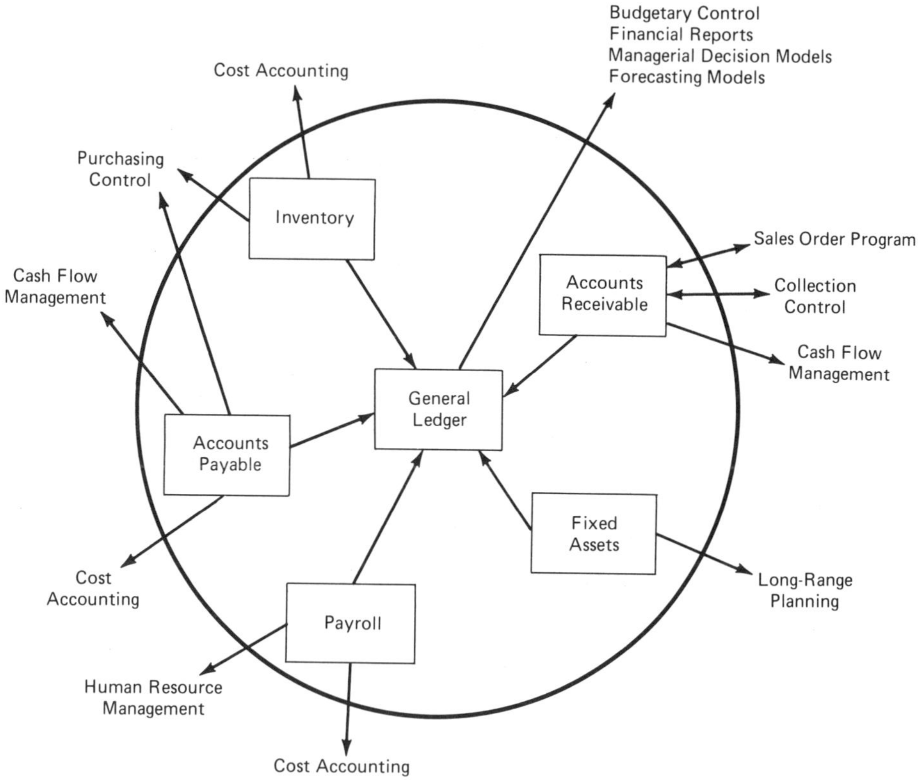

FIGURE 6–5 An AIS-centered View of Applications Software

thoughtful reader will correctly infer from this fact, financial accounting software provides the backbone of an organization's accounting information system. Data are collected, stored, and processed into information primarily to meet the financial accounting requirements of management and external agencies. A well-conceived system design will permit the additional functions of cost and managerial accounting to be supported with minimal additional expenditure of funds and effort. The specific needs of financial accounting information software will vary widely with the size of the organization, the purpose of the organization, and the degree of responsibility the organization has to report its activities to the general public. As a comparison of extremes, we would not expect the accounting needs of a small privately held foundry to be the same as those of U.S. Steel; neither would we expect the needs of a local hospital to compare to those of Blue Cross-Blue Shield. However, the accounting requirements imposed by the Securities and Exchange Commission, the Financial Accounting Standards Board, the Internal Revenue Service, and other regulatory agencies have resulted in certain minimally acceptable standards for firms and agencies subject to their rules. To the extent that these rules codify

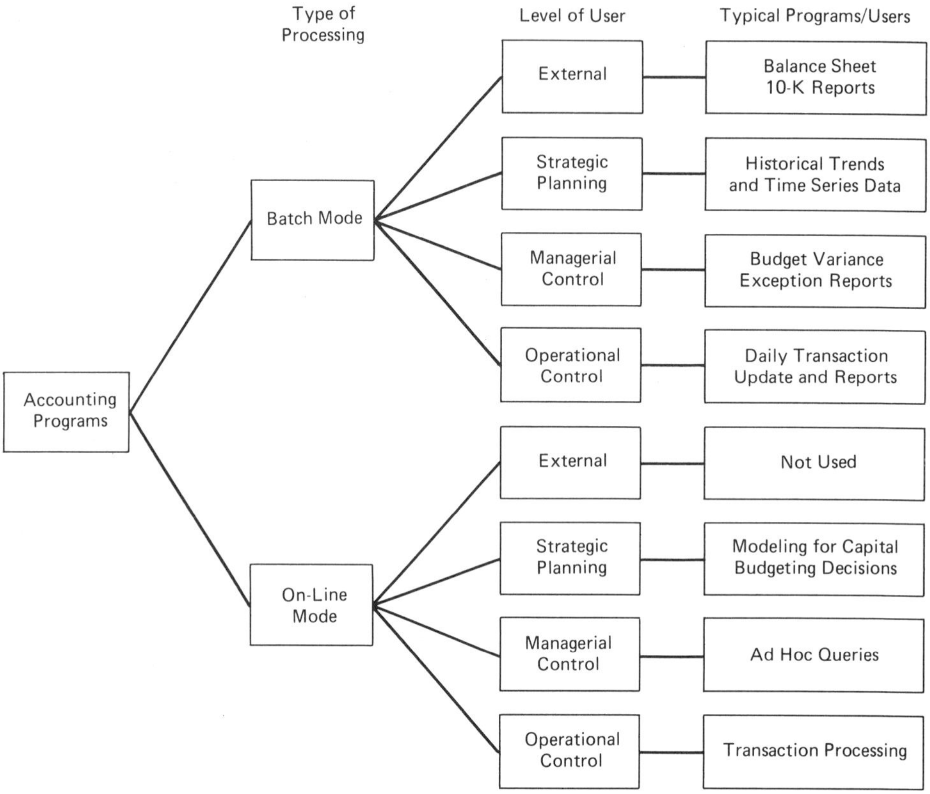

FIGURE 6–6 Accounting Applications Software Tree

good business practice, they have been voluntarily accepted by organizations not directly subject to regulation. Therefore, it is possible to form some generally applicable statements about the characteristics of well-designed financial accounting software.

The central feature of any such accounting system will be the general ledger. In addition, most financial accounting systems will include one or more of the following components:

- Accounts payable
- Accounts receivable
- Payroll
- Inventory
- Fixed assets

Figure 6–7 illustrates the interrelationships among these components in a mid-sized organization.

Financial accounting systems may be either batch-oriented or interactive. The software may be procured as a package, or it may be

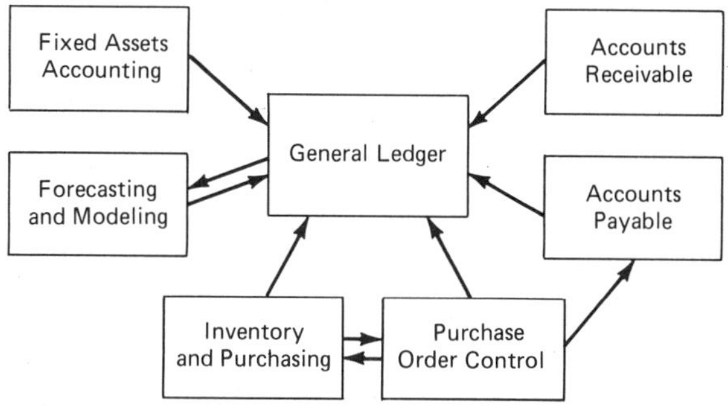

FIGURE 6–7 A Typical Financial Accounting Information System

designed for a particular organization. It may be implemented as a single entity, or in a modular fashion. In the latter case, a rational organization will implement the modules in order of descending return on investment. For example, a firm that is experiencing great difficulties in closing the ledger accounts and preparing financial reports might elect to automate its general ledger while maintaining all subsidiary ledgers with traditional manual procedures. If it next found that it was having severe problems in billing and tracing aging receivables, it might opt to automate accounts receivable. At this stage, postings to accounts receivable would be transcribed onto machine-readable media, processed by the A/R programs, and then automatically summarized and posted to the general ledger without human intervention.

Automation of the entire financial accounting function will continue in this modular fashion as it becomes cost-effective to purchase or develop programs for the other ledgers. The need for centralized planning and control of this process should be apparent. An accounts receivable program which provides output that is incompatible with the input requirements of the general ledger is hardly a major step forward. The desirable characteristics of the major components of financial accounting software follow.

General ledger programs provide an accurate database for all required financial reports to management, shareholders, and regulatory agencies. Requirements for internal control include a trial balance, a transaction register, and departmental accounting reports. External requirements for publicly held corporations include balance sheets, income statements, and statements of changes in financial position, among many others. Many governmental and nonprofit organizations and privately held corporations use similar reports; however, there is a great deal of variation in these areas. A well-designed general ledger system will provide for automatic interfaces with all subsidiary ledger systems and, in addition, may provide support for other management control functions, such as budgetary control, financial analysis models, and forecasting models.

Accounts payable programs maintain records of all outstanding claims against the assets of an organization. A well-designed accounts payable system will establish a list of validated vendors, provide a time-sequenced list of payables that optimizes cash flow, print checks and maintain a check register, prevent duplicate payment of invoices, forecast cash requirements; and maintain a payables transaction listing. The accounts payable programs should provide an automated interface with the general ledger system and may provide automated interface with and support of the purchasing function of the organization.

Accounts receivable programs maintain records of all amounts due to the organization. A well-designed system will maintain customer records to include current balance and credit status information, prepare invoices and statements, produce aging reports, and maintain a receivables transactions register. The accounts receivable programs should provide an automated interface with the general ledger and maintain such subsidiary ledgers as may be required by the organization.

Payroll programs maintain records of all amounts due to the salaried, hourly, and commission employees of an organization. At a minimum, payroll systems must maintain accurate records of employee data related to pay, deductions, and benefits; compute all federal, state, and local tax deductions; print paychecks; print checks to tax authorities and other payees authorized by employee deductions; maintain year-to-date totals of pay and deductions; provide tax reporting forms at year end; and print a payroll register. The payroll programs should provide for automatic interfaces with the general ledger and may provide such additional features as distribution of labor costs to departments and/or projects. In an integrated system, the payroll programs will interface automatically with the master personnel file maintained by the organization's personnel department.

Fixed assets accounting programs maintain the records necessary for property control. At a minimum, fixed asset accounting systems will maintain property records to include identification and location, depreciation schedules for tax and financial reporting, and provide for leased property. The system should have the flexibility to adjust for changes in tax regulations that may be advantageous to the organization over the useful lifetime of the property held. Fixed asset programs should generate automated inputs to the general ledger for depreciation expenses, additions, transfers, adjustments, and retirements.

Inventory accounting programs maintain records regarding the status, use, and costs of supplies. A well-designed inventory system will calculate economic order quantities, reorder points, and safety point levels. The inventory accounting system should provide an automated interface with the general ledger.

Managerial Accounting Software

Managerial accounting software will, in general, consist of programs that extract and manipulate data from the files and databases established in support of financial accounting functions. The requirements for managerial accounting information must be included with the specifications of the financial accounting developments if they are to be fully realized.

The area of managerial accounting and reporting is much less structured than that of financial accounting, and the lack of structure gives rise to a far greater variety in software. We will mention four sets of programs that have found wide use. Many additional programs are unique to a particular industry, government sector, nonprofit group, or to a single organization within any of these classes. The four to be described here are:

1. Budgetary control programs
2. Ratio analysis programs
3. Cash flow management programs
4. Forecasting programs

Budgetary control programs are probably the most widely used of the managerial accounting systems. These programs record annual, quarterly, and monthly expectations for expenditures of labor, material, and other costs based on approved managerial estimates. The actual expenditures are then extracted from the general ledger system, summarized according to cost center or other budgetary unit, and compared with the estimated values. Managerial attention is then required to explain or correct any significant variances. Budgetary programs exemplify the concepts of first- and second-level feedback noted in Chapter 2, and may be further used to adjust the organization's processes and objectives.

Ratio analysis programs are widely used to track particular features of an organization's financial health. A computer program may be used to generate a large number of ratios which may be relevant to an organization and to report only those which fall outside a specified range or show a significant trend over time. Ratio analysis programs are based on data available in the general ledger system.

Cash flow analysis and projection programs are used to prevent cash crises from arising. Cash outflows can be monitored and predicted with a high degree of accuracy based on data available from the accounts payable files of the financial accounting system. Cash inflows can be predicted from analysis of the accounts receivable files. Periods of potential excesses or deficiencies can be predicted well in advance, and plans laid to invest the excess or borrow to cover temporary shortages.

Forecasting programs are based, in part, on historical data available from the general ledger system. Forecasts are based on a variety of modeling techniques that may range from simple linear extrapolation to highly sophisticated smoothing algorithms which may be adjusted for cyclical phenomena. Such programs usually have the facility to enter a variety of planning parameters and to record changes in the forecast as different assumptions are made regarding the parameters.

Cost Accounting Systems

Cost accounting systems are supported by the data gathered for financial accounting. Costs of labor, material, and other items of interest may be allocated to products or to jobs based on data encoded into the payroll, inventory, and accounts payable programs. The allocated costs may then be compared to standard or estimated costs, and corrective actions initiated where variations exist.

Processing Modes

A set of programs to support any of the accounting functions noted above may include programs to operate in either *batch* or *interactive* processing modes. The two methods may be used in a combination that best supports the needs and budget of the organization. A system that consists only of batch programs is characteristic of older software systems designed to run in a large mainframe environment. The principal advantages of all-batch programs are that they make the most efficient use of available hardware resources; they can be used with relatively simple operating procedures; they provide excellent security; and they have inherently simple backup and recovery procedures.

An organization that exists in a static environment and has little or no occasion for rapid response to internal management or to external authorities may find an all-batch system sufficient. However, such organizations are becoming increasingly rare in today's world. Customers are not satisfied to wait until the end of the next reporting period for information on accounts or shipments; employees are unwilling to wait for changes in their status to be recorded at the end of the month; managers must have the latest cash flow projection right now. There is little market today for pure-batch systems, and no manufacturer of accounting packages is writing such systems today.

A significant step forward in responsiveness is a system that uses batch update programs but has provision for on-line retrieval of information. Such systems retain many of the advantages of the pure batch mode. They can use machine resources efficiently—batch updates are usually scheduled during off-peak business hours—and they retain the security and recovery features of the earlier systems. A recent case illustrates this point. "Hackers" were able to compromise the access codes to the databases of a major national credit reporting agency. They were able to discover a great deal of information about individuals and, perhaps, use this information to perpetuate fraudulent transactions. However, the files could be updated only from magnetic tape input, and therefore it was impossible for the unauthorized users to alter any existing information. The potential for damage was serious, but limited.

Many of these hybrid systems were originally programmed for batch-only operations but have been modified to interact with a communications software package. The combination of batch input and on-line retrieval is ideal for applications that are characterized by high volume of update transactions where a degree of obsolescence of retrieved data can be tolerated. In these systems, the high volume of input data is transferred into machine-sensible format in an off-line mode (key-to-disk, key-to-tape, optical character reader), collected into a periodic batch of transactions, and then entered into the accounting files via a batch update run.

A significant drawback of such a system is that erroneous transactions may not be discovered until the batch is run against the master files. The resulting error listing will have to be formatted into a new batch and run again. Also, there is a need in accounting systems to enter adjusting entries in a timely manner to facilitate closings. These needs have resulted in systems which are primarily batch-oriented for update but have the capability to enter lower-volume transactions in an on-line mode. Note that this additional capability is purchased at the cost of simplicity of computer operations, increased security concerns, and more sophisticated backup and recovery procedures.

Many modern accounting information systems are designed for all-interactive processing operations. Such systems are characteristic of smaller organizations using mini and microcomputers. Often, these machines are not equipped to operate in a batch mode. Programs at this level are usually menu and screen driven; the operator simply has to know how to enter the system and is then guided through a series of questions to enter data, make an on-line query, or produce a variety of hard copy reports.

Management Support

Accounting information supports the operational, managerial, and strategic planning levels of management. Return to Figure 6–5 for some typical examples of support at each level. Programs written to establish and maintain the files of the accounting system will include extensive edit and control features to relieve first-line supervisors from the onerous and time-consuming tasks required to maintain quality control of posting entries. Routine reports will be generated to provide accounting and line managers with the detailed information needed for daily operations. Summarized and exception reports will be provided to mid-level managers in support of their planning and control functions, and on-line access to data provides additional capabilities to generate one-time reports or to respond to immediate needs for information of top management or customers. Top management is further served by summaries of historical data, forecasting programs based on projections of this data, and computer models which permit rapid evaluation of the likely results of a variety of managerial decisions in areas such as cash flow, change in product line mix, or proposed physical expansions.

Make or Buy

The decision of whether to produce software customized to the needs of an organization or to purchase a prepackaged product is an important one in AIS. There are numerous strong arguments for buying packaged programs:

1. Package vendors gain considerable experience in their areas of specialization and have encountered and solved many problems that may not be foreseen in custom development.
2. The cost of developing the software is spread among many users.
3. The package is immediately available and can be installed and operating in a relatively short time.
4. The vendor will have expertise in training accounting and data processing personnel in use of the package.
5. The programs will be largely error-free.
6. Program documentation will be available for inspection.

There are equally valid points to be made in favor of custom systems:

1. Custom-designed software conforms to existing organizational procedures.
2. Packages frequently require extensive modification for local use—this may result in an inability to install vendor-supplied updates.

3. Internal information systems development personnel will be more responsive to the organization's need to update programs.
4. Not all package vendors are stable and reliable. (There is a strong tendency for vendor marketing departments to anticipate successful performance of their technical departments. Performance claims should be verified before signing a contract.)

The correct decision will vary with each organization and with each proposed application within the organization. There are a number of excellent accounting packages on the market, but none may meet the requirements of a given organization. This issue will be addressed further in Chapter 8. For now, we will note that an investigation of the availability and suitability of packaged software should always be considered as one option in applications development.

Applications Software Summary

Accounting applications software has been the focal point of our discussion of applications software in general. The reader is reminded again that accounting applications software systems are subsystems of both the accounting system and the information system of the overall organization. For purposes of exposition we have chosen to consider accounting applications of primary interest. This is, in fact, the case in many organizations, especially at the headquarters level, where financial information provides the common language among a variety of divisions or agencies. In other organizations, the production function, the marketing function, the patient care function, the distribution function, or any of a number of other subsystems may be the focus of development, and accounting software may be ancillary. The correct emphasis will depend upon the parent organization's goals and objectives. The systems approach demands that we consider the interfaces among all subsystems as development proceeds. Planning and control must be exercised at the general management level to ensure that all applications that are developed will be capable of interacting in an automated fashion wherever interactions are required. The DBMS and data dictionary systems discussed under the general purpose software category are major elements in this planning and control.

SUMMARY

Three levels of software are relevant to the accounting information system. Operating systems software is that set of programs essential to controlling computer resources and maintaining the internal efficiency of computer operations. A second layer of software, designated as general purpose, is necessary to provide for efficient use of machine resources by programmers and end users. Although the AIS practitioner is not directly involved with operating systems or the mechanics of general purpose software, he or she needs to be aware of the existence of these programs, their range of capabilities, and the effects they may have on selection and utilization of applications programs. Applications software comprises those programs which accomplish some organizational purpose for line or staff managers. Our discussion has centered on financial accounting software. A general ledger system is the centerpiece of financial accounting, and all software installed to support subsidiary ledger operations should be fully compatible with the general ledger programs. With sound planning, the data files established for financial accounting purposes can be used to support both managerial and cost accounting. Certain interfaces between financial accounting programs and some categories of nonaccounting software can be implemented in an organization, and effective use of the systems approach to software development can ensure the necessary compatibility among subsystems. (We caution the reader again that the centrality of accounting software as presented here is a bias deliberately introduced to support the purposes of this text; it may or may not occur in any given organization.)

REVIEW QUESTIONS, DISCUSSION QUESTIONS, AND PROBLEMS AND CASES

A. Review Questions

A6.1 Name and provide a brief description of the three levels of software.

A6.2 What is the significance of an operating system to an AIS practitioner? How does the operating system promote and/or constrain the AIS?

A6.3 What are the four categories of general purpose software? What is the significance of each to the AIS?

A6.4 Describe the evolution of computer languages through four generations.

A6.5 What is a DSS generator? What features would you expect to find in a DSS generator ? What level of management control is supported by the DSS?

A6.6 What is a DBMS? What three characteristics are necessary for a DBMS to be useful in the AIS context. What types of programs are required?

A6.7 List the capabilities that data communications software may have.

A6.8 Define a LAN. What are the implications of a LAN for the AIS?

A6.9 An AIS is developed initially to support the requirements of financial accounting. What functions are likely candidates for such an AIS?

A6.10 Describe the program modules that would comprise a complete financial accounting AIS.

A6.11 A managerial accounting system is less standardized than its financial accounting counterpart. What are the advantages and disadvantages of this in terms of systems development?

A6.12 Some organizations still maintain pure batch-mode accounting software. What are the advantages and disadvantages of this mode of operation?

A6.13 What are the primary decision criteria governing the choice between batch and interactive processing in the AIS?

B. Discussion Questions

B6.1 At the present time, there is a relatively high degree of standardization of operating systems software at the microcomputer level and none at all at the mainframe level. There is strong sentiment that standardization should be extended to the larger machines. Who would benefit from this? Who would be likely to resist such a movement?

B6.2 If operating systems and general purpose software are essentially transparent to the AIS practitioner, why do you suppose they are included in this text?

B6.3 What is the significance of an organization moving from a third-generation language environment to a fourth-generation environment? Consider applications software development, hardware requirements, operating procedures, and control in your discussion.

B6.4 What is meant by DBMS? Are the varying definitions of this term of significance to accountants? Why or why not?

B6.5 The text discussion of applications software takes an accounting-centered view. How would this change if we used top management's perspective in a manufacturing firm? An insurance firm? A bank? A hospital? The welfare division of a state government?

B6.6 The decision to make or buy applications software is an important and sensitive one in most large organizations. What does your school (or business, if you are a part-time student) do in this regard? Why?

C. Problems and Cases

C6.1 Assume you are the accounts receivable manager for a large department store. Your computerized support system was originally developed for batch processing and has been patched over the years to provide a degree of on-line access. You are able to retrieve customer status data in the interactive mode, but all updates are made in the batch mode at the end of each day's business. You have requested that the information services department (ISD) update your automated support. The ISD manager fully supports your request, since maintenance of the current system is a major drain on programming resources. All costs of development and computer operations are charged back to user departments in accordance with the following schedule:

Analyst time	$35/hour
Programmer time	25/hour
CPU time	50/minute
Terminals	25/month

The ISD manager has presented you with three alternatives in regard to replacing the A/R software: (A) Alternative 1 is to develop the software in-house, using traditional COBOL programming techniques. (b) Alternative 2 is to develop the software in-house using a newly acquired fourth-generation language. (c) Alternative 3 is to purchase an A/R package from a reliable vendor at a cost of $18,500. The requirements for each alternative are as follows:

	Alternative 1	*Alternative 2*	*Alternative 3*
Analyst time	300 hr	300 hr	200 hr
Programmer time	400 hr	100 hr	20 hr
CPU time/month	20 min	28 min	15 min
Terminals used	8	8	8

Which development alternative would you select? What are its strong and weak points? What other information would you like to have in regard to this decision?

C6.2 Intermountain Express is a large interstate trucking firm that has offices and freight terminals in 10 western states. In addition to moving freight between its terminals, Interstate also makes direct on-site deliveries to its larger customers. The company is currently having serious problems keeping track of deliveries and billing its customers. Under the current system, drivers are responsible for maintaining manual records of deliveries to customers and submitting the forms to the next company office on their route. This has resulted in difficulties in matching loading and delivery records, delays in billing, and discontent among the drivers who are held liable for any shortages. A data processing consultant has recommended that the firm replace the manual system with a portable microcomputer system. Each driver would be issued a microcomputer with a database consisting of his or her cargo and its destination. The micros would have a built-in modem so that the driver could call in directly to the mainframe computer at each delivery site and simultaneously update his or her own database and that of the company. The instructions for using the terminal are only slightly more complex than those for using an automatic teller machine. What software would be required to implement this system? How would you propose to coordinate the delivery system with the accounting system? What difficulties might you anticipate in implementing this system?

SUGGESTED READINGS

BOEHM, BARRY W. *Software Engineering Economics*. Englewood Cliffs, N.J.: Prentice-Hall, 1981.

ESSICK, EDWARD L. *Business Data Processing,* 5th ed. Chicago: Science Research Associates, 1986.

LOOMIS, MARY E. *Data Communications*. Englewood Cliffs, N.J.: Prentice-Hall, 1983.

MARTIN, JAMES, AND C. MCCLURE. *Software Maintenance: The Problem and Its Solutions*. Englewood Cliffs, N.J.: Prentice-Hall, 1983.

chapter seven

The Data Component: Characteristics, Storage, and Retrieval

CHAPTER OUTLINE

INTRODUCTION

We have now seen how the human component of the AIS initiates and controls AIS actions and permits the AIS to adapt to a changing environment; how the hardware component sets an upper limit on the systems capability; and how the software elements combine to enable us to use the hardware capability in support of organizational goals. The data component of the AIS remains to be addressed. The concept of data and its role in information systems has undergone a revolution hardly less significant than the more obvious changes in hardware and software. Early applications developments centered about the automation of a particular process. In these developments, data were seen as a subordinate element—something to be manipulated by and essentially a part of a set of programs. More recent concepts visualize data as a prime resource of the organization—an entity to be managed with the same care accorded to personnel, raw materials, or financial assets. The data-centered approach breaks the bond between application programs and data storage, allowing widespread sharing of data among end users.

Here, we discuss the elementary properties of data stored within the CAAIS, the ways data may be organized for storage, and the ways data may be accessed to support organizational objectives. As recently as the early 1980s, much of the information in this chapter would have been considered esoteric, of interest only to data processing professionals intent upon the internal design of programs. The advent of the microcomputer and fourth-generation languages requires that all managers understand these fundamentals if they are to use the newer capabilities effectively.

The primary subject of this chapter is data, as distinct from information. However, the retrieval process is necessarily concerned with providing information. Therefore, we include a final section which emphasizes the difference between data and information and notes the characteristics that are essential if computer-processed information is to be used effectively throughout an organization.

THE NATURE OF DATA

Data are commonly defined as the raw material of information processing. At the most elementary level, data in an automated information system are represented by the presence or absence of a given level of voltage or by the orientation of a microscopic magnetic field at a specified location. A single such location is the familiar binary digit, or *bit*. A single bit can assume only two states; either it is on or it is off; it can represent only two characters. Since this is not very useful, we group bits together into coded units called *bytes*. A byte usually consists of 8 bits, which permits the encoding of 2^8, or 256 characters. The most commonly used codes in data storage are the EBCDIC (Extended Binary Coded Decimal Interchange Code) used in IBM machines and the ASCII (American Standard Code for Information Interchange) used in most other systems.

In general, a byte represents one character of information. It is the most commonly used unit for specifying the capacity of primary and secondary storage devices. A simple example using textual data may strip some of the mystery from the byte. A page from a book selected at random was found to have 75 characters per line (remember that a blank space is a character in computer code) and 40 lines per page. If we wish to enter 100 pages of the book into a word processor memory, we may compute a first approximation of the space required by multiplying: 75 characters $\times$ 40 lines $\times$ 100 pages $=$ 30,000, or approximately 30k bytes of storage. In actual practice, there may be data compression techniques that reduce this number, and a need for control characters that will increase it; however, the simple computation will not be far off the mark.

It does not advance our purpose to dwell on the bits and bytes level of data storage; nevertheless, it is sobering to realize that the greatest portion of the financial assets of any modern organization exist only as microscopic magnetic spots in the secondary storage system of the organization's banking institution. This is true for organizations as small as your local grocery store and as large as the United States of America.

The smallest logical unit of data, the unit which has meaning to a user, is the *field*. This is also referred to as a *data item* or *data element*. Data fields are aggregated in some manner so that they describe a particular entity or event. The result of this aggregation is the *record*. If we assemble all data records of a particular type, we have a data *file;* and if we further assemble all files that are logically related, we have a *database*. Let us assume for the sake of simplicity that each of the sets of programs in the accounting applications system of Chapter 6 produces a transaction file and a master file. This will result in 2 accounts payable files, 2 accounts receivable files, 2 inventory files, 2 fixed assets files, and 2 payroll files. (This is an oversimplification. An operational accounting database would contain a considerably greater number of files.) Each of these files would contain a number of records. Within a given file, the format of each record would be specified in terms of the names, type of allowable characters, and size of each of its composite fields. The record structures to be used in processing data must be specified precisely. Suppose that we wish to establish an accounts receivable master file as part of our accounting database. For brevity, we will limit the A/R record to the following fields: Customer Identification, Customer Name, Street Address, City, State, Zip Code, Credit Limit, and Current Balance. Figure 7–1 is an extract from a COBOL program that defines this record.

```
DATA DIVISION
FILE SECTION
FD ACCTS-RECEIVABLE-MASTER
      BLOCK CONTAINS 5 RECORDS
      LABEL RECORD IS STANDARD
01 ACCTS-RCVBL-MAST
      05 CUSTID                        PIC(X)7
      05 CUSTNAME                      PIC(X)25
      05 STRADDRESS                    PIC(X)30
      05 CITY                          PIC(A)15
      05 STATE                         PIC(A)2
      05 ZIP                           PIC9(9)
      05 CREDLIM                       PIC99999V99
      05 CURRBAL                       PIC99999V99
```

FIGURE 7–1 Data Record Specification (COBOL Example)

Do not be concerned if you do not understand COBOL; the purpose of this illustration is to emphasize the reality of the data structure concept and the degree of detail the AIS user must provide to use computerized support. The entry "01 Accts-Receivable-Master" defines the record name. The following 8 entries define the 8 fields that comprise the record. For example, the first of these lines uses the mnemonic "CUSTID" to represent the Customer Identification code. The entry "PIC X(7)" of this line describes the CUSTID field. In this case the "X(7)" indicates that the field will accept any combination of alphabetic or numeric characters 7 characters in length. An "A" entry in the PIC clause indicates it will accept only alphabetic characters, and a "9" entry indicates that the field is numeric. A "V" embedded in a numeric clause indicates the location of the decimal point.

We use COBOL for this illustration because it is the language most widely used in business data processing. However, it is not necessary to know COBOL or any other language to establish file and record structures in many modern systems. End users, accountants in the AIS context, can establish their own systems with a variety of fourth-generation languages. Figure 7–2 illustrates an end-user-generated equivalent to the COBOL data section of Figure 7–1. To use this language, the user needs to know a few commands—in this case, "CREATE-FILE" and the details of the fields he or she wishes to establish. After the "CREATE-FILE" command is typed, the user enters the desired information, one line at a time.

```
FOURTHGEN READY:

CREATEFILE
FILE TYPE ? ENTER SEQUENTIAL, INDEXED, OR RANDOM

RANDOM
TYPE HASHING ? ENTER A IF PRIMARY KEY IS NUMERIC, OR B IF PRIMARY KEY
IS ALPHABETIC

B
ENTER RECORD STRUCTURE IN FOLLOWING SEQUENCE:
FIELDNAME, TYPE, LENGTH, DECIMAL PLACES
THE FIRST FIELD ENTERED MUST BE THE PRIMARY KEY

? CUSTID, C, 7
? CUSTNAM, C, 25
? STRADDRESS, C, 30
? CITY, C, 15
? STATE, C 2
? ZIP, N, 9
? CREDLIM, N, 8, 2
? CURRBAL, N, 8, 2
? (RETURN)
```

FIGURE 7–2 Data Record Specification (Fourth-Generation Language)
Note: Underlining indicates user response.

Such interactive procedures bring the creation of file structures into the area of responsibility of functional managers. They require a much lower level of technical data program expertise, but they increase the end users' responsibility to consider optimal data structures. Let us examine this subject in some detail.

DATA STRUCTURE

Concepts of data structure have evolved along with the development of direct-access storage devices and the advances in software that permit us to exploit the new hardware capabilities. Prior to the development of magnetic disks, all business data were arranged in records stored serially on magnetic tape. Records might be kept in chronological order; more likely, they would be sorted in sequence by one particular field. There were few other choices. In this environment, the main effort in regard to data structure was to compress data to make the most efficient use of the limited storage capacities of the machines of that time. The emphasis was on efficient processing rather than the business use of the data. The structure of records was essentially an afterthought—something necessary to support the particular procedure currently being automated. Managers had to be content with listings based on batch processing. Although considerable progress was made in developing summary and exception reports, many of these listings were voluminous and required additional manual processing to determine answers to questions of managerial concern.

As technology advanced, competition required managers to develop more rapid response capabilities. Consider, for example, a high-visibility application, such as customer service in a department store. If store A operates in a batch mode, the following sequence is required to respond to a customer's query in regard to the status of an order. The customer service representative must obtain the necessary information from the client's telephone call, hang up, search through a batch listing, locate the required information, and return the customer's call with the shipment information. If there were any errors or misinterpretations in the initial contact, the process had to be repeated. In addition, the file might not be up to date for this customer. If store B operates in an on-line mode, the customer service representative can key the information into a terminal and provide an immediate response. Any misunderstanding or request for further information can be handled immediately. The store B customer service representative can service more calls and provide a higher degree of customer satisfaction. Such immediate on-line response requires direct-access storage devices, sophisticated software, and a well-conceived data structure.

The Logical Record

The logical record is the fundamental unit of all business data processing; therefore, we will begin our discussion of data structure at this level. We have seen that a record is composed of a group of related fields that describe an entity or event of interest. Business data processing requires the ability to identify each record in a file uniquely. Therefore, at least one field (or perhaps a combination of two or more fields) on the record must have a set of values such that a given value will occur only once in a particular file. Employee numbers, part numbers, and invoice numbers are common examples of such fields. If there is no field in the record which has a built-in uniqueness property, an arbitrary sequence field may be established for identification purposes. The field or combination of fields that has this property is called *the primary key* of the record.

All transaction processing depends upon identifying a record by its primary key. A new record is created in the main storage area of the central processing unit and then moved in its entirety to a secondary storage location determined by its primary key. If an existing record is to be updated, the primary key is used to locate the record in secondary storage, the entire record is moved to the CPU, the desired changes are entered, and the record is rewritten to secondary storage, again to a location determined by its primary key. Recall the principle of nondestructive readout from your introductory course in data processing. It is more correct to say that a *copy* of the existing record is moved from secondary to main storage for update. The original record remains in its original place with its original content until and unless the revised record is rewritten in the same space.

If we wish to delete a record from the file, a similar procedure is required. The record is identified by its primary key and read into main storage. Subsequent action depends upon whether we are using sequential- or direct-access secondary storage media. In the former case, we will be creating a new magnetic tape, and we may simply not write the record being deleted into the updated file. When using direct-access media, we may return null values to the location to be deleted. In either case, we may also elect to keep the data in the file, and set a delete indicator (a field included in the record for precisely this purpose) so that the deleted record will not be processed by applications programs, but can still be retrieved for historical purposes.

Location of a record by its primary key will suffice for processing activities which deal with data items contained in a single record. For example, if we wish to produce monthly invoices from our accounts receivable file, we may produce an invoice for every customer; nevertheless, we deal with only one record for each transaction. Similarly, if we wish to know the address of employee 591228, we retrieve the record for the employee based on the primary key and display or print the desired information. However, the primary key is often inadequate to answer queries that involve multiple records. For example, suppose we wish to know the names of all employees who live in zip code 97113. If our employee master file does not have additional structural features beyond the primary key, the only way to retrieve this information is to read each record from secondary storage into main storage, compare the value of its zip code with the value 97113, and display the desired information whenever we find a match. In a large file, this will require a considerable amount of time and use a large amount of computer resources. To facilitate such retrievals, we may designate any field of interest as a *secondary key*.

A secondary key may or may not have unique values within a file. If it has unique values, it may be used as an alternate way to sort a file. For example, if we disallow duplicate names among our employees, the employee name field of an employee master record could be a unique secondary key. We may list the file in order of its primary key, employee number, or we may sort on the secondary key and list the file alphabetically by employee name. Secondary keys are not usually unique. In these cases, the secondary key is used to aggregate records having the same value in the secondary key field. The zip code example could be effectively addressed if zip code were a secondary key in the record. The techniques for secondary key processing will be discussed in the data retrieval section later in this chapter.

Normalized Record Structure

A further consideration at the record level is to determine just which fields should be included within each record. This is not a critical factor when each application maintains its own files or when the number of records within a file remains small. However, the composition of records becomes increasingly important as organizations move into large, shared-data operations. Suppose, for example, that we have a purchase order system used to generate inputs to accounts receivable and inventory control applications in addition to its primary role in sales. Typically, a purchase order may be used to order several items, and it will have a provision for the customer to elect cash or charge payment.

Figure 7–3 suggests three ways we might structure our files to

					Repeating Group				
Purchase Order No.	Date	Customer ID	Customer Address	Number of Items	Line No.	Item ID	Quantity	Unit Price	Type Payment

A. Purchase order treated as a single record

Purchase Order Master Record (One per purchase order)

Purchase Order No.	Date	Customer ID	Customer Address	Type Payment

Item Record (One per item in a purchase order)

Purchase Order No.	Line No.	Item ID	Quantity	Unit Price

B. Purchase order representation using two record types

Customer Master (One for each customer of the firm)

Customer ID	Customer Address

Purchase Order Master (One for each purchase order)

Purchase Order No.	Customer ID	Date

Purchase Order Item Record (One for each item in a purchase order)

Purchase Order No.	Item ID	Quantity

Item Master Record (One for each item sold by the firm)

Item ID	Unit Price

C. Purchase order representation with two related permanent files

FIGURE 7–3 Alternate Record Structures

support such an application. Figure 7–3a aggregates all information regarding any one purchase order into a single record. The purchase order number serves as the primary key. This approach seems to be simple and straightforward, and was widely used in early batch systems. It has the advantage of maintaining all the information about a single purchase order in a single record. However, it has some serious drawbacks. Details about the customer (name, address) and about the items (description, price) must be repeated in each purchase order. This results in redundancy in the files and introduces the possibility of inconsistencies in the data. For example, it is possible for the same firm to have different addresses, or the same item to have different prices. Also, the practice of having repeating fields leads to records of variable length. A purchase order with 10 items will result in a much longer record than a purchase order with a single item. This leads to complexity in processing and inefficient use of secondary storage. Further, we have no way to maintain a file of customers for whom we do not have a current purchase order. This could have serious implications for follow-up activity in the sales division.

Figure 7–3b improves on Figure 7–3a by eliminating repeating groups. It achieves this by establishing an individual record for each line item in the purchase order. The primary key for each record is a concatenation of the purchase order number and the line number. This is an improvement over Figure 7–3a in that it relieves the problems associated with variable length records; however, the improvement is offset by an increase in the redundancy of the customer and item deails, and the new record structure retains the disadvantage of requiring an open purchase order if we are to maintain the basic customer information.

Figure 7–3c eliminates the need to repeat the details relating to the customer and the item by separating these data into individual records. All the nonkey fields in each of the four records of 7–3c are directly related to the key field(s) of their respective records. The process of organizing fields in records so that each nonkey field is dependent upon the record key, all elements of the record key, and nothing but the record key is known as *normalization*. In this case, the normalized records have the following advantages over the other structures: (1) The company file is not dependent upon having an open purchase order; (2) the item unit price is maintained centrally, eliminating the possibility of inconsistent pricing; and (3) the responsibility for maintaining currency of individual record items can be more easily assigned. The advantages of this structure are achieved at the cost of an increase in the complexity of application programs. On balance, the normalized structure has been found to be most suitable for supporting managerial functions, particularly at the middle and upper levels of organizations.

Files

The manner in which records are organized within a file is a critical factor in determining efficiency of operations. Three fundamental file organizations are in wide use in data processing operation today: sequential, indexed-sequential, and random. The managerial use of the information to be derived from the file is the primary determinant of the appropriate organization. Within this constraint, selection is based on economic criteria. If the data are accessed once a month to produce standardized reports, then a simple sequential organization will suffice. If the data are accessed to provide up-to-the-minute response, a random file is necessary. The AIS practitioner should understand the cost and efficiency tradeoffs involved in producing higher performance.

Sequential. Sequential files are those in which records are stored contiguously on secondary storage in ascending or descending order of a designated field. This will most commonly be the primary key; however, in the pure batch environment it is not unusual to maintain duplicate files sorted on alternate fields. Sequential files may be stored on either magnetic tape or magnetic disk. In the former case, the records must be processed sequentially; that is, each record must be read from secondary storage to main storage, examined to see if it is the record of interest, and then acted upon. If the file consists of 1000 records and we wish to examine only record number 750, then we must examine 749 records of no interest to us. On an average, 50 percent of the records in a file will be read whenever we wish to retrieve any single record.

If a sequential file is stored on magnetic disk, we may process it sequentially, or we may utilize a search strategy to improve the single-record retrieval performance. Binary or block techniques, discussed in the data update and retrieval section of this chapter, can be used with sequential data files. Although these search techniques result in considerable improvement over sequential processing, they require moving the entire data record into main storage. A data record may contain several hundred bytes of information. Therefore, if we anticipate that a file will be used extensively for retrieval of individual records, an organization other than sequential is in order.

Indexed-Sequential. Indexed-sequential files are those that maintain the sequential ordering of the data records, but in addition establish index records to facilitate the search for an individual record. The index records are arranged in the same order as the data records, but they contain only two fields—the primary key of the data record and the address of that record in the secondary storage media. The index records can be searched much more rapidly than the data records because (1) there is much less movement of data, and (2) the indexing technique can be extended; we may have several layers of indexes to support more efficient search algorithms. Indexed-sequential files must be stored on direct-access storage devices. They improve the ability of the system to locate a specified record quickly while maintaining the capability to access the records sequentially when a high percentage of the records in the file are to be used. The improvement in response is achieved at an additional cost in terms of storage capacity required and in complexity of file maintenance procedures.

Random. Random files dispense with physical contiguity of records. In a random file, the records are placed into a designated area of secondary storage based upon a mathematical procedure, called *hashing,* that transforms the primary key into a physical storage address. When it is necessary to locate a record previously stored for update or retrieval, the same mathematical operation is performed on the key, producing the same address and permitting immediate access. Random files provide the fastest access to any single record, but they become extremely inefficient if a high percentage of the records are to be used on a single program run. Loss of sequential processing efficiency is the primary price paid for the high-speed access. Random files are also relatively inefficient in their use of secondary storage space.

DATABASE STRUCTURES

The need for database structure can be traced to the fact that different functional managers in an organization use the same data in different ways. The need is illustrated by the inventory management problem in a production environment. An inventory system can be based on a set of files consisting of records stored sequentially by part number. Such a system can be used to report stock levels by part number, to maintain usage data, and to compute economic order quantities and reorder points for each individual part. This may fulfill the needs of the inventory control manager very well. However, the production manager is also interested in inventory levels. He or she needs to know how many of each part used in a particular product or subassembly are on hand in order to facilitate production planning. A file organized by part number is not equipped to support this function; what is needed is a file organized as a bill of materials for the firm's products. A file organized hierarchically would meet this need.

The problem does not stop there. Surely, in most organizations many parts are used in more than one product or subassembly.

Therefore, a single hierarchy will not suffice; we will require a number of interrelated hierarchies. Such interrelated hierarchies are commonly called *networks*. We can carry the problem one step further if we consider that it is impossible to determine in advance all possible uses of all the parts in the inventory. If we wish to cover all contingencies, we must be able to relate one part to another without prior knowledge of how the parts will be assembled. These considerations have given rise to the three most widely used data models in database management systems: the hierarchical, the network, and the relational models.

The Hierarchical Model

The *hierarchical* model was conceived as an answer to the bill of materials problem. The original concept was developed during the period when magnetic tape was the available secondary storage medium and records had to be processed sequentially. For production control purposes, the file was arranged in hierarchical order based on the bill of materials rather than part number sequence. Figure 7–4 illustrates the difference between these approaches. A purely hierarchical model is based upon a one-to-many, often called a parent-child, relationship between record types. In a hierarchy, a parent may have many children, but a child may have only one parent. We may have as many layers in the hierarchy as we wish. Figure 7–5 illustrates the hierarchical relationship. Figure 7–5a is a hierarchy as it might appear naturally; Figure 7–5b is an occurrence of the hierarchy; and Figure 7–5c is the commonly used shorthand to represent the general relationship.

No purely hierarchical database management system exists today. Given the limitations of tape storage, the hierarchical model was a major advance in information processing. However, the advent of magnetic disk has permitted the early single-hierarchy systems to evolve into multiple hierarchy systems. Although often referred to as hierarchical, they are in fact network systems.

The Network Model

The network structure is most often associated with the work of the Database Task Group (DBTG) of the Committee on Data Systems Languages (CODASYL). CODASYL is an association of industry and government representatives formed to promote standardization of data processing procedures. Although it does not have authority to approve standards, its recommendations are generally influential. In the 1970s, the DBTG made an extended effort to establish the network data structure as an industry standard. In this case, the attempt was not

Consider a Product P, which is composed of Subassemblies A and B. In turn, Subassembly A is composed of Parts 001 and 002, and Subassembly B is composed of parts 003 and 004. This relationship can be diagrammed as

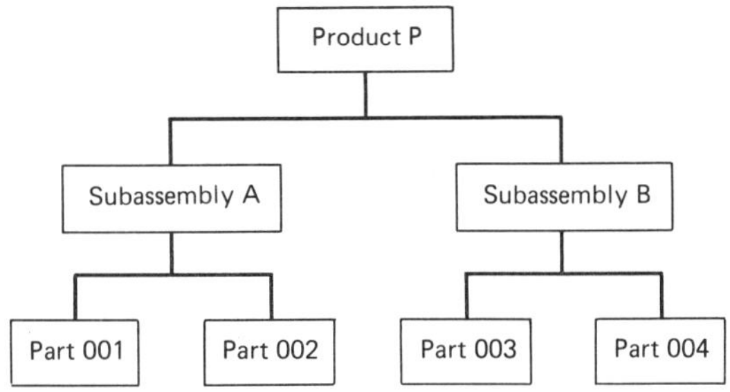

A. This may be represented in computerized storage as three independent files:

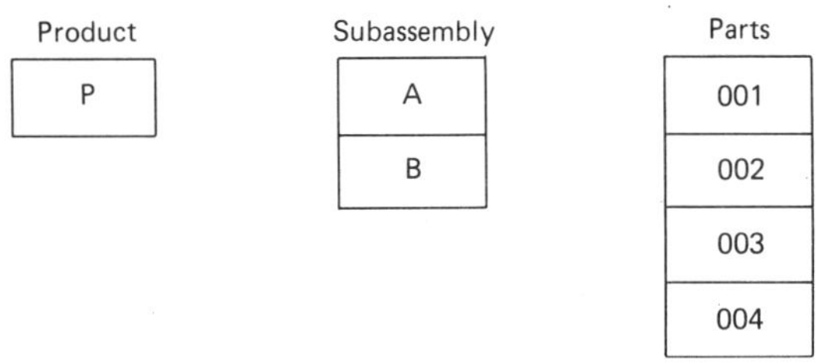

B. Alternatively, it may be represented by a single hierarchical file:

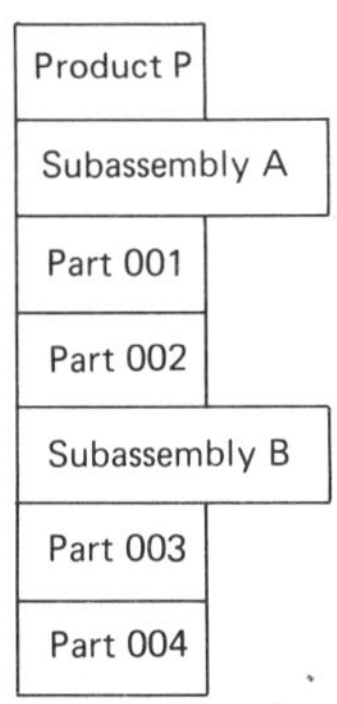

FIGURE 7–4 Independent versus Hierarchical Record Storage

successful; nevertheless, the effort resulted in a dialogue that significantly advanced the development of database management in general and in a network model that has several major commercial implementations.

As an example of network complexity, consider a typical undergraduate program in which each student declares a single major. This results in a hierarchical relationship where one major has many students (Figure 7–6a). However, each student is also assigned to a

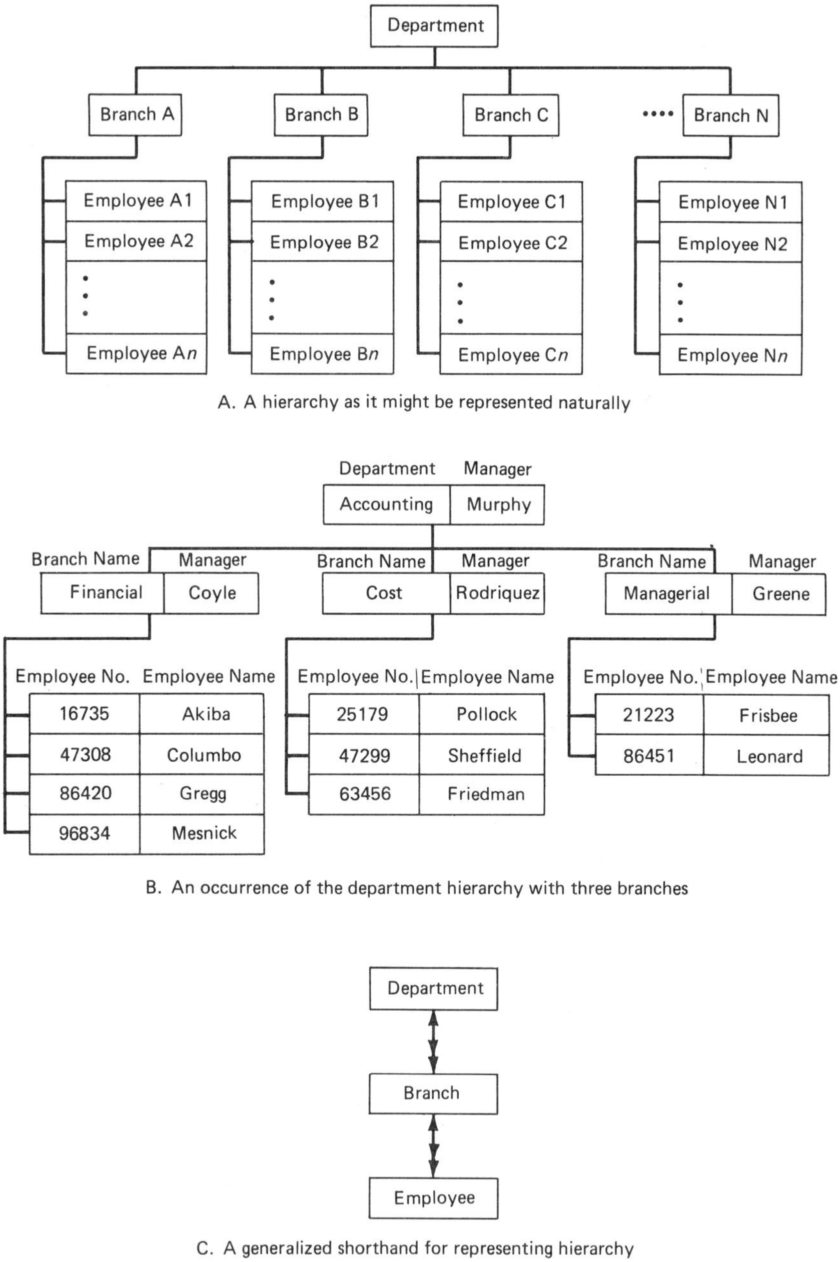

FIGURE 7–5 The Hierarchical Relationship

Note: The single-head arrow points to the parent record type, and the double-head arrow points to the child record type in the one-to-many relationship.

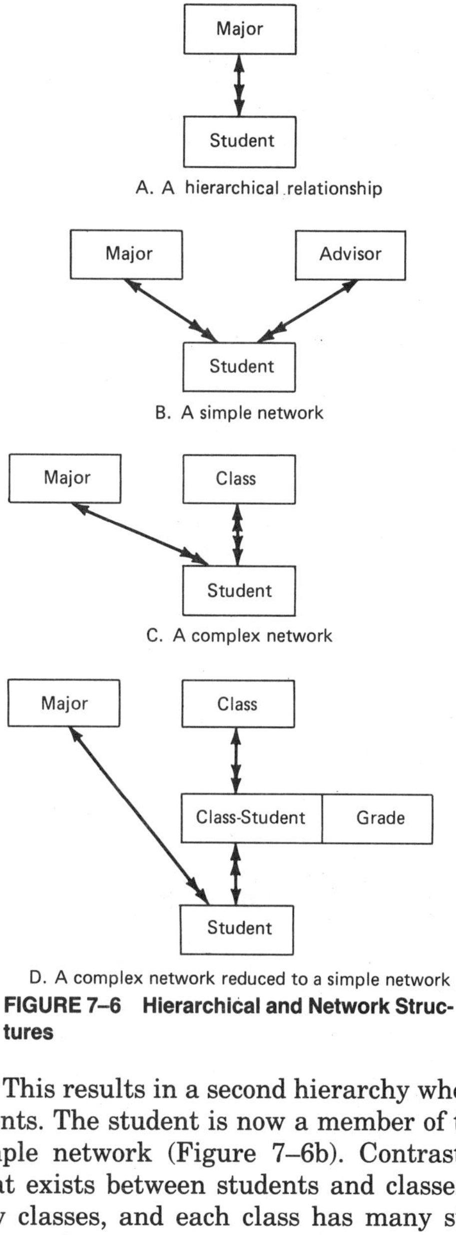

FIGURE 7–6 Hierarchical and Network Structures

faculty advisor. This results in a second hierarchy where each advisor has many students. The student is now a member of two hierarchies, which is a simple network (Figure 7–6b). Contrast this with the relationship that exists between students and classes. Each student enrolls in many classes, and each class has many students (Figure 7–6c). This is a complex network.

Consider the need to record each student's grades in each of the classes the student takes. This could be represented as a repeating group in the student record; however, we have seen that repeating groups lead to undesirable processing characteristics. A preferable data structure is that shown in Figure 7–6d. Here we create an intersection record. The primary key of the intersection record consists of two fields, the Class ID and the Student ID. We have reduced a complex network to a simple network. The only additional fields in an intersection record should be those that depend upon both fields of the primary key for full identification. In this case, it would be the grade field. This is in accordance with the normalization principle cited earlier. Although normalization is not strictly a requirement of network structures, it is widely accepted as the most desirable way to group fields in any system that encompasses multiple record types. In a network system, each relationship must be defined as the database is implemented and included in the data structure description.

Hierarchical and network structures have proved to be major improvements over unrelated file structures; they can be designed to support the most common uses of data in a highly efficient manner. However, the need to predefine the relationships between and among record types limits the ability of systems based on these models to respond to unanticipated needs. And in middle and top management applications, the unanticipated use of existing data is the norm rather than the exception.

The Relational Model

The relational database structure fulfills the need for flexible response. Whereas the hierarchical and network structures are abstractions from the reality of organizational structure and the uses of data within organizations, the relational structure is an outgrowth of the mathematical concepts of set theory. The former approaches are useful in supporting existing needs for information; the latter is essential for supporting future needs. On first inspection, the relational structure appears to be a lack of structure. A relational database consists of a group of logically related files without any predefined interconnections. To understand how the relationships among records are established, we will introduce some of the vocabulary of relational systems. A *relation* is essentially a table which conforms to certain limitations; notably, its rows may not include any repeating groups, they must be normalized, and no two rows may be identical. In the data processing terms we have been using, a relation is a file. The rows of the relation are called *tuples.* A tuple is a record within a file. The columns of the relation are called *attributes,* which we have identified as fields or data items. Figure 7–7 illustrates these fundamental terms.

The values a particular attribute in a relation may assume must be drawn from the *domain* for that attribute. For example, the domain for an attribute Zip Code might be the set of all positive nine-digit

Attribute

CUSTID	CUSTNAME	CUSTADDRESS	CREDLIM
01245	JONES, INC.	BALTIMORE	10000
15378	DALY BROS.	JACKSONVILLE	15000
35419	BILL'S BAR	KANSAS CITY	10000
96380	VAN'S VANS	SAN DIEGO	12000

Tuples — A Relation

FIGURE 7–7 Relational Database Terminology

integers, or the domain for an attribute Sex might be M or F. The domain is the basis for establishing relationships among the relations in the database. A relation A may be combined with a relation B to form a new relation C if an attribute of A shares the same domain as an attribute of B. Such a combination is called a *join*. Figure 7–8 illustrates a join. The join is based on a comparison of all values of the two attributes. Figure 7–8 shows a join based on equality of values. This is, perhaps, the most common use; however, joins based on inequalities can be performed equally well.

Relation A (Abbreviated Customer Master)

CUSTID	CUSTNAME	CUSTADDRESS	CREDLIM
01245	JONES, INC.	BALTIMORE	10000
15378	DALY BROS.	JACKSONVILLE	15000
35419	BILL'S BAR	KANSAS CITY	10000
96380	VAN'S VANS	SAN DIEGO	12000

Relation B (Abbreviated Invoice Master)

INVOICENUM	CUSTID	AMOUNT
006431	35419	345.50
005841	01245	7000.00
003782	01245	542.99
002456	96380	888.98
009847	35419	666.67

The result of relation A joined with relation B on the CUSTID field is:

A.CUSTID	B.CUSTID	CUSTNAME	CUSTADDRESS	CREDLIM	INVOICENUM	AMOUNT
01245	01245	JONES, INC.	BALTIMORE	10000	005841	7000.00
01245	01245	JONES, INC.	BALTIMORE	10000	003782	542.99
35419	35419	BILL'S BAR	KANSAS CITY	10000	006431	345.50
35419	35419	BILL'S BAR	KANSAS CITY	10000	009847	666.67
96380	96380	VAN'S VANS	SAN DIEGO	12000	002456	888.98

FIGURE 7–8 Combining Relations: A Join

Note: A.CUSTID and B.CUSTID represent the Customer Identification fields from Relations A and B, respectively. This is an example of an equijoin. In most cases, one of the ID columns is suppressed. The result is called a *natural join.* DBMS implementations allow us to select any of the fields in the join. It is not necessary to produce the full array of attributes. Attributes can be arranged in any order.

DATA UPDATE AND RETRIEVAL

Primary Key Processing

All additions, changes, and deletions to records in business data processing are based upon the affected records' primary key. A new record is established in main storage based upon the key field and moved to a location in secondary storage determined by the value of that field. If the record is subsequently to be updated, deleted, or retrieved for information purposes, it must be located or identified by its primary key and moved back to main storage for the desired action. The precise means of search and identification vary with the secondary storage media and the file structure in use.

If the secondary storage medium is magnetic tape, all records must be processed sequentially. An update file is created by sorting all current transactions into the same order as the existing master file based on their primary key. The update process consists of comparing the key values of records in the update file with the values of the keys from the old master file. New records are inserted into their correct location in the new file in what is essentially a merge operation. Changes and deletes occur when the transaction record key equals the old master record key. The update process creates an entirely new master file without changing the data resident on the old master file. The necessary backup for this procedure consists of maintaining the old master tapes and the transaction tapes for as many batch runs as may be prudent.

If the secondary storage medium is magnetic disk or other direct-access equipment, the update options depend on the file structure employed. A sequential or an indexed sequential file may be updated in the batch mode, as described above. Batch updates may be used when any number of changes are to be made; however, they are desirable whenever a high percentage of records in the file will be affected. One important difference between disk and tape operations is that an updated record is written over the old master record when using disk. This requires greater attention to backup procedures.

If a relatively small number of records are to be updated, a disk file may be changed by interactive processing. This requires locating the specific record to be updated. If the file is sequential, data records must be searched to locate the desired record; if the file is indexed, the index is searched until the data record's address is located and then the data record is retrieved directly; if the file is random, a hashing algorithm is employed to compute the address of the desired record.

Data records may be searched using either binary or block search techniques. A *binary search* divides the total number of records in the file into two equal segments, determines which segment contains the record of interest, and then repeats the halving process until the record is found. For example, if we have a file of 1000 records and we wish to locate record 631, we first inspect the record at location 500. We find that the record of interest is in the 500–1000 segment; therefore, we next check at location 750. The process is indicated in Figure 7–9a. A binary search is most efficient if all records in a file have equal probability of being retrieved.

A *block* search is carried out by dividing the total file into smaller segments or blocks, searching for the block that contains the record, and then continuing the search within that block. If we wish to use a block search to find record 631 in the file of 1000 records, we might search in blocks of 100 until we locate the correct block. Once within the block, we may elect to read records sequentially until we find the desired record, or we may subdivide the block of 100 into blocks of 10. Figure 7–9b illustrates this process.

Index records may be searched using the techniques above. Because the index records are much shorter than the data records, the search is much faster. In addition, indexes may be layered. This permits us to search a high-level index to determine which detailed index contains the record of interest, further reducing search time.

Secondary Key Processing

We process a file by one or more secondary keys whenever we wish to produce information in a sequence other than that of the primary key or whenever we wish to aggregate information based on one or more data fields.

A magnetic tape file can support secondary key processing only if time is not of the essence. Tape records can be read from the master file, sorted on one or more nonkey fields, and written to a new tape or presented to the user in the revised sequence. The process is unwieldy and time-consuming and cannot support many managerial needs. Therefore, we will restrict further discussion of secondary key processing to direct-access storage media. There are two primary means of secondary key processing: inverted files or indexes, and linked lists.

Inverted Files or Indexes. The *index* technique establishes an index of record addresses for each value of each designated secondary key. Figure 7–10 is a data file that we might establish as an accounts receivable master file, together with indexes on credit limit and zip code fields. By establishing the index records, we can answer such questions as these: What are all the names of firms we do business with in Zip Code 02114? or What firms have a line of credit in excess of $10,000? without examining every record in the data file. Notice also

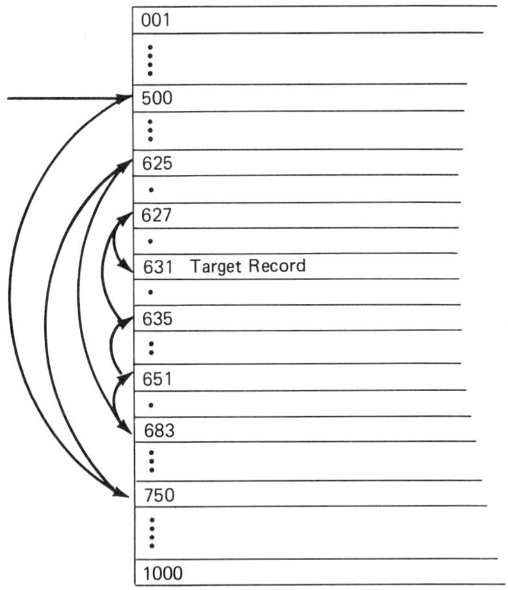

A. A binary search to locate Record 631. Eight accesses required (10 would be the maximum)

B. A two-stage block search to locate Record 631. Fourteen accesses required (28 maximum)

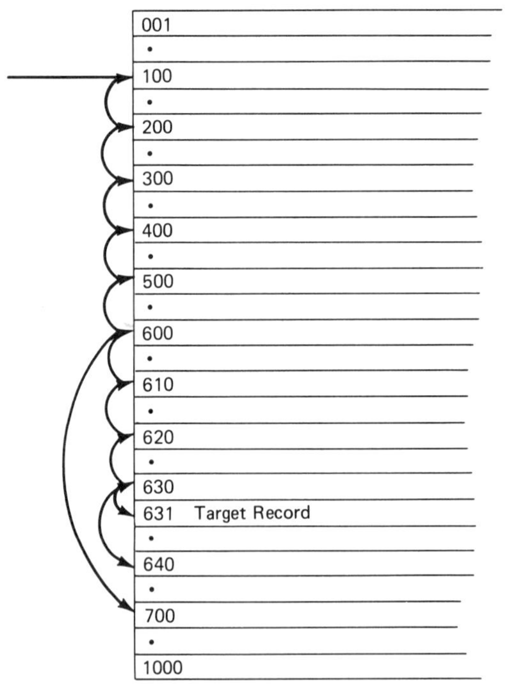

FIGURE 7–9 Search Techniques

Data Records

CUSTID	CUSTNAM	CUSTADDRESS	ZIP	CREDLIM
00279	DOC'S DELI	BOSTON	02108	5000.00
01437	SMITH, INC.	BOSTON	02114	5000.00
11326	JOHNSON	BOSTON	02118	10000.00
21999	O'LEARY	BOSTON	02108	10000.00
88456	SUNDBURY	BOSTON	02118	5000.00
93455	DELUCA	BOSTON	02114	15000.00

ZIP Index Records

ZIP	CUSTID	
02108	00279	21999
02114	01437	93455
02118	11326	88456

Credit Limit Index Records

CREDLIM	CUSTID		
5000.00	00279	01437	88456
10000.00	11326	21999	
15000.00	93455		

FIGURE 7–10 Secondary Key Processing by Use of Indexes

that we may answer questions such as What firms in Zip Code area 02108 have a credit limit of less than $20,000? without accessing data records at all.

Secondary key indexes provide the capability to respond rapidly to many managerial queries. This rapid response is achieved at the expense of additional storage space required for the index records—in a fully indexed file, the indexes may use as much space as the data itself—and a more complex operating system.

Linked Lists. The *linked list* technique for processing secondary keys uses a system of pointers to link records. A *pointer* is simply a field added to the record structure that holds the address of another record. Pointers may indicate the next record, the previous record, the first record, or the last record in the list. Figure 7–11 indicates one way

Data Records

CUSTID	CUSTNAM	CUSTADDRESS	ZIP	CREDLIM	NEXT ZIP POINTER	NEXT CREDLIM POINTER
00279	DOC'S DELI	BOSTON	02108	5000	21999	01437
01437	SMITH, INC.	BOSTON	02114	5000	93455	88456
11326	JOHNSON	BOSTON	02118	10000	88456	21999
21999	O'LEARY	BOSTON	02108	10000	*****	*****
88456	SUNDBURY	BOSTON	02118	5000	*****	*****
93455	DELUCA	BOSTON	02114	15000	*****	*****

FIGURE 7–11 Secondary Key Processing by Use of Linked Lists

in which linked lists might be constructed to provide a capability equivalent to the index technique of Figure 7–10. Linked lists generally require less additional storage capacity than indexes; however, they are somewhat slower in response for most applications, and they require complex update algorithms.

The primary and secondary key processing operations available to the AIS developer depend upon the operating system in use. These capabilities may exist in a stand-alone capacity for improving access to data files, or they may be incorporated into a database management system.

Multiple User Environment

Traditionally, data processing applications have been developed to respond to a procedural need of a particular individual or functional group within an organization. Our discussion of the development of an automated accounting system in Chapter 6 is typical of this approach. Each functional manager specifies the requirements for processing in his or her area of responsibility and submits a request for development to the information services department (see Chapter 9 for a full discussion of this process). Given that the request is approved, the information services department assigns one or more analysts to investigate the problem.

Consider the plight of the systems analyst in the procedure-oriented environment when asked to automate a new procedure in a business area that is already using the computer extensively. Much of the data necessary for the new application will already be available on existing files. The analyst may elect to draw this information from the existing sources. However, the new client will not have control over updating or changing the structure of records in these files. If the file owners are tardy in update, information generated by the new application will be out of date. Worse still, if the owner of the file changes as much as one byte in the record structure, the new application will not run at all until it has been modified.

As an alternative, the analyst may elect to establish new files for the new application. This results in duplication of data in the files, redundant update procedures, waste of storage space, and it introduces the possibility of inconsistencies in reports that purport to be based on the same data. Any large, established data processing operation will contain programs that use a mixture of these approaches. The result is a database that contains a high degree of redundancy, uncontrolled interdependencies among files and programs, the production of unreliable information for management, and excessive program maintenance costs for the information system.

DATABASE MANAGEMENT

Data Dictionaries

The need to control the proliferation of data fields and files has long been recognized. Initial attempts to achieve this control centered about the use of data element dictionaries. Early dictionaries were data files maintained separately from other automated files. Their currency depended upon effective managerial control over applications development, and the conscientiousness of systems analysts and programmers in using and updating the dictionary as part of applications development documentation. Even the best intentioned programmer/analysts were hampered in their efforts to use the dictionaries because of the ambiguity inherent in defining data fields. Often, in an organization the same data element is known by different names by different users, and equally often different users use the same name to identify entirely different data items. For example, in an information requirements analysis done recently by a leading insurance company, it was discovered that the term "policy number" had five different meanings in common usage.

The need for better control over data fields led to the development of active data dictionaries. The characteristics of these tools were discussed in Chapter 6. The effective use of a data dictionary is a major step toward recognizing the importance of data as a corporate resource and establishing centralized control over that resource. The dictionary can increase the reliability and integrity of stored data and reduce redundancies in storage; however, additional software is needed to support the effective use of the data.

Database Management Systems

The purpose of a database management system is to support the information needs of the various members of an organization by providing effective and efficient access to the organization's data. The development of DBMSs is based on the premise that data are an organizational resource rather than the exclusive property of any individual or functional group within the organization. In Chapter 6 we defined a DBMS as a set of programs that would (1) provide a data structure that supports multiple user views of the stored data, (2) provide independence between the physical storage of data and end user application programs, and (3) provide for ease of information retrieval.

We will consider the familiar university setting to examine what is meant by the first two of these requirements. The rows of Figure 7–12 are a sampling of data items that might be maintained for each

Data Item	Registrar	Bursar	Housing	Financial Aid
Student Name	X	X	X	X
Student ID	X	X	X	X
Street Address	X	X	X	X
City	X	X	X	X
State	X	X	X	X
ZIP	X	X	X	X
Verbal SAT	X			
Quant SAT	X			
Cum GPA	X			
Current Balance		X		X
Veteran Status			X	X
Marital Status			X	X
Dependency Status		X	X	X
Parent Name		X	X	X
Parent Address		X	X	X
Requests Housing		X	X	

FIGURE 7–12 Data Fields and Multiple Users

student. The columns of the figure represent the interests of each of the university agencies that are directly concerned with students. A mark in the row and column intersection indicates that the agency uses the data field. The summation of marks in a column is an agency's view of the student. The number of marks in a row indicate how widely the field is used. Ideally, a database system will store the data item only once, but make it available to all concerned agencies. Further, if an agency does not use a particular field, it should not have access to it, or indeed even be aware of its existence.

Data independence means that if a field is changed in size or deleted from the database, only the programs that use this field should be affected in any way. (This point seems trivial; however, it cannot be achieved in a traditional file structure. In a file environment, every program that uses the file, not just those that use the field, will be affected.)

These two objectives are achieved by using a three-level database structure. Figure 7–13 illustrates the concept. An *external* level supports the end user programs that depend upon a single view of the database. In our university example, there would be four external views, each of which would have its own logical data description. The

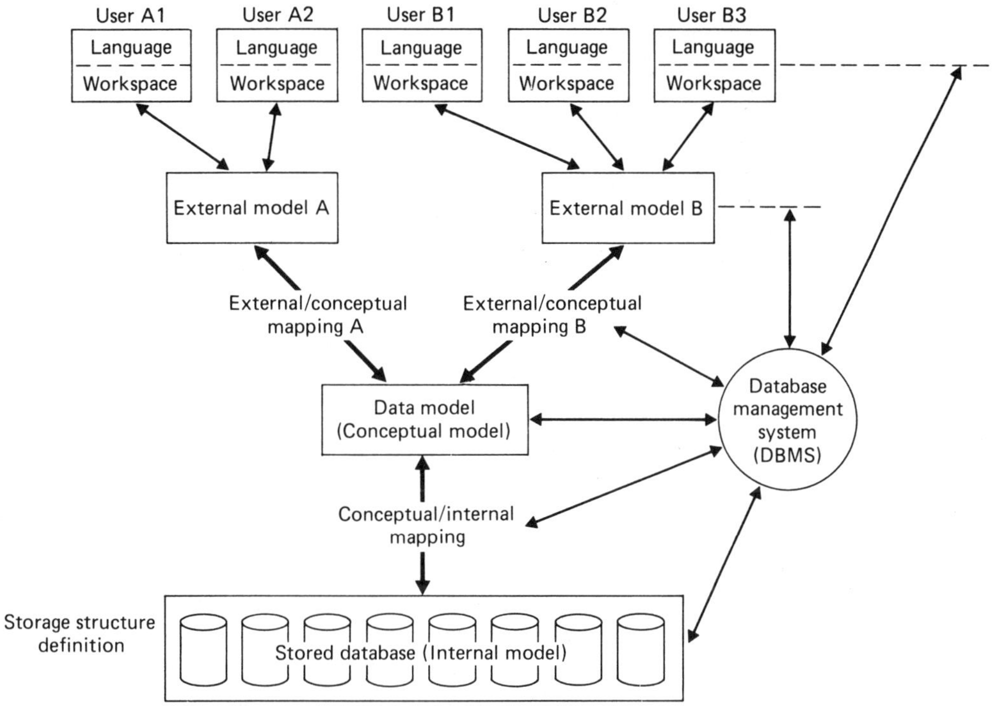

FIGURE 7–13 Three-Level Database Structures
Source: Adapted from C. J. Date, *An Introduction to Database Systems,* 3rd ed. (Reading, Mass.: Addison-Wesley, 1981), p. 20. © 1981 Addison-Wesley Publishing Company, Inc. Reprinted with permission.

summation of these views is the *conceptual* level. There is one conceptual data description for a database. Each of the external views can be derived from the conceptual level.

The external and conceptual levels are logical representations of the data; that is, they represent data relationships as users understand them. The records at this level do not necessarily have a physical storage counterpart; they exist only during program execution. The final level of the database is the *physical storage* level. This is what in fact exists on secondary storage media. The boundary between the physical storage level and the conceptual level insulates end user programs from changes in physical data structure; the boundary between the conceptual level and the external level insulates end user programs from changes in the conceptual structure.

The three-level structure can be applied to any of the three database models—hierarchical, network, or relational. Virtually all commercial DBMSs adhere to the three-level concept and are based on one of the three data models.

The advantages of a DBMS include these:

1. Ease of program maintenance. When a field is deleted or changed in size, only those programs that use the field are affected. The internal programs of the DBMS protect other application programs from the change.
2. Enhanced data integrity. The quality of data entered into the database is improved by centralized control.
3. Improved security. The use of external views restricts users to those data fields defined in their data description. Further, security restrictions can be uniformly enforced at record or data field level.
4. Elimination of data inconsistencies. All users of any given data item are using a single data source.

DBMSs that embody the three-level structure meet the first two requirements of our definition and will improve the use of information systems at the operational level of management. The third requirement—ease of information retrieval—must be met if the DBMS is to improve the effective use of information systems at the higher managerial levels. Ease of retrieval depends upon data structure. DBMSs based on hierarchical or network models are excellent vehicles for retrieving information that conforms with their underlying structures. However, retrieval from these systems requires detailed knowledge of the database structure; the systems cannot respond efficiently to requests for information other than that for which they were specifically designed. DBMSs based on the relational model utilize the mathematical concepts underlying the software to provide automatic access to data without requiring knowledge of complicated access paths. Therefore, relational systems can outperform other systems in the ease of retrieval category whenever the retrieval is not one anticipated during the design stage.

DATA VERSUS INFORMATION

We have defined *data* as the raw material of information processing, and *information* as the result of operating on data to give it meaning and context. A simple example illustrates this distinction effectively. Let us start with the symbols 3 and 7. This is certainly data at an elementary level. As a first process, we may place them together to form 37. This provides some context. Most people will interpret this as a number in which 3 represents the number of tens and the 7 represents the number of units. However, it remains data. As a second process, let us write 37°. This will generally be understood to be 37 degrees. It may be a temperature, or perhaps a latitude or longitude. The symbols begin to acquire meaning. If we continue the process to write 37°C, virtually everyone will accept this as a temperature on the Celsius scale. Finally, if we note that 37°C = 98.6°F, most readers of this text will perceive the context and meaning of the figure as the average body temperature of a human being. At what point in the process did the data become information? This question cannot be answered precisely because of the human element in the equation. The same condition holds true in business data processing. A poorly designed system may provide information that can be interpreted only after lengthy review by a select group of users.

If computer-based information is to be used effectively, it must be based on data that are (1) accurate, (2) timely, and (3) complete in all essential aspects. Further, the information must be:

1. Relevant to the needs of the user at the time it is to be used.
2. Immediately understandable.
3. Brief.
4. Trustworthy: The nature of the data manipulation should be understood and accepted by the user.
5. Appropriately presented. For example, a tabular presentation may be required for detailed review, whereas the same data should be presented as a graph to higher management levels.
6. Easily accessible: Printouts must be delivered to the users' desk and terminals must be located at or very near the users' normal work space.

SUMMARY

The need for AIS practitioners to understand the fundamentals of data structures has become greater as advances in technology make end user computing increasingly available.

At its most elementary level, data is stored in binary digits (bits). Bits are combined into units called bytes. Each byte represents one character of data. The smallest unit of data that has logical meaning to a user is the data field, also known as a data item or data element. Fields that are logically organized to represent the characteristics of an entity or event become a data record. When like records are assembled, they are called a file. A group of files that have some logical relationship among them constitutes a database. A record can be uniquely identified within its file by its primary key. A secondary key is often used to aggregate records that have the same value of that key. Secondary keys can be processed by establishing indexes or by imbedding pointer chains in the data records. Normalization of the fields in records is a process which results in all the fields in the record being dependent on the record key. Normalization is an important consideration when structuring files that will be shared by multiple users.

Files have three basic structures: sequential, indexed-sequential, and random. The sequential structure is best suited for files that will be processed in the batch mode. The random structure is best suited for files that will be processed in an interactive mode. The indexed-sequential structure is a compromise that provides both batch and direct-access capabilities.

Database management systems have evolved in response to the need to improve access to data. They provide additional benefits in terms of reducing program maintenance costs. The price paid for these improvements is additional software overhead. Three data models are used in current database management systems (DBMS): the hierarchical, network, and relational models. The first two of these reflect organizational structures and can be tuned to support recurring operational uses of data. The relational model provides the greatest flexibility of response and can better support unanticipated information needs.

Database management systems and data dictionaries are two tools essential to a data-centered approach to systems development and information resource management.

It is important to distinguish between data and information. Data are the raw material from which information is derived. Information must be accurate, timely, and complete. If it is to be used effectively in organizations, it must have additional features that make it convenient and easy to use.

REVIEW QUESTIONS, DISCUSSION QUESTIONS, AND PROBLEMS AND CASES

A. Review Questions

A7.1 Define data and information. Clearly state the distinction between the two concepts.

A7.2 The following terms are encountered in discussions of data storage. Define each and give its significance to the AIS practitioner:

- **a.** Byte
- **b.** Data element
- **c.** Logical record
- **d.** Database
- **e.** Primary key
- **f.** Secondary key

A7.3 Why is an understanding of data structure of increasing importance to accountants?

A7.4 Describe the use of the primary key in locating a record in a sequential file, an indexed-sequential file, and a direct access file.

A7.5 What are the characteristics of a record that is normalized? Why is normalization considered important?

A7.6 What are the three data models that underlie database management systems?

A7.7 What is the distinguishing characteristic of the hierarchical data model?

A7.8 How is the network model similar to the hierarchical model? How does it differ?

A7.9 What is the fundamental difference between the relational model and either the hierarchical or the network models? When might the relational model be preferred to either of the other models? When might it be less desirable?

A7.10 What are the differences between primary and secondary key processing?

A7.11 Describe secondary key processing by the use of indexes. By the use of linked lists. What are the relative merits of each technique?

A7.12 What is the primary purpose of using a database management system? What are some attendant advantages? What are the drawbacks?

B. Discussion Questions

B7.1 What is your understanding of the differences between a process-centered and a data-centered approach to information processing? Which do you feel will best support accounting functions?

B7.2 What are the advantages of normalized data record structures? Are there any offsetting limitations?

B7.3 Random storage file structures provide the fastest access to data maintained in secondary storage. Why is any other structure used?

B7.4 It is generally conceded that hierarchical and network database management systems can be "tuned" to provide highly efficient retrieval of data in preplanned formats, and that relational database systems provide the greatest flexibility for unplanned data retrievals. What are the implications of these statements in regard to Anthony's levels of management?

C. Problems and Cases

C7.1 A large government agency was recently required to cut its budget by 6 percent with only 24 hours notice. The quick response precluded a systematic review of each item in the budget; therefore, the cut was made across the board and all 4000 items in the budget were reduced proportionally. This was achieved by applying a simple mathematical algorithm to the agency's automated database. Subsequently, a line item review was conducted and it was found that the actual reductions could be applied to only 500 of the items. (The legislature did not care how the cuts were made, as long as the required top line was met.) The only way that this final adjustment could be made was with individual adjustments to all 4000 items. How could a properly operating DBMS have minimized this workload?

C7.2 The general manager of a large manufacturing plant became exasperated with the differences between inventory and work-in-process accounts as reported by the production department and by the controller. The MIS manager advised him that this was because each department worked from its own set of files, which were updated independently of each other. A DBMS vendor convinced the GM that the discrepancies would be eliminated if the GM would implement her relational database system. Further, the vendor offered a conversion package that would automatically convert all existing files to run under the new DBMS. The package was bought and installed, and the files were successfully converted. However, the general manager still receives reports with conflicting data. What has gone wrong?

SUGGESTED READINGS

DATE, C. J. *An Introduction to Database Systems,* 3rd ed. Reading, Mass.: Addison-Wesley, 1981.

HICKS, JAMES O. *Information Systems in Business: An Introduction.* St. Paul, Minn.: West Publishing, 1986.

KRONKE, DAVID M., AND KATHLEEN DOLAN, *Business Computer Systems: An Introduction,* 3rd ed. Santa Cruz, Calif.: Mitchell, 1987.

MARTIN, JAMES. *Computer Data-Base Organization,* 2nd ed. Englewood Cliffs, N.J.: Prentice-Hall, 1977.

———. *An End-User's Guide to Data Base.* Englewood Cliffs, N.J.: Prentice-Hall, 1981.

part three

The Dynamics of the AIS

The reader who has mastered the fundamentals of the AIS's components is now prepared to address the topic of how this system functions to support the information needs of its parent organization.

Chapter 8 addresses the principles that underlie information processing and discusses two primary modes of processing—batch and interactive. This chapter is concerned with the operations of the existing CAAIS.

Dynamic considerations must also address how the CAAIS changes over time to meet the information needs of the broader AIS and the still broader parent organization. This again highlights the primacy of the human element in automated systems. Chapter 9 addresses the traditional systems development life cycle, which is presented as a management planning and control device in its most common organizational context. We have chosen to limit our discussion to the evolution of software, as virtually all accountants will become involved in this aspect of systems change. The principles of the chapter apply equally well to hardware changes, but a thorough discussion of the technical considerations in this area is beyond the scope of this text.

Shortcomings of the traditional approach to the development of software have led to a variety of alternative approaches to meeting the information needs of end users. Chapter 10 deals with these newer and generally more responsive techniques. Accountants should pay particular attention to the control issues associated with these alternative methods.

chapter 8

Processing Principles and Practices

CHAPTER OUTLINE

INTRODUCTION

The objectives of this chapter are to examine the processes a computer system carries out in order to transform data into information and the ways in which we may use these processes to achieve the goals of the CAAIS. We start by defining five fundamental processes the computer can perform: input, output, move, compare, and compute. We will then see that the fundamental processes can be executed in three ways—sequentially, selectively, and repetitively—to solve any business problem. This is followed by a review of batch and interactive processing modes. Finally, we examine the revenue-generating subsystem of an organization as it might be carried out in three data processing environments.

COMPUTER OPERATIONS

A modern digital computer is best described as a fast and reliable symbol-manipulating machine. The internal symbols the computer can sense are binary in nature; that is, the computer can detect only the existence of two states or levels of signal. These internal signals are either levels of electrical voltage or polarization of microscopic magnetic spots. A single signal, one high or low voltage or one magnetic spot, is known as a binary digit or bit. We have seen how bits are encoded into bytes to form the EBCDIC and ASCII codes. The internal architecture of computers is based upon the parallel flow of bits through the computer system in units of one or more bytes. Thus, an 8-bit machine, the smallest of home microcomputers, processes one byte at a time, a 16-bit machine two bytes at a time, and so on. Data may also be transferred externally for short distances in the parallel mode; however, for distances greater than a few miles, they must be transmitted serially and then reformed into bytes upon arrival at the new location. The transfer and processing of data can be summarized in five fundamental processes: input, output, move, compare, compute.

The Five Fundamental Processes

The digital computer can perform a range of functions that appear to be limited only by human imagination. Nevertheless, the most complex of these functions can be reduced to five processes.

1. *Input* converts data from some real-world characteristic into the electrical or magnetic symbols that can be interpreted by the computer's circuitry. These characteristics may be physical quantities, such as heat or velocity of a vehicle; in the world of business data processing, we are usually concerned with converting words and numbers from some natural language, most likely English for the readers of this text, into EBCDIC or ASCII characters. The commonly available devices for doing this were examined in Chapter 5. The input process is activated in programming languages by such words (or more precisely, the electrical symbols generated by these words) as INPUT or READ.

2. *Output* is the reverse of the input process. Again, in general, output from a computer can take a great variety of forms, including control of a spacecraft or manipulation of robots. In business data processing we are generally concerned with the more mundane forms, such as printouts and cathode ray tube displays. The commonly used output devices were reviewed in Chapter 5. Output processes are activated by programming language words such as PRINT or WRITE.

3. *Move* describes a variety of actions that take place within a computer system. Data and instructions must be moved from permanent storage locations to the registers of the arithmetic and logic unit of the computer, where all data transformation and logical comparisons take place. Data are moved from secondary storage to an input buffer in primary storage. GET, FETCH, or OBTAIN are typical commands to activate this process. Data and instructions may be moved several times within primary storage. For example, they might be moved from the input buffer to an initial storage location. If the computer architecture includes an accelerator or cache memory, data may be moved from an initial position into one of these addresses prior to actual use. The data are then moved into the processing registers of the arithmetic and logic unit, back to another primary storage location, to an output buffer, and finally perhaps returned to secondary storage. The movements internal to the CPU are governed by hardware configurations and microcode programs under the control of the operating system. Movement back to secondary storage is typically controlled by a FILE, SAVE, INSERT, or REPLACE command. Instructions themselves undergo similar movements into, through, and out of primary storage. Recall that computer processes employ destructive write-in and nondestructive readout methods. Therefore, there may be multiple copies of a data element or instruction in the system as a program executes.

(In standard data processing usage, the movement of data between primary and secondary storage is known as input/output. For our purposes, we prefer to reserve these terms for the human/machine interface. We do not believe this will result in any confusion for the managerial user of computers, and the student who elects to continue his or her education in computers should have little difficulty in mastering the transition in terminology.)

4. *Compare* provides the computer with an apparent reasoning capability. A comparison is used as part of the program control to determine which of two sets of program instructions are to be executed. Comparisons can be nested as deeply as necessary to carry out the most complex sets of decision criteria. Comparisons are widely used in the editing and verification of data. Comparisons can be made between any pair or combination of pairs of data elements as long as the elements are in the same computer code. Hence, comparisons that have no inherent logic to a person may be perfectly sensible to the machine. For example, the question "Is DOG equal to or greater than CAT?" is nonsense to a human being but perfectly sensible to the computer if both DOG and CAT are expressed as ASCII (or both as EBCDIC) coded symbols. The computer can test for equality or any degree of inequality between symbols. In programming languages, the comparison can be expressed by mathematical signs (=, =>, =<, >, <, <>) or by word equivalents, generally abbreviated (EQ, GT, LT, UNEQ). All comparison processes take place in the arithmetic and logic unit of the computer's CPU.

5. *Compute* provides the capability to transform an incoming symbol to some other symbol. All general purpose computers carry out all the basic mathematical operations of multiplication, division, addition, and subtraction. These operations can be combined to perform mathematical operations of any complexity under program control. As with the compare processes, the compute processes may be expressed mathematically (+, −, *, /) or in word equivalents (ADD, SUB, MULT, DIV), and they take place in the arithmetic and logic unit of the CPU.

The Three Control Processes

Three methods are used in business data processing to control the order in which the five fundamental processes are executed by the computer.

1. *Sequential processes* specify that one action follows another in the sequence in which they are entered into the computer's control unit. Unless some other control instruction is provided, the fundamental process will be executed in this order.

2. *Selective control* requires that some condition be tested for its truth or correctness. If the condition tested is true, then one set of instructions will be executed; if the condition is not true, then an alternate set of instructions will be executed. Selective control is achieved in computer programs by some variation of the IF . . . THEN . . . ELSE statement. For example, if we wish to use the computer to determine whether or not to fulfill a customer's order for goods or service, we could check his or her credit rating in the following manner:

```
IF (customer credit status = "good")
THEN process order
ELSE return order to sender
ENDIF
```

Selective structures combined with the comparison process permit users to carry out the logic of a real-world activity with the computer. They give computer systems the appearance of intelligence.

3. *Repetitive control* causes a given set of fundamental processes to be executed repeatedly for a given number of times, until some condition is met, or while some condition exists. They are the bread and butter of business data processing. We would hardly need computer assistance to credit interest to one customer's bank balance; however, when we wish to credit the interest to several thousand accounts using the same logic and computations, the computer comes into its own. Repetitive control permits us to continue to execute a specified group of processes until we have no more records which require attention. Three forms of repetitive control are in common use: REPEAT FOR (*n* times) where *n* is known in advance or can be computed by some previous process; REPEAT WHILE causes repetition until a specified condition no longer exists; and REPEAT UNTIL causes repetition until a specified condition exists.

A Pseudolanguage

Armed with the processes described above, we can write our own version of a rudimentary computer language. It simply consists of the five fundamental processes operating under the direction of the three control processes. Of course, it will not run on any computer unless we are capable of writing a language translation program to convert our choice of words to represent the processes into computer-sensible symbols; however, we can use it to communicate the logic of our solution to a problem to other human beings in a form that can easily be coded into an existing computer language. This is precisely the nature of pseudocode, a tool of systems analysis which is explained in relation to the software development life cycle in the next chapter.

Batch and Interactive Processing Revisited

The fundamental and control processes detailed above may be executed on a computer in either a batch or an interactive mode. In the batch mode, transactions are accumulated over a period of time and then processed in a single computer update run. In the interactive mode, transactions are entered into the computer's data storage as they occur. The batch mode is the more economical of the two. It permits efficient use of computer resources; it requires relatively inexpensive storage media; and it uses simple operating procedures. Further, it lends itself to straightforward backup and recovery procedures. However, in this mode information available to users is always somewhat out of date. The interactive mode provides information based on current data, but at a major increase in hardware and software costs and in more sophisticated operating procedures. The easy availability of interactive terminals and disk storage has led to widespread use of the interactive mode, often in cases where immediate access to current data is not required. Cost justification of interactive updating and access to information should be a continuing concern for all those connected with an AIS.

A Range of Support. The organization that decides to seek automated assistance in developing accounting information or to upgrade an existing automated capability has a wide variety of options from which to choose. The range of support extends from hand-held calculators with a printing capability to multimillion-dollar installations that integrate communications networks and distributed databases. The AIS configuration most appropriate to a particular organization will depend upon the organization's size, the nature of its business, its degree of physical dispersion, the requirements for support, the data processing experience of its personnel, its potential for growth, its philosophy of management, and its view of accounting information. A small entrepreneurial firm may properly view its AIS as an overhead function necessary to keep historical records and to satisfy legal requirements. A governmental agency or a large firm in a relatively static environment may view its AIS as having an additional important function in establishing and maintaining cost controls. A government planning body or the planning staff of an expanding firm will sense an additional requirement for accounting information to support long-range objectives.

Data entry procedures for each mode, batch and interactive, were discussed in Chapter 5, and software considerations relating to each mode were discussed in Chapter 6. A full consideration of these alternative modes requires that we integrate the previous discussions into a systems view. There are many ways to combine manual, batch, and interactive processes. We will limit our discussion to an overview of the principles involved.

Batch updates are accomplished by collecting business transactions over some period of time and then entering the resulting batch as an input transaction file to a file update program. The result is an updated master file, a listing of any transactions that fail to process correctly, and a series of control and management reports. The original transactions may be in one of the following forms:

1. *A standard business form.* These forms will be collected by a designated person in the functional area and submitted to key operators for preparation as computer input. Forms may be specifically structured for the keying operation, with each item on the form specifying its location in the transaction file record to be generated. If the forms do not have this feature, it may be necessary for the functional area representative to enter the data into a standard keying format.
2. *An optical character reader (OCR) form.* Recall that these forms are directly readable by machine. The same documents that are used in the business transactions are batched for machine processing.
3. *A computer-prepared form.* This may be either in punched-card or OCR format. The form is originally produced by the computer using information that is resident in the permanent files of the organization. The form is completed by adding data from the current transaction.

Batch Retrievals

Information from batch processing is always provided to the user at the completion of an update run. This information will include the number of transactions processed, the number of error-free transactions entered into the permanent files, and a list of any errors that may have prevented a transaction from being processed. Errors may be corrected by resubmitting a new batch immediately. If the errors are not time-sensitive, they can be included in the next routine update.

Any number of control and managerial reports can also be generated at this time. Additional reports can be generated from a batch file at any time; however, it is essential that the user understand that such reports do not reflect any transactions that have taken place since the last update. There is little limit on the variety of detailed, summary, and exception reports available from a batch system as long as the general format and content of the report was anticipated and programmed in advance. Batch reports may include data from all records in the file or any subset of those records under control of parametized variables in the applications programs. *Parametization* consists of setting selection variables to their desired values prior to the retrieval run. The parameter values are specified by the functional area manager and inserted into the program by information systems professionals. If a new format for a report is required, or if a retrieval is requested on a variable that has not been parametized, programming action will be required and there may be a significant delay in getting the desired information.

Interactive updates are accomplished by functional area personnel interacting directly with the master file as each business transaction occurs or is received at the data input station. Interactive updates can be edited for data integrity, and in some systems they do not update the master file until a transaction that requires more than one entry is completed. Interactive update is facilitated by fourth-generation languages and database management systems. This mode of operation requires a considerably greater commitment of data processing resources than does batch update, and its use should be carefully considered in each application area.

Interactive retrievals can be made from files that are updated by either batch or interactive processing. Users must be alert to the fact that interactive retrievals from batch-maintained files will produce information that is somewhat out of date.

A CAAIS EXAMPLE

We have selected the revenue generation subsystem (RGSS) as a vehicle for examining the processes and procedures that take place in three data processing environments. This selection is arbitrary, but not without reason. The RGSS is an essential activity of all commercial enterprises, charitable organizations, hospitals, and public agencies. Details of how a receivable is generated will vary widely among organizations, but the provision of a good or service must be recorded, billed, and paid for if the organization is to survive. The RGSS is a boundary-spanning activity that interacts with the organization's environment at one extreme and with numerous internal subsystems at the other. Again, the internal subsystems with which the RGSS will interact will vary with the nature of the organization. We will generalize this to three functions: operations, cash flow management, and the AIS. (Extension of the example to other organizational subsystems is suggested as an exercise for the reader.)

The three data processing environments have been selected as representative of the variety of processing techniques the reader may encounter in the late 1980s and into the early 1990s. The first environment is that of traditional batch processing. This was the dominant mode of automated accounting in the 1970s and early 1980s. It still persists in organizations that cannot justify the major investment in capital and personnel resources necessary for installation of a more modern system. In general, those organizations are in fields that are protected from competition or have a relatively low volume of transactions. The first category can pass the costs of inefficient methods on to clients, and the second can survive because the costs are incidental. Ironically, many of these organizations were technological leaders in the 1970s. Their investment in obsolete technology now prevents them from updating. Because the accounting function was among the first to be computerized, accountants are more likely than other managers to encounter this environment. The second environment is a hybrid interactive and batch system characteristic of those encountered in small to medium-sized organizations. Such systems were developed for and tailored to the capabilities of mini- and super-minicomputers. The last environment to be considered is a fully integrated interactive system. These systems are found at the extremes of organizational size. They are used on large mainframe computers by high-volume retail firms using point-of-sale data capture technology, and they are used on microcomputers by very small organizations using keyed input.

The RGSS

Figure 8–1 defines the RGSS in its organizational setting. The other organizational subsystems with which the RGSS must interface include the AIS, represented by the general ledger; the comptroller, represented by the cash flow manager; the treasurer, represented by the cashier; and the operational units which supply the goods or services. The RGSS also interacts with customers across the organizational boundary, accepting orders and payments from the customer and issuing invoices and bills to the customer.

Figure 8–2 expands the black box presentation of the RGSS depicted in Figure 8–1. (Figure 8–2 is in the form of a dataflow

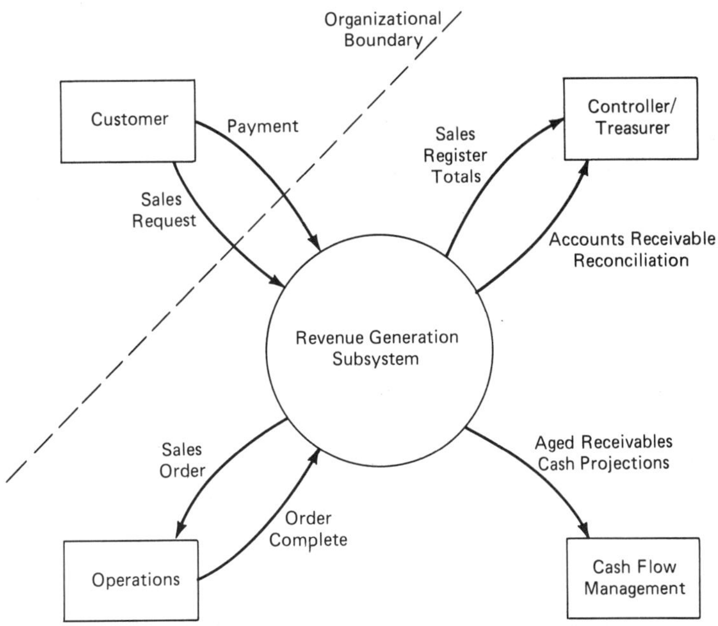

FIGURE 8–1 A Systems View of the Revenue Generation Subsystem

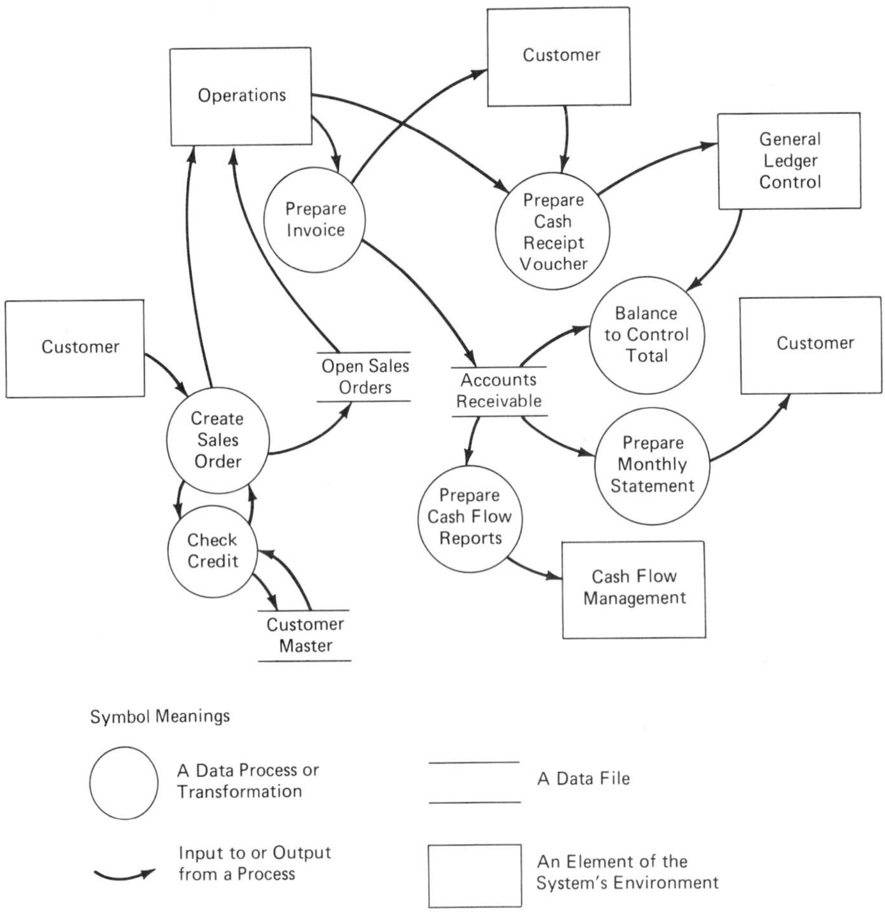

FIGURE 8–2 Dataflows within the RGSS

diagram rather than the more familiar flowchart. Dataflow diagrams have replaced flowcharts in structured systems analysis. A brief explanation of the symbols used is included in the figure.) The components necessary to examine the operations of this subsystem include order processing, billing, accounts receivable, and the cashier. Note that each component of the RGSS may also be a component of one of these other internal subsystems. In a level of detail not diagrammed, we consider the order processing activity to include the preparation of sales orders and the verification of customer credit. As an illustration of the systems definition problem cited in Chapter 2, we considered including the finished goods inventory account in the system because it is of interest to the CAAIS; however, we elected to leave this in the operational environment because it is not essential to revenue generation.

The dataflow depicted in Figure 8–2 is initiated upon receipt of a customer order for goods or services. The order processing group completes a sales order form and, if the transaction is not paid for in advance, initiates a credit check. Upon receipt of credit approval, the customer order is entered into an open order file. The open order file is used by the operations department to respond to the customer request. If the organization is distributing merchandise, this would be used to develop a warehouse packing slip; if it is a service organization, a schedule of services; and so on. When the goods or services have been provided, the operations department notifies the billing department and an invoice is prepared. The invoice is forwarded to the customer, the customer's account in the accounts receivable file is updated, and a sales or services rendered journal is updated. Periodically, this journal is closed to the general ledger, and the general ledger receivables control account is balanced against the totals in the accounts receivable subsidiary ledger.

The accounts receivable file is processed at the end of a billing period to produce a bill for each customer and to provide aging of receivable information to the cash flow manager and the credit approval group.

A second dataflow process in the RGSS is initiated when the customer renders payment. This is received by the cashier, who endorses the check and prepares a cash receipt voucher for posting to the cash and accounts receivable accounts.

The RGSS in the Batch Environment. The revenue generation function in a batch environment is carried out much as it was before the introduction of automated data processing. Typically, these systems were developed piecemeal; the sales department has its programs, files, and reports relating to sales; the billing office has its programs, files, and reports to control invoicing; the accounting department has its programs, files, and reports to support accounts receivable and financial reporting. However, these programs are usually not coordinated, and many data items are repeated in each department's files. The RGSS still relies heavily on multipart forms for interdepartmental communication and control. As in the general discussion, the RGSS is activated when a salesperson or customer contacts the order processing group. The order will be recorded on a multipart form. The complete form will be routed to the credit approval desk. The credit department will have a computer printout of customer credit status. This listing is updated weekly or monthly on the computer and annotated by hand to keep it up to date.

After credit is approved, the sales order is returned to order processing. The first copy will be pulled and kept with the first copies of all other sales transactions for the day. At the end of the day, the batched orders will be submitted to data processing's keying branch for creation of a card, tape, or floppy disk transaction file. As part of this submission, the sales order clerk will submit a batch control form specifying the date, the number of order forms, and the total value of the sales represented by the forms as calculated manually. These data will be entered onto the magnetic transaction file and used as batch check totals. The transaction file will be run daily to update the open orders file. A number of reports can be generated from this file. A Daily Sales Transaction Report can be used for sales analysis and for control purposes in other organizational locations that receive copies of the sales order. The sales transactions can be sorted in a number of ways; for example, a sort by date permits management to determine how many days it takes to fill an order; a sort by customer name facilitates response to customer inquiries by customer service representatives; a sort by sales representatives can be used to evaluate salespersons and compute commissions.

The second copy of an approved sales order is sent to the operations department to authorize the delivery of goods or services. Operations also receives a copy of the Daily Sales Transactions Report and uses this to ensure that all authorized sales orders have been received. When the goods or services are provided, operations notes this fact on its copy and forwards it to the billing office.

The third copy of the approved sales order is sent directly from the order processing group to the billing office. It is held there in suspense until the second copy is received from operations. Billing may also use the Daily Sales Transactions Report as an additional control. When the second copy is received, billing returns one copy of the sales order to order processing so that the order may be removed from the open order file during the next batch run. Billing also generates a multipart invoice. The original is sent to the customer, and the second copy is kept with all other second copies of invoices until the close of business. The batched invoices are then sent to data processing and in a manner analogous to the sales order batch are used to update the sales (or service) journal. The third copy of the invoice is sent to accounts receivable, where the accounts receivable clerk assembles a batch of invoices, submits the batch to data processing, and orders the batch to be run to update the customer receivable accounts. The sales journal is closed weekly to the general ledger receivables account. This value is used as a control total for reconciliation with the accounts receivable subsidiary ledger.

The accounts receivable file is processed monthly to compute customer bills, to provide an aged receivables report for collection control, to provide cash inflow projections for cash flow management, and for reconciliation for monthly financial statements.

The cash receipts portion of the RGSS operates similarly, but is considerably simpler. Whenever a payment is received, the cashier creates a cash receipt voucher. These vouchers are batched throughout the day, submitted to data processing for keying, and processed to produce a cash receipt register and to update the cash and accounts receivable subsidiary ledger.

The system is tedious, and the multiple handling of forms and numerous data preparation steps are conducive to creating errors. Much time in a batch accounting system is devoted to reconciling out-of-balance accounts. The computer has not been used to great advantage; essentially, it has replaced the manual functions of a bookkeeper in posting and totaling accounts. The sorting capabilities of the machine have provided some improvement in managerial control. In all fairness, we should state that the operation described above is a worst-case situation. With a minimum of coordination across departments, many of the steps can be simplified or eliminated.

The RGSS in a Hybrid Environment. The advent of interactive processing has facilitated streamlining of the revenue generation function. The invoicing function has been incorporated into order processing; the order processing subsystem produces magnetic media inputs for the accounts receivable systems, and the accounts receivable programs automatically produce bills at the end of the billing cycle. Typically, in such a system order processing is conducted in an interactive mode; the invoices generated will be maintained on disk as a transaction file, and this file will be used as a batch input transaction file to update accounts receivable as required to produce customer bills and managerial reports.

As in the batch example, the RGSS is activated by a customer's request for goods or services. The order processing clerk enters the order data at a visual display terminal. The entries are edited to ensure that they are reasonable, and the order is automatically checked against an on-line customer credit status file. If the customer's credit is good, the order is added to the open order file and a hard copy of the order form is printed. A copy of this form is sent to operations. When the good or service has been supplied, the sales order is completed and returned to order processing. The completion transaction is entered interactively, causing the order to be removed from the open order file, an invoice to be generated for the customer, and a magnetic image of the invoice to be entered into the sales transactions file. The transaction file can be inspected visually, or it can be printed as an invoice register if desired. In its magnetic form, the file is used to update the sales account of the general ledger and the accounts receivable subsidiary ledger. This batch process is executed in accordance with policies set by management.

The cash receipt function operates similarly to the invoicing function. The receipts are entered at a VDT to create a transaction file on magnetic disk. This file is then used in the batch mode to update the cash and accounts receivable accounts, as determined by management.

The hybrid environment is a major improvement over batch operations in simplicity of data handling. This in turn reduces the transaction error rate and eliminates many reconciliation problems. However, it also eliminates many of the controls that we have built into the traditional accounting system. Therefore, while the more modern environment is less susceptible to inadvertent error, it is more susceptible to fradulent transactions. This susceptibility can be offset by additional control measures. (These measures are discussed in Chapter 14.)

The RGSS in the Fully Integrated Environment. It is a relatively short step from the hybrid environment to the fully integrated environment. Instead of having our order processing subsystem write its output to a disk transaction file, we simply keep our accounts receivable file on-line and write the results directly to this file. This process requires more complex programs and greater storage capacity, but if immediate access to information is needed, the additional capabilities are available. All other files involved in the RGSS can be similarly on-line and interactively updated. Other features of integrated systems vary with the nature of the organization. Features frequently encountered include these:

1. Automatic capture of sales data from credit/debit cards
2. Terminals located at all internal offices to eliminate paper flow
3. Terminals located at customer locations so that customers can enter their own sales orders into the vendor's system; this can be refined so that funds are automatically transferred when the transaction is confirmed

At the retail level, the RGSS has reached what may be the ultimate limit in integration in the area of gasoline sales. A customer may now use a debit card to pay for gasoline directly from a bank account. The customer inserts the debit card into an electronic funds transfer terminal located at the gasoline pump, and enters the correct password and the dollar amount of the gasoline desired. The terminal sends the customer data to a central processing site via satellite relay to confirm that sufficient funds are available. (The site may be on the other side of the country.) If the customer has enough money in the account to cover the proposed sale, the pump is activated. The correct amount is then transferred from the customer's account to the oil company's account. The entire authorization transaction takes less than 10 seconds.

DATA PROCESSING ISSUES

The Service Bureau Option

The first question an organization must address is its need for on-site processing capability. The decision to establish an in-house capability requires a significant commitment of time, space, personnel, and dollars. If the total processing requirements of the organization do not justify this commitment, a full range of accounting information services is available from external sources.

Service bureaus are firms dedicated to providing processing capabilities. The services provided may vary from a single function which handles input and output services in a batch mode, such as payroll services, through a full batch processing capability, such as a remote job entry station that can execute prestored or newly entered programs, to a complete menu of interactive services. The services may be limited to prepackaged programs executed under control of the service center, or may encompass a complete database and programming capability. Some service bureaus simply provide the hardware capabilities and permit the client to handle software; others provide specialized software and custom programming. Computer services are also available through a variety of firms that market excess capacity. Excess capacity is often found in financial institutions that require extensive on-line services during peak workload times but cannot profitably use the resulting computer system for internal purposes in off-peak hours.

The principal advantage of the service bureau approach is that the client organization can select and pay for only those services that it needs. It may be particularly cost-effective for a small organization or for one that is expanding rapidly. It is most effective in providing the services essential to operational level control. The principal disadvantage of the service bureau is that the client organization has only limited control over its AIS function. Recently, a Fortune 1000 company was faced with a tenfold increase in costs of services provided by a service center in a single year. The internal needs of the processing institution had caught up with its capacity; the excess capacity had simply disappeared. The client company faced with this situation elected to establish its own in-house capability. In this particular instance, the client had been operating a full batch terminal in the remote job entry mode and was able to convert to in-house operations with a minimum of chaos. At the other extreme, a client firm that wished to terminate its contract with a service bureau discovered that its data tapes were the property of the service bureau and had to be purchased at a very large fee. Although such problems are rare enough to be newsworthy, the point remains that it is essential for the user organization to understand the terms of its service contract.

In-House Processing Options

If the organization elects to have an on-site processing capability, it will need to consider the advantages and disadvantages of purchasing versus leasing its computer. As a fully operational AIS can be developed with either option, the decision will be based primarily on the financial status of the organization. Such considerations as alternate investment opportunities, tax benefits, and cash flow analyses will be paramount. There may be a perception that the firm will have greater stability of operations if it owns its processor; however, this is likely to be illusory in that the term of a lease may be very nearly equivalent to the expected useful life of a processor. In either case, a major concern of the AIS is that software purchased or developed for the current system should be transportable to the widest possible variety of hardware and operating systems. The large, tightly integrated software systems that provide the best accounting support are likely to be quite inflexible in this regard. The systems that are most efficient and effective in meeting today's needs often increase the difficulty of adjusting to tomorrow's requirements. This is one of many tradeoffs AIS personnel must evaluate carefully.

Centralization versus Decentralization

A second issue that must be addressed in regard to in-house computer operations is the degree of centralization of control to be exercised over computerized operations. Control, in all senses of the word, is an essential concern of the accounting profession. In the sense of centralization or decentralization of computing power, control will be a major determinant of the method of developing AIS software, the integrity of accounting data, and the auditability of the organization's financial transactions. There is a continuous range of possibilities for the centralization or decentralization of data processing, from the total centralization of planning, processing, and development to total autonomy for divisions or departments for any one or more of these functions. As we will repeatedly find in our examination of the AIS, there is no one "best" solution to this issue. In general, it can be stated that the degree of centralization of data processing should correspond with the managerial philosophy of the organization.

CONTROL ISSUES IN THE CAAIS

Planning Level

The need for control permeates the information systems of all large organizations. Information systems require long-range planning; they consume large amounts of financial and human resources, and their reliability and responsiveness are crucial to the health of the organization. Computing resources must be rationed. The existence of extensive programming backlogs and the rapid proliferation of personal computers in the work setting are two measures of an apparently insatiable appetite for computer-assisted information processing. The first level of control concerns controlling the growth and direction of the overall information system.

How much computing power is enough? Microeconomic theory provides a simple but glib answer to this question: We should expend funds on the information system until the marginal rate of return on IS investment is precisely equal to the marginal rate of return from alternate investment opportunities. In practice, this value is not easily determined, primarily because the long-range rate of return on investment in information systems is difficult to estimate to management's satisfaction. The point to be made remains that the information systems function must compete with alternate uses of available resources. In this competition, the information system is often at a disadvantage because its benefits are indirect and difficult to quantify. This disadvantage is offset for the AIS, in part, by the fact that many AIS requirements are mandated by law and that the existing AIS is an important source of input for managerial control and strategic planning decisions. Expenditure of funds for information systems development cannot be controlled effectively unless the organization has an operative long-range strategic plan and a supporting MIS master plan.

Managerial Level

The Information Systems department may operate as either a cost center or a profit center. The internal control of existing resources is most often accomplished by a combination of two policies: (1) managerial approval of applications developments and (2) charge-back of information systems cost to users. The managerial approval process is used to establish the priority of projects within successively higher levels in the organization. In a properly operating system, this priority will be in consonance with the overall development scheme as established in the MIS master plan. Charge-back procedures vary widely among firms. Cost categories often include developmental costs, CPU time used, amount of on-line and off-line storage used, and the time that input/output devices are in use. The CAAIS, as a subsystem of the organization's IS, is a client in charge-back schemes. One of the most important features to strive for in any charge-back system is to be certain that users clearly understand what the charges represent.

Operating Level

The AIS has a participative role in the long-range development of the overall information system and the allocation of existing computerized resources. It has full responsibility for the control of accounting data. Inputs to the CAAIS must be checked and edited to ensure that they are complete and accurate. If erroneous data are permitted to enter the system and are subsequently processed, incalculable damage may be done. Required accounting reports will be in error, and managerial decisions will be based on faulty information. It is difficult and expensive to locate errors in a file and to correct information that has been developed from the erroneous data. Further, it delays ongoing processing. For these reasons, as many as two-thirds of the lines of code in production software systems may be devoted to checking the completeness and accuracy of input data.

Data will be checked to be sure they satisfy specified characteristics for individual fields—that they are of the correct type and length and are within the range of allowable values; they will be checked for logical consistency with other related data items; and whenever appropriate, they will be checked against existing values in master records already resident in the system. Software checks and edits will detect most inadvertent errors; however, no amount of automated checking can fully protect the AIS against deliberate input manipulation by a skilled human. Therefore, it is essential that traditional manual procedural controls be continued to the extent possible when implementing machine procedures. For example, no one individual should be allowed to program, operate the computer, and enter data. This fundamental principle of separation of functions is often violated, particularly in relatively small organizations, when automation is introduced.

The programs themselves must be carefully controlled. Accountants and auditors must test program modules during development to ensure that the programs do precisely what they are intended to do. As the modules are assembled into subsystems and finally into the total application system, testing must continue. Once the programs are introduced into the production cycle, they must be tested periodically to ensure that only authorized changes have been made. In large installations, the operating system software will record access to programs, files, records, and perhaps even to fields within records. These records must be inspected for irregularities. In smaller systems, the automated controls will be less extensive and greater reliance must be placed on periodic testing and maintenance of sound physical and procedural controls.

Control over processing is particularly difficult in decentralized operations. The user of information in a decentralized environment cannot be sure that the information has been produced by properly controlled programs. The extensive use of microcomputers exacerbates this problem. The AIS retains control over information entering financial accounting reports, but control is easily lost over information in the managerial accounting area.

Control over computer output is the final area to be discussed in this overview. If input data are complete and accurate and processing is accomplished in accordance with management's direction, then it follows that the information output must be accurate and reasonable. Nevertheless, we continue to encounter news items describing computer output that is obviously erroneous. The clerk who receives a weekly paycheck of a million dollars or the patient who receives a bill for a $100,000 for one emergency room visit are familiar examples. These errors are usually traced to a breakdown in input controls; however, they could not occur if adequate output controls were in place.

Output as well as input must be checked for reasonableness, and any unusual value should be isolated for management attention and checked before the output is released. Software controls over output should check that values are within expected limits and should limit access to stored information to properly authorized users. A number of means are available to accomplish this function. Access can be limited by password at the file, record, or field level of data; it can be limited by user identification; it can be limited to selected terminals or even to certain hours of the day. As with input controls, the software output controls must be supplemented by sound physical and procedural controls. Visual display terminals should be located so that only authorized personnel can see and read the screen. Distribution of hard copy reports should be strictly in accordance with prescribed directives.

SECURITY AND PRIVACY IN COMPUTER PROCESSING

Computer security is concerned with the loss or alteration of data from accidental or deliberate events. It includes measures to prevent these events and, if they occur, to detect and correct them. As we will see, an organization that has installed and maintains the developmental, input, processing, and output controls noted earlier has taken a major step in securing its data. A leading authority in the field of EDP security cites three areas of concern: (1) physical security—the protection and control of access to the data processing environment; (2) operational and procedural security—the constraints placed on personnel within the systems environment; and (3) internal security—the safeguards built into the hardware, software, and communications elements of the system.

Physical Security

Physical security of data is threatened by natural forces, such as floods, fires, and earth movements; by malicious attacks, such as arson, sabotage, and terrorism; and by unauthorized access to computer spaces or terminals. Physical security is enhanced by careful selection of computer sites, installation of fire detection and automatic fire-fighting equipment, and restriction of entry to computer spaces by locks, guards, badges, and other identification systems. Loss of data is prevented by maintaining backup copies at a remote location. Physical security is significantly more difficult in a distributed processing environment than in a centralized system.

Weak physical controls contributed to one of the more spectacular recent computer-related crimes. The crime consisted of the unauthorized transfer of $10.2 million from a California bank to a New York City bank for further payment to the account of a Soviet diamond brokerage firm in Zurich. The "virtual" money that exists in the magnetic and electrical impulses of the computer world was converted to real value when the perpetrator of the transfer traveled to Zurich and collected most of the $10.2 million in diamonds. He was able to obtain the necessary account numbers and authorization codes to execute the transfer because he was allowed to enter the California bank's wire transfer room, although he had no clearance to do so. Based on prior acquaintance, the manager of this facility accepted his pose as a consultant to the Federal Reserve System without checking for credentials. A further breakdown in operational and procedural security contributed to this crime.

Operational and Procedural Security

Operational and procedural threats to data include manipulation of computer input data, alteration of programs, alterations in master files, and interception or misuse of teleprocessing communications. These threats may be offset by separation of responsibilities, adherence to standard procedures, monitoring of computer logs, management of program changes, and encryption of sensitive data before filing or transmission. In the case of the $10.2 million transfer, the account number the intruder obtained in the wire transfer room proved to be incorrect. He called the international banking department of the California bank and, by giving the incorrect number, identified himself as a person authorized to have access to the numbers. He was then provided with the correct number over the telephone.

Internal Security

Internal security threats to data include equipment malfunctions and unauthorized electronic access to files. Internal security measures include the use of passwords, selective terminal permissions, isolation of user programs and data, redundancy of critical processing components, backup and recovery procedures, and the maintenance of computer logs. The most commonly reported violations of internal security relate to overzealous computer science students penetrating university computer systems or misusing data processing networks. The ease with which this has been accomplished suggests that there may be a significant amount of more insidious penetration. Another common problem in this category is referred to as a head crash. This occurs when the floating read/write head of a disk comes into contact with the disk surface, and it results in the destruction of data recorded on that surface.

Degree of Security

No computer system can be made 100 percent secure. The degree of security that is desirable depends upon (1) the cost to the organization if the data are lost, improperly manipulated, or made available to unauthorized parties; and (2) management's assessment of the probability that a particular breach of security is likely. In the case of accounting information, the stakes are relatively high. The loss of a single transaction or part of a transaction can result in high use of man-hours to detect and correct the error. A loss of any significant portion of data can result in major manual efforts, severe financial losses, legal entanglements, or even bankruptcy. Erroneous entries have an effect similar to the loss of a transaction. Standard accounting and data processing procedures are usually adequate to prevent or minimize the cost of accidental loss or input errors.

A recent case involving a small manufacturing concern illustrates the potential costs of not following sound procedure. Payments to the company were posted against accounts receivable balances but were not posted against payments, credits, or returned merchandise. After approximately one year, the company had $2 million of unreconciled balances. At this point, the computer's memory holding the balances was accidentally erased. No backup files were maintained. With no information to validate the receivables, the company was faced with the choice of depending on customers to pay what their records showed, or simply writing off the $2 million.

Similarly, there is a relatively high probability that an unscrupulous employee or a professional criminal will select the AIS as a point of penetration. The financial assets of an organization are more easily turned into cash than other assets and therefore present the most attractive target. Protection of accounting information from deliberate alteration requires controls over the control system. It is not enough simply to design the system; it must be monitored continuously.

Privacy

An organization that has established and maintains effective control and security procedures has the physical attributes necessary to ensure privacy of information. *Privacy* involves releasing information about a person or an organization only to those who have a legitimate right to that information. Information in the AIS regarding customers, suppliers, and personnel is clearly of a sensitive nature. The release of AIS information to unauthorized persons or its use for purposes other than those for which it was gathered is subject to legal and ethical constraints.

SUMMARY

All computer processes can be analyzed as falling into one of five fundamental processes which can be controlled in three ways. The fundamental processes are INPUT, or conversion of human sensible symbols to computer sensible symbols; OUTPUT, the opposite process to input; MOVE, the repositioning of data for manipulation and storage; COMPARE, a logical operation; and COMPUTE, a transformation. The order of execution of the fundamental processes may be controlled by a combination of sequential, selective, and repetitive processes. Taken together, the fundamental and control processes constitute a pseudolanguage that is easily understood by people and easily encoded into a formal computer language.

A computer program can be executed in either a batch or an interactive mode. The batch mode makes efficient use of machine resources, but results in data files that are always somewhat out of date. The interactive mode is essential for applications that must have the latest information.

A continuous spectrum of data processing environments supports the CAAIS. They range from pure batch processing through hybrid combinations of batch update with interactive retrievals to fully interactive systems. Selection of the appropriate support technology depends upon the requirements and capabilities of the organization.

A number of data processing issues must be addressed when implementing or updating an AIS. These include: (1) whether to conduct processing in-house or through a service bureau; (2) if an in-house capability is required, whether the organization should buy or lease equipment; (3) what degree of centralization of processing is desired; (4) what controls are appropriate to the operation; (5) what security measures must be considered; and (6) what privacy factors are involved.

REVIEW QUESTIONS, DISCUSSION QUESTIONS, AND PROBLEMS AND CASES

A. Review Questions

A8.1 What is a bit? A byte? The EBCDIC code?

A8.2 What is the significance of a byte to the internal operation of a computer?

A8.3 What are the five fundamental computer processes? Describe each briefly.

A8.4 What are the three control processes?

A8.5 What are the components of a pseudolanguage? Why is a pseudolanguage of any interest or value?

A8.6 What is the major limitation of batch processing in regard to the production of information?

A8.7 What outputs should be expected from a batch update?

A8.8 Should an organization's goal be to convert all data processing to the interactive mode? Why or why not?

A8.9 What problems may arise from the extensive manual data handling required in a traditional batch-processing operation?

A8.10 What, if any, advantages does the traditional batch-processing mode have vis-à-vis more modern modes?

A8.11 What advantages do the more modern data processing modes have vis-à-vis batch processing?

A8.12 How does a debit card system operate?

A8.13 What is a service bureau?

A8.14 What are the relative advantages of buying an in-house computer as opposed to leasing one?

A8.15 What is meant by planning level controls? By managerial level? By operating level?

A8.16 What are three levels of security that must be considered in regard to data processing?

A8.17 Why do we not strive for 100 percent secure operations?

A8.18 What is meant by privacy?

B. Discussion Questions

B8.1 The text states that a modern digital computer is best described as a fast and reliable symbol-manipulating machine. What does this mean to you? How else might you describe a computer?

B8.2 Consider an information system with which you are familiar, such as the production of your grade report at the end of a semester. How would you describe this process for a single individual in terms of the fundamental and control processes of this chapter? For every student in the school?

B8.3 Parallel processing is a fourth possible means of controlling the fundamental processes. It is not included in this chapter. What do you suppose accounts for this omission? How would you envision using parallel processing in the CAAIS?

B8.4 In a modern data processing facility, virtually all files are maintained on direct-access storage devices. This provides the potential for fully interactive update of all files. When should this potential be exercised? If your answer is other than "at all times," why not? In either case, provide concrete examples within the CAAIS.

B8.5 Consider the payroll function. How would this operate in a pure batch environment? Could the function be carried out in a completely interactive mode? If so, how? What implementation problems would you foresee?

B8.6 With the widespread availability of cheap and powerful microcomputers, why would any organization consider using a service bureau?

B8.7 What conditions would you consider when deciding whether to buy or lease a large computer system?

B8.8 Assume for a moment that you are a mediocre but totally unscrupulous student. You wish to change your academic records to indicate a level of performance considerably higher than the grades assigned by your professors. How would you attack your school's record system?

B8.9 Your state's Registry of Motor Vehicles sells a listing of licensed drivers to an automobile sales agency. Assuming that you are a licensed driver, has your right to privacy been invaded?

C. Problems and Cases

C8.1 The Storage Technology Division of a large computer manufacturer produces disk drives that are sold as part of the initial computer installation of the firm and are also marketed directly to users. The Material Requirements Planning Department of the division is assigned responsibility for ensuring that all necessary materials are on hand when they are needed for the assembly of the drives. This requires coordination with the corporate planning staff and the Peripherals Sales Division in order to forecast demand. Tasks that must be accomplished include:

1. Maintaining an authorized vendor list for all raw materials and subassemblies
2. Placing orders for materials
3. Verifying receipt of materials
4. Storing materials until required for use
5. Approving vendor invoices for payment
6. Timing payment of invoices to conserve cash flow while taking advantage of discounts for prompt payment
7. Issuing materials to the production department, decrementing raw materials inventory, and incrementing work-in-process

Describe how this function could be supported in a pure batch environment.

C8.2 Describe how the Material Requirements Planning Department in Case C8.1 could be supported in a completely interactive environment.

C8.3 Assume you are the head of the MRP Department as the transaction from batch to interactive processing is to be implemented. In what order would you convert the functions from batch to interactive? Would you recommend leaving any activities in the batch mode if that were an option?

SUGGESTED READINGS

BENFOROOZ, ALI, AND ONGAR P. SHARMA. *An Introduction to Computer Science: A Structured Problem Solving Approach.* Englewood Cliffs, N.J.: Prentice-Hall, 1986.

GILHOOLEY, IAN. "Defining the Scope of DP Controls," in *A Practical Guide to EDP Auditing,* ed. James Hannan. Pennsauken, N.J.: Auerbach, 1982.

HOUSLEY, TREVOR. *Data Communications and Teleprocessing Systems,* 2nd ed. Englewood Cliffs, N.J.: Prentice-Hall, 1987.

KRONKE, DAVID M., AND KATHLEEN A. DOLAN. *Business Computer Systems: An Introduction,* 3rd ed. Santa Cruz, Calif.: Mitchell, 1987.

PARKER, DONN B. *Crime by Computer.* New York: Charles Scribner's Sons, 1976.

chapter nine

The Traditional Software Development Life Cycle

CHAPTER OUTLINE

INTRODUCTION

The AIS exists in a highly volatile environment. New needs for accounting information arise in response to regulatory actions, business problems, and perceived new opportunities. The rapid evolution of technology provides a continuously improved capability to meet these needs and in turn widens management's perception of what information is potentially available and useful. In this chapter we will concentrate on the traditional software development processes which support an organization's changing needs for information. Most modern medium to large firms use custom-designed software to support their accounting information needs. The overall software system is developed incrementally in projects of a manageable size. In a well-managed organization, these projects will be modules, or subsystems, of the AIS which will interface with other modules of the organization's total information system. The process of developing this component of the AIS is known as the software development life cycle (SDLC). Although the SDLC is the main topic of this chapter, we will first discuss the broader topic of the management of systems development so that the SDLC can be understood in its context.

THE CONTEXT FOR THE TRADITIONAL LIFE CYCLE

Management control practices, in general, vary widely among organizations. So does management control of software development. Organizational theory suggests that appropriate control measures will be contingent upon a number of factors. Space does not permit a complete discussion of this topic, but two factors will serve to place our SDLC discussion in context. The first of these is the size of the organization, and the second is the stage of data processing.

Organization Size

A small organization is likely to use relatively informal control procedures both in its selection of applications for development and in the subsequent development process. This is entirely appropriate, because in a small organization it is possible for senior management to perceive needs directly, establish priorities, and control resources directly. In larger organizations these issues become more complex. No single manager or single group of top managers can be aware of all relevant information affecting the organization's welfare. The managers in the several functional areas of an organization develop, filter, and summarize information from their particular perspectives, and a formal set of procedures becomes essential to resolve the resulting conflicts in the best interests of the total organization. The discussion in this chapter is more applicable to these larger, more formal organizations than to the smaller, less formal ones.

Stage of Data Processing

The second factor of prime interest is the experience of the organization in the use of information processing technology. Nolan[1] has provided useful guidelines in this area by identifying six stages of data processing development. In brief, these are:

1. *Initiation.* A computer is introduced into an organization in a limited capacity. Typically, the initial use is in support of accounting needs. In virtually every case, the installed computer has more capacity than the single function can use. In this stage, the data processing manager becomes a salesperson for this excess capacity.

2. *Contagion.* This stage results from the successful efforts of the data processing manager in stage 1. Several managers outside the initial functional area receive automated support. This results in a deluge of requests for applications developments. The data processing manager, previously embarrassed with excess capacity, now becomes short of human and computer resources. This, in turn, results in requests for additional commitment of resources to the information systems function. In this stage, the data processing manager has a free hand in establishing priorities for application development.

3. *Control.* The control stage results from rising data processing costs and dissatisfaction with the data processing manager's sense of priorities. It is at this stage that top management becomes concerned with data processing. Planning is initiated. The DP function is removed from its location within a functional area and established as an independent department. Control methods imposed at this stage typically include some sort of top-management review process and the institution of a charge-out policy to recover all data processing development and operating costs. In this stage, application development remains strongly functionally oriented. A large number of files are established, many of which contain overlapping data. The control stage slows, and in some cases even halts, the pace of information systems development. It is in this stage that the applications backlog begins to become significant.

4. *Integration.* The proliferation of files in the earlier stages of development results in inconsistencies in the database of the organi-

[1] Richard Nolan, "Managing the Crisis in Data Processing," *Harvard Business Review* (March–April 1979).

zation. Because of differences in file update cycles, the same data item may have two or more different values at any point in time. This leads to contradictory reports to management. In addition, it results in inefficient data processing and leads to severe problems in program maintenance. In the integration stage these problems are addressed by consolidating files into some scheme of area databases. Data are shared among several users rather than being the property of any individual. Database management systems are introduced. Teleprocessing and distributed data processing are often part of the integration stage.

5. *Data administration.* This stage results from the broadening perception that data is a major organizational resource to be handled with the same care allotted to human, financial, or material resources. Superficially, it may seem to be a continuation of the integration stage; however, it represents a basic shift in philosophy from a bottom-up integration of existing applications to top-down management of structured systems. Technologically, it is characterized by widespread use of database management techniques and extensive on-line access to data.

6. *Maturity.* The mature stage of information systems development remains highly speculative. In this stage, information processing is totally integrated with the activities in the firm. The state of hardware and software technology is such that the information needed by all members of the organization is immediately available with a minimum of effort. Databases may be updated dynamically so that there is no need for major systems replacement. As of this writing, no organization is operating in this mature stage.

In terms of Nolan's stages, the principles of management control of software development set forth in this chapter apply most appropriately to the control and integration stages. In the earlier stages, the controls have not been implemented; in the later stages, they will be less than adequate. This limitation is not as stringent as it may first appear. A few leading firms have started to operate in the data administration stage; however, the vast majority of medium and large organizations in the United States are in the late control and early integration stages of information systems development. Figure 9–1 illustrates Nolan's stages in regard to data processing planning and control.

THE MIS MASTER PLAN

The development of software to meet the needs of an organization requires a significant commitment of organizational resources. This

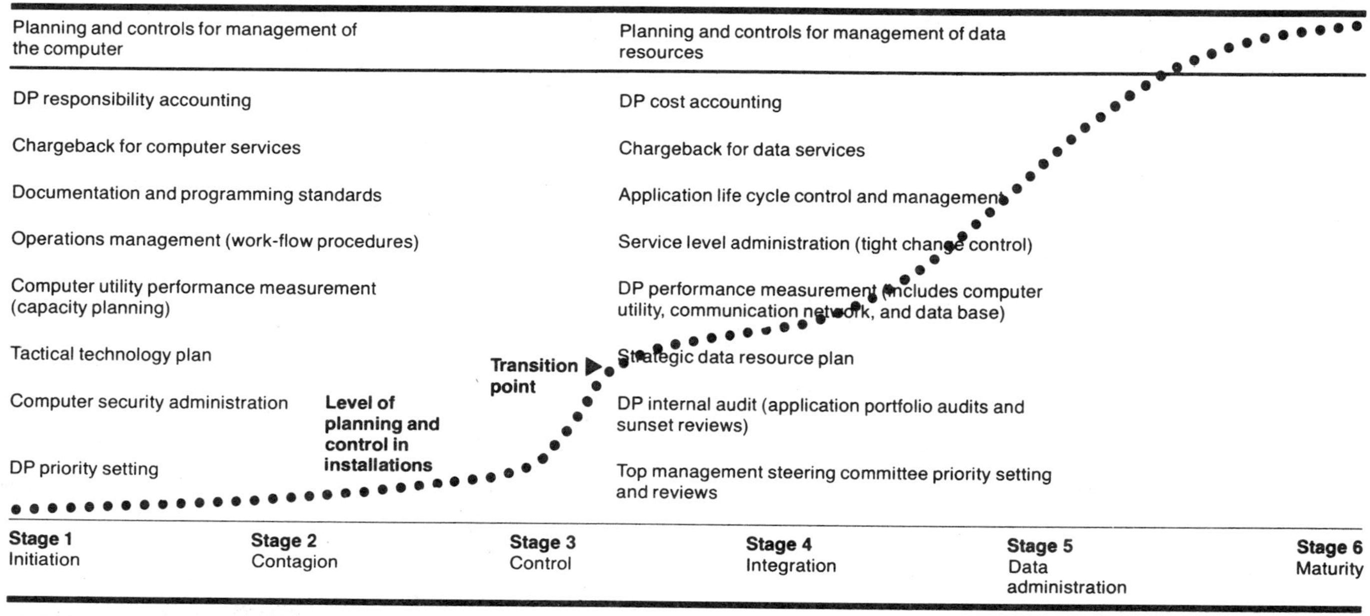

FIGURE 9–1 Nolan's Stages of Growth

Source: Reprinted by permission of the *Harvard Business Review.* An exhibit from "Managing the Crisis in Data Processing" by Richard Nolan (March–April 1979).

commitment is often formalized as part of the long-range information systems development plan of the organization. Methods for developing an MIS master plan vary widely. We will examine the two extreme approaches, and then suggest one of several possible syntheses that is in relatively wide use.

Centralized Planning and Control

This approach is based on an organizationwide information requirements analysis that will identify all potential software development and establish priorities based on the potential each has to contribute to organizational effectiveness and efficiency. The centralized approach has considerable merit from the viewpoint of rational management. It permits the logical, balanced, and coordinated development of an overall system that will support the goals of the organization. Early attempts at employing the centralized approach were severely handicapped by inadequate development techniques. More recently, improved analysis tools and database management technology have made possible a major step forward in the feasibility of implementing a planned sequence of developments. Nevertheless, formidable obstacles remain to implementing the centralized, or top-down approach.

It is extremely difficult to perform a comprehensive information requirements analysis in a large organization. Even with the assumption of a static environment, the need to select between competing demands for limited resources requires a firm set of organizational objectives for guidance and active top management support to resolve conflict. Organizations, of course, do not exist in a static environment. In the time it takes to complete an organizationwide information requirements analysis, unforeseen problems and opportunities and the rush of technological change may cause a considerable change in information needs. If we further extend the time horizon to include design and implementation delays, then information needs may have changed radically. This is particularly true with the AIS, where unanticipated legislative and regulatory actions are frequently the source of information requirements. A second major drawback of fully centralized development is that the approach creates a high level of user resistance. Resistance to change is a widespread phenomenon in all aspects of organizations; it is particularly prevalent in regard to automation of information systems, which poses a threat to job security and to existing formal and informal organizational structures. The ability to impose top-down solutions has consistently been oversold by data processing technicians. Although such total systems solutions are appealing to managers and may be technologically feasible, they usually fall short of expectations because of organizational complexity and behavioral considerations. There does not appear to be any breakthrough in analytical techniques or design methods that will overcome these nontechnical considerations in the foreseeable future.

Decentralized Development

Some organizations have taken a totally decentralized approach to information systems development. This is based on the philosophy that a profit center manager should be held accountable for attaining a desired level of performance within his or her area of responsibility and that the end is best achieved by allowing the manager responsible freedom to allocate available resources. Under this concept, each manager submits development requests to the information systems department. The ISD selects those it is best staffed to complete internally and contracts the remainder out to software development firms. In extreme cases, the functional area manager may contract directly with a time-sharing service for the needed support.

This approach has the advantages of keeping responsibility for functional performance with the functional manager; it identifies critical short-term needs for information and satisfies those needs quickly; and it lowers the level of user resistance. However, it has several drawbacks. Programs developed in this manner often lack standardization and are incompatible with programs developed for other managers. The quality of documentation may vary widely, and it may prove economically infeasible to maintain those that are poorly documented. There will be severe imbalances in computerized support among the functional areas. Those managers comfortable with technology may develop programs that provide a minimal return on investment, whereas less technically inclined managers may fail to use automated assistance in even the highest payback areas. Most significant, an organization which permits this type of development cannot effectively use information to improve its overall performance.

In spite of these considerable shortcomings, many firms continue to operate in this mode. In a recent survey, the ISD manager of a major division of a Fortune 100 company noted: "We have no master plan, no approval process and no backlog. If a manager wants something programmed, we get the job done. We serve mainly a brokerage and quality control function with software houses doing the bulk of the programming to our specifications. The profit center manager has the sole responsibility for cost effectiveness of the projects." While few firms have such a policy of total decentralization for their large systems operations, the widespread introduction of the microcomputer into organizations in the mid-1980s produced the same de facto effect.

A Common Synthesis

Many organizations have selected the more desirable features from the centralized and decentralized extremes and integrated them with their usual business planning practices. A common synthesis is to establish the general goals for the management information system and to set standards for all applications developments as part of an overall systems development plan. Within this broad centralized scheme, individual managers and departments are encouraged to submit requests for application developments. The requests are processed in accordance with the procedures the firm uses to reach any other resource allocation decision. Under these procedures, the functional department is usually responsible for estimating the benefits and organizational feasibility of the project, and the ISD is responsible for estimating the cost and technical feasibility of the development. When requests for development exceed the resources the organization is willing or able to commit to its information systems support, the ISD manager recommends the priority for development in consonance with the strategic IS plan. This recommendation is reviewed and approved by top management. The result of this process is a firm plan for software development for a 6- or 12-month period.

The synthesis approach ensures a reasonable balance of development across functional departments. It also ensures that the projects selected for development contribute to the overall goals of the organization, that they meet reasonable cost-effectiveness criteria, and that they are endorsed by operational-level management. However, it too has potential drawbacks. One is that the process tends to become rigid. The IS manager is evaluated on how well he or she sets and attains goals. Therefore, once a project is established in the development sequence, it may be difficult to reorder priorities to meet changing needs. Perhaps more significantly, the lengthy justification process contributes to the widely observed applications development backlog commonly acknowledged to be from 2 to 4 years and found to be as great as 7 years in some organizations. Nevertheless, this latter environment is the one most likely to be encountered by the AIS practitioner, so we will discuss the software development life cycle in this setting.

THE SOFTWARE DEVELOPMENT LIFE CYCLE (SDLC)

The concept of a life cycle implies that any software development passes through periods of conception, growth, maturity, decline, and finally termination. The process is usually divided into phases or stages. The definition of the SDLC phases is essentially arbitrary, and terminology varies from one organization to the next. The idea of the SDLC approach is to develop a rational plan of action which will (1) identify those applications which have a significant impact on organizational effectiveness or efficiency, (2) identify potential problems in the development as early in the cycle as possible, (3) involve all interested parties in the development, (4) examine a reasonable range of alternative actions, (5) provide for controlled programming and implementation of the selected option, and (6) provide effective management control throughout the development and subsequent operation.

The SDLC is a managerial response to an earlier laissez-faire approach to applications development—an approach that often led to expensive and spectacular failures, to developments that were technologically challenging but of little value to the organization, or to applications that were initially useful but soon fell into disuse. The SDLC is best viewed as a managerial planning and control device that embodies many of the systems concepts introduced in Chapter 2.

We will describe the SDLC in terms of four major phases: (1) project request and feasibility determination, (2) development, (3) implementation, and (4) operation. We will further subdivide the development phase into three stages: (1) project definition and analysis, (2) preliminary design, and (3) detailed design and programming. Figure 9–2 summarizes this structure, together with the activities and outputs characteristic of each stage and phase.

In regard to the AIS, we wish to emphasize the role of the accountant in the successful completion of the SDLC. It is the accountant who identifies the organizational problem to be solved or the opportunity to be exploited. It is the accountant who knows the details of the operational specifications and must transmit these to a systems analyst. It is the accountant who must ensure that the design proposed by the information systems specialists will be responsive to the specifications. It is the accountant who must be sure that validity checks will accept valid transactions and reject those that are invalid. It is the accountant who must maintain continuity of operations during conversion from old to new procedures. Finally, it is the accountant who must evaluate the software product and provide feedback essential to keeping it in tune with evolving managerial information requirements.

Phase 1: Project Request and Feasibility Determination

The object of phase 1 is to establish and justify the need for a particular software development. It is initiated by a request from the accounting department to the information systems department. The request may be in response to guidance from an information requirements analysis; it may result from a need for greater operational efficiency; it may be the result of a need for more sophisticated analysis at higher managerial levels; or it may be generated by changes in government

FIGURE 9–2 The Software Development Life Cycle

	Project Request and Feasibility Determination	*Project Development: Project Definition and Analysis*	*Project Development: Preliminary Design*	*Project Development: Detailed Design and Programming*	*Implementation*	*Operation*
Activities	Accountant initiates request Determine objectives Determine technological feasibility Determine organizational feasibility Preliminary cost-benefit analysis	Study existing procedures Specify functional requirements Initial software concept Intensive interactions between accounting and info systems	Refine objectives Refine specifications Develop alternative approaches	Structure program modules Code modules Program tests Module tests Write manual procedures Systems test Begin training	Conduct acceptance test Train users, operators, maintenance programmers Complete all documentation Change over to new software	Feedback discrepancies Request updates and modifications Evaluate software Evaluate development process
Tools	Narrative memos and reports Operational research techniques	Dataflow diagrams I/O charts Responsibility matrices Pert techniques	Systems flowcharts Decision tables Structure charts	Program flowcharts Nassi-Schneidermann charts Pseudocode Programming language		
Outputs	Study report Decision to proceed	Specifications documents Program schedule Pert charts	Output formats Selected approach Decision to proceed Freeze design	Tested programs	User's manual Operator's manual Program maintenance manual New system operational	Program maintenance log Evaluation reports

regulations or accounting standards. Whatever the source of the request, the initial effort must be to define the project objectives, determine that the proposal is technically and organizationally feasible, and make a preliminary assessment of likely benefits and costs. The extent of the study done at this time will be in proportion to the scope of the proposed project.

Key activities of the accounting staff in this first phase include identifying and defining any necessary assumptions, identifying alternative approaches, assessing the organizational impact of the project, identifying other affected functional areas, and providing both qualitative and quantitative estimates of the benefits to be expected from the development. King and Schrems[2] have proposed a useful typology of benefits that are likely to accrue from information systems development. Benefits may be measured in terms of cost reduction (CR), error reduction (ER), increased flexibility of operations (IF), increased speed of activity (IS), or improvement of management planning and control (MP). Figure 9–3 is a matrix of tasks often associated with AIS developments and their possible benefits.

At this stage, the information systems department will assign a planner or business systems analyst to work with the accounting users. The ISD representative will determine if the proposed project is technologically feasible within existing or planned hardware, software, and programming resources and provide a preliminary estimate of project costs. It is essential that accounting and information systems personnel establish a sound working relationship at this initial stage. The output from this stage is a study report that documents project requirements, establishes its feasibility, and includes a preliminary cost-benefit assessment. This report is the formal documentation which supports the request for development through the entire project selection process. The need to establish the importance of the project at this stage cannot be overstated, for this is the point at which numerous projects will be competing for limited programming resources. Only those judged to be highly significant to the overall organization's needs will proceed into the following phases of the SDLC. Only those deemed to be essential will receive a favorable place in the development queue.

Phase II: Development

Definition and Analysis. The definition and analysis substage is characterized by the detailed study of existing procedures, reports, and data structures; the detailed specification of the functional requirements stated in the project request; the detailed specification of the reports and data which will be required by the new system; and a software development plan. In this stage, the accountant retains primacy in reviewing existing procedures, proposing new procedures, and specifying performance criteria in regard to accuracy, validity checks, timing, and operational feasibility. Accounting personnel are also responsible for an assessment of the improvements projected for the new software and for defining the organizational impacts that must be anticipated.

Information systems department personnel are responsible for converting the functional requirements into an initial definition of the

[2] J. L. King and E. L. Schrems, "Cost Benefit Analysis in Information Systems Development and Operation," *Computing Surveys* (March 1978).

FIGURE 9–3 Typology of Data Processing Benefits

Task Category/Typical Tasks	*CR*	*ER*	*IF*	*IS*	*MP*
Benefits from Contributions of Calculating and Printing Tasks					
Reduction in per-unit costs of calculating and printing	X				
Improved accuracy in calculating tasks		X			
Ability to quickly change variables and values in calculation programs			X		
Greatly increased speed in calculating and printing				X	
Benefits from Contributions to Recordkeeping Tasks					
Ability to "automatically" collect and store data for record	X	X		X	
More complete and systematic keeping of records	X	X			
Increased capacity for recordkeeping in terms of space and cost	X				
Standardization of recordkeeping	X			X	
Increase in amount of data that can be stored per record	X			X	
Improved security in records storage	X	X			X
Improved portability of records	X		X	X	
Benefits from Contributions to Record-Searching Tasks					
Faster retrieval of records				X	
Improved ability to access records from large databases			X		
Improved ability to change records in databases	X		X		
Ability to link sites that need search capability through telecommunications			X	X	
Improved ability to create records of records accessed and by whom		X			X
Ability to audit and analyze record searching activity		X			X
Benefits from Contributions to System Restructuring Capability					
Ability to simultaneously change entire classes of records	X		X	X	
Ability to move large files of data about			X	X	
Ability to create new files by merging aspects of other files			X	X	
Benefits from Contributions of Analysis and Simulation Capability					
Ability to perform complex, simultaneous calculations quickly		X	X	X	
Ability to create simulations of complex phenomena in order to answer "what if" questions			X		X

Task Category/Typical Tasks	*CR*	*ER*	*IF*	*IS*	*MP*
Ability to aggregate large amounts of data in various ways useful for planning and decision making			X		X
Benefits from Contributions to Process and Resource Control					
Reduction of need for manpower in process and resource control	X				
Improved ability to "fine tune" processes such as assembly lines	X	X		X	X
Improved ability to maintain continuous monitoring of processes and available resources		X	X		X

Source: John L. King and E. L. Schrems, "Cost Benefit Analysis in Information Systems Development and Operation," *Computing Surveys* (March 1978). Copyright 1978, Association for Computing Machinery, Inc., reprinted by permission.

software to be developed. Documentation is written to ensure that there is a mutual understanding of the problem to be solved and to control the phases of development. Much of the documentation at this point is narrative in nature and may take a form similar to that of Figure 9–4 for specifying functional requirements or of Figure 9–5 for specifying data requirements.

The data to flesh out this outline are obtained by extensive and intensive interaction between the accounting and information systems staffs. At the risk of redundancy, we emphasize again that people remain the most important element in the information system. Inadequate communication between the parties involved at this stage will preclude success in meeting the project goals. The modes of communication used include memos, surveys, interviews, and observation of operations.

In addition to the narrative material, a number of graphic presentations may be used to enhance system descriptions. Use of graphic aids is a standard part of the training of all systems analysts. The accountant who wishes to communicate effectively with his or her information systems counterparts must be familiar with the fundamentals of these tools. The two most widely encountered aids in the early analysis stage are dataflow diagrams (DFDs) and input/output charts.

The dataflow diagram is the first tool used in structured systems analysis. It is a graphic presentation of data movement, processing functions, and the data stores necessary to support an information system. A dataflow diagram strives for clarity and simplicity in representing the system or subsystem under study. The number of symbols used is held to a minimum in the interest of emphasizing the logical solution to the problem. Only four symbols are used:

1. A labeled arrow is used to indicate an input to a process or an output from a process.

The purpose of the Functional Requirements Document is to provide a basis for the mutual understanding between users and designers of the initial definition of the software, including the requirements, operating environment, and development plan.

Contents

SECTION 1. GENERAL INFORMATION
- 1.1. Summary
- 1.2. Environment
- 1.3. References

SECTION 2. OVERVIEW
- 2.1. Background
- 2.2. Objectives
- 2.3. Existing Methods and Procedures
- 2.4. Proposed Methods and Procedures
- 2.5. Summary of Improvements
- 2.6. Summary of Impacts
- 2.6.1. Equipment Impacts
- 2.6.2. Software Impacts
- 2.6.3. Organizational Impacts
- 2.6.4. Operational Impacts
- 2.6.5. Development Impacts
- 2.7. Cost Considerations
- 2.8. Alternative Proposals

SECTION 3. REQUIREMENTS
- 3.1. Functions
- 3.2. Performance
- 3.2.1. Accuracy
- 3.2.2. Validation
- 3.2.3. Timing
- 3.2.4. Flexibility
- 3.3. Inputs-Outputs
- 3.4. Data Characteristics
- 3.5. Failure Contingencies

SECTION 4. OPERATING ENVIRONMENT
- 4.1. Equipment
- 4.2. Support Software
- 4.3. Interfaces
- 4.4. Security and Privacy
- 4.5. Controls

SECTION 5. DEVELOPMENT PLAN

Figure 9–4 Functional Requirements Document
Source: Guidelines for Documentation of Computer Programs and Automated Systems (*FIPS 38*), U.S. Department of Commerce/National Bureau of Standards, 1976.

The purpose of the Data Requirements Document is to provide, during the definition stage of software development, a data description and technical information about data collection requirements.

Contents

Figure 9–5 Data Requirements Document
Source: Guidelines for Documentation of Computer Programs and Automated Systems (*FIPS 38*), U.S. Department of Commerce/National Bureau of Standards, 1976.

2. A circle or a rectangle with rounded corners is used to indicate some process or transformation of data.
3. A pair of parallel lines is used to indicate a data store.
4. A rectangle is used to indicate an element of the system's environment. The rectangle represents an interface with some other subsystem; it is either the source of an input or a destination of an output from the system being developed.

Dataflow diagrams are organized hierarchically; that is, there will be a master DFD (designated diagram 0) which will indicate the overall flow of data within the system. Each of the circles in diagram 0 may be viewed as a black box. At this level we are concerned only with inputs and outputs. Each circle is then expanded to show its internal processes and transformations. The DFDs at this level are designated diagram 1, diagram 2, and so on. These numbered diagrams may include circles which represent black boxes expanded in diagram 1a, diagram 1b, and so on. The process of expansion can continue in as many hierarchical levels as may be required to represent the complexity of the system. Figure 9–6 illustrates diagram 0 for a payroll system and Figure 9–7 illustrates the expansion of one of its transformations. The dataflow diagram divorces the concepts of the system under study

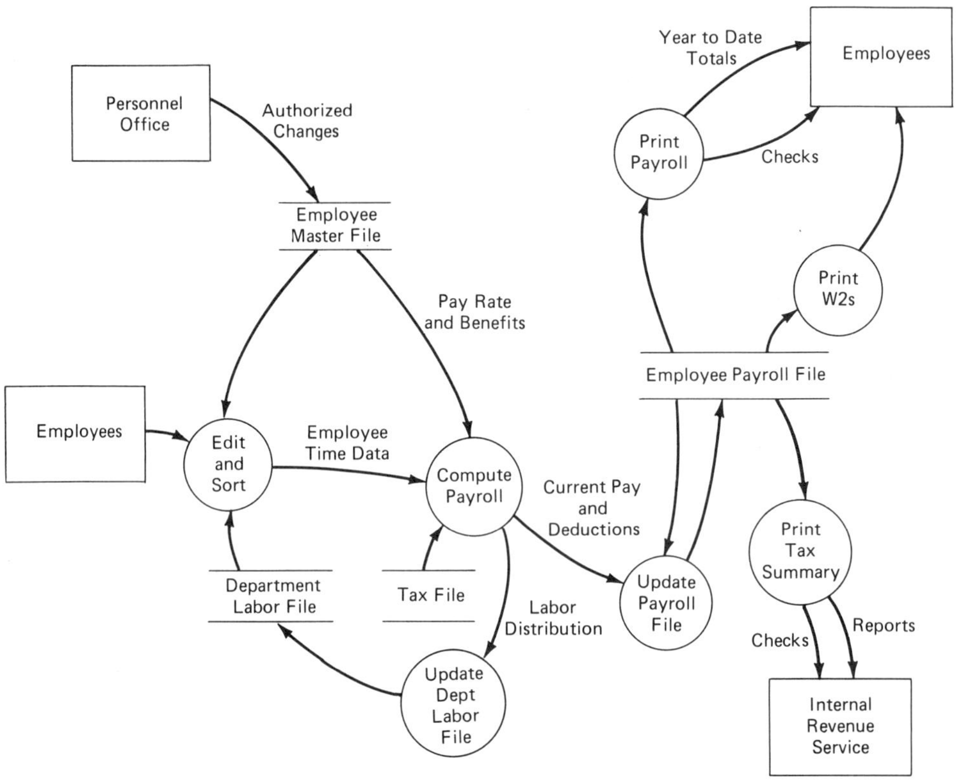

FIGURE 9–6 Diagram Zero for a Payroll System

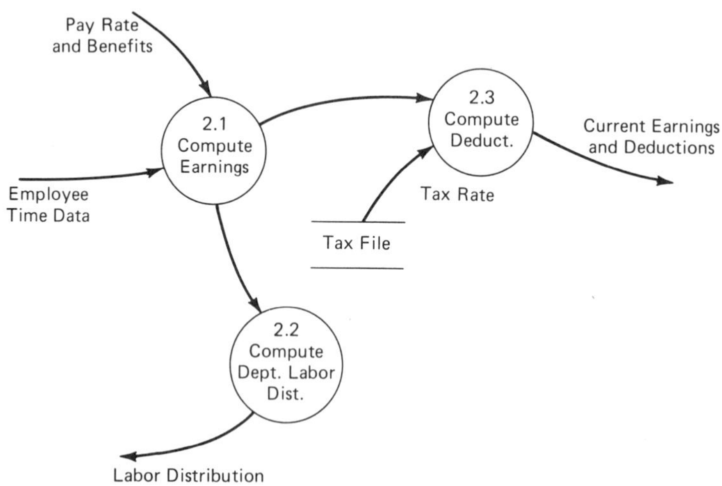

FIGURE 9–7 Diagram 2: Compute Payroll. An Expansion of Figure 9–6

from any hardware or software constraints. It is particularly appropriate when undertaking the design of a totally new system.

Input/output charts may be used for a number of purposes. Typically, systems development proceeds in what might be considered a back to front manner; that is, we start by specifying the outputs we want from a system and then determine if we have, or if we can develop, all the inputs necessary to generate the end products. A realistic input/output table for an accounting application would cover several pages of this book. Figure 9–8 is an abbreviated version that will illustrate the principle. The central column identifies all the data

Application: Payroll Subsystem												
Source(s)						Data	Use(s)					
Dept. Code	Current Emp. Master File	Tax Table	Payroll Master	Time Card	Computed	Element Name	Update Emp. Payroll Master	Update Emp. Master File	Update Dept. Labor File	Paychecks	Emp. Pay Summary	Tax Summery
						Employee ID						
						Employee Name						
						Department Code						
						Pay Rate						
						Hours Worked						
						Current Gross Pay						
						Tax Rate: Current Fed. Tax						
						Current FICA						
						Current State Tax						
						Current Deduct. 1						
						Current Deduct. 2						
						Current Deduct. 3						
						Current Deduct. 4						
						Current Net Pay Year to Date						
						⋮						

FIGURE 9–8 An Input/Output Table

items required by the application being considered. The columns to the right identify the reports(s) in which each item appears, and the columns to the left indicate the source of the item.

In addition to developing functional and data specifications, the project team will produce a schedule which establishes a series of milestones for completion of the project and a time-phased breakdown of the planned expenditure of project resources. The information developed in project definition and analysis often results in a change of scope of the project—automation of a function is rarely as simple as first envisioned.

For relatively simple projects, a Gantt chart may be sufficient to represent the project phases. For a more complex project, detailed program evaluation and reporting technique (PERT) or critical path method (CPM) charts may be necessary to control the development process. If the change in scope requires a significant change in the initial estimates of cost or time to complete the project, most organizations require a management review before the project can continue.

Preliminary Design. The object of the preliminary design stage is to convert the requirements formulated in the preceding stage into a programmable solution for the following stage. As the project moves from analysis to design, the accountants become increasingly dependent upon the information systems personnel for success of the project. Systems analysts will convert the dataflow diagrams into job streams and identify all major subfunctions that must be carried out. The accounting staff must be prepared to review the analysts' interpretations to be sure that the resulting structures will meet operational requirements and incorporate essential controls. Sections 1 through 4 of Figure 9–9 represent a typical output from this stage. As analysts and accountants improve their understanding of the problem, the requirements are continually refined.

The needs for accuracy, validation, timing, and flexibility will largely determine how the system will be subdivided into logical modules for programming. Final approval of these considerations remains with the accounting staff. Similarly, the needs for interfaces, security, privacy, and controls are within the accountant's domain.

During preliminary design, the information systems staff will examine several means of satisfying the requirements. The selection from among these alternatives is based upon the technical recommendations of the ISD and the operational recommendations of the accounting department. This decision is the final checkpoint before entering the detailed design and programming stage. Any errors or omissions which go undetected will result in less than fully satisfactory software. Typically, the design is frozen at this point so that detailed design and programming can be managed efficiently. Minor logical

The purpose of the System/Subsystem Specification is to specify for Analysts and Programmers the requirements, operating environment, design characteristics, and program specifications (if desired) for a system or subsystem.

Contents

FIGURE 9–9 System/Subsystem Specification
Source: Guidelines for Documentation of Computer Programs and Automated Systems (*FIPS 38*), U.S. Department of Commerce/National Bureau of Standards, 1976.

and cosmetic changes identified after this will be consolidated for the initial maintenance review. Major changes that might invalidate the design may be cause for reevaluation of the project. Most institutions require a formal "signoff" on the part of ISD and accounting to the effect that the system can be completed within specified resource constraints and that it will meet all stated requirements.

The most important parts of the documentation produced at this stage will be precise descriptions of the printer reports and/or CRT screen formats that will result from the applications development. These must be carefully reviewed to ensure that they provide all the information necessary to support the control and decision-making functions of the intended users. In addition, the accountant needs to be familiar with several tools systems analysts use to represent logical flows and decision processes. Those most widely used are these:

1. Systems flowcharts
2. Decision tables
3. Structure charts

Systems flowcharts are used to illustrate the input/process/output relationships of a specified job stream within a system under development. A variety of symbols relate logical job stream flow to physical devices. Figure 9–10 illustrates the systems flowchart symbols that conform to the International Organization for Standardization (ISO) International Standard 1028, or the American National Standards Institute (ANSI) Standard X3.5. Figure 9–11 illustrates the use of the flowcharting symbols to depict the biweekly submission of employee pay cards, preparation of paychecks, and updating of related files within a payroll system.

Systems flowcharts make use of the black box approach—they are concerned with describing the overall process, and not with the details of any one operation. When properly drawn, they provide an excellent presentation of subsystem logic, interfaces, and controls. However, these flowcharts tend to become cluttered and unwieldy if the process is complex or requires numerous selective operations. The limitations of systems flowcharts have led to the development of other techniques for displaying system logic and structure.

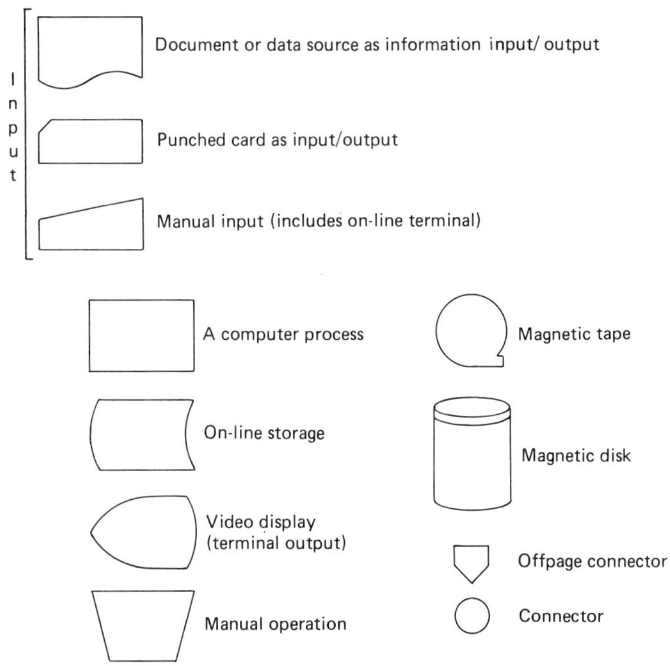

FIGURE 9–10 Systems Flowchart Symbols

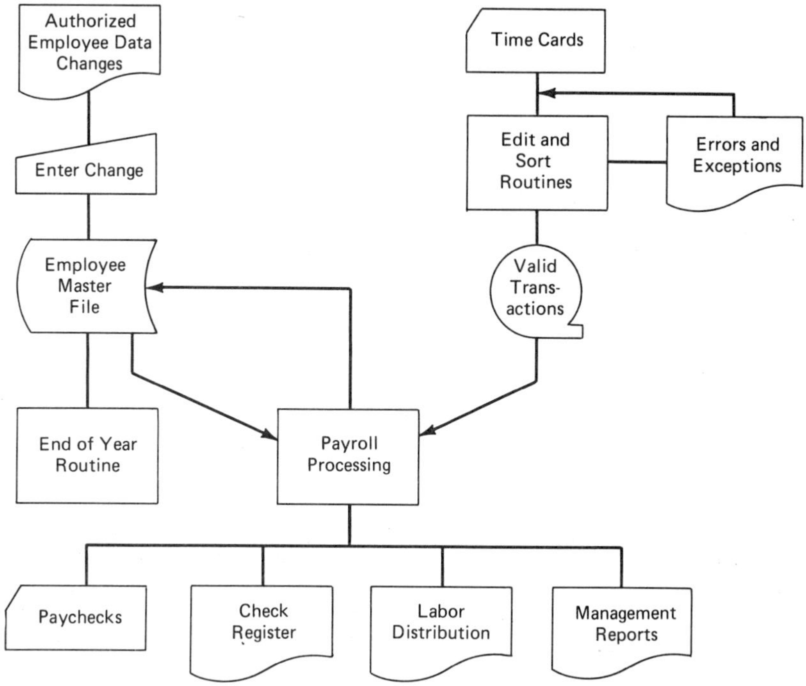

FIGURE 9–11 A Simplified System Flowchart: A Hybrid Payroll System

A *decision table,* for example, is often used to represent those portions of a system which examine a multiplicity of decision criteria and select courses of action based on the states of variables at a given time. In general, a decision table consists of a set of conditions, a set of actions, and a set of decision rules. Conditions and actions are stated in the rows of the table, and a decision rule consists of a column including both the states of the conditions and the resulting actions. The decision rule is read as a series of compound IF-THEN conditions and actions. Figure 9–12 shows a decision table that might be used to verify the validity and reasonableness of the data extracted from an employee's time card.

The *structure chart* is an intermediate step in converting dataflow diagrams into programmable specifications. Like the systems flowchart, it takes advantage of the black box approach. It is concerned with *what* needs to be done, leaving *how to do it* for later consideration. Unlike the flowchart, the structure chart explicitly supports structured analysis and design techniques. Figure 9–13 illustrates the use of a structure chart in developing the modules of a payroll program. The control module is assigned a name representative of the function to be accomplished by the diagrammed structure. Its purpose is to call the subfunctions represented by the working modules. Each working

		Decision Rules									
		1	2	3	4	5	6	7	8	9	
Conditions	Employee number valid?	Y	Y	Y	Y	Y	Y	Y	Y	N	
	Employee name match employee number?	Y	Y	Y	Y	N	N	N	N	Y	
	Dept. code valid?	Y	Y	N	N	Y	Y	N	N	Y	
	Hours worked equal to or less than 50?	Y	N	Y	N	Y	N	Y	N	Y	
Actions	Accept transaction	X	X								
	Call supervisor		X								
	Reject transaction			X	X	X	X	X	X	X	
	Call internal audit					X	X	X	X		

FIGURE 9–12 A Decision Table
Note: This table is truncated. In this case, an invalid Employee Number will result in an action to reject the transaction; therefore, there is no need to test the remaining seven possible decision rules.

module is a black box at this level of depiction. The structure chart is concerned only with inputs and outputs. This allows each working module to be independent of all others as far as its processes are concerned. As long as its output meets the systems specification, any internal modification does not affect any other module.

The structure chart uses symbols sparingly. Each process is represented by a square. The long arrows leading from the control module to the worker modules indicate a connection for the flow of information and control. The shorter arrows with open ends indicate that data are passed between the control module and the worker module; those shorter arrows with solid ends indicate the exchange of control information. Any working module that can be called by more than one control module is indicated by vertical columns in each end of

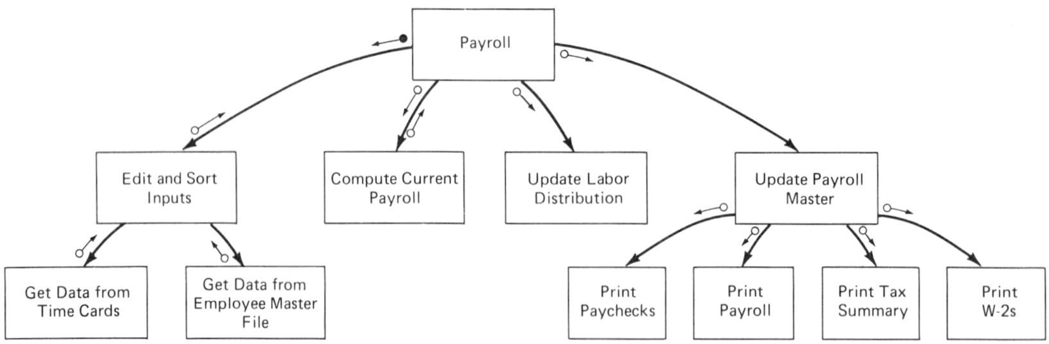

FIGURE 9–13 Structure Chart for Payroll System (See Figure 9–6 for corresponding dataflow diagram)

the module symbol. The structure chart is primarily a tool for the internal use of the information systems department; nevertheless, a review of this level of documentation by the user can assist in detecting system flaws or ineffective processes.

Detailed Design and Programming. The object of this substage is to produce the programs that will implement the problem solution and the essential supporting documentation. This substage is often considered to be the exclusive concern of the information systems department. We strongly disagree. In one of the most famous articles in the field of data processing, Ackoff[3] cited the case of an inventory control program that confused the reorder point with the maximum allowable stock level. This logical error occurred in the programming stage of development and was undetectable with the normal controls employed by the information systems department. It would, however, have immediately been detected by the user.

Regardless of who is conducting the actual work, the responsibility for the accuracy of accounting reports remains a responsibility of the accounting department. There are two means of establishing that reports generated by an automated system will have this essential property: (1) The detailed processes to be used in computing output values must be reviewed; and (2) the programs written to support the processes must be tested exhaustively. The first requires that knowledgeable managers check the logic to be programmed; the second requires that knowledgeable managers participate actively in program, module, subsystem, and system testing.

A review of the logic systems analysts develop to address a problem is time-consuming, but not difficult. The tools used in this process are the result of concerted efforts to represent complex processes as simply as possible. Three techniques are in widespread use: program flowcharts, Nassi-Schneidermann diagrams, and pseudocode. These detailed design techniques permit a programmer to encode the logic of the solution into the computer language best suited for the application. The level of detail required at this stage precludes illustrating the use of these techniques for a complete module. However, our discussion and the accompanying diagrams should serve as an introduction and guide.

Program flowcharts are the oldest technique. They can be used effectively for relatively small or logically simple processes, but they become confusing and difficult to follow when longer or more complex tasks must be represented. In such cases, the analyst is faced with the alternatives of producing a chart with a large number of connector

[3] Russell Ackoff, "Management Misinformation Systems," *Management Science,* Vol. 14, No. 4.

symbols or one that becomes a veritable maze of interconnecting symbols. Program flowchart symbols are few in number and easily understood; however, they require a large amount of space to represent the process logic. It is not uncommon for a single flowchart to fill 10 or more pages. Figure 9–14 illustrates a program flowchart for a portion of a payroll program.

The shortcomings of program flowcharts led to the search for improved graphic presentation techniques for detailed design. The Nassi-Schneidermann diagram is one widely used solution. These diagrams embody the three basic components of structured programming in a concise and easily interpreted form. Figure 9–15a illustrates the N-S symbols for the separate structures and Figure 9–15b applies the symbols to the same portion of the payroll program addressed by the program flowchart of Figure 9–14.

Pseudocode is the last and perhaps the most widely used design tool. At first inspection it does not appear to be a graphic representation at all, since it uses standard English phrases rather than other symbols. However, these phrases are precisely defined and are assembled to represent the logical structuring of the required program. In effect, pseudocode represents the precise logic of the solution in a programming language without the distractions of having to comply with the syntactical limitations of any particular language. There is no universal standard for pseudocode, but all versions will have set phrases to indicate the beginning and the end of sequential, selective, and repetitive processes. Indentation from the left margin is used to indicate the nesting of processes. Figure 9–16a suggests a set of phrases for a generalized pseudocode system and Figure 9–16b applies this set of phrases to the same problem addressed in the previous two figures.

The accountant's review of the detailed design will ensure that the analyst has correctly interpreted the users' needs and presented a correct solution to the programmer; however, the only way to be sure that the problem solution has been correctly encoded is to develop and run test data that test every feature of the programs after they are written. This requires that accountants participate fully in the development of the test data and the analysis of the results. Each module must be tested to ensure that it performs its transformations as prescribed; each subsystem must be tested to ensure that all modules interface correctly; and the entire system must be tested to ensure that all subsystems interface as designed and that there are no unanticipated impacts on other parts of the total organization's information system. Tests at all levels must include valid transactions, and the results from the new programs must be compared with the results from a process known to be correct. Tests at all levels must include invalid data to ensure that such transactions will be rejected and that appropriate error messages will be generated.

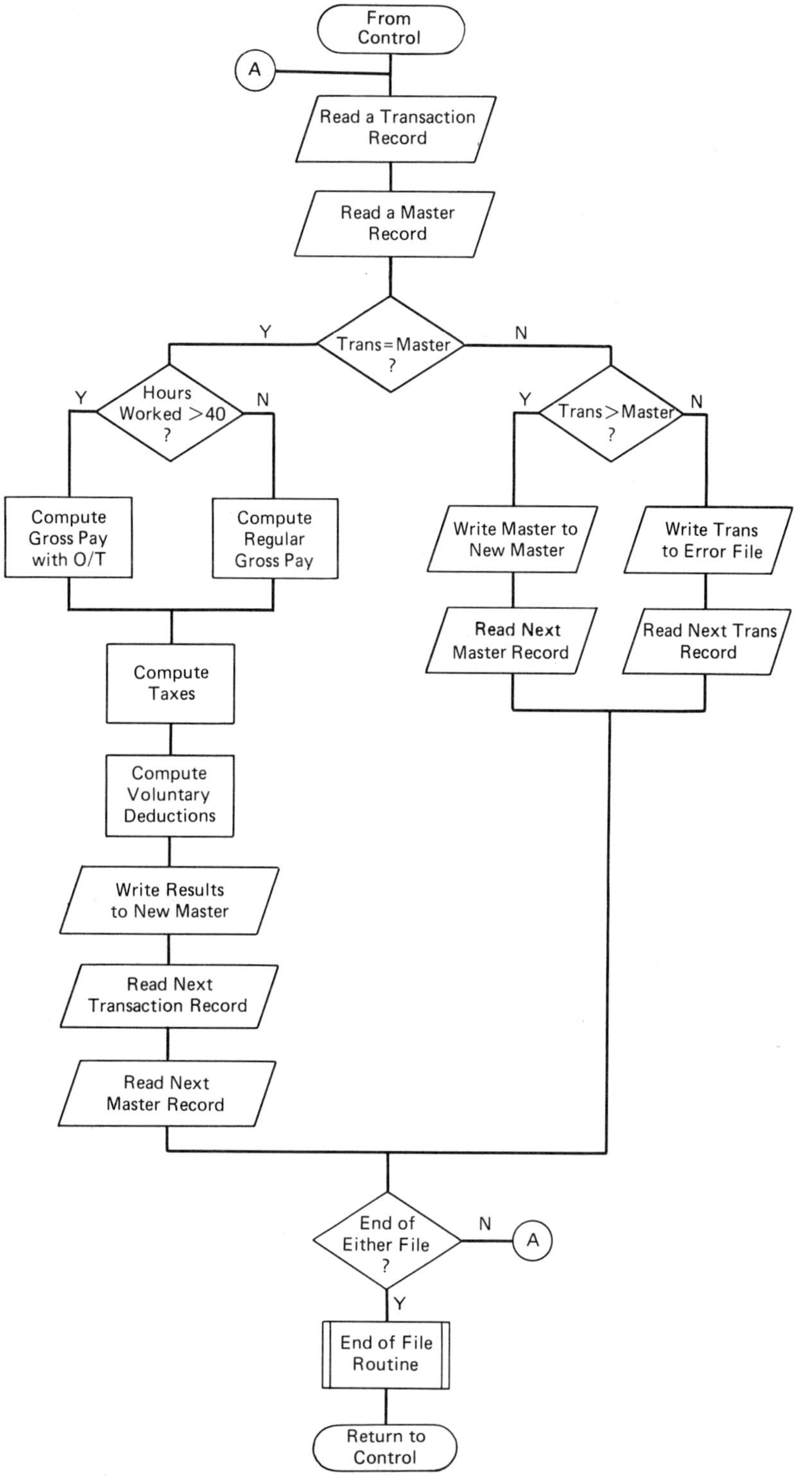

FIGURE 9–14 An Abbreviated Program Flowchart for the Current Pay Module

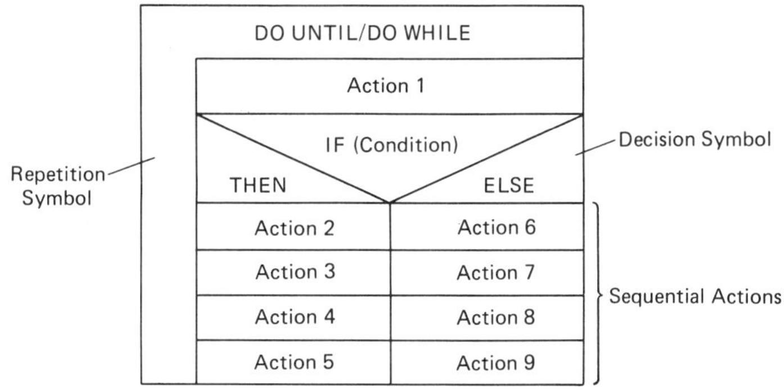

FIGURE 9–15a Nassi-Schneidermann Symbols

In addition to the technical development, other activities take place during this stage. No accounting information system is totally automated. At some point, human intervention is required to operate the system or interpret its output. These manual procedures must be specified by the accounting staff. These necessary desk and standard operating procedures must be developed along with the programming effort if the implementation phase is to be executed efficiently.

Phase III: Implementation

The object of the implementation phase is to convert from the existing support system to the new system. The essential activities in this stage include training, development of operational documentation, final systems test, and changeover to the new software.

Training and documentation must proceed on three levels simultaneously: the user level, the operator level, and the program maintenance level.

The user's manual will incorporate the input and output formats from the technical development and the manual support procedures developed by the accounting staff. It should be as free of data processing jargon as possible and should serve as a reference document for determining the applicability of the software to a user's problem, preparing input data, selecting appropriate output options, and interpreting the results of processing. Figure 9–17 shows a typical contents page for a user's manual.

The operator's manual will include the information necessary for computer operations personnel to set up and run the programs. It is particularly important that the operator's manual include instructions for abnormal conditions, restart, and recovery procedures. This level of documentation is not directly used by accountants, and it will be beyond the level of technical competence of most accountants to evaluate its quality; nevertheless, it is incumbent upon the user to

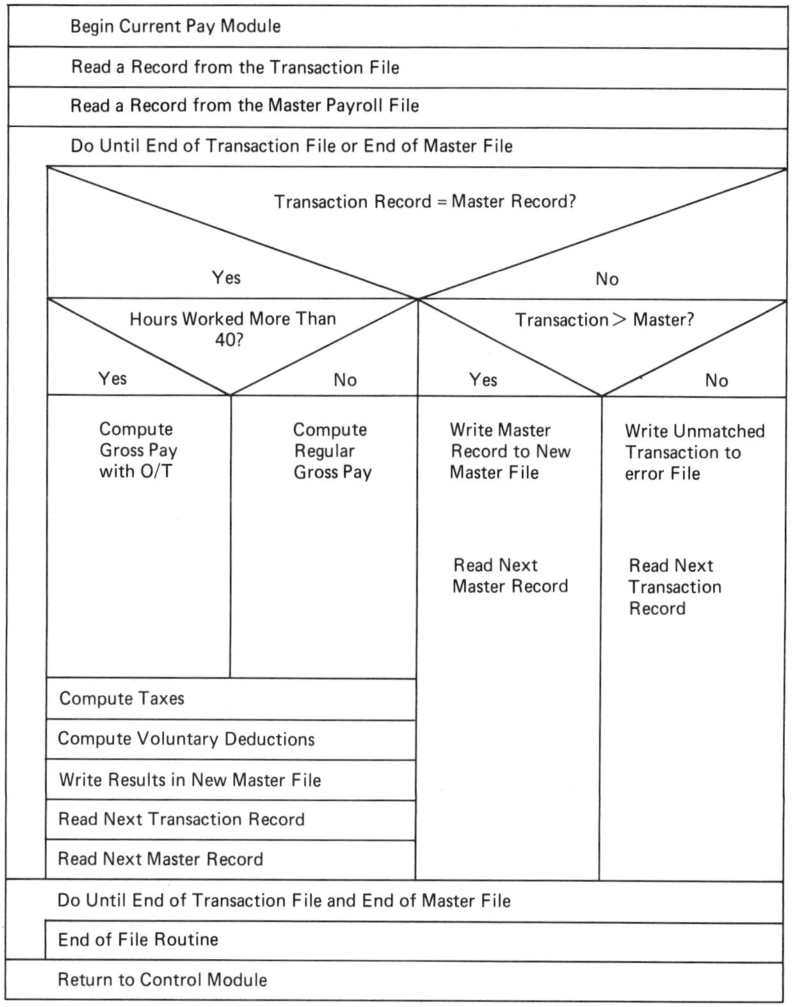

FIGURE 9–15b Nassi-Schneidermann Chart for Payroll Module

ensure that the new software can be run properly by any trained operator before that software becomes an integral part of the user's procedures. An operating manual that addresses the areas suggested by the contents given in Figure 9–18 should be in existence before the software is accepted for operational use.

The position stated earlier to the effect that all software features should be exercised during systems tests is normative. In practice, time and cost constraints usually preclude testing all of the nearly infinite number of conditions that may occur in a sizable software system. It is axiomatic in data processing that some untested conditions will arise during system operation. The result will be aborted runs or erroneous processing. There are well-documented cases of

```
Do Sequentially
.
.
.
End Sequence
IF
  ELSE
  End IF
Do Until
Do While
Do For
```

FIGURE 9–16a Typical Pseudocode Control Statements

```
BEGIN Compute Current Pay Module
READ First Transaction Record
READ First Master Record
REPEAT UNTIL End of Transaction File or End of Master File
  IF Transaction Record EQUALS Master Record
    IF Hours Worked GREATER THAN 40
      COMPUTE Gross Pay with Overtime
    ELSE
      COMPUTE Regular Gross Pay
    END IF
    COMPUTE Taxes
    COMPUTE Voluntary Deductions
    WRITE Results to New Master File
    READ Next Transaction Record
    READ Next Master Record
  ELSE
    IF Transaction Record GREATER THAN Master Record
      WRITE Master Record to New Master File
      READ Next Master Record
    ELSE
      WRITE Unmatched Transaction Record to Error File
      READ Next Transaction Record
    END IF
  END IF
END REPEAT
CALL End of File Routine
RETURN to Control Module
```

FIGURE 9–16b Pseudocode for Payroll Module

programs running satisfactorily for years before encountering some untested condition. When this occurs, it is essential that the programs be examined and corrected. The program maintenance manual provides the programming staff with the information essential to understand the programs and to expedite correction of inadequate code. As was the case with the operations manual, accountants do not use the program maintenance manual directly, but they do need to be sure the

The purpose of the User's Manual is to sufficiently describe the functions performed by the software in non-ADP terminology, such that the user organization can determine its applicability and when and how to use it. It should serve as a reference document for preparation of input data and parameter, and interpretation of results.

Contents

FIGURE 9–17 User's Manual
Source: Guidelines for Documentation of Computer Programs and Automated Systems (FIPS 38), U.S. Department of Commerce/National Bureau of Standards, 1976.

manual exists in sufficient detail so that any competent maintenance programmer can make corrections and updates as they are needed.

Training to use, run, and maintain the software will be conducted concurrently with and generally be based on the corresponding manuals. As these activities proceed during the implementation phase, there should be a strong synergistic effect between questions developed in the training sessions and improvements in the draft versions of the documentation.

The testing begun in the detailed design and programming stage reaches its culmination in an operational acceptance test during implementation. Operational testing is performed in the organizational environment with the purpose of ascertaining that all elements of the system—software, hardware, people, and data—are integrated into a functional system. Operational testing of a new system is often done with the live data from a previous reporting period. This ensures

The purpose of the Operations Manual is to provide computer operations personnel with a description of the software and of the operational environment so that the software can be run.

Contents

FIGURE 9–18 Operations Manual
Source: Guidelines for Documentation of Computer Programs and Automated Systems (*FIPS 38*), U.S. Department of Commerce/National Bureau of Standards, 1976.

that the new manual and automated procedures interact to provide a known result.

When all parties are satisfied with the results of operational testing, implementation continues to bring the new system into use. Timing is the first element to consider in bringing new software on-line. Software that is essential to support financial reporting should be scheduled for initial operation as far in advance of quarterly or annual closing dates as feasible. Many companies have firm policies prohibiting even minor updates to systems or applications programs within 30 days of annual closings. It has been found preferable to live with a small but known discrepancy in the existing system than to risk introducing some unforeseen problem at a critical time.

The conversion should be carefully planned and alternate procedures specified in the event the new system fails to function fully. There are several methods of introducing new programs; selection will depend upon a number of factors, particularly the extent of change being introduced, the urgency of getting the new system operational, the risk that can be accepted in the conversion, and the resources that may be expended in the process.

The most conservative crossover involves running the new system in parallel with the old system until all users are satisfied with the new system results. This is essentially a continuation of the operational test using live data. It minimizes the risk of new system inadequacies; however, it nearly doubles the costs of performing the function during the conversion period, and it incurs the risk that the new system will never be accepted. This parallel running approach is used for functions where reliability is essential. At the other extreme, the use of the old system can be terminated as soon as the new system is brought into operation. This incurs the greatest risk, but minimizes the crossover costs if the new system performs to specifications.

In between such extremes, the new system may be gradually phased in by one of several schemes. In cases where some new system modules are compatible with existing procedures, a modular approach may be used by implementing the compatible modules first and then introducing those that produce more profound changes. Some organizations operate multiple sites. In these cases, one site may be selected as the pilot for implementation, with further installations dependent upon resolving any problems discovered in the pilot operation. In still other cases, the new software may serve several functional areas. It may be possible and desirable to introduce these systems in increments that support one function at a time.

Phase IV: Operation

The primary object of the operation phase is to get on with the business of the organization with a minimum of concern for data processing. Nevertheless, certain activities are required to keep the software abreast of organizational needs, and others are beneficial to the long-range improvement of information systems support.

The principal item in the first category is a program change request policy which provides for adjustments, improvements, and changes that may be required. Errors will exist, and they must be corrected. Users will become more knowledgeable, and they will request more information. Times will change, and information requirements will change with them. The organization must adopt a policy and establish procedures to record these ongoing events and to incorporate the necessary changes in the programs. Collectively, these actions are known as *system maintenance.*

Evaluation is the key item in the second category. Evaluation should be conducted at several levels. From management's viewpoint, the objective must be to improve the organization's ability to implement software systems. Two criteria are of interest: (1) Did the development provide the benefits projected at the beginning of the SDLC? (2) Was the development completed within time and cost estimates? At the outset of the evaluation, it should be understood that very few SDLC projects meet both criteria, for many reasons. Some common ones are:

1. Environmental changes required a major change in scope or specifications.
2. The accounting staff did not fully describe the specifications in the initial request.
3. The ISD over/underestimated the resources necessary to complete the project.
4. The development was interrupted for one or more higher priority programming actions.
5. Unforeseen changes in hardware or software required a major redesign.
6. Documentation was not adequate in scope or not produced when needed.
7. The system was not accepted by users.

Many of the issues in managerial evaluation are extremely difficult. Skillfully done, the evaluation can result in feedback that will improve the SDLC; poorly done, it can result in defensive behavior by all concerned parties and a deterioration in intra-organization communications.

At the accounting level, the overriding evaluation criterion is user satisfaction. Typical questions to be addressed are these: Does the new software provide the information required? Is the information accurate? Is the information timely? For interactive systems, is the response time satisfactory? In short, the accountants are concerned with the effectiveness of the new system.

At the information system level, evaluation criteria will be more concerned with efficiency of the development process and the resulting products. Questions to be asked are these: Did we use an appropriate language? Did we employ productivity aids when possible? Are the programs designed to conserve CPU cycles and storage space? Is documentation complete and easily interpreted by its intended audience?

SUMMARY

The traditional software development life cycle (SDLC) is the most widely accepted means of controlling the development of custom-designed software in medium to large organizations and may be effectively employed by any organization that does in-house programming. The use of some variant of the SDLC is most appropriate to organizations that are currently in the middle stages of data processing growth—the control and integration stages as defined by Nolan.

Projects to be developed using the SDLC discipline are most often carefully screened and integrated into the organization's overall MIS master plan. Typically, the master plan is generated by combining top-down guidance, which defines the overall organizational goals and priorities, with bottom-up requests for application development.

The SDLC consists of a series of phases or stages. The end of each phase is a checkpoint which permits management to determine whether the proposed objectives are being achieved on time and within cost estimates. If not, corrective action can be taken in a timely manner. While the specific terminology relating to phases and stages is arbitrary and varies from one organization to the next, all versions of the SDLC follow the pattern of conception, growth, maturity, decline, and termination. Successful use of the SDLC process will result in selection of those application developments which have the greatest value to the organization, identification of all interfaces and potential problems at an early stage, control of the development in an orderly fashion, and integration of the resulting products into the organizational environment with a minimum of disruption.

If the SDLC is to be fully effective in supporting the AIS, accountants must be active participants in the process. They must take the lead in developing specifications that accurately portray accounting needs. They must ensure that the logic developed by systems analysts responds to the specifications. They must provide input to and analyze the results of program, module, subsystem, and system tests. They must develop and implement the user portion of the training schedule. They must develop office procedures that complement the automated procedures, and they must have final approval of operational test and changeover procedures.

To accomplish these tasks, accountants must be conversant with the tools used by their information systems counterparts and be prepared to review the documentation produced during the SDLC. The tools described in this chapter are those most commonly used today.

REVIEW QUESTIONS, DISCUSSION QUESTIONS, AND PROBLEMS AND CASES

A. Review Questions

A9.1 Briefly describe Nolan's six stages of development of the data processing function in organizations. How do these stages relate to the traditional SDLC?

A9.2 What is an information requirements analysis? Why is it important to the AIS practitioner?

A9.3 Describe the bottom-up approach to software development. What are its advantages and disadvantages?

A9.4 What are the relative advantages and disadvantages of the centralized and decentralized approaches to developing an MIS master plan?

A9.5 What is the significance of the term *life cycle* as applied to the development and use of software? In general, what are the periods in a life cycle?

A9.6 What are the objectives of the SDLC?

A9.7 What are the primary concerns of accountants during the SDLC? How do these compare with the concerns of the information systems professionals?

A9.8 What is the advantage of using dataflow diagrams rather than systems flowcharts in the definition and analysis stage of development? Are there times when a systems flowchart might be more appropriate?

A9.9 Why is the black box approach useful in the design process?

A9.10 What three techniques are commonly used to depict logical procedures in the detailed design and programming substage? Why should an accountant be familiar with these?

A9.11 Who is responsible for developing data for a program test? For a module test? For a full system test?

A9.12 What are the three areas of training that must be addressed if implementation is to be successful?

A9.13 What must an accountant know about user documentation? About operator documentation? About program maintenance documentation?

A9.14 What methods are used to introduce new software into the operational environment?

A9.15 Why is it necessary to establish a program change request policy and procedure?

A9.16 What are some of the reasons cited in the text for failure of SDLC projects to fully meet their cost and benefit projections?

B. Discussion Questions

B9.1 The validity of Nolan's stage development theory is somewhat controversial in data processing circles. What factors might permit an organization to bypass one or more of the stages? Could different departments in an organization be at different stages of development?

B9.2 Many organizations exist without an operative MIS master plan. What are some implications of not having such a plan?

B9.3 The text emphasizes that accountants must bear responsibility for successful AIS software development. Do you agree? Support your position.

B9.4 Which of the graphic methods for describing overall applications systems structure do you find most beneficial? What are some of the factors that would govern the selection of a particular method? Is it feasible to mix and match methods within a single development?

B9.5 Review Figures 9–14 through 9–16. Which figure provides you with the greatest information after a one-minute inspection? Do all your classmates concur with your selection? If you were to study the figures for a longer period of time, would your selection of the most informative method change? Which type of presentation is the easiest to develop?

B9.6 Suppose you are assigned the task of evaluating an AIS development project that was completed 6 months ago and has been in operational use ever since. How would you proceed?

C. Problems and Cases

C9.1 Archaic Paper Mills, Inc., has approached your professor for consulting assistance. Archaic has a 10-year-old mainframe computer that operates in a batch mode to service the accounting department. The mainframe is operated by the data processing department, which consists of a manager, one systems analyst, two applications programmers, and three computer operators. The DP manager reports to the vice president for administration. In addition to supporting all accounting functions, the DP department also produces a series of weekly printouts for the production department; however, these are rarely used, as they are perceived to be badly out of date. About two years ago, the sales department installed its own minicomputer in order to improve its performance in monitoring sales and following up on customer leads. The mini is a turnkey system provided by a small local company that specializes in sales support programming. The sales personnel are pleased with their system; however, the sales orders generated by the mini have to be manually keyed into the mainframe for accounting purposes. Last year the personnel department procured a microcomputer complete with a personnel management package. This has resulted in greatly improved service to employees in terms of maintaining benefits packages, performance reviews, and promotion data. As with the case of sales, the outputs from the personnel micro must be manually keyed into the mainframe for accounting purposes. Production is left out of the DP support picture. The production manager has heard of many productivity aids that could be used in his area, but he has neither the time nor the expertise to evaluate their use.

As a class project, your assignment is to plan a course of action that will result in an integrated MIS master plan for Archaic at the end of 6 months.

C9.2 Investigate the student registration and billing process at your college or university. At a minimum, your investigation should include the processes of (1) establishing a file of applications, (2) registering full- and part-time students, (3) preparing student bills, (4) establishing accounts receivable, (5) assigning grades at the end of a semester.

a. Describe these processes using a level zero dataflow diagram.

b. Expand the billing and accounts receivable function at the next level of detail.

C9.3 Repeat exercise C9.2 using systems flowchart symbols.

C9.4 Assume that as part of your investigation of the registration process, you encounter the following set of conditions: (1) If the student is registering for the first time, a new record must be established for recording grades and for maintaining financial status data. (2) If the student has attended classes in a previous semester, his or her records must be updated. (3) If registering for three or more courses, the student is billed at the full-time student rate of $6000 per semester for tuition and fees. (4) If registering for one or two courses, the student is billed at the rate of $400 per semester hour. (5) If the student is a teaching or research assistant, tuition charges are waived. Only full-time students can be assigned to these positions. (6) If the student is receiving financial aid, the amount of the aid is deducted from the bill before the bill is presented to the student.

Write a section of pseudocode that will satisfy these conditions.

SUGGESTED READINGS

DEMARCO, TOM. *Structured Analysis and System Specification.* New York: Yourdon, 1978.

DOLAN, KATHLEEN. *Business Computer Systems Design.* Santa Cruz, Calif.: Mitchell, 1984.

GINZBERG, MICHAEL J. "Key Recurrent Issues in MIS Implementation Processes," *MIS Quarterly* (June 1981).

Guidelines for Documentation of Computer Programs and Automated Systems (*FIPS 38*), Federal Information Processing Standards series, U.S. Department of Commerce/National Bureau of Standards, 1976.

NOLAN, RICHARD M. "Managing the Crisis in Data Processing," *Harvard Business Review* (March/April 1979).

YOURDON, E., AND L. CONSTANTINE. *Structured Design: Fundamentals of a Discipline of Computer Program and Systems Design.* Englewood Cliffs, N.J.: Prentice-Hall, 1979.

chapter ten

Applications Development Alternatives

CHAPTER OUTLINE

INTRODUCTION

The traditional software development life cycle described in Chapter 9 has brought order and control to the process of developing applications software. Unfortunately, it has also contributed to an applications backlog estimated to be from 2 to 4 years in most large organizations. This backlog, in turn, has contributed to a widespread perception that the information systems department is unresponsive to user needs.

The hardware and software advances noted in Chapters 5 and 6 have made it possible for users to condense or bypass portions of the SDLC without incurring a major expenditure of resources and without exposing the organization to serious consequences in the event of failure. These new capabilities range from relatively simple on-line retrievals of information, through the development of prototype systems, to complete end user autonomy in developing or selecting applications programs. The extent to which these alternatives can be employed in any specific organization depends upon the state of information processing technology in the organization and the ability and willingness of functional area managers to utilize this technology. The extent to which these alternatives should be employed depends upon broader organizational considerations.

In addition to the increased potential for end users to access and manipulate data interactively, software vendors provide a wide variety of packages that can replace much of the design stage of the SDLC. Appropriate use of these packages can be of great advantage to an organization. In this chapter, we examine these alternatives and related issues.

INTERACTIVE ALTERNATIVES

The data processing technology that existed prior to the mid-1970s limited accountants and other end users to the traditional software development life cycle approach whenever they required new or revised automated assistance. An apparently trivial request—for example, to consolidate two existing reports into one—would initiate a full cycle of activity and might require a significant commitment of analytic and programming resources. The hardware, software, and data storage advances introduced into organizations since that time permit a much wider range of developmental possibilities. We will briefly review these advances in the applications development context.

Technological Considerations

Hardware. The most apparent hardware development is the proliferation of visual display terminals (VDTs) throughout most organizations. The VDT provides the capability for an interactive human-machine interface. The quality of this interface varies widely. The most commonly used mode is via traditional keyboard operations, but this may be enhanced by preprogramming functions to minimize keystrokes, by the use of electromechanical devices, or by touch-sensitive screens. Other, less obvious, hardware enhancements are also required if the applications development process is to be improved. The installation must have direct-access storage devices and, if acceptable response times are to be maintained, an enlarged main storage capability and a very fast processor. Steady and dramatic reductions in hardware costs have brought these capabilities within the range of most medium to large organizations. Microcomputer technology has brought many of the benefits of improved information handling to even the smallest sole proprietors. The microcomputer operating in a stand-alone mode permits the accountant to employ a large number of programs totally independent of the information systems department. These generally fall into three categories: word processing, spread sheets, and database management programs.

Software. Advances in general purpose software are also essential to support applications development alternatives. The products needed fall under the general rubric of fourth-generation languages. This title covers an ill-defined but generally agreed-upon category of products that includes complete nonprocedural languages, applications generators, report writers, query languages, decision support system generators, data dictionaries, and database management systems. Each of these products is described in Chapter 6. Different application development alternatives require different software products. A specific application may be completed with a limited set of software tools; however, the general purpose products—complete languages, data dictionaries, and database management systems—are necessary to facilitate and broaden the applicability of developments.

Databases. The alternative modes of application development can be executed in a file-oriented environment. However, limited access to data will limit the usefulness of such developments to a few users. Therefore, interactive system development is most satisfactory when conducted in a database environment.

End-User Considerations

From a functional viewpoint, the AIS end user is easily defined as any non-information systems professional who uses computer-generated information to facilitate his or her performance within an organization.

When we translate this definition into the realm of business data processing skills, a variety of levels of end users emerges.

Nonprogramming End Users. These are personnel whose requirements for information can be satisfied by predetermined formats. With respect to batch processing, they receive standard printouts that may be more or less detailed, depending upon the user's managerial level. In regard to interactive operations, their needs may be satisfied by responding to a series of preprogrammed questions (a menu-driven approach), or they may have preprogrammed functions which display the required information in response to a few keying operations. If this class of end users wishes new or additional information, they must request assistance from information systems professionals or more technically sophisticated end users. Nonprogramming end users range from clerical personnel who need routine, recurring information to support daily operations to senior executives who wish to review summarized performance data on a periodic basis.

Retrieval Language Users. These are personnel whose needs for information vary and cannot be fully specified in advance. The information requested by users at this level must exist in the database at essentially the same level of detail required by the user, although some simple summary and mathematical operations may be permissible. Further, the data must be structured and the performance designed so that the data can be accessed with little or no knowledge of its structure on the part of the user. Retrievals are made in the interactive mode. The results may be displayed at a VDT for immediate use and discarded, or they may be routed to a printer or graphics terminal for hard-copy output. In the former case, the supporting software will usually be programmed to select a suitable format by default. In the latter case, the user may have considerable control over how the data will be presented. The language used may be a query language or report generator limited to this specific use. Increasingly, entry and mid-level managers in a wide variety of organizations are expected to be proficient in the use of retrieval languages. An AIS practitioner in the 1980s should plan to attain this skill level.

Nonprocedural Language Users. These are personnel who need to create models, one-time applications, or prototypes of production software systems in support of their functional or staff responsibilities. In addition to the data retrieval capabilities of fourth-generation products, they are conversant with the full range of data structure, database access, and modeling capabilities. This level of skill is usually limited to staff assistants who use the full language capability on a regular basis or to systems analysts who are assigned to functional areas. The accountant who is familiar with the retrieval features of a fourth-generation language can often function at this level with some assistance from a product expert.

Procedural Language Users. The need for non-information systems professionals to program with procedural languages is questionable. Programming in these languages is a time-consuming activity that can severely affect other activities more traditionally associated with functional area management. In addition, programming in procedural languages requires precise program definition and frequent cross-checks to ensure that the programs execute the desired logic. The SDLC has evolved to ensure that the commitment of resources to this activity is not undertaken lightly and that adequate quality controls are built into the professional programming activities. It makes little sense for an end user to bypass these controls. Nevertheless, this level of user involvement may be appropriate as an interim solution in organizations where a significant programming backlog exists, where there is no nonprocedural language available, and where an end user has the necessary programming skill. Procedural language end users are most likely to be found in technical or engineering areas. The increasing availability of fourth-generation languages suggests that this category of end user will not be a significant factor in the AIS.

ALTERNATIVE DEVELOPMENT MODES

We will examine the alternative modes explicitly in this section and suggest some AIS examples.

Direct Query

Direct query refers to the capability for an end user to retrieve information directly from files or databases without assistance from the information systems department. It permits the end user to respond to his or her needs for information by reformatting existing data. In essence, it replaces the SDLC in those cases where all data to support a request for information exist on magnetic media and can be accessed by retrieval language tools. Direct queries may be structured or unstructured. Structured query capabilities will usually suffice for operational and some lower-level managerial requirements. The minimum requirements to support direct query operations are these:

1. An interactive terminal. This must be located at or very close to the user's normal work station. Experience has shown that personnel,

particularly those at managerial levels, will not willingly use terminals that are remote from their desks.

2. A menu-driven or screen-driven presentation. Although menu- and screen-driven applications presuppose a degree of structure in the information to be retrieved, they can provide a large number of options. Menu-driven systems present the user with a series of screens and instructions to select the desired category on each screen. Figure 10–1 illustrates a nesting of three such screens. An operational query can present as many as may be required to select the desired fineness of detail.

   Form-driven systems present the user with an outline of a form that may be more or less detailed. The user enters appropriate data into

A. After signing into system, the accountant is presented with the general ledger system main menu. Accountant enters 4 at cursor position.

GENERAL LEDGER SYSTEM
Main Menu

1. Establish Chart of Accounts
2. Make Journal Entries
3. Establish Reporting Periods
4. Print Financial Reports
5. Compute Managerial Accounting Ratios
6. Terminate Session

ENTER NUMBER FROM ABOVE

4

B. The accountant is now asked to select reports for display on the visual display terminal or to print in hard copy. The accountant enters 3.

GENERAL LEDGER SYSTEM
Financial Reporting System

1. Display Balance Sheet
2. Display Income Statement
3. Print Balance Sheet
4. Print Income Statement
5. Print Balance Sheet and Income Statement
6. Return to Main Menu

ENTER NUMBER FROM ABOVE

3

C. The accountant must now select the period of interest. Option 4 provides a listing of previous periods that may be retrieved. The accountant enters 2 and the balance sheet from the latest quarter will be output at the accounting department printer.

GENERAL LEDGER SYSTEM
Print Balance Sheet Menu

1. Print Latest Month
2. Print Latest Quarter
3. Print Latest Fiscal Year
4. Type "Help" to display other reporting periods available
5. Return to Main Menu

ENTER NUMBER FROM ABOVE

2

FIGURE 10–1 Three Levels of Menus in a Typical Interactive Accounting System

the spaces, as indicated by the preprogrammed movement of a cursor. Supplemental instructions and/or help facilities may be provided. Perhaps the ultimate in flexibility for screen-drive systems is Query By Example, a product of IBM. It is possible for a QBE user to examine and retrieve any data to which he or she has access rights without prior knowledge of any data item or file names. Figure 10–2 illustrates a query and response that would produce the names of all employees in the accounting department with a salary greater than $25,000 per year.

3. Access to functional area files. A file-oriented system can support direct query operations. However, retrievals will be severely limited in scope.
4. A nonprogramming end user. Simple direct query operations require some knowledge of terminal conventions; however, there is no need to have programming capability to perform a wide range of retrievals.

Although this level of query may seem elementary, it provides wide access to required information with the minimum requirement for end user training and relieves the information systems development staff from frequent interruptions to satisfy one-time requirements for reports.

The minimum requirements described above will not generally be adequate to support the needs for unstructured information that frequently arise in managerial and strategic planning activities. The more complex nature of these needs will require a query language. A query language is often a subset of a comprehensive fourth-generation language. Most require the user to formulate a verbal request for the data to be retrieved in some variation of a SELECT-FROM-WHERE

Pay	Emp#	Emp Name	Dept	Title	Salary
		P. Smith	Accounting		>25,000

1. The QBE program presents the accountant with a blank template. The accountant enters the name of the interest in the leftmost position of the title line. (In the example, the word "pay".) Assuming that the user account has the required permissions, the program then prints the names of the fields of the pay file in the remaining title row positions.

2. The accountant then makes the entries on the second line. The "P" entry is a command to print employee names. The "Smith" entry is an example of what the program should locate. The "Accounting" and "> 25,000" entries condition the reply to limit the names printed to those personnel in the accounting department who make an annual salary greater than $25,000.

3. The result of this query will be a list of employees' names that meet the conditions specified.

FIGURE 10–2 A Query by Example Inquiry

format, as illustrated in Figure 10–3. The SELECT clause includes the data elements which the user wishes to display, the FROM clause specifies the record type or types where the data elements are stored, and the WHERE clause may be used to select subsets of the data. The values in Figure 10–3 will select the same data for retrieval as the QBE example of Figure 10–2. Additional features of query languages permit the user to sort the data selected into a desired order, and to perform simple mathematical operations such as summing and averaging for numerical data elements. The user must know the query language commands and have at least a rudimentary knowledge of data structure and mnemonics to use the language effectively. On-line HELP facilities are usually provided to assist in retrievals. Continuing developments in artificial intelligence will make this level of inquiry accessible to less technically oriented users in the near future.

Report Generation

Report generation is an extension of the direct query capability. The usual response to a direct query is presented to the user in a standardized format referred to in data processing jargon as a *default option.* If the information being retrieved is to be reviewed by personnel other than those making the query, it becomes desirable to tailor the report to the intended audience. Thus the immediate user's needs may be satisfied by a simple columnar listing, but if the report is to be submitted to the user's seniors, it may require headings, more formal nomenclature for data items, date of preparation, titles, and subtitles. If it is to be used in presentations, it may be further processed into any of a number of graphic forms. Graphs, bar charts, histograms, or pie charts are among the options widely available. The use of a report generator requires a broader knowledge of data processing capabilities, but does not require greater in-depth knowledge of either procedures or databases. The capability to produce graphic output requires additional software and hardware, but again it does not require greater knowledge on the part of the end user.

```
SELECT EMPNAME
FROM PAY
WHERE DEPARTMENT = "ACCOUNTING"
  AND SALARY > 25000
```

FIGURE 10–3 A Typical Verbal Retrieval System
Note: This request will produce the same result as the QBE example of Figure 10–2.

Prototyping

Prototyping is a technique that employs interactive processing to produce a working model of a projected system in a very short time, usually a few days. Prototyping is particularly effective in situations where the users cannot specify exactly what information they need at the outset of the systems development process. It is also appropriate in areas where system requirements may be unstable. The initial working model is not expected to be complete. It provides the user with sample procedures and output products that can be quickly and inexpensively modified based on the user's interactions with the prototype. A series of iterations is at the heart of the concept. When the prototype performs to the satisfaction of the users, it is documented and delivered to the information systems applications group for detailed design and subsequent implementation. The key to successful prototyping is rapid turnaround, which requires extensive technological and personnel support.

The technology includes interactive terminals, a database management system, and a comprehensive fourth-generation language. The need for a conveniently located interactive terminal has been discussed above. A database management system, which facilitates access to all stored data necessary for the application, is essential to support the broad access to data implicit in most applications suitable to the prototyping approach. However, there may be isolated instances where prototyping operational control applications in a file environment would be effective. A fourth-generation language is required to create and modify file structures, to integrate library programs and models into the application, and to generate suitable output formats in the limited time expected.

Prototyping requires personnel who have a thorough knowledge of the business function under consideration, the underlying database structure, and the full features of a fourth-generation language. Success depends upon the active participation and immediate response of the proposed end users. For a small project, a single individual might possess all these required skills. In an AIS, such an individual would be an accountant with strong interest in data processing technology or a systems analyst assigned to the accounting department. A larger project will require a two- or three-member team. In the case of the AIS, this will be an accountant, a database specialist, and a language specialist. This team may be structured like the one used in the traditional SDLC, but it will function entirely differently. There will be no extensive interviews, and no pages of detailed specifications. Instead, the team will work together at a terminal to produce a live version of the application under consideration.

Prototyping can collapse the weeks or months normally expended on systems analysis and preliminary design into a few days. In organizations where these phases of the SDLC constitute the development backlog, the entire development process will be accelerated.

Full Applications Development by End User

Full development by end users is an extension of the prototyping capability. The significant difference is that the prototype becomes the operational system. The requirements for end user participation are essentially the same as for prototyping; however, in most cases the need to use the modeling features of the fourth-generation language will be greater. Applications developed in this manner will not utilize machine resources as efficiently as will those developed using second- or third-generation languages, so they are not appropriate for the high-volume operations typical of operational control. They may be highly effective in support of managerial and strategic planning activities. The most familiar category of end-user-developed systems is the Decision Support System generator discussed at length in Chapter 13.

Appropriate Use of Alternatives

There is no one best way to develop applications software. Three major factors affect the decision to use the SDLC or one of the alternatives suggested in this section: (1) the nature of the application, (2) the available technology, and (3) the level of expertise in the user community.

OTHER CONSIDERATIONS

The Information Center (IC)

The Information Center is an organizational structure designed to bring together the latest technological developments and the potential users of that technology. The center houses the necessary hardware and provides technical consultation in using software and accessing data. The hardware may consist of terminals operating off the central computer, microcomputers operating in a stand-alone mode, or microcomputers using data downloaded from the central computer. The software environment consists of the fourth-generation products noted above and ideally will also include an on-line data dictionary.

Human resources are critical to the success of an IC. Three types of personnel are necessary: a manager, one or more business systems analysts, and one or more product specialists. The manager's role is to organize the IC assets and to market its capabilities. IC managers play a key role in overcoming managerial reluctance to using keyboard devices. The business systems analysts must have a sound overall knowledge of the organization's business and a general knowledge of available software and databases. They play the role of catalyst, connecting the user who has a problem to the product specialist who can solve it. The technical specialist plays the role of advisor and consultant. He or she must be familiar with the details of the software products and available data in a specific area.

The original concept of the IC precluded any hands-on participation by the product specialist; the objective was to have the user learn the necessary system characteristics. However, in practice, the specialists usually play a somewhat more active role. The specific division of responsibilities between IC personnel and the users varies from organization to organization, but there is general consensus that the center personnel should provide assistance, and that the users should do the main body of the development. The formalization of end user computing in the IC provides the user with an entry into the information systems world and relieves the applications development branch of the information systems department from interruptions in its planned development schedule. It has proved very satisfactory in a wide variety of organizations.

Microcomputer Considerations

In the 1980s, the widespread use of microcomputers in organizations has provided additional alternatives to large systems applications developments and has accelerated the use of the other alternatives already discussed. The microcomputer operating in a stand-alone mode is an extremely powerful tool. In large organizations it may be used in a wide variety of tasks in support of managerial information needs. This reduces pressures for augmenting or changing existing large system applications. Common examples are creating and manipulating small databases, employing the ubiquitous spreadsheet programs to perform "what-if" operations, and using packaged programs in support of auditing and inventory evaluation. In smaller firms, the complete AIS function can be accomplished using a microcomputer and prepackaged software. The principal constraint in the stand-alone mode is that the data entry function is often tedious.

The advent of the microcomputer has had the additional effect of raising the information systems awareness of user personnel. Hands-on experience with the micro has led to an appreciation of the functions of data entry, data integrity, access to operational data, and the need for backup and recovery procedures. This new awareness has improved communications between users and information systems professionals in most organizations.

As microcomputer memories have increased in size, it has become increasingly feasible to download a significant portion of the mainframe database for manipulation at the micro level. This solves the data entry limitation noted above. Some experts in the field predict that this mode of operation will become dominant in the future, with the information system function having responsibility for the maintenance and integrity of the database and the user departments having responsibility for all applications developments.

Packaged Software

Many functions are sufficiently standardized across a variety of firms so that it has become profitable for companies to develop applications and sell them to prospective users. This has numerous advantages over custom development. It spreads the cost of the development effort over a number of organizations. It permits the prospective user to examine the final product as part of the evaluation process. The input requirements, output products, supporting procedures, and state of documentation can be known completely before committing to the product. If commitment is made, the application software is available for immediate implementation; there is no lengthy design and coding period.

Packaged software has gained acceptance slowly in large organizations, for a number of reasons. Historically, such products were not available when the need for them first arose. Therefore, those organizations that have had established data processing activities for a long period of time have developed large libraries of custom software. Data processing managers often prefer to continue this tradition. Another frequently cited reason for not using packages is that the organization must adjust its procedures to conform to the needs of the software. This is often unacceptable. Nevertheless, a major banking institution in the Northeast United States recently reached a policy decision that all new applications must use packaged products. The rationale for this was based on two considerations. First, the bank's experience with custom software was less than satisfactory. Many developments were overtaken by events before they could become fully implemented, in spite of the most careful review process. Second, the banking industry's needs are highly standardized. This bank's managers felt that any function that needed to be performed could be covered by a packaged product. If there was no product available, then there was no bona fide need to perform the function. While one may take issue with the validity of this position, it clearly makes the point that packaged products should be considered as a first alternative to any new applications development request. Table 10–1 summarizes the advantages and possible pitfalls of using packages.

TABLE 10–1 Advantages and Pitfalls of Purchased Software Packages

Advantages
- Lower costs—Development costs are spread among all clients
- Faster implementation—Programs are already written
- Personnel savings—Fewer in-house programmer-analysts required
- Reliability—Can verify with other customers
- Documentation—Available for inspection
- Training—Part of package buy as required
- User group may exist

Pitfalls
- Incompatibility—May not be compatible with existing procedures or other installed software
- Maintainability—Customization may lead to difficulties in updating programs
- Vendor stability—May abandon product or go out of business

SUMMARY

The time and cost limitations of the traditional software development life cycle have contributed to the need for alternative means of developing applications programs.

Alternative development techniques require interactive hardware and software technology. Visual display terminals (VDTs) and fourth-generation languages are the most apparent of these needs; however, they must be supported by direct-access storage devices, database management systems, data dictionaries, nonprocedural languages, and sophisticated operating systems if they are to be used effectively.

Proficiency with the hardware and software tools is another factor in effective use of the alternative techniques. End user capabilities vary from using menu-driven retrieval systems through developing a complete operational system using fourth-generation languages.

The Information Center is an organizational development which has assisted end users to satisfy their processing needs. It has been employed successfully in a wide variety of organizations. The widespread use of microcomputers has presented still another alternative to centralized systems development. At the same time it has led end users to a higher level of computer knowledge and a greater understanding of the capabilities of larger systems.

The availability of a wide variety of well-written, documented, and supported software packages permits an organization to bypass the design stage in the software development life cycle when these packages meet the organization's needs.

REVIEW QUESTIONS, DISCUSSION QUESTIONS, AND PROBLEMS AND CASES

A. Review Questions

A10.1 What are two factors limiting the use of applications development alternatives?

A10.2 What hardware components are necessary to support fully interactive development alternatives?

A10.3 What general purpose software products are essential to support fully interactive development alternatives?

A10.4 In the context of applications development alternatives, why is a database environment superior to a file-oriented environment?

A10.5 Name four categories of end user. Are these categories discrete, or do they represent an arbitrary division of a continuous spectrum of abilities?

A10.6 How does a menu-driven system differ from a forms-driven system?

A10.7 What are four modes of interactive end user applications development?

A10.8 What is prototyping? What is its role in applications development?

A10.9 What are three factors to be considered in selecting an applications development mode?

A10.10 What is an Information Center? What are its objectives?

A10.11 What types of personnel are needed in an Information Center?

A10.12 What are the current and projected effects of the microcomputer on the applications development process?

A10.13 What parts of the SDLC are replaced when an organization elects to buy a packaged software product? What are the advantages of using packages compared to following a custom-designed development path?

B. Discussion Questions

B10.1 Why has the SDLC described in Chapter 9 been supplemented by other means of applications development in many organizations?

B10.2 Refer to Nolan's stages of development described in Chapter 9. In what stage(s) is interactive development of applications most likely to be found? Why?

B10.3 What level of ability in the use of such third-generation languages as COBOL, FORTRAN, BASIC, Pascal is appropriate for an AIS practitioner? Support your position.

B10.4 What level of ability in the use of fourth-generation languages such as FOCUS, RAMISII, MAPPER, NOMAD is appropriate for an AIS practitioner? Support your position.

B10.5 An entry-level accountant is expected to be proficient in the use of microcomputers with prepackaged software. What effect will this have on the traditional SDLC? On the relationships between the accounting and IS departments?

B10.6 What phase(s) of the traditional SDLC are most affected by the prototyping process? By a decision to buy a packaged program rather than developing custom software? By the ability of an end user to generate his or her own reports? Which of the alternative development techniques substitutes for the implementation and operations phases?

C. Problems and Cases

C10.1 The Midlands National Bank was among the first institutions in its area to establish an Information Center. The IC manager insists that her staff is to consult with and assist users, but in no circumstances are they to perform the "hands-on" features of a development. The center had great success for about 12 months, but it is now beset with problems. Many of the staff consultants have left, and those remaining are looking for new assignments. The flow of users is steadily decreasing. The MIS manager has expressed the opinion that the Information Center has completed its mission of training functional area managers to use their software effectively, and has recommended that the center be disbanded. Personnel currently assigned there could be reassigned to functional departments or to the MIS Department. What are some of the implications if this recommendation is adopted? If the IC is retained, what do you think should be its charter?

C10.2 The Josiah Bartlett Insurance Company has one of the most comprehensive information systems organizations in the insurance industry. A senior vice president has overall responsibility for all information systems matters. A vice president for data processing and a vice president for applications development report directly to him.

The Applications Development Division has the following capabilities: (1) A 20-person team devoted to program generation and maintenance in the assembler language in use on the company's large mainframe computers. (2) A 40-person team devoted to developing and maintaining programs in COBOL. (3) A 15-person team using a fourth-generation COBOL code-generating language. (4) An Information Center staffed by 20 persons knowledgeable in the entire range of mainframe and microcomputer software products available to end users. In addition, they are thoroughly cognizant of all database structures.

The Data Processing Division operates two large mainframe computers. In addition, it supports departmental minicomputers that are linked to the mainframes via high-capacity local area networks. It approves all departmental purchases of microcomputers to ensure that these products are compatible with the company network and can be economically maintained.

At the present time, the company has 13 million policies of various types in effect. Company policy permits customers to pay premiums on a lump sum, monthly, or quarterly payment schedule. Until June of this year, those customers electing a delayed payment schedule were charged 14 percent interest on the outstanding balances. A recent regulatory ruling has found this to be excessive and has directed the company to reduce this charge to 12 percent retroactive to the first of the year. Refunds must be made to all customers within 60 days, or the company faces additional punitive measures. You have been assigned the responsibility for completing this action. In view of the legal aspects, it has first priority for resources in the company. How would you utilize the resources available to attack this problem?

SUGGESTED READINGS

IVES, B., AND M. H. OLSON. "User Involvement in Information System Development: A Review of Research," *Management Science* (May 1984), pp. 586–603.

MARTIN, JAMES. *Application Development Without Programmers.* Englewood Cliffs, N.J.: Prentice-Hall, 1982.

SPRAGUE, RALPH J. JR. "A Framework for the Development of Decision Support Systems," *MIS Quarterly* (December 1980), pp. 1–26.

———, AND ERIC D. CARLSON. *Building Effective Decision Support Systems.* Englewood Cliffs, N.J.: Prentice-Hall, 1982.

part four

The AIS at Work

Controls in accounting generally focus on techniques and procedures to ensure that assets are safeguarded, transactions are authorized, and appropriate accounting principles applied. As a result, accounting controls are developed around the accounting functions—inventory control, cash control, and so on. When each of these controls is considered separately, it provides a fragmented and partial view of organizational control. The traditional view of AIS limits its domain to accounting controls and fails to address different levels of organizational controls. In this part we discuss AIS within Anthony's framework of organizational controls—operating controls, management controls, and strategic planning. The use of AIS at different levels of organizational control cannot be overemphasized, though the degree of use may vary significantly. To contribute to effective organizational controls, accounting students need appropriate exposure to the broader domain of AIS, which is the objective of the chapters in Part IV.

chapter eleven

AIS in Operating Controls

CHAPTER OUTLINE

INTRODUCTION

Controls in organizations have been viewed in many different ways. We have used Anthony's framework, which discusses three levels of organizational controls: operating controls, management controls, and strategic planning. This chapter deals with AIS in operating controls.

We begin with an overview of organizational control. To acquaint you with the most current view of organizational control, we have used Flamholtz's control model.[1] The overview is followed by a discussion of the characteristics of operating controls from the AIS perspective. The last part of the chapter includes useful and practical examples of operating controls in the AIS.

Accounting controls are basic organization controls—they do not exist in a vacuum. Accounting controls are influenced by the forces of higher-level controls. The higher-level controls that exist in an organization emanate from the (a) structure, (b) culture, and (c) environment of the organization. The basic controls, of which accounting controls are parts, are called core controls. The core controls are at the center of all controls.

CORE CONTROLS

Core controls are basic and involve the processes of planning, operation, measurement, evaluation, and reward. Accounting controls fall within the classification of core controls. Subsequent chapters on control, which discuss operating controls, management controls, and strategic planning, also deal with core controls.

The Context

Structure. Organizational structure is commonly viewed as a set of rules, procedures, roles, and relationships. Accounting systems are designed and operated within the structural framework of an organization. For example, a centralized organization where decision-making authority is concentrated in one place employs an AIS that facilitates the flow of information as unabridged and primary data towards the center location. On the other hand, a decentralized organization where decision-making authority is delegated to different segments of the organization processes more information at the segment levels; only summary reports and figures are transmitted upward.

[1] Eric G. Flamholtz, "Accounting, Budgeting and Control Systems in Their Organizational Context: Theoretical and Empirical Perspectives," *Accounting, Organization, and Society*, 8, 2/3 (1983), pp. 153–169.

Culture. Each organization develops certain cultural niches for its people. The cultural norms comprise the value systems, beliefs, assumptions, and procedures within the organization. For example, Sears Roebuck's belief in customer satisfaction has many implications for control systems. It must make sure product quality and customer services are provided as guaranteed.

Environment. The environment of the organization sets the outer boundary for the organizational culture, and that in turn influences the structure and core control systems. Competition and technology are two very important environmental factors that have significant influences on organizational culture and structure. Organizational culture and structure have profound effects on the AIS design and operation.

The Core Control System

A fully developed core control system has five basic elements:

1. Planning and standards
2. Operations
3. Results
4. Measurement and evaluation
5. Feedback and correction

1. *Planning activities and setting performance standards.* These provide the base for a control system. Examples: (a) Setting budget targets for production or salespeople is the planning component of the budgetary control; (b) setting cash retrieval procedure for an automatic teller machine; (c) setting minimum stock level for inventory control.

2. *Operation.* The actual functioning of the subsystem, such as (a) Withdrawing money from the automatic teller machine; (b) achieving actual production or making sales; issuing, ordering or receiving stores.

3. *Results.* Reports of operating performance, such as (a) Actual production quality and quantity; (b) sales made in units and dollars; (c) stores used and stock level maintained.

4. *Measurement and evaluation.* Comparison of the results achieved with the planned standards and targets to evaluate the performance variance (deviation) as satisfactory or unsatisfactory: for example, (a) production is below the budget; (b) lack of adequate inventory; (c) auto teller wrongly processes certain customers.

5. *Feedback and correction.* The results when compared with the standards may indicate weaknesses in the control system, which are

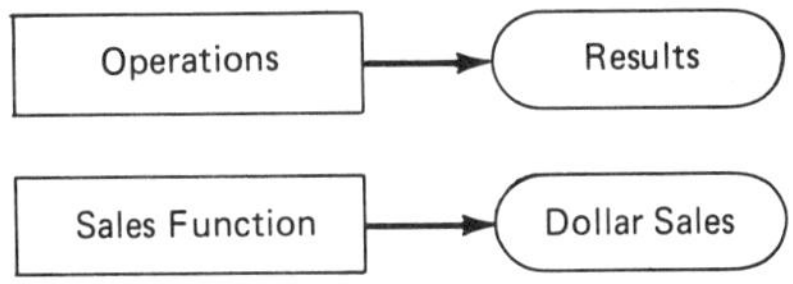

FIGURE 11–1

corrected at the time of the subsystem evaluation. Examples: *Production budget deviations due to:* (a) incorrect prediction of sales; (b) nonavailability of raw materials; (c) other, e.g., a strike. *Corrective actions:* (a) improve sales forecasting technique; (b) review minimum inventory level, purchase order system, or other variables.

This framework may be used to explain control systems at any level of operating control, managerial control, and strategic planning.

Some forms of control exist in all organizations. For example, the cash register used in almost all businesses is an example of a simple operating control for a cash and accounting information subsystem. If the cash register provides a printed tape of transactions, it can be analyzed at day's end to determine (a) cash sales, (b) cash balance, and (c) different items sold. Superior systems will have higher capabilities for data manipulation and versatile uses, such as the point of sale system (POS) discussed later in this chapter.

Accounting controls work with AIS support. AIS support determines the extent of accounting controls an organization can have. Organizations invest in AIS as they need, and prescribe the degree of controls desired. A first-degree control is a simple operating report that can be achieved by any simple system. Higher degrees of controls add more steps to the system. The following paragraphs illustrate first-degree and second-degree core controls accompanied by accounting examples.[2]

A first-degree control system has a simple relationship between results and operations, as Figure 11–1 shows. This is usually observed in small businesses like grocery stores, professional services, and restaurants.

A second-degree control adds planning to precede the operation or measurement as corrective feedback to the operation, as Figure 11–2 shows.

When purchases of inventory and supplies involve substantial financing, consideration for lead time and capacity utilization become imperative; usually sales planning is included to precede the operation stage. As business begins to grow, a planning stage becomes essential. Organizations may choose to add a measurement loop for corrective feedback instead of a planning loop (see Figure 11–3). Here, accounting

[2] Ibid.

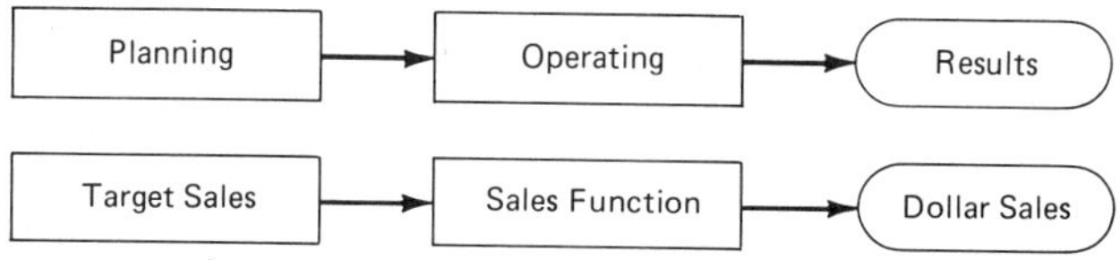

FIGURE 11–2

reports provide corrective feedback, which primarily indicates the correctness of sales and inventory and the discrepancies, if any. Measurement is made only for corrective feedback.

Organizations needing more information and capable of handling a higher level of manipulation incorporate planning functions with operations, results, and measurement loops (Figure 11–4). Here the AIS functions at two places: (a) in the planning process, developing a sales budget; and (b) in the measurement process, preparing sales reports for corrective actions.

Finally, an organization willing to motivate people by applying rewards and sanctions includes a measurement and evaluation loop for evaluative feedback (Figure 11–5).

Measurement provides feedback for evaluating the performance of people, along with feedback for corrective actions. Organizational reward systems and performance evaluation systems rely on evaluative feedback (see, for example, Figure 11–6). At the planning stage, accounting data are prepared for individual segments like sales territory, sales personnel, products, and product groups. These are then compared with the accounting reports prepared from the actual results incorporating the evaluative feedback (3 and 5, and 4 and 5 in Figure 11–6). This turns out to be a completely developed form of organizational control. A user or a designer of AIS should be careful to select the appropriate level of control configuration for an organization. This will save a lot of resources and wasted energy.

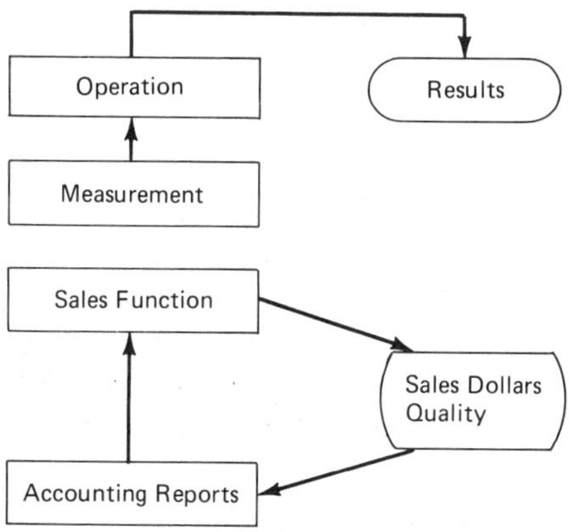

FIGURE 11–3

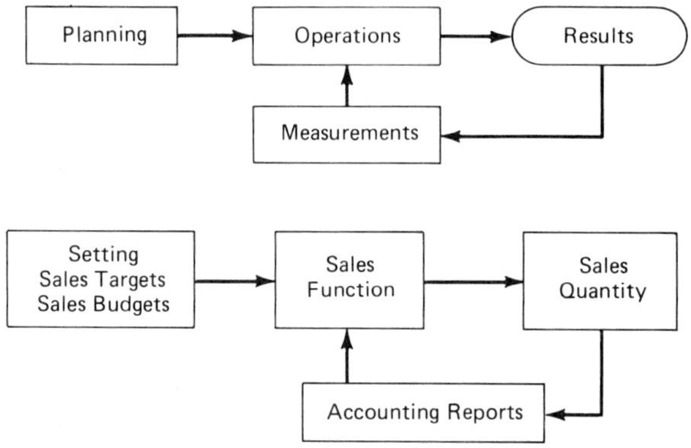

FIGURE 11–4

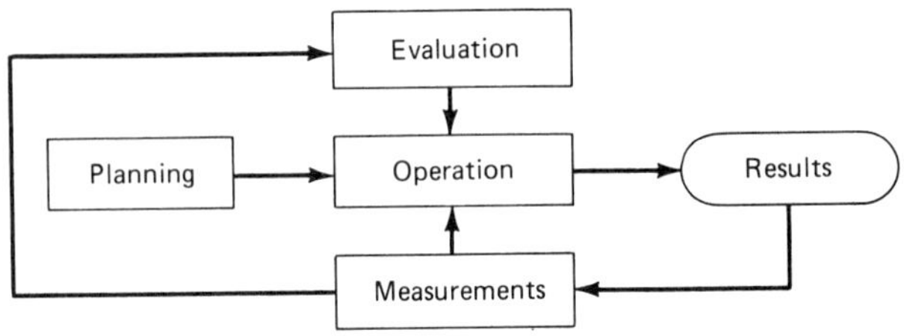

FIGURE 11–5

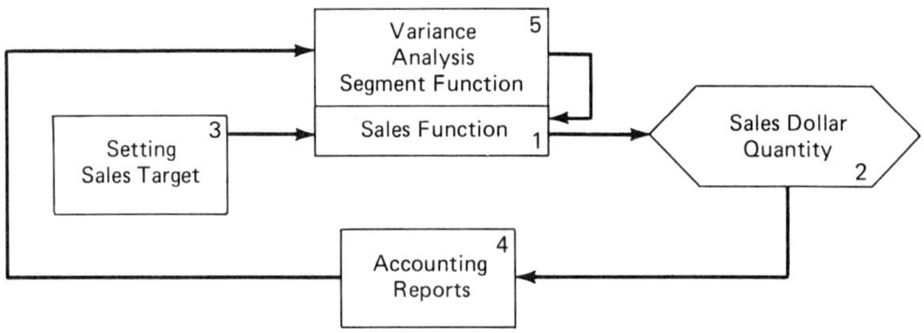

FIGURE 11–6

Behavior Control and Output Control

When the output is measured, monitored, and evaluated, it is called output control; when behavior of people within an organization is measured, monitored, and evaluated, it is called behavior control. Selective rewards are an essential part of behavioral control. Rewards are administered on the basis of a comparison between demonstrated behavior or achieved output and the present standards.[3]

[3] William G. Ouchi, "The Relationship Between Organizational Structure and Organizational Control," *Administrative Science Quarterly,* 22, March 77, pp. 95–110.

A CONTROL FRAMEWORK: OPERATING CONTROL

The study of control in an organization may be approached from different perspectives.[4] The control framework advanced by Anthony is widely used.[5] Anthony's control framework, defined in Chapter 1, has three levels: (a) operating control, (b) management control, and (c) strategic planning.

Operating control focuses on individual tasks or transactions. Management control focuses on a complete function and activity. Operating control works through defined rules and procedure, whereas management control is based on judgment and uses guidelines. Strategic planning deals with long-range planning, which provides direction for management control of potential products, services, markets, and resources. Table 11–1 shows the information characteristics of different levels of controls.

TABLE 11–1 Information Characteristics and Controls

Characteristics of Information	*Operational Control*	*Management Control*	*Strategic Planning*
Source	Largely internal	⟶	External
Scope	Well defined	⟶	Very wide
Level of aggregation	Detailed	⟶	Aggregate
Time horizon	Historical	⟶	Future
Currency	Highly current	⟶	Quite old
Required accuracy	High	⟶	Low
Frequency of use	Very frequent	⟶	Infrequent
Decision points	Subordinates and operating supervisor	⟶	Top management and the board of directors
Complexity	Simple	⟶	Very complex

Management controls fall in between operating controls and stategic planning from the decision and information perspectives. For example, inventory, credit, and quality control decisions fall into the operating control category; budgetary control, personnel development, production planning, marketing decisions (pricing), and accounting choices fall into the management control category.

[4] Post action controls, input controls, and specific actions are three control perspectives used by the following researchers, respectively: W. H. Newman, *Constructive Control: Design and Use of Control Systems* (Englewood Cliffs, N.J.: Prentice-Hall, 1975); R. L. Simons, "Control in Organizations: A Framework for Analysis," *Proceedings of the Canadian Academic Accounting Association Conference,* 1982, pp. 101–103; K. Merchant, "The Control Function of Management," *Sloan Management Review* (Summer 1982), pp. 43–44.

[5] R. N. Anthony and John Dearden, *Management Control Systems,* 4th ed. (Homewood, Ill.: Irwin, 1980).

Table 11–1 shows that data in operating controls are unabridged, detailed, internal, current, well-defined, and simple. For example, in inventory controls, the reorder points (ROP) and economic order quantity (EOQ) are preestablished. The stock clerk prepares purchase requisitions when the inventory level approaches ROP. A perpetual inventory record shows the current level of inventory; ROP and EOQ set the requisition criteria, and the preestablished ordering procedures define the steps to be taken. The stock clerk acts almost mechanically to prepare an order for merchandise. In many organizations this type of activity is performed by a computer, which will prepare the purchase order.

At the operating control level, the stock clerk deals with each item individually. At the management control level, total inventory costs are the focus, rather than the individual inventory item. Total investment may be reported by product line and by manufacturing and nonmanufacturing classifications. Strategic planning does not need any of these historical data on inventory. On the contrary, long-term future inventory needs are the focus. These are based on future products and markets, and may not relate at all to existing conditions.

Some characteristics of operating control decisions are outlined below:

1. They are based on a rational control system.
2. They employ a set of logical rules.
3. They employ economics and physical science as basic principles.
4. The focus of attention is a single task or transaction.
5. They use preestablished rules and procedures to provide direction.
6. They are repetitive and do not rely on judgment.
7. They are highly stable and predictable because they are based on prescribed rules.
8. They are based on a short-run current perspective.
9. They use monetary and nonmonetary units of measurement.
10. They are based on reports in the nature of "scorecard" and "attention directing." (*Scorecard:* What am I doing? *Attention directing:* Where have I gone wrong?)

Specific Accounting Operational Controls

A large number of accounting subsystems contribute to operating controls. The basic elements in accounting subsystems for operating controls consist of transaction processing, general ledger, subsidiary ledger, internal control procedures, standardized forms, and periodic reports. Common accounting operating controls include:

1. Accounts payable accounting
2. Accounts receivable accounting
3. Cash receipt accounting
4. Cash payment accounting
5. Payroll accounting
6. Inventory accounting

This list could be enlarged by including functional subtasks in areas such as production, marketing, research, and services. Nevertheless, we have decided to restrict ourselves to these six.

FRAMEWORK FOR OPERATION AND CONTROL OF PURCHASES

From the operating control perspective, a purchase transaction involves several functions, such as: (1) purchasing, (2) receiving, (3) inventory, and (4) accounts payable. Organizationally, these four functions are performed by four separate departments. Each department head is responsible for the efficient and effective operation of his or her department. For control purposes, each department is a basic control unit. Within these units, output controls and behavior controls are achieved through forms, procedures, standards, internal controls, audits, supervision, and formal evaluation. The location of supervisory control of the purchasing functions varies from organization to organization. In organizations where production activity is dominant, receiving and issuing inventory remain within the production area, and purchasing is located within logistics. Accounting for payables obviously is an accounting function. In service organizations, these four functions are supervised by the controller or treasurer's department. Sometimes conflict may arise in defining a boundary between the AIS and the MIS. The AIS usually includes accounting functions like accounts payable and inventory records, while the rest remains within the MIS domain.

The steps in a purchase transaction are:

1. Preparation of a purchase requisition
2. Preparation of a purchase order
3. Receipt of the merchandise
4. Updating the inventory record
5. Bookkeeping: (a) accounts payable function, (b) cash disbursement function

The following sections provide examples of purchase-related functions, which may be different in different organizations.

Purchase Requisitions (PR). PR is an essential part of the purchase function. In fact, no purchase function is initiated without a formal PR. It serves as an internal control vehicle by including authorization, approval, and budget comparison in the process, and also by dividing the purchase order and purchase requisition functions between two departments. Usually the user department or the inventory clerk prepares the PR in multiple copies on a prenumbered form. The PR is checked by the head of the department for correctness, budget provision, and requirements, and then the PR is authorized and approved. Depending on the system, one to two copies of the PR are sent to the purchasing department.

Purchase Order. The purchasing department examines the PR, selects the vendor, updates the vendor records, and then prepares the purchase order in six copies. The copies of the purchase order are distributed as follows:

1. Vendor's copy—Complies with vendor's ordering formalities. It informs the vendor about quality, quantity, and the price at which the order is placed, address to be delivered, expected time (if any), and billing address.
2. File copy—File alphabetically.
3. Receiving department's copy—Informs the receiving department about the incoming materials.
4. Inventory clerk's copy—Makes store management aware of the incoming materials.
5. Requisitioning department's copy—Informs the department that an order has been placed.
6. Accounts payable's copy—Inform the department in advance about the payable liability.

The internal copies are filed temporarily until the ordered merchandise is received.

Receipt of the Merchandise. Upon receipt of merchandise, the receiving department compares the shipping bills or packaging slip and the invoice with the actual merchandise received and also with the purchase order. Once things are found to be in order, a receiving report (RR) is prepared in four copies. If there are deviations, these are reported and appropriate actions are taken.

The copies of the RR are distributed as follows:

1. Purchasing department's copy—A copy goes to the purchasing department for the vendor's file.
2. Receiving department's copy—Filed with the purchase order and packaging slip.

3. Accounts payable's copy—One copy with the vendor's invoice. To assure control, in some cases the vendor's invoice is sent directly to accounts payable.
4. Inventory manager's copy—Tells the manager to update the inventory records and store the merchandise.

The receiving department is responsible for ensuring that the quality, quantity, and specifications of the merchandise received match the purchase order data. Any discrepancy that remains undetected by the receiving department will eventually be revealed from the accounts payable, inventory, or user department actions.

Accounts Payable. The accounts payable department performs the last step in the cycle. Accounts payable compares the purchase order, invoice, and receiving reports. Once they are found in order, a payment voucher is prepared, ledger posting is done, and the accounts payable record is updated. Accounts payable forwards the voucher package to the cashier for payment. The treasurer's office will make the payment when due, taking advantage of any cash discount.

Purchasing, receiving, inventory, and accounts payable departments prepare weekly and/or monthly reports which are used for control purposes. Procedure and form flow charts are used to illustrate the purchase procedure. Sample flowcharts are included in the appendix illustrations.

In a computerized system most of the controls and checks are achieved through subroutines and a set of on-line programs that edit input, record transactions, print purchase orders, distribute data, update records, prepare daily and other periodic reports, provide status inquiry, and interface with other operating routines and data files.

Internal controls issues are discussed in Chapter 14. For each operating subsystem, the AICPA outlines three broad control objectives: (1) authorization, (2) accounting, and (3) assets safeguard. The AICPA's outline includes criteria establishing the objectives for control and examples of control procedures and techniques. An example of an *authorization objective* for the purchasing function—adjustments to vendors accounts and accounts distributions should be properly *authorized.* An example of control procedures and techniques—the use of approved debit memo to notify vendors of goods returned to them and other adjustments to their accounts. An illustration of an *accounting objective*—all goods, other assets, and services received should be accounted for properly on a timely basis. The use of receiving reports is an example of a control procedure which satisfies the *accounting objective.*

FRAMEWORK FOR OPERATION AND CONTROL OF SALES

Sales transaction activities fall into six subtask categories:

1. Preparation of sales order
2. Customer credit check
3. Finished goods inventory adjustment
4. Shipping functions
5. Customer billing
6. Accounts receivable functions

When a customer's purchase order is received, if it is not prepaid a customer credit check is made by the credit department. The credit department may approve or disapprove the credit request on the customer's purchase order. The credit department sends back a disapproved purchase order to the customer, citing the reasons for disapproval. An approved purchase order goes back to a salesclerk for preparation of a multiple-copy sales order.

Two copies of the sales order go to the finished goods inventory department for inventory check. The inventory department approves the sales order if appropriate inventory is available in stock, updates the inventory record, and posts the inventory transaction.

The shipping department combines two copies of the sales order: (1) one copy with credit approval, and (2) one copy with inventory approval, checks the copies for authorization and correctness, and prepares a bill of lading (transit bill) in three copies. It files one set of forms and transmits one set to the billing department. A copy of the sales order and the bill of lading accompany the shipment. The billing department again checks the approved customer's purchase order, approved sales order, and the bill of lading and prepares the sales invoice in three copies. It posts the transaction to the sales journal and general journal, files one set of documents, and sends the other set to accounts receivable. Accounts receivable checks, posts, and updates the accounts receivable journal and general ledger.

The operating control module that works at every stage of sales transaction processing aims to achieve (1) authorization, (2) asset safeguard, and (3) accounting. For a credit sale transaction, credit authorization is a must before any order is prepared. A sales order form includes detailed sales data—price, quantity, specification, customer's name, address, account number, the terms of credit, shipping instructions, freight charges, discounts, salesperson, and the date of sale. These items of information are used by the different departments responsible for processing the sale order. Customer billing, shipping, and inventory records are usually done by different people, and at each point there is a control check for authorization and accuracy.

TABLE 11–2 Examples of Output Control and Behavior Control Criteria for Sales Order Processing Subtasks

Subtasks	*Output Control Criteria*	*Behavior Control Critera*
Sales order	1. Number of sales orders processed	1. Reduce mistakes in sale order
	2. Lost sales due to sales order processing reasons	2. Improve processing time
Credit approval	1. Number of customers credit check	1. Improve credit evaluation
	2. Bad debt	2. Reduce bad debt
		3. Increase credit volume
Finished goods inventory	1. Regular and accurate account-perpetual inventory record	1. Reduce investment in inventory
	2. Number of inventory checks	2. Reduce lost sales
	3. Lost sales due to lack of inventory	3. Improve inventory planning data
Shipping	1. Number of times right shipping done	1. Improve shipping efficiency
	2. Number of times goods returned	2. Reduce backlog
	3. Order backlog	3. Shipping checks
Customer billing	1. Number of bills prepared	1. Improve efficiency
	2. Mistakes in billing	2. Improve correctness
	3. Delays in billing	3. Reduce delay
Accounts receivable	1. Number of receivable transactions	1. Prompt receivable accounting
	2. Number of accounts receivable	2. Reduce investment in receivables
	3. Investment in accounts receivable (e.g., accounts receivable turnover)	3. Use receivable feedback reports (e.,g., aging of accounts receivable)

Table 11–2 shows some examples of output control and behavior control criteria for sales transaction subtasks. These are for illustration only; different organizations may use different criteria.

Operational control criteria for sales transactions are developed around the individual subtasks. Organizations differ in grouping the subtasks and selecting criteria. The subtasks groups and criteria selected determine the domain of operating controls. Furthermore, the use of electronic data processing influences the framework for subtask grouping, criteria selection, authorization, accountability, and accounting.

FRAMEWORK FOR OPERATION AND CONTROL OF CASH TRANSACTIONS

Control of cash is achieved primarily through accounting procedures. A well-designed accounting system, either manual or computerized, can achieve adequate cash control. Cash is necessary because it provides liquidity to the business to meet current obligations and to make long-term investments. On the other hand, cash is susceptible to fraud and misappropriation. Maintaining a regular flow of cash receipts and cash disbursements is a major concern for a financial manager. No financial manager likes to have more or less cash than he or she needs. Thus, cash management is a significant part of financial planning and control. The operating functions of cash management fall into two groups: (a) cash receipts and (b) cash disbursements.

For internal control and operating efficiency, cash receipt and cash disbursement functions are separated in all organizations except small businesses. Cash receipt functions are related to accounts receivable and cash disbursement functions are related to accounts payable.

Cash Receipt Functions

Cash receipts arise from customers' payments for accounts receivable, cash purchases, and advances. Payments are generally made by credit customers through bank checks. The cash receipt function can be seen as having several independent subtasks.

Mailroom	1. Receives checks and a copy of invoice returned with the check. 2. Records checks received, prepares batch totals. 3. Sends the checks and a copy of the batch total to the cashier.
Cashier's office	1. Compares the batch total invoices and checks for any mistakes. 2. Endorses the checks. 3. Prepares journal voucher debiting cash and crediting accounts receivable.
Bookkeeping: Accounts receivable ledger	1. Compares remittances receipt advice from the mailroom with the batch total. 2. Uses journal voucher prepared by the cashier's office to post transaction entries to the customer's accounts. 3. Makes credit department alert about overdue customers' accounts.
Bookkeeping: General ledger	1. Gives entry to the general ledger control accounts—accounts

receivable control accounts and cash receipts ledger.

2. Prepares periodic statements of accounts receivable and cash.

Internal audit	Internal audit functions as the control valve in cash operations: Receives deposit slips from the cashier, batch total from the mailroom, and bank statements from the bank.

Cash Disbursement Functions

The objective of an efficient cash disbursement procedure is to establish control for appropriate payment and to check for any fraudulent payment. A good disbursement procedure ensures that payments are made for the authorized obligations, to the right persons, and at the appropriate time. It also ensures that records of obligations and payments are made correctly, so that a single obligation is not paid out more than once, nor an account paid more than the balance outstanding. Timely payment of obligations is necessary to take advantage of cash discounts, avoid penalty, and maintain good credit standing.

The cash disbursement function concerns several subtasks. The sources of the cash disbursement function include accounts payable, cash purchases, and advances paid.

Bookkeeping: Accounts payable

Accounts payable performs its functions in two stages. In stage I, it prepares the papers for payment; and in stage II, it records the payments in accounts.

Stage I:

1. Receives copies of the purchase order, receiving reports, and invoices for all credit purchases of inventory.
2. Prepares payment vouchers and files the vouchers and other documents according to the payment dates.
3. Sends the payment voucher package to the cashier for payment on due date.

Stage II:

1. Receives the voucher package from the cashier to file.
2. Uses journal voucher to post debits to the accounts payable.

	3. Prepares batch totals. 4. Sends journal vouchers to the general ledger section.
Cashier	1. Receives supporting documents from the accounts payable section. 2. Checks them for correctness. 3. Prepares checks and stamps each supporting document. 4. Prepares journal vouchers and returns the package to accounts payable.
Bookkeeping: General ledger	1. Compares batch total and journal voucher received from cashier and accounts payable. 2. Posts the transaction to the general ledger control account, like accounts payable control, and cash disbursment control.
Internal audit	1. Receives canceled checks, bank statements, and batch totals from accounts payable. 2. Compares them for correctness and reports irregularities.

PAYROLL ACCOUNTING

Payroll accounting includes a wide range of activities involving several functions and accounting steps. The activities are broadly classified as follows:

1. Collection of base data
2. Calculation of wages and salaries
3. Recording and distribution
4. Payment

Base Data

The calculation of payroll requires certain base data. Three bases are used to collect and compute the payroll obligations:

1. Hourly basis: usually paid weekly or biweekly
2. Periodic basis: usually paid weekly, biweekly, or monthly
3. Piece basis: usually paid weekly or biweekly

An *hourly rate* is applied to the wage computation of factory workers and certain service workers. Where an hourly rate is used, wages are paid weekly or biweekly. A *periodic basis* is applied to office staff and administrative people, who are paid on a weekly, biweekly, or monthly basis. A *piece rate* basis is applied when the wage calculation is made on output counts and not on inputs. Output wage plans incorporate various types of bonus plans to provide incentive to workers to achieve higher outputs and quality standards.

Factory Payroll System

The following example illustrates the basic steps of a simple, manual factory payroll system. The payroll activities of a factory payroll system originate from the factory department. The factory department prepares two data cards: (1) a job time ticket, and (b) an employee clock card. The *job time ticket* records the time spent on each job by individual employees. The *employee clock card* records time worked by each employee. After the manufacturing cost accountant compares the job time ticket with the employee clock card and checks for any discrepancy, a *cost distribution sheet* and journal vouchers are prepared. The journal vouchers debit work-in-process and factory overhead and credit payroll payable. Work-in-process is debited to direct labor and factory overhead for indirect labor.

The payroll department is responsible for the accounting necessary to meet payroll obligations. The payroll department keeps the *payroll master file,* which records all hiring information about an employee. It compares the *payroll data sheet* with the payroll master file and prepares journal vouchers by debiting payroll payable and crediting cash (a separate payroll bank account) and other accounts for deductions. After achieving the required accuracy, the payroll department prepares checks for individual employees.

The general ledger clerk compares the two journal vouchers prepared by the cost distribution clerk and the payroll clerk (or accounts payable clerk); one shows debits to the payroll control account, and the other shows credits. This provides a reconciliation between the payroll costs debited to the work-in-process account, and the payroll prepared for payment. The checks, statements, and posted journal vouchers are sent to the cashier for disbursement.

Internal control prepares reconciliation from the payroll bank statement, deposit tickets, and canceled paychecks. Internal control periodically compares payroll data and personnel data. Sometimes there are unclaimed checks. Internal control makes an attempt to distribute these to the original payees and traces their preparation as a safeguard.

INVENTORY CONTROL

Inventory is termed a "necessary evil." It absorbs funds, becomes obsolete, is susceptible to theft and pilferage, and is a fire hazard. Yet investment in inventory is necessary for smooth production and sales operations. Inventory control helps achieve:

1. Appropriate accounting
2. Adequate physical control
3. Optimum financial planning

In a manufacturing concern there are usually three types of inventory to account for: raw materials inventory, work-in-process inventory, and finished goods inventory. In contrast, a merchandising business has one type of inventory—merchandise.

The appropriate accounting and adequate physical control over inventory are achieved through inventory methods that include: (a) procedures for recording inventory receipts and issues; and (b) methods of inventory valuation and bookkeeping.

Procedures for Recording Inventory Receipts and Issues

The procedures for recording inventory follow a sequence, as outlined below:

1. Purchase requisition and ordering
2. Receiving materials
3. Issuing materials
4. Costing raw materials inventory
5. Tracing ending balance

The tasks involved in this cycle are performed by several departments, such as (a) stockroom, (b) ordering department, (c) purchasing department, (d) receiving department, and (e) cost accounting.

The stockroom or ordering department prepares purchase requisitions based on inventory needs. The purchasing department selects vendors and issues purchase orders. Two control techniques are available to determine when to order and the optimum quantity to order; these are economic order quantity (EOQ), and reorder point (ROP). *Economic order quantity (EOQ)* is the optimum quantity of inventory to order that minimizes the inventory ordering costs and carrying costs. The *reorder point (ROP)* calculation relies on average weekly or daily needs, and the lead time for an order to arrive. A longer lead time will mean a higher reorder point.

For example, if the average daily need is 700 units and it takes 10 days to get an order, then the ROP is 700 × 10 = 7000 units; it assumes that the use of inventory is uniform over the periods and that the inventory will arrive on the tenth day. However, in reality this may not be true; there may be fluctuations in needs, and also in order filling time. In such cases there are risks of incurring stockout costs. The *safety stock* serves as a cushion. The reorder point (ROP) in that case includes a safety stock level, which can be computed by estimating the maximum expected use, the average use, and the lead time.

Methods of Inventory Valuation

Materials costing uses one of the following cost flow assumptions: (1) last in first out (LIFO), (2) first in first out (FIFO), (3) weighted average, and (4) specific identification. These methods are discussed in elementary accounting texts. Briefly, LIFO gives the current cost of goods sold or manufactured; FIFO gives the historical costs; weighted average gives average cost of purchase during any period; and specific identification gives the actual costs of purchases.

Cost flow assumptions in accounting and the physical flow of goods may not have any relationship. Accounting traces the physical flow of goods and assigns dollar amounts to the physical units based on a cost flow assumption. Furthermore, accountants use periodic or perpetual inventory costing for inventory valuation. The perpetual costing method requires recording and costing after each inventory transaction, whereas the periodic method requires inventory costing and recording after a given period.

COMPUTER-ASSISTED OPERATING CONTROL SYSTEMS

So far we have discussed some basic accounting operating controls. These operating controls can be performed manually or electronically. Application of computers in these subsystems does not eliminate human involvement; organizations try to create a balance between computer use and human involvement to achieve the optimum efficiency. For example, inventory control can be fully automated. The computer can start the ordering procedure when the inventory level reaches the ROP, determine the EOQ, select vendors, and generate purchase orders automatically. Yet organizations rarely rely completely on computers for this. They will involve people to assign responsibility, motivate employees, and make necessary adjustments for any changes in policy, price, and other conditions.

EFTS—Electronic Fund Transfer Systems

The most widely used computer-assisted operating system is the EFTS. EFTS uses computerized electronic impulses rather than papers and checks in manipulating financial transactions or transactions such as: (1) remote banking service, (2) retail point of sale service (POS), (3) direct deposit, and (4) preauthorized payment service.[6]

Remote Banking Service (RBS). Remote banking service may be viewed as a revolution in commercial banking. A customer can withdraw cash, deposit money, make transfers between accounts, pay bills, and make status inquiries through the RBS. The steps used are: (1) Insert a plastic card, (2) enter the identification number, (3) press the function keys, and (4) accept cash, receipts, and the card.

RBS telephone uses are limited to bill paying, transfers, and account status inquiry. Steps include: (1) dialing the system phone number, (2) entering account number, (3) entering payer's identification number and account number, and (4) confirming the transaction from computer's voice response (using precoded phrases).

Remote banking terminals are called Automated Teller Machines (ATM) or Customer-Bank Communication Terminals (CBCT). Remote banking services are available in two forms: proprietary systems and switch systems. Proprietary systems are operated by commercial banks. Such systems communicate with only one institution (bank). The switch system terminal communicates with more than one institution. For example, *Moncec* terminals, which communicate with more than one bank through a control computer, are part of a switch system.

Retail POS Service. Retail point of sale service is another revolution in retail marketing. In a supermarket, POS service is employed to perform three types of services: (1) check verification and guarantee, (2) fund transfer, and (3) data capture—inventory, sales, and cash control.

Customers' checks are verified by the cashier through the identification numbers and personal codes of the customers. Data capture through EFTS is simplified through the use of the Universal Product Code (UPC), which is used by supermarkets for inventory records and product prices. When the cashier draws the product across an optical scanner, the computer reads the product code, records and displays the price on the sales register tape and display, and simultaneously updates inventory records and sales records. For products for which UPCs are not available, the cashier uses codes provided by the store.

[6] This section is based on Carol A. Schaller, "The Revolution of EFTS," *The Journal of Accountancy* (October 1978), pp. 74–80.

Direct Deposit. An employee may choose to use the direct deposit service for his or her weekly or monthly pay check. The payroll office, upon authorization by the employee, instructs its bank to transfer the employee's pay directly to the employee's bank account. The employee receives a confirmation and details of pay computation from the payroll office. Direct deposit service automatically credits the employee's bank account and makes funds available without any delay.

Preauthorized Payment Service. A customer can authorize his or her bank to pay bills for utilities, mortgages, and other installments, which will be done automatically on every bill payment cycle until the customer changes the instructions.

SUMMARY

The accounting information system is the major vehicle of information in planning and control. Organizational controls provide the base and background for the AIS. Organizational controls have four levels. Viewed as a hierarchy of concentric circles, at the center is the core control, bounded by the structure, culture, and environment of the organization. The elements of core controls are: (1) planning and standards, (2) operation, (3) results, (4) measurement and evaluation, and (5) feedback and correction. A fully developed core control is a configuration of all five elements. A basic core control includes only operations and results. Organizational control focuses on two types of variables: behavior and output. The organizational control framework comprises a hierarchy of controls such as operating controls, management controls, and strategic planning. These three types of controls exist in a continuum from high certainty to least certainty.

Operating controls include a large number of accounting controls. Accounting for operating controls covers transaction processing, ledger accounting, internal controls, forms, and periodic reports. This chapter included accounts payable, sales and accounts receivable, cash receipts, cash payments, payroll, inventory control procedures, and remote banking systems.

REVIEW QUESTIONS, DISCUSSION QUESTIONS, AND PROBLEMS AND CASES

A. Review Questions

A11.1 What is the accountant's view of controls? Is that sufficient for the students of AIS?

A11.2 How do organizational structure, culture, and environment relate to organizational control?

A11.3 What is a core control? What are the basic elements of a fully developed core control system?

A11.4 Classify the following actions into five basic elements of core control: (1) sales made in units, (2) purchase procedure, (3) preparing purchase order, (4) issuing materials, (5) actual production for the period, (6) cash withdrawal limit, (7) cash budget, (8) actual cash above the budget, (9) review the cash budget, (10) sales forecast, (11) stock issued, (12) processing customer by auto tellers, (13) customer complaint, (14) minimum stock level set.

A11.5 Fill in the blanks:

a. A first-degree control includes —— and —— as core control elements.

b. A second-degree control includes ——, ——, and —— as the control elements.

A11.6 Give examples of first-degree controls and second-degree controls.

A11.7 A company's controls include setting the sales target for salespeople, preparing the weekly sales report and comparing the actual performance, and reporting the performance feedback to the salespeople. What is the degree of control?

A11.8 What are the only two things in control that are available to monitor and measure?

A11.9 Define behavior control and output control.

A11.10 From the control framework discussed in this chapter, define:

a. Operating control.

b. Management control.

c. Strategic control.

A11.11 (a) List the information characteristics for operating controls. (b) Repeat the same thing for management control and strategic control.

A11.12 List some characteristics of operational control decisions.

A11.13 Briefly describe the functions of the following accounting control subsystems:

a. Accounts payable.

b. Accounts receivable.

A11.14 Briefly describe the functions of the following accounting control subsystems:

a. Cash receipts.

b. Cash payment.

A11.15 Briefly describe the functions of the following accounting control subsystems:

a. Payroll accounting.

b. Inventory accounting.

A11.16 What are the subtask points for cash receipts? Describe the mailroom functions for cash receipt.

A11.17 What do the (a) account receivable ledger clerk and (b) general ledger clerk do with respect to the cash receipt function?

A11.18 Describe the cash disbursement functions of:

a. Accounts payroll clerk.

b. Cashier.

c. General ledger clerk.

A11.19 Describe the tasks of the payroll accounting department.

A11.20 How is internal control for payroll payment achieved where payments are made through bank checks?

A11.21 Name the types of inventory in (a) a manufacturing business and (b) a merchandising business.

A11.22 What is an inventory control cycle? Illustrate an inventory control cycle.

A11.23 What is an EOQ? Why is it used?

A11.24 List the five steps involved in a purchase transaction.

A11.25 Describe:
- **a.** Purchase requisition (PR).
- **b.** Purchase order (PO).
- **c.** Receiving report (RR).

A11.26 Why are multiple copies of a purchase order prepared? What persons or departments receive copies of a purchase order?

A11.27 What are the six subtask categories involved in a sales transaction?

A11.28 What information is included in a sales order form?

A11.29 Give examples of output control criteria and behavior control criteria for the following: Example: Sales order = Number of sales orders processed/ reduced mistakes in sales order.
- **a.** Purchase order.
- **b.** Billing.
- **c.** Payment of invoice.

A11.30 What is EFTS? What are the uses of EFTS?

A11.31 What services does the remote banking service (RBS) of a commercial bank offer to its customers?

A11.32 What is a POS service? Where and why are POS used?

Questions 11.33–11.39 relate to Appendix 11B.

A11.33 What are the major files in the computerized payroll/personnel system?

A11.34 Redraw the payroll/personnel processing flowchart shown in Figure 11B–2 and explain the steps involved.

A11.35 What are the major files in a computerized accounts payable system? Narrate their functions.

A11.36 Give examples of some of the standard reports that can be generated by a computerized accounts payable system.

A11.37 List the contents of the accounts receivable master file, and the customer master file.

A11.38 Name the management reports that are generated by the Accounts Receivable/Cash Management System.

A11.39 What are the three basic types of processing the Accounts Receivable/ Cash Management System employs?

B. Discussion Questions

B11.1 Five Star Groceries uses cash registers with printed customer receipts and a copy tape that prints all transactions. Discuss the core control elements for cash control in the Five Star Groceries.

B11.2 Discuss the degree of control and the relationship of the core control elements to degree of control.

B11.3 Do you think that all companies must include all core control elements? Why or why not?

B11.4 Can AIS influence both behavior control and output control in an organization? Why?

B11.5 What type of control is involved when managers look at the total costs of the department and not the individual transactions for cost incurred? Why?

B11.6 Review the characteristics of operating controls and explain them with reference to specific accounting control subsystems.

B11.7 Discuss the processing of a customer order from the order receipt to the shipping of merchandise.

B11.8 Explain the operation of a remote banking service you are familiar with.

B11.9 Do you think EFTS is a revolution in financial transactions? How is an AIS effected by the EFTS?

B11.10 Appendix 11A shows salesman and bookkeeper procedures. Write a narrative of the procedures shown in this appendix.

B11.11
a. What are the control weaknesses in the salesman procedure shown in Appendix 11A?
b. Do you see any weaknesses in the bookkeeping procedure?

B11.12 In Appendix 11B, how does Software International's Accounts Receivable/Cash Management System give users maximum control over inflow of cash?

C. Problems and Cases

C11.1 (SMA, Canada) During an investigation of the receiving procedures of a large manufacturing company, the following was found: (1) The receiving department prepares six copies of the receiving report for the following distribution: one copy to Stockroom, one copy to Purchasing, two copies to Accounts Payable, one copy is retained and filed in numerical order, one copy to Inspection. (2) The goods are sent with a copy of the receiving report to Inspection. After the quality control check, they are sent to the Stockroom, and the Inspection copy of the receiving report is destroyed. If the goods do not meet specifications, Inspection prepares a rejection report. The goods are returned to the receiving department, together with one copy of the rejection report and the receiving report copy. Three other copies of the rejection report are sent to stockroom, purchasing, and accounts payable (one copy each), for cancellation of the receiving report. (3) Purchasing uses the receiving report copy to update purchase order records. The copy is then filed by receiving date. (4) Accounts payable attaches one of its copies to the vendor's invoice for vouchering. The other copy is used to maintain numerical control of the receiving reports.

a. What improvements, if any, can be made to the receiving report procedure?

b. Prepare a flow process chart of the receiving report procedure incorporating the improvements you made in part (a). Use the following symbols:

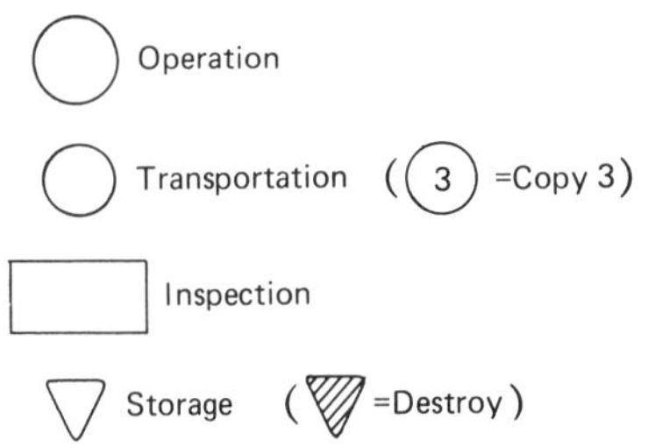

C11.2 (CMA) Over the past several years, the Programme Corporation has encountered difficulties estimating its cash flows. The result has been a rather strained relationship with its banker. Programme's controller would like to develop a means by which he can forecast the firm's monthly operating cash flows. The following data were gathered to facilitate the development of such a forecast. (1) Sales have been and are expected to increase at 0.5% each month. (2) 30% of each month's sales are for cash; the other 70% are on open account. (3) Of the credit sales, 80% are collected in the first month following the sale and the remaining 20% are collected in the second month. There are no bad debts. (4) Gross margins on sales average 25%. (5) Programme purchases enough inventory each month to cover the following month's sales. (6) All inventory purchases are paid for in the month of purchase at a 2% cash discount. (7) Monthly expenses are: Payroll, $1,500; rent, $400; depreciation, $120; other cash expenses, $5 of that month's sales. There are no accruals. (8) Ignore the effects of corporate income taxes, dividends, and equipment acquisitions.

Using the data above, develop a mathematical model the controller can use for his calculations. Your model should be capable of calculating the operating cash inflows and outflows for any specified month.

C11.3 (CMA) The Vane Corporation is a manufacturing concern that has been in business for 18 years. During this period, the company has grown from a very small family-owned operation to a medium-sized manufacturing concern with several departments. Despite this growth, a substantial number of the procedures employed by Vane have been in effect since the business was started. Just recently, Vane computerized its payroll function.

The payroll operates in the following manner. Each worker picks up a weekly time card on Monday morning and writes in his or her name and identification number. These blank cards are kept near the factory entrance. The workers write on the time card the time of their daily arrival and departure. On the following Monday, the factory foremen collect the completed time cards for the previous week and send them to data processing.

In data processing, the time cards are used to prepare the weekly time file. This file is processed with the master payroll file, which is maintained on magnetic tape according to worker identification number. The checks are written by the computer on the regular checking account and imprinted with the treasurer's signature. After the payroll file is updated and the checks are prepared, the checks are sent to the factory foremen, who distribute them to the workers or hold them for the workers to pick up later if they are absent. The foremen notify data processing of new employees and terminations. Any changes in hourly pay rate or any other changes affecting payroll are usually communicated to data processing by the foremen. The workers also complete a job time ticket for each individual job they work on each day. The job time tickets are collected daily and sent to cost accounting, where they are used to prepare a cost distribution analysis.

Further analysis of the payroll function reveals the following: (1) A worker's gross wages never exceed $300 per week. (2) Raises never exceed $0.55 per hour for the factory workers. (3) No more than 20 hours of overtime is allowed each week. (4) The factory employs 150 workers in 10 departments.

The payroll function has not been operating smoothly for some time, but even more problems have surfaced since the payroll was computerized. The foremen have indicated that they would like a weekly report indicating worker tardiness, absenteeism, and idle time, so they can determine the amount of productive time lost and the reason for the lost time. The following errors and inconsistencies have been encountered the past few pay periods:

1. A worker's paycheck was not processed properly, because he had transposed two numbers in his identification number when he filled out his time card.

2. A worker was issued a check for $1,531.80 when it should have been $153.81.

3. One worker's paycheck was not written, and this error was not detected until the paychecks for that department were distributed by the foreman.

4. Part of the master payroll file was destroyed when the tape reel was inadvertently mounted on the wrong tape drive and used as a scratch tape. Data processing attempted to reestablish the destroyed portion from original source documents and other records.

5. One worker received a paycheck for an amount considerably larger than he should have. Further investigation revealed that 84 had been punched instead of 48 for hours worked.

6. Several records on the master payroll file were skipped and not included on the updated master payroll file. This was not detected for several pay periods.

7. In processing nonroutine changes a computer operator included a pay rate increase for one of his friends in the factory. This was discovered by chance by another employee.

Required:

Identify the control weaknesses in the payroll procedure and in the computer processing as it is now conducted by the Vane Corp. Recommend the changes necessary to correct the system. Arrange your answer in the following columnar format:

Control Weaknesses   *Recommendations*

C11.4 (CMA) Huron Co. manufactures and sells eight major product lines with 15 to 25 items in each product line. All sales are on credit, and orders are received by mail or telephone. Huron has a computer-based system that employs magnetic tape as a file medium.

All sales orders received during regular working hours are typed on Huron's own sales order form immediately. This typed form is the source document for the keypunching of a shipment or backorder card for each item ordered. These cards are employed in the after-hours processing at night to complete all necessary recordkeeping for the current day and to facilitate the shipment of goods the following day. An order received one day is to be processed that day and night and shipped the next day.

The daily processing which has to be accomplished at night includes the following activities: (1) Preparing the invoice to be sent to the customer at the time of shipment. (2) Updating the accounts receivable file. (3) Updating the finished goods inventory. (4) Listing of all items backordered and short. Each month the sales department would like to have a sales summary and analysis. At the end of each month, the monthly statements should be prepared and mailed to customers. Management also wants an aging of accounts receivable each month.

a. Identify the master files Huron should maintain in this system to provide for the daily processing. Indicate the data content that should be included in each file and the order in which each file should be maintained.

b. Using the symbols shown below, prepare a systems flowchart of the daily processing required to update the finished goods inventory records and to produce the necessary inventory reports (assume that the necessary magnetic tape devices are available). Use the annotation symbol to describe or explain any facts that cannot be detailed in the individual symbols.

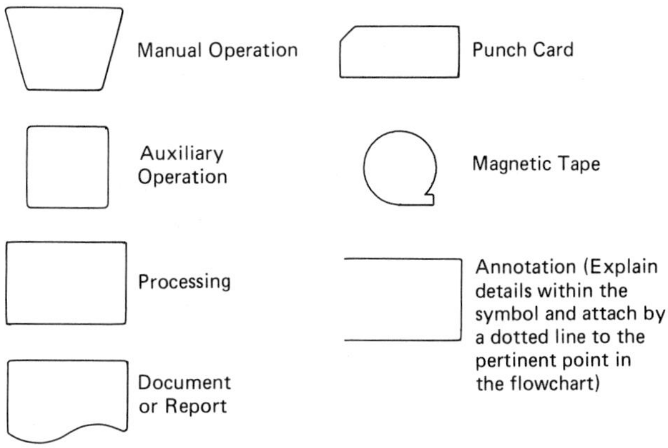

c. Describe (1) the items that should appear in the monthly sales analysis report(s) the sales department should have, and (2) the input data and master files that would have to be maintained to prepare these reports.

SUGGESTED READINGS

AICPA. *Special Advisory Report on Internal Control.* New York: American Institute of Certified Public Accountants, 1978.

ANTHONY, R. N., AND JOHN DEARDEN. *Management Control Systems,* 4th ed. Homewood, Ill.: Richard D. Irwin, 1980.

MCCOSH, A. M., MAWDUDUR RAHMAN, AND MICHAEL J. EARL. *Developing Managerial Information Systems.* New York: Wiley, 1981.

SIMON, H. A., et al. *Centralization vs. Decentralization.* New York: Controllership Foundation Inc., 1954.

appendix 11A

A Manual AIS of a Small Business: Sales and Cash Received Procedure*

SALESMAN PROCEDURE

Elwood Flynn's sales procedures are based on a lot of salesman input, which begins the procedure (see Exhibits 11A–1 and 11A–2.) Upon completing his sale the salesman prepares a sales invoice. The invoices are prenumbered and prepared in two copies, incorporating data on price of merchandise sold, names and addresses of the customers, date of sale, and the terms of the sale.

Terms of sale are either cash or charge. In the case of a cash sale, the salesman enters the sale in a manual cash register and then gives the customer the original copy of the sales invoice. The second copy of the invoice is then stored sequentially and given to the bookkeeper at the end of the day. In a charge sale situation, the salesman does not enter the sale in the cash register. The original copy of the invoice is again given to the customer, while the second copy is filed sequentially as in the cash sale situation.

Two other conditions warrant the preparation of a sales invoice. First, when a customer makes payment on his account. In preparing the invoice, the salesman notes the date of the transaction, name and address of the customer, a description of either "payment on account" or "on account," and finally the amount of the payment. The salesman then records the transaction in the cash register, gives the customer the original copy of the invoice and files the duplicate sequentially.

The second situation is the case of a sales return, when an invoice is prepared. The return may involve a direct refund or a credit to the customer's account. In a cash refund situation, again the salesman who originally sold the merchandise makes the refund. The customer must present the copy of the original sales invoice. The salesman prepares a new sales invoice indicating the date of transaction, name and address of the customer, description of merchandise being returned, and an

* This case was prepared with contributions from Robert Korol.

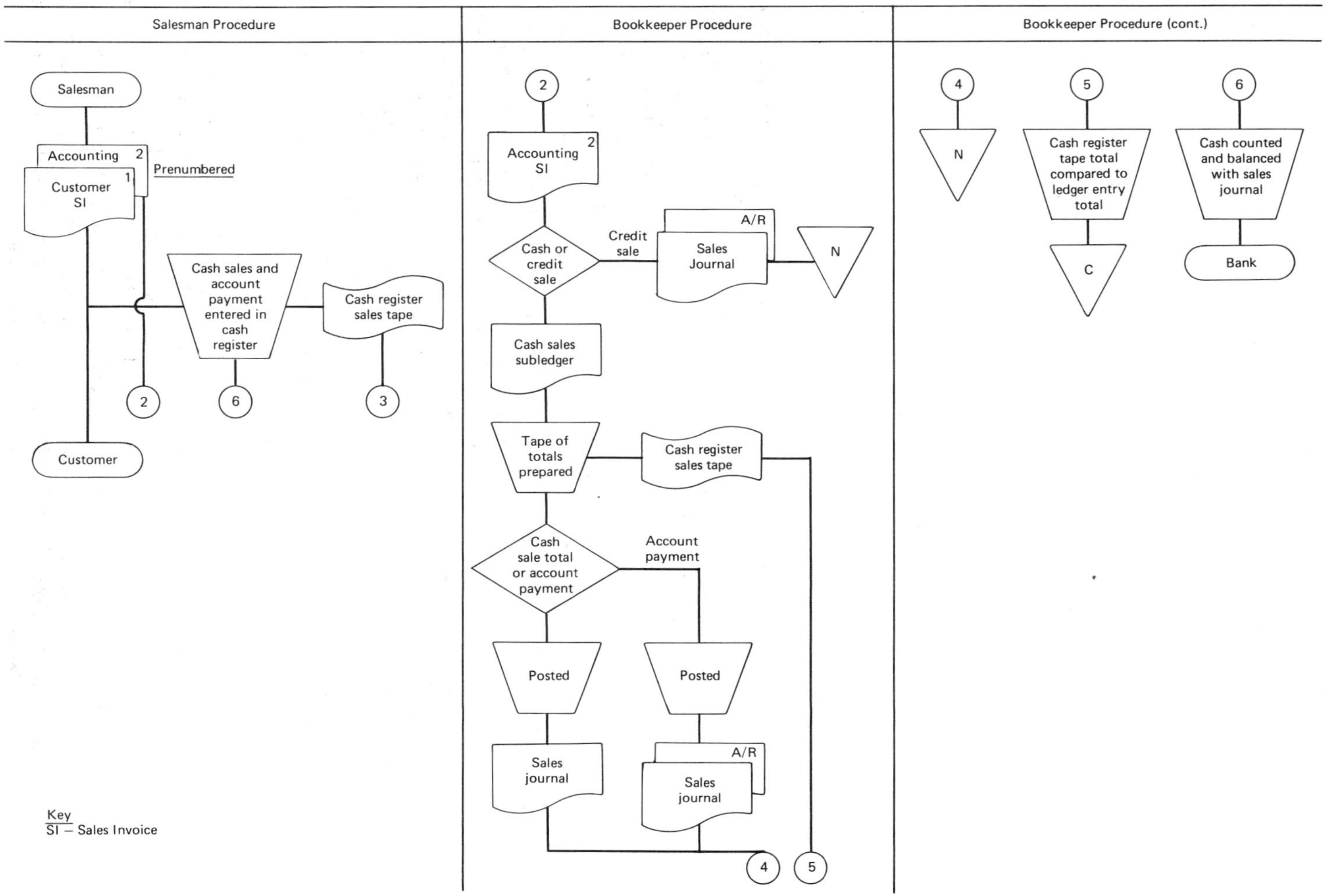

 EXHIBIT 11A–1 Sales and Cash Received Procedure

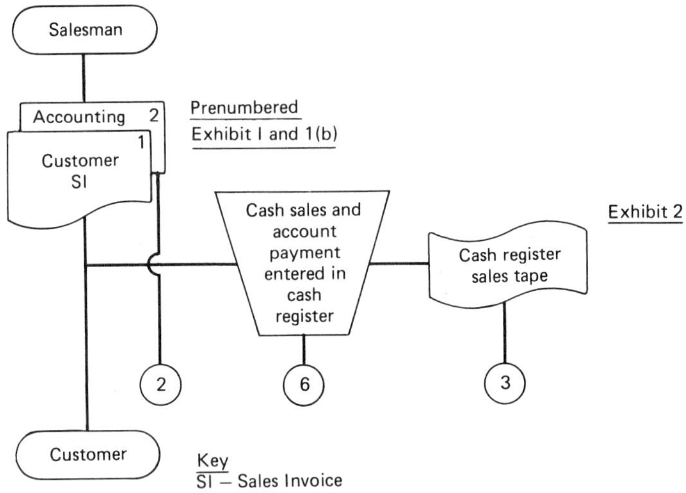

EXHIBIT 11A–2 Salesman Procedure

indication that cash was refunded. The salesman compares the items of the original sales invoice with those on the current refund invoice to ensure that they correspond. Finally, the salesman documents the transaction by receiving the customer's signature on the refund invoice and thus authorizing the refund of cash. In turn, the refund is entered and subtracted in the cash register. The customer receives the cash refund, along with the original copy of the sales invoice, and the duplicate copy is then filed sequentially as in any other situation. Where a credit to a customer's account is involved, the original salesman handles the return. The customer must again present his copy of the original sales invoice. Once this condition is met, the salesman prepares a new sales invoice indicating the date of transaction, customer's name and address, a description of merchandise being returned, and an indication that the transaction is to be credited to the customer's account. The salesman compares the original and refund invoices to ensure their accuracy. The invoice is then signed by the customer to authorize the account credit. Finally, the original copy of the refund invoice is handed to the customer, while the duplicate copy is filed sequentially.

In all four situations, the duplicate copy of the sales invoice is filed sequentially. Upon completion of the day's transactions, all duplicate copies are given to the bookkeeper as an indication of the day's transactions. The bookkeeper totals the cash register tape and takes the cash received from the business for the day. A cash float of \$100 remains in the cash register to accommodate the subsequent day's transactions. The duplicate invoices, the cash register tape, and all applicable cash are given to the bookkeeper.

BOOKKEEPER PROCEDURE

Due to the problem of limited staffing, the assistant manager-bookkeeper must participate in both the sales and bookkeeping procedures. (See Exhibit 11A–3.) The inputs to the bookkeeper procedure are the duplicate sales invoices, cash register tape, and cash received.

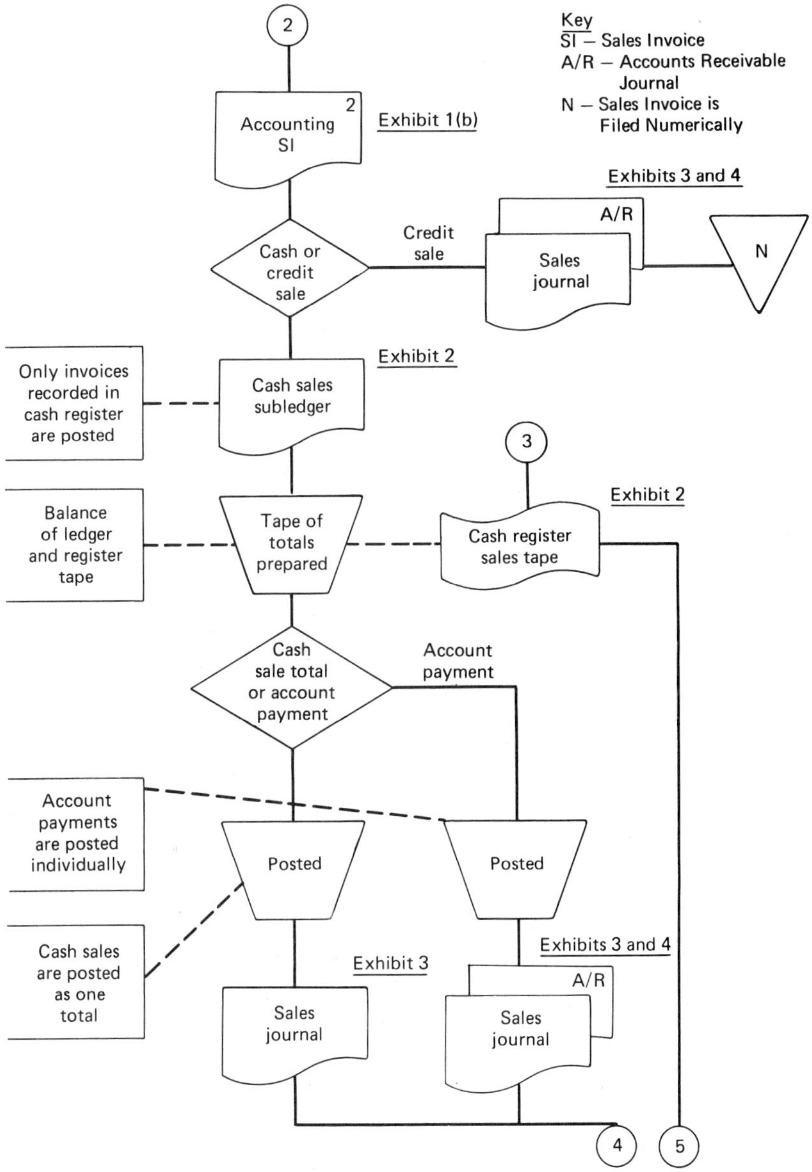

EXHIBIT 11A–3 Bookkeeper Procedure

EXHIBIT 11A–3 (cont.)

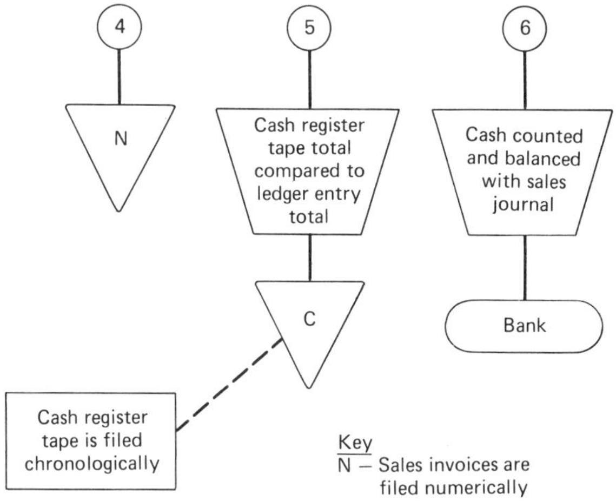

The initial process is to document the sales invoices individually. The bookkeeper then prepares the daily cash sales subledger. (See Exhibits 11A–4 and 11A–5.) This ledger includes all entries of sales invoices with the following conditions: (1) sale paid in cash (this includes cash refunds), and (2) payments on account.

Sales which are paid in cash are recorded in the sales subledger with a breakdown of actual sales and tax given. Payments on account are recorded separately from cash sales. Upon completion of the entries applicable to the sales subledger, totals of sales, tax, and payments on account are posted to a summary in the cash sales subledger. A grand total of these three entries is made and compared with the cash register tape total to ensure that all cash entries have been accounted for. At this point, only cash sales and tax totals are posted to the sales journal. (See Exhibit 11A–6.)

Once total cash sales and tax have been posted to the sales journal, the bookkeeper repeats his routine with charge sales, payments on account, and the credit account for merchandise returns. The bookkeeping system currently employs a Systematic One Write System. This system enables the posting of entries to both the sales journal and the accounts receivable journal at the same time.

In the case of a charge sale, the customer's account card (Exhibit 11A–7) is pulled from the receivable ledger and an entry is made to both the sales and the receivables journals. A breakdown is given of sales and education tax in the sales journal. In an account payment situation, the customer's account card is pulled and the entry is made in both the sales and receivable journals. In a situation where merchandise returned is to be credited to the customer's account, the

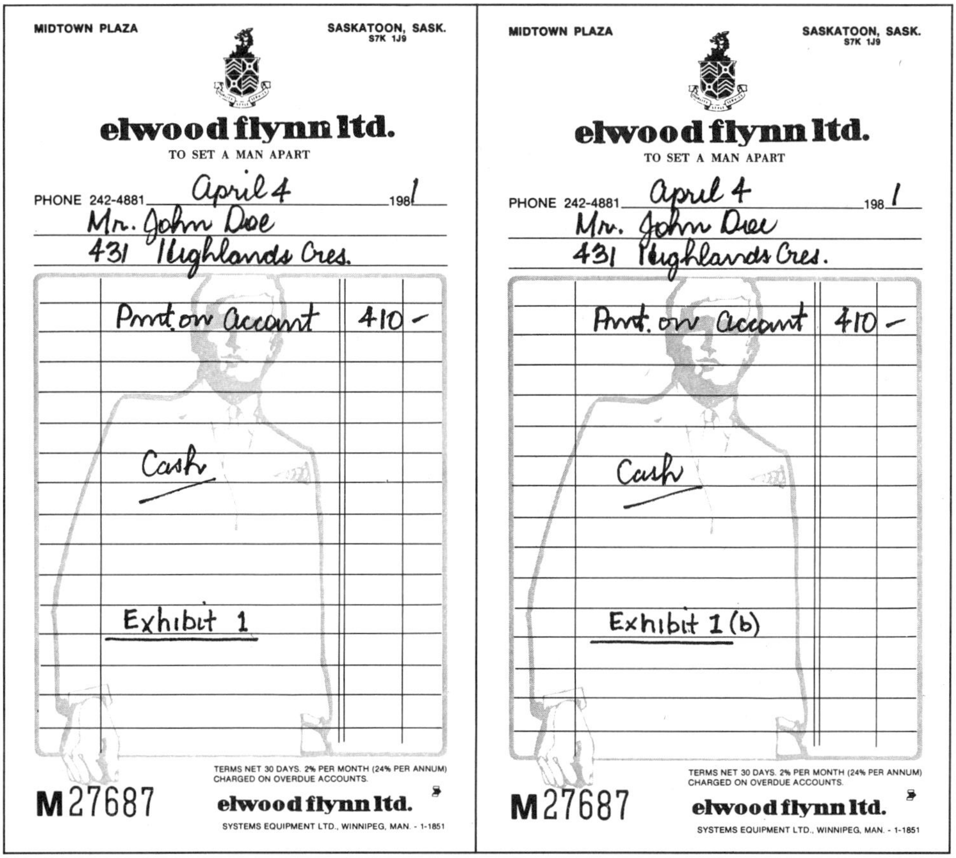

MIDTOWN PLAZA SASKATOON, SASK. S7K 1J9

elwood flynn ltd.

TO SET A MAN APART

PHONE 242-4881 April 4 1981

Mr. John Doe

431 Highlands Cres.

Pmt. on Account 410 -

Cash

Exhibit 1

TERMS NET 30 DAYS. 2% PER MONTH (24% PER ANNUM) CHARGED ON OVERDUE ACCOUNTS.

M27687 **elwood flynn ltd.**

SYSTEMS EQUIPMENT LTD., WINNIPEG, MAN. - 1-1851

MIDTOWN PLAZA SASKATOON, SASK. S7K 1J9

elwood flynn ltd.

TO SET A MAN APART

PHONE 242-4881 april 4 1981

Mr. John Doe

431 Highlands Cres.

Pmt. on Account 410 -

Cash

Exhibit 1 (b)

TERMS NET 30 DAYS. 2% PER MONTH (24% PER ANNUM) CHARGED ON OVERDUE ACCOUNTS.

M27687 **elwood flynn ltd.**

SYSTEMS EQUIPMENT LTD., WINNIPEG, MAN. - 1-1851

EXHIBIT 11A–4 Sales Invoices

same procedure is followed. Thus, cash refunds are posted individually to the sales journal only, with a breakdown of sales and taxes paid.

At this stage, all sales (cash or charge), payments on account, credit account returns, and cash refunds should be posted to the appropriate journals. To ensure correct entry, a total of all cash entries is made and compared with the cash register tape.

In finalizing the procedure, cash received totals are compared to actual sales journal entries. The cash over or short is entered in the sales journal. Finally, a bank deposit slip is prepared in duplicate, and cash is deposited in the bank. The owner-manager's involvement in the entire bookkeeping procedure is limited to checking the duplicate bank deposit slip returned by the bank. Duplicate copy sales invoices are then filed sequentially for reference at a later date.

Daily Recap
April 4, 1981

Sales	Tax	On Account
50.00	2.50	323.50
75.00	3.75	410.00
450.00	22.50	278.75
60.00	3.00	1012.25
12.50	.63	
647.50	32.38	

Summary:

Cash Sales	647.50
Education Tax	32.38
Total Cash Sales	679.88
On Accounts	1012.25
Total Cash.	1692.13

Elwood Flipm Ltd.
Cash Register
Sales Tape
April 4, 1981

```
  50•00 +
   2•50 +
 323•50 +
  75•00 +
   3•75 +
 410•00 +
 450•00 +
  22•50 +
 278•75 +
  60•00 +
   3•00 +
  12•50 +
   0•63 +
1692•13 ◇
1692•13 *
```

EXHIBIT 11A–5 Cash Sales Subledger

DATE	DESCRIPTION	1 CHARGES	2 CREDITS	3 BALANCE	4 PREVIOUS BALANCE	NAME	5 CASH—	6 SALES	7 BANK	8	9 SALES— CR	10 TAX CR	11	12 CASH OVER/ SHORT
4-481						CASH SALES	67988				64750	3238		
4-481	27687		410-	Ø	410-	JOHN DOE	410-							
4-481	27690		32350		32350	BILL SMITH	32350							
4-481	27694		27875	100-	37875	TOM JONES	27875							
4-481	27696	63-		63-	Ø	JOHN DOE					60-	3-		
4-481						CASH OVER/SHORT		3-						3-
4-481						DEPOSIT		168913	168913					
									169213					
4-681	28061-CREDIT	63-		Ø	63-	JOHN DOE					<60->	<3->		
	CREDIT ACCOUNT MERCHANDISE RETURNED													
4-681	28066					BILL BROWN		21-			<20->	<1->		
							CASH REFUND— MERCHANDISE RETURNED							
	TOTALS													
		CHARGES 1	CREDITS 2	BALANCE 3	PREVIOUS BALANCE 4	RECONCILIATION: COL 4 + 1 − 2 = 3	5	6	7	8	9	10	11	12

EXHIBIT 11A–6 Sales Journal

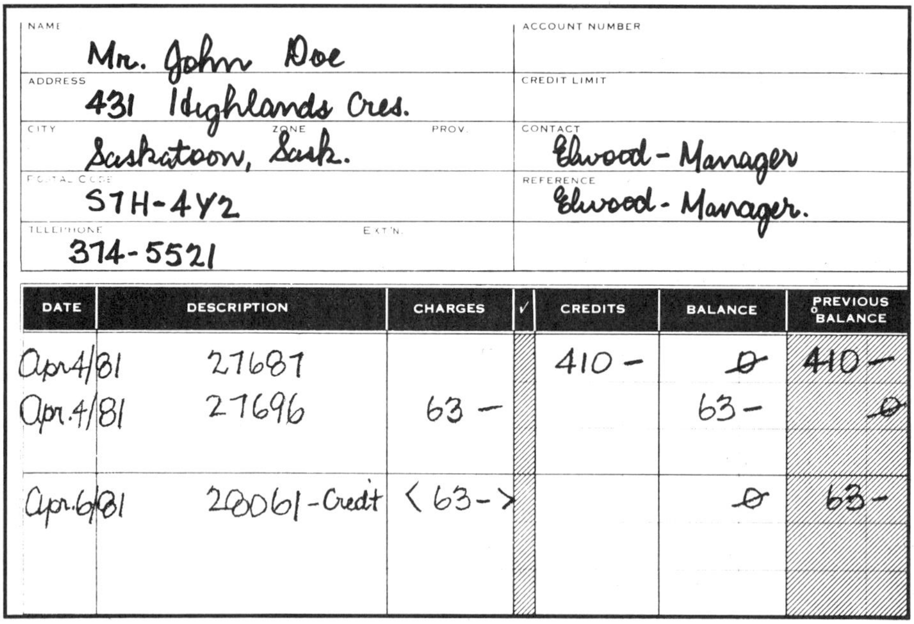

NAME: Mr. John Doe | ACCOUNT NUMBER:

ADDRESS: 431 Highlands Cres. | CREDIT LIMIT:

CITY: Saskatoon, Sask. ZONE PROV. | CONTACT: Elwood - Manager

POSTAL CODE: S7H-4Y2 | REFERENCE: Elwood - Manager.

TELEPHONE: 374-5521 EXT'N.

DATE	DESCRIPTION	CHARGES	✓	CREDITS	BALANCE	PREVIOUS BALANCE
Apr.4/81	27687			410 -	0	410 -
Apr.4/81	27696	63 -			63 -	0
Apr.6/81	28061 - Credit	⟨63 -⟩			0	63 -

EXHIBIT 11A–7 A/R Ledger Card

appendix 11B
Computerized Operating Controls

There can be as many computerized systems as there are minds. Users and vendors design their systems by focusing on the points they think critical to their systems. Here we reproduce the systems designed by one software vendor, Software International.* Because systems are continuously revised and improved, we reproduce those aspects that are of an enduring nature, particularly those most beneficial to beginning learners. These include: (a) an overview of the payroll/personnel system, (b) an overview of the computerized accounts payablesystem, and (c) an overview of the accounts receivable/cash management system.

* Materials in this section are taken from Software International publications, with permission.

AN OVERVIEW OF PAYROLL/PERSONNEL SYSTEM

Data Processing Information

The Payroll/Personnel System is a sequential system that provides rapid processing to handle multiple user requirements while requiring a minimum of program changes. The Control file allows this capability by providing the user with a mechanism for varying processing options to meet specific needs. The System can be equally responsive to a small, single payroll retail outlet and a multi-payroll service bureau.

Major File Descriptions. The Payroll/Personnel System is based on the interaction of the following files and tables (see Figure 11B–1).

- Employee Master
- Control File
- Tax Tables
- Rate of Pay File
- General Ledger Table

Employee Master. Based on an 1800-character record, this file contains necessary payroll information for each employee, such as salary, deductions, leave, union or job class, etc. In addition, it holds personnel data such as: sex, birth date, hire date, marital status, number of dependents, termination date/reason, salary change date/reason, position change code, last paid date, position description, ethnic code, permanent-temporary code.

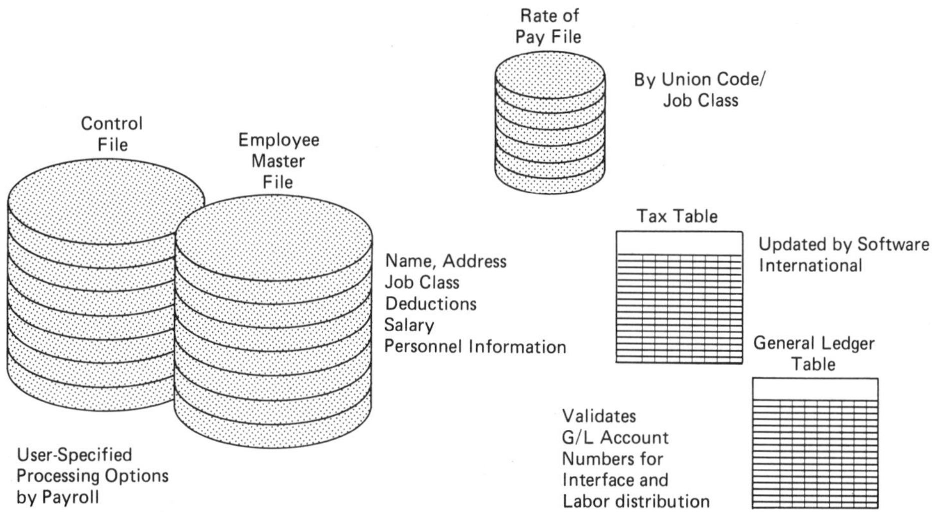

FIGURE 11B–1 Overview of Files and Tables

Control File. This file contains variable information that allows users to specify, for each payroll: deduction names, frequencies, whether deductions are flat monetary amount, percentage of gross pay, or cents per hour, which deductions are non-taxable, pay frequencies, and the account periods to which labor is to be charged.

General Ledger Table. This is used to edit for valid general ledger account numbers and to determine the appropriate account numbers for payroll distribution to the general ledger.

Tax Tables. All U.S. and Canadian tax information, as it affects the payroll function, is stored for easy access. Software International supplies updates on a regular basis so users are assured of processing with current tax information.

Rate of Pay File. Organized by job, union class, or any user-specified category, this table stores up-to-date hourly and shift premium rates of pay for calculating gross earnings. Rates of pay for each employee can also be stored permanently in the Employee Master record, or entered as an override rate on the time input document.

Processing. Based on a sequential processing system the Payroll/Personnel capability provides a rapid and efficient method of handling a broad range of payroll needs as well as supplying basic personnel information and control. Figure 11B–2 is a graphic representation of system processing flow.

The system is responsive to user needs. Pay can be automatic or triggered with the input of a time document. Sequential processing of each payroll assures control; audit trails and edit reports are thorough. Checks are produced accurately and on time. The System offers a large library of standard reports, plus a report writer that allows each user to modify standard reports and prepare additional reports unique to the user's organization. The personnel base supports the production of many history and employee-information reports.

Implementation Support

Software International is committed to the successful implementation of each user. They offer a variety of important support services, including:

- Complete documentation—this system-produced documentation is easily referenced and logically organized. It supplies step-by-step guidance for both data processing and Payroll/Personnel Departments.
- Fully warranted software products—Software International provides

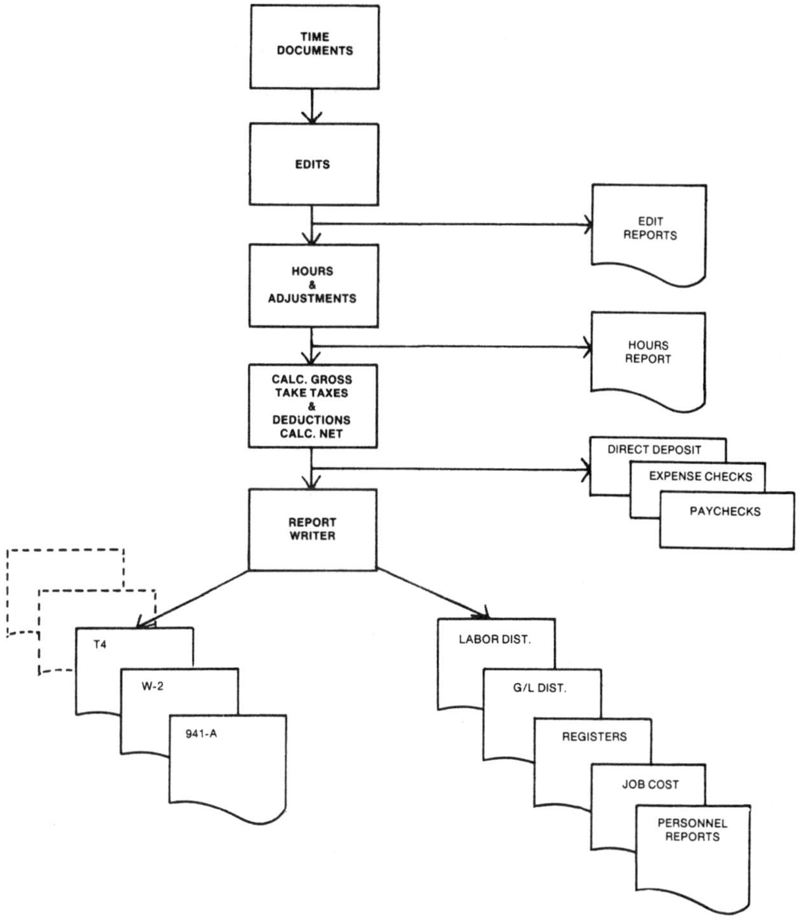

FIGURE 11B–2 Payroll/Personnel Processing Flow

modifications to or replaces any module found to be defective within one year of the date of installation.

- Maintenance Agreement—The included maintenance agreement provides for new releases, allows a 100% trade-in on a higher level version of the system, and gives continuous insurance for high level performance.
- Enhancements—issued on a regular basis, additional capabilities are added frequently and releases are generally made on an annual basis.
- Full technical installation and support services—users get the benefits of our staff of proven, technical professionals for pre-installation planning, technical surveys, on-site assistance, and system review.

Checks

The user is assured of total accuracy and processing thoroughness through the system's careful handling of the production of checks and audit reports throughout the check-writing cycle.

Standard paychecks and stubs are system-produced with many features to suit a wide range of user requirements. (See Figure 11B–1 for a typical example.) Specific capabilities are:

- User-specified deduction names
- Check numbers computer-generated *or* pre-printed
- Period-ending and check dates entered via control transactions

At each step in the check-generating process, user reports are produced to carefully highlight and audit system processing. Proper audit trails for proof of check calculations are provided in registers. Figure 11B–3 is a representative Payroll Check Register, sequenced by check number, which assists users to account for each check. Figure 11B–3, a Detail Payroll Register, gives comprehensive detail information for each check. A Direct Deposit Register is also provided for cross-checking amounts for which no corresponding system-produced pay check was generated.

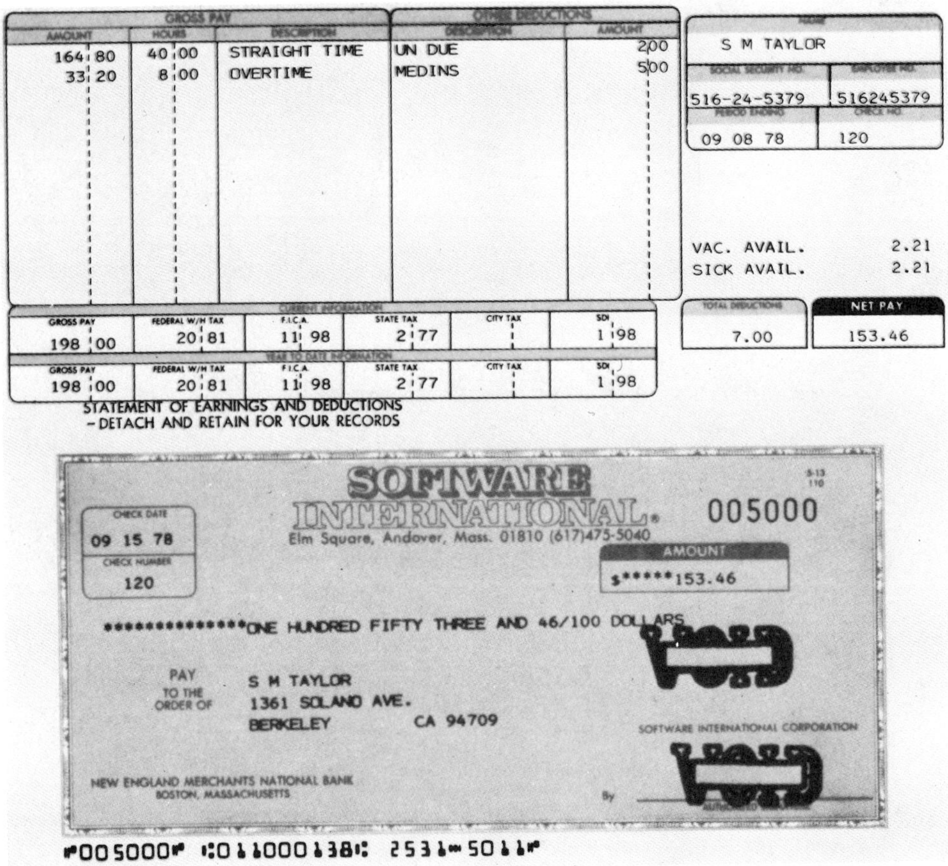

FIGURE 11B–3 Check (Actual checks and paystubs are attached side-by-side.)

Check Reconciliation. The system provides reconciliation reporting to monitor all checks in the system, whether voided, cancelled, replaced, entered manually, or outstanding (see Figure 11B–3). From production to final disposition, each check is fully visible for user monitoring.

AN OVERVIEW OF COMPUTERIZED ACCOUNTS PAYABLE SYSTEM

Complete Control Through Accounts Payable File Relationships

An extensive yet simple relationship among the system's files provides the user with considerable flexibility in obtaining information from the Accounts Payable System. For example, the user can review the vouchers which are due to be paid on a given day, or for a range of dates. The user can retrieve *only* those vouchers associated with a particular vendor. (See Figure 11B–4.)

Vendor File

The vendor file contains one master record for each vendor in the system. Each record contains the following data fields:

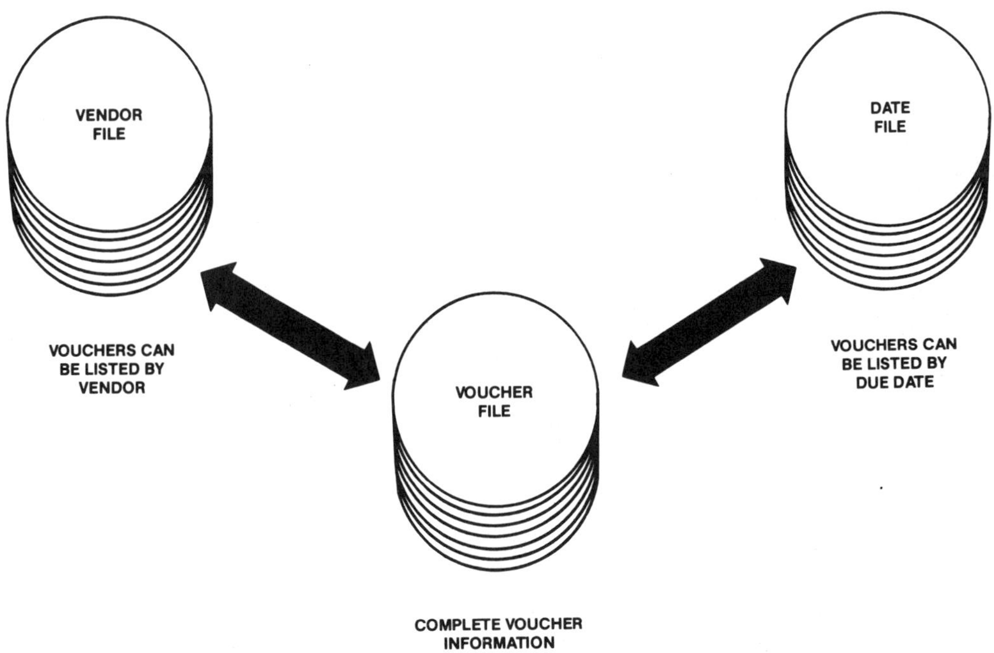

FIGURE 11B–4 Accounts Payable File Relationships

- Vendor number
- Vendor name
- Street address
- City
- State
- Zip code
- Vendor optional address I
- Vendor optional address II
- Vendor's telephone number
- Contact name
- 1099 indicator
- Employee indicator
- Standard industry code
- Activity date
- A/P payments—year-to-date
- A/P payments—month-to-date
- A/P outstanding commitment
- Discounts taken—year-to-date
- Discounts taken—month-to-date
- Outstanding discounts
- Payments made—last year
- Discounts taken—last year
- Discount terms—days
- Discount terms—percent
- Cross reference
- Bank
- Hold indicator
- Temporary vendor

Date File

The date file contains the following summary information associated with particular due dates:

- Total outstanding amount due
- Total outstanding discounts
- Number of open vouchers
- Number of paid vouchers

Voucher File

The voucher file is composed of records which contain all relevant information relating to a particular transaction with a particular vendor. Included in this information is:

- Vendor number
- General ledger account number
- Discount date
- Vendor invoice number
- Vendor invoice date
- 3 optional data fields
- Voucher gross dollars
- Voucher discount amount
- Voucher bank code
- Voucher check number
- Check amount
- Check date
- Entry date
- Distribution date
- Accounting period
- 1099/Tax indicator

Supplemental Files

Outstanding Check File. This is a file of checks not yet cleared through various bank accounts. Cleared checks are processed against this file to produce a reconciliation of checks generated through the accounts payable system.

YTD Distribution History File. This is a detail file of all transactions entered and distributed year-to-date.

YTD Paid Voucher History File. This is a detail file on all transactions paid, disbursed, and retired from the active voucher file year-to-date.

Vendor Invoice File. This is a sequential file containing vendor invoice records which are used to report multiple usage of a vendor's invoice.

Standard Reporting

Entry Cycle

- Edit report
- Add report
- Duplicate invoice

Commitment Reports

- Commitment by vendor
- Commitment by voucher
- Summary commitment by date

Cash Requirements Report
Check-Writing Cycle

- Check sample
- Check register

Check Reconciliation

- Reconciliation edit
- Check reconciliation
- Outstanding check journal
- New check add report

User Aids

- Vendor master list
- Rotary card file
- Labels
- Vendor credit statement

End-of-Period Processing

- Period ending vendor history report
- Paid voucher report
- Distribution report
- Open accounts payable report

Audit Reports

- Accounts payable control log balance report
- Check exception list
- Batch suspense report
- Vendor/voucher file control

Maintenance

- Vendor file maintenance
- Voucher file maintenance
- Date file maintenance

Minimal Input Requirements

The user controls transaction information entered into the accounts payable system through:

Payment vouchers
Manual vouchers
Adjustment/memo vouchers

The system requires only the following information to process voucher transactions:

Batch number (number-total-date)
Vendor number
Voucher number
Amount
General ledger account number

The following voucher transaction information is provided by the system, and is entered only at the discretion of the user to meet unique requirements:

Payment date
Bank code
Discount information
1099/tax indicator
Bank information
Miscellaneous user defined information

See Figure 11B–5.

AN OVERVIEW OF ACCOUNTS RECEIVABLE AND CASH MANAGEMENT SYSTEM

Database Design

Software International's accounts receivable/cash management system is a comprehensive database designed system, utilizing advanced file handling techniques which allows the user department maximum control and flexibility in processing cash payments and controlling accounts receivable. Major systems files include:

1. *The Accounts Receivable Master File.* This contains one record for each invoice, memo, adjustment, and cash transaction posted by the system. All transactions pertaining to a customer are linked to the customer master with an unlimited number of transactions per customer. It includes such items as:

- Customer number
- Date of transaction
- Transaction number
- Due date
- Discount amount

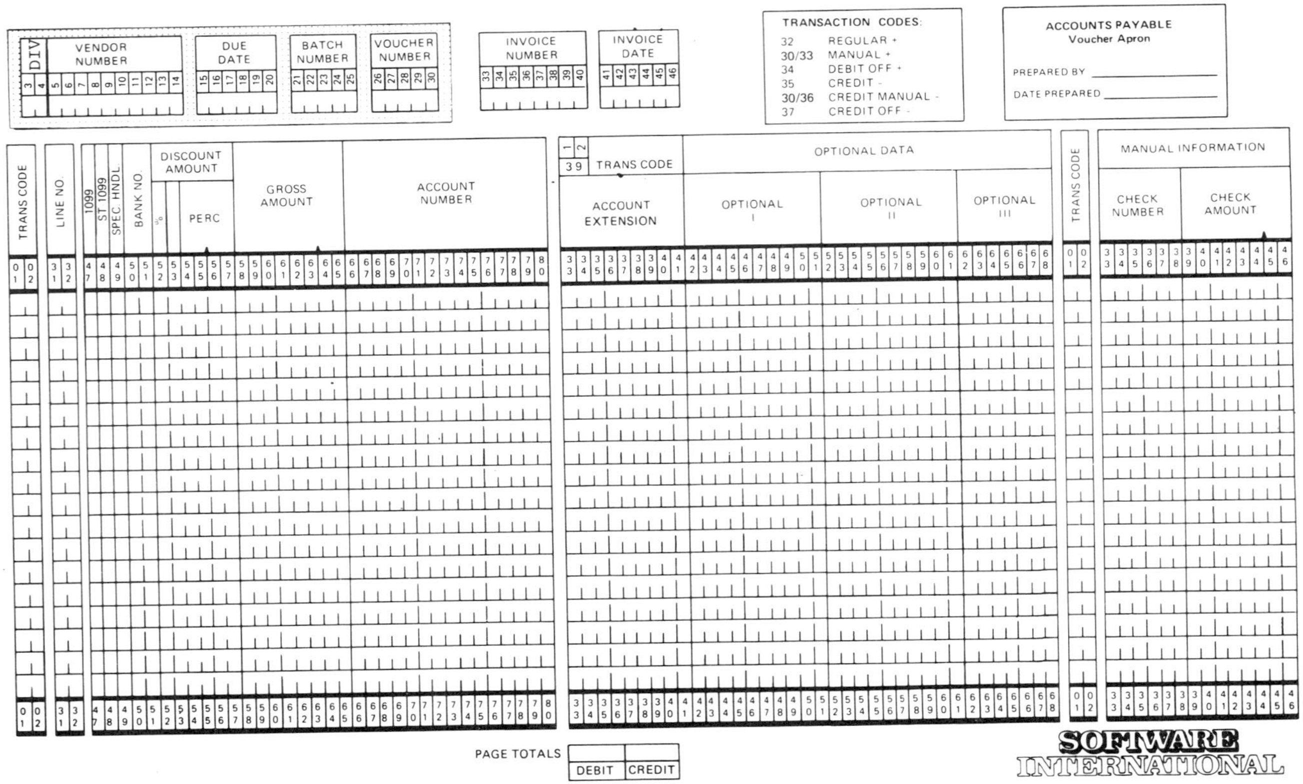

EXHIBIT 11B–5 Transaction Input Sheet

- Terms code
- "Apply to" number
- Date of last activity
- Original amount
- Remittance data
- Net amount due
- Optional fields for information or control descriptions

2. *The Customer Master File.* This contains one master record for each customer and reflects associated transactions on the accounts receivable file. It holds basic customer information such as:

- Customer number
- Customer name
- Customer address
- Credit limit
- High historical balance
- Current accounts receivable balance
- Date customer record established
- Date of last activity
- Complete overview of customer's payment history
- Invoice/credit summary history
- Optional fields

3. *The Cross Reference Master File.* This feature is unique to the Software International accounts receivable/cash management system. This file allows the financial manager to match a payment to the proper account when the only information available is the invoice number. This assures the ability to maintain invoice integrity and enhances cash application.

4. *The Customer History File.* This includes zero balance items removed from the accounts receivable master file.

5. *The General Ledger Interface Master File.* This is used to collect accounts receivable entries to generate journal entries to interface with the Software International general ledger system. An accounts receivable summary report containing a recap of all transactions posted into the system for the period is also produced.

6. *The Suspense Master Files.* These are used at the user's option to hold and maintain transactions (either individual or entire batches) containing errors until the user makes the necessary corrections. There are two suspense master files: one for cash transactions and one for noncash transactions.

Reporting

The accounts receivable/cash management system has been designed to produce a variety of valuable standard reports to provide management with all the necessary information required for complete audit, control, and up-to-date detailed and summary analysis of accounts.

In addition, certain reports such as cash management, customer history, customer inquiry, credit control, and audit trails can be generated "as required" (any time during the accounting period), and can be requested by various criteria:

- By customer
- By range of customers
- By any three parameters on the customer master file (for example, customer number, customer name, credit limit, high balance, current accounts receivable balance, date customer record established, date of last activity, or payment history

Daily Reports. These are standard reports that are produced to reflect daily processing. Included are such reports as:

- Customer master listing
- Customer file maintenance
- Accounts receivable maintenance
- Accounts receivable edit listing
- Accounts receivable G/L account number error listing
- Accounts receivable register
- Customers exceeding credit limit
- Cash edit listing
- Cash register
- Unauthorized discounts
- Charge-back report
- Accounts receivable batch control report

The following daily reports can also be produced selectively as required:

- Customer master listing
- Customer status report

Period-End Reports. Reports such as the A/R purge, customer status, and A/R history are produced at the end of the accounting period after all zero-balanced records have been purged. Standard period-end reports include:

- Accounts receivable summary by control date
- Accounts receivable purge report
- Accounts receivable history report
- General ledger distribution report
- Accounts receivable summary report

The following period-end reports can be selectively produced:

- Unapplied cash
- Unresolved deductions
- Detail aged trial balance
- Summary aged trial balance
- Accounts receivable past due report
- Forward aging of accounts receivable
- Cash forecast
- Accounts receivable open item listing
- Accounts receivable statement
- Accounts receivable dunning letter

System Processing

Software International's accounts receivable/cash management system utilizes three basic types of processing: "daily"; "as required"; and "period ending." See Figure 11B–6.

Daily Processing. In addition to normal maintenance of customer information (that is, change of address, updated credit limits, and so on) the system accepts input for maintenance of accounts receivable information such as invoices, memos adjustments, transfers, and cash transactions.

During the *edit phase,* all necessary editing is performed. The system automatically calculates amounts, discount dates, and payment due dates based on the term codes shown on the invoice transactions or customer master file. Individual transactions or entire batches containing errors may be held in suspense until corrective action is taken. The batch control report provides an analysis of the edit phase, indicating out-of-balance and error conditions.

During the *posting phase,* all appropriate data files are updated for each transaction accepted by the edit. The user can supply the criteria for which the charge-back will be utilized. Charge-back transactions can automatically be generated for short payments, overpayments, and unearned discounts if desired. Transactions from the various periods can be posted simultaneously. All data posted is retained to produce journal entries and historical reports when required.

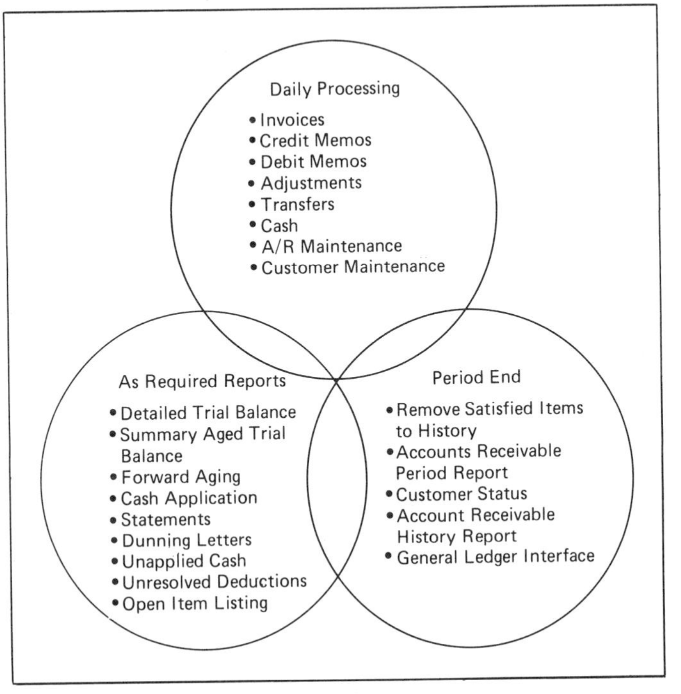

FIGURE 11B–6 Daily, As-Required, and Period-End Overview

The *maintenance phase* provides the ability to add new (and update existing) customers. Accounts receivable master and audit trails (including before-and-after listings) are provided. Specific transactions or all transactions can be transferred from one customer to another. Reports generated during daily processing include accounts receivable maintenance, A/R edit, and A/R batch control report, which reflect the transaction control and highlight conditions requiring corrective action. Exception reports are generated when unearned discounts, unauthorized deductions, and credit-limit-exceeded conditions are detected. The accounts receivable register and cash register provide the user with a detailed audit trail of transactions posted by the system.

As Required Processing. This involves generating reports at any time based upon the user's requirements. These reports can be produced for the entire accounts receivable file or can be run selectively through inquiry control reflecting the current status of each customer. Detailed and summary aged trial balance reports are produced with flexible aging capability through seven user-defined aging periods. If desired, a past due aged trial balance, a forward aging of the accounts receivable, a cash forecast report statement, and/or dunning letters can be issued. Also, if required, a cash application document can be produced.

Period-End Processing. This involves the clearing of satisfied accounts receivable master records, which are those records containing a zero balance amount due because of payment or adjustment entries. The A/R purge report provides an audit trail of records removed by the system. All purged records are retained on a detailed history file under user control and can be printed on the A/R history report if desired. In the final phase of period-end processing, a customer status report can be generated and history data on the customer master transferred to the customer summary history file as required. Journal entries may be created to interface with Software International's general ledger system.

Overview

Software International's accounts receivable cash management system gives users maximum control over inflow of cash. Advanced *system processing* fully supports comprehensive *cash management* procedures, including cash application and cash projections. A complete *customer information* base provides solid data for historical analysis and credit inquiries. The system offers many *user controls* for varying aspects of processing to satisfy individual requirements. *Audit controls* ensure the integrity of system information and the complete *reporting* capability supplies a wide range of management reports, statements, and dunning letters. *On-line* data entry and access give immediate answers to key management concerns. The database designed accounts receivable/cash management system interfaces with Software International's general ledger and financial reporting system. Full *customer support and documentation* ensure that each user receives maximum benefit during installation and in the future. See Figure 11B–7.

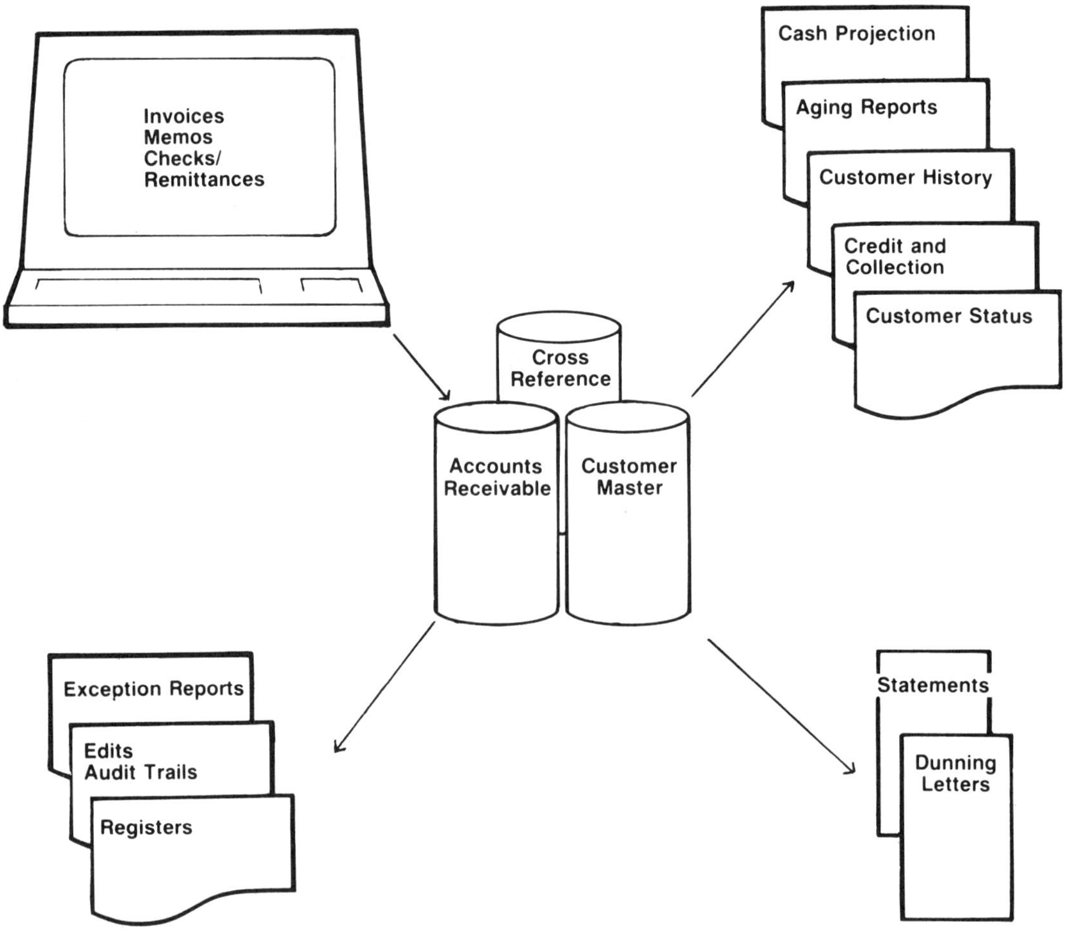

FIGURE 11B–7 Accounts Receivable/Cash Management System Overview

chapter twelve

AIS in Management Control

CHAPTER OUTLINE

INTRODUCTION

AIS CHARACTERISTICS AND CRITERIA FOR MANAGEMENT CONTROL

AIS DATA SUPPORT FOR MANAGEMENT CONTROL

AIS–MIS USE MIX IN MANAGEMENT CONTROL

ACCOUNTANTS AND MANAGEMENT CONTROL INTERFACE

MANAGEMENT CONTROL DECISIONS USING AIS

SUMMARY

REVIEW QUESTIONS, DISCUSSION QUESTIONS, AND PROBLEMS AND CASES

SUGGESTED READINGS

APPENDIX 12A: GTE'S COST AND SCHEDULE PERFORMANCE SYSTEM

APPENDIX 12B: MANAGEMENT CONTROL CYCLE OF THE SYNEX CORPORATION

INTRODUCTION

Traditionally, AIS has been regarded as a distant contributor to management control, and accountants were not expected to have as much involvement with management as they do in the case of operating control. This situation is changing fast with the rapid growth in information technology. As a result, the domain of AIS is expanding and being redefined. Accountants have to be prepared to assume a bigger role and wider responsibility.

This chapter on AIS in management control serves two purposes. First, it is important to recognize that there has been a shift in the role of accountants in organizations. In most organizations computers are now used in recordkeeping and routine manipulations, freeing accountants' time and enabling them to get more involved in nonroutine and managerial work. As a result, accountants are increasingly participating in the management process, where they interact with middle management people and decision problems. Accountants now face the challenges of coping with people. A successful accountant needs to have sufficient exposure to issues of management control that deal with information and motivation. Accountants provide information for many management control decisions and also contribute to motivation systems.

Second, the chapter provides illustrations of management control decisions where accounting information is used. These are functional level decisions—marketing, production, and financial management decisions. In the past, the functional nature of these decisions was the only focus, and the AIS as the information system employed was hardly stressed. AIS now plays an important role in functional level management control decisions.

AIS CHARACTERISTICS AND CRITERIA FOR MANAGEMENT CONTROL

A management control system "assists, guides and motivates management to make decisions and act in ways that are consistent with the overall objective of the organization."[1]

A number of structural and behavioral variables dominate the domain of management control.[2] In the interplay of these variables, accounting data provide a partial but important input to the solution of management control problems.

[1] Edward E. Lawler III and John G. Rhode, *Information and Control in Organizations*. Pacific Palisades, CA: Goodyear, 1976, p. 6.

[2] William J. Bruns, Jr., and John H. Waterhouse, "Budgetary Control and Organization Structure," *Journal of Accounting Research*, Autumn 1975.

Accounting information useful to management control must have certain qualities: measurement criteria, and reporting characteristics.

Measurement criteria include the following factors: (1) validity, (2) sufficiency, and (3) stability.

It has always been a problem in accounting to provide a "valid" measurement of certain facts for planning and control purposes. Accounting measures are *surrogate measures*. For example, in many situations people will use *residual income* other than ROI as valid measures of performance. The question of *sufficiency* is as relevant as validity. Whether a measure adequately represents all aspects of the control situation is a matter of sufficiency. Almost all accounting measures will fail to fulfill the sufficiency criterion if considered individually. That is why managers use several accounting and nonaccounting measures as supplements to any accounting measures used for management control.

Stability in measures means that the same results should be achieved from repeated use of the measure on the same data. Accounting measures satisfy the stability condition if assumptions and principles are not altered.

The reporting characteristics include the following: (1) complexity, (2) aggregation, and (3) frequency. Accounting information for management control is moderately complex. There are analytical and conceptual difficulties in the use of accounting information for management control. For example, if a variance analysis report is used to evaluate budget performance, an understanding of variances, establishing tolerance limits, and using management by exception cause essential conceptual and analytical difficulties.

Management control accounting information is mostly aggregates rather than details. Accounting reports summarize accounting data to meaningful numbers like ROI, accounting ratios, variances, and percentages.

The frequency of reporting accounting data depends on the review periods. Most accounting reports for management control are prepared monthly, quarterly, and yearly.

Lucas has summarized the characteristics of management control in Table 12–1. A brief review of the table will help us to understand the nature of the accounting information used as input to management control.

Management control decisions are middle-level management decisions. Most of the internal input for management control decisions comes from operating controls. Chapter 11 discussed the nature of operating control decisions. For example, in credit operations the tasks of preparing credit bills, receiving payments, and updating credit records are routine operating controls. Credit decisions like increase or decrease in credit line and credit approval extend beyond routine

TABLE 12–1 Information Dimension of Different Control Types

Information Dimensions	*Operating Control*	*Management Control*	*Strategic Control*
Decision points	Subordinates and operating supervisors	Middle management	Top management and the board of directors
Data source	Internal	Internal and external	Largely external
Complexity	Simple to manipulate and use	Moderately complex	Complex
Aggregation	Detailed	Moderately aggregated	Fully aggregated
Frequency	Very frequent	Reasonably periodic	Not frequent

Adapted from H. C. Lucas, "An Empirical Study of a Framework for Information Systems," *Decision Science* 5 (1974), pp. 102–103. Reprinted by permission of the American Institute for Decision Sciences, Atlanta, Georgia 30303.

activities and are based on internal and external data that fall within the category of management control. For an existing customer, managers will rely on internal credit reports, which may provide the following information from the AIS:

1. Credit limits
2. Outstanding balance
3. Payment regularity
4. Number of overdue payments
5. Overall credit rating
6. Delinquent payments (if any)

External data are collected from various sources, like credit bureaus, present and past employers, and banks. These include:

1. Credit bureau reports
2. Income verifications
3. Employment verifications
4. Bank account verification

The manager's credit decisions are influenced by both external and internal data about the customer, and by overall industry data and company policy.

AIS DATA SUPPORT FOR MANAGEMENT CONTROL

Management control data needs are both external and internal, and both AIS and MIS provide these data supports. AIS data support for management control comes from a variety of internal AIS data sources. Although the exact nature of these data sources will vary among systems, in general they include the following:

1. Operating control database and reports, such as credit reports, credit database, payroll reports, payroll database
2. Financial accounting database, such as the cost ledger system.

MIS data support for management control comes from

1. Personnel database
2. Marketing database
3. Research and engineering database
4. External database on (a) market and competition, (b) economic conditions, (c) political decisions, and (d) demographic factors

AIS–MIS USE MIX IN MANAGEMENT CONTROL

Based on the nature of data used, management control decisions can be classified as financial or nonfinancial. Financial management control decisions rely heavily on AIS databases, while nonfinancial decisions rely on AIS databases to a lesser degree. However, all management control decisions depend to some extent on both AIS and MIS. Figure 12–1 illustrates the possible mixes of uses of AIS and MIS in some selected management control decisions. It shows that there is some AIS input in all management control decisions and that some decisions use AIS more than others. Appropriate data capture and manipulation techniques are necessary to feed AIS data into the relevant decisions. For example, a decision to invest in a pollution control plan needs financial data on the costs of implementing such a decision, and its long-run revenue implications are among the more relevant social and political data.

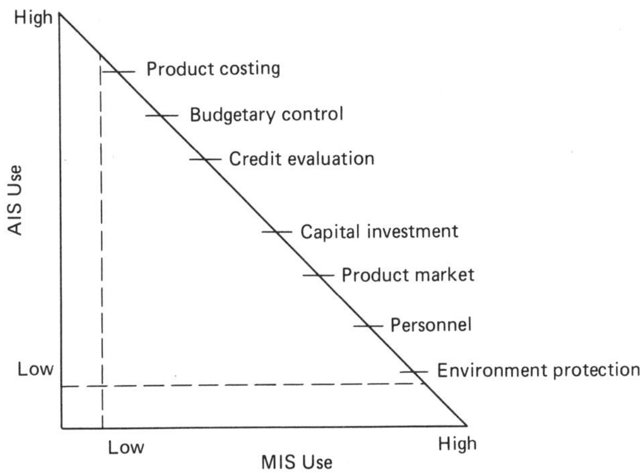

FIGURE 12–1 Use of AIS in Management Control Decisions

Data Organization for Management Control

AIS serves a host of varying management control decisions in different functional areas. Sometimes it is difficult to organize data to support these decisions, and it requires prior plans and preparation to meet the information needs effectively. An effective way to organize data for management control is given below:

1. Classify management control decisions by functional areas, such as production and marketing, and as either AIS or non-AIS decisions by using the following tabulation:

AIS Use	*Functional Areas*
A. High AIS use	1. Marketing
	2. Production
	3. Research
	4. Finance
	5. Sales budgeting
	6. Cost control
	7. Investment
B. Low AIS use	1. Market segmentation
	2. Protection and employee welfare
	3. New Product development

   This classification scheme can be further expanded, depending on the needs. Based on this scheme, a decision can easily be identified; for example, 2A means a high AIS use production decision. This helps to assess the data need and to relate the databases.
2. Identify AIS databases and relate them to decision classification; for example, production cost database or cost ledger relates to the 2A classification.
3. Make available all data needed by establishing relationships to primary and secondary databases with AIS and MIS.
4. Establish reporting formats and periods. For example, monthly budget reports compare monthly actual with the budget for the current month and year to date with variances.
5. Format irregular special reports, identify data sources, and make data available.
6. Make available appropriate computer packages, programs, and modeling languages. Example: For investment decisions, interactive financial planning system packages may be used.
7. If models were developed and used, save the decision models developed for future reference.
8. Keep track of past decisions and the accounting databases used for future reference.
9. Take feedback from decision makers on the adequacy of the information supplied and on needs for new information.
10. Review, revise, and update AIS data supports for management control.

Data Manipulation in Management Control

Management control needs data manipulation beyond routine accounting manipulations. It needs applications of tools and techniques that do not normally fall within the accounting domain. Accountants should have appropriate expertise and at least familiarity with these techniques so that they can organize data, apply the relevant technique, and interpret the results. Some manipulation techniques are cited below:

1. Statistical manipulations—simple average, standard deviations, test of significance, probability and expectations, correlation, regression, and time series analysis
2. Algebraic manipulation—matrix algebra, algebraic models, linear programming models
3. Present value models
4. Econometric models

Examples of uses of these techniques can be found in advanced management accounting and cost accounting texts.

ACCOUNTANTS AND MANAGEMENT CONTROL INTERFACE

Accountants perform a staff function in a management control process. They participate in the process through data capture, data manipulation, and periodic reporting. In order to perform these functions, they interact with more than one management level. Figure 12–2 shows a schematic representation of the accountant's interface with the management control process. For example, Figure 12–2 shows management controls in a sales function, where budgets are used as the control tools. The AIS is employed to prepare sales budgets, collect and manipulate actual sales data, prepare reports, and provide feedback to the three levels of management. The figure shows two-way flows of

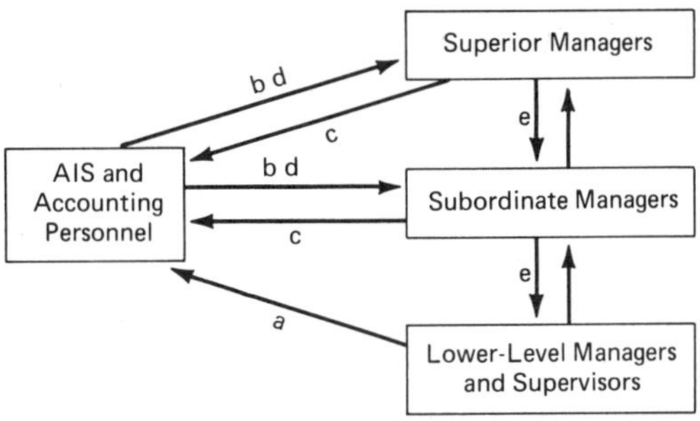

FIGURE 12–2 Accountant's Interface

information between AIS and management levels and excludes operating control levels.

The control system works this way:

a. Sales data are fed to the AIS routinely.
b. AIS manipulates data, and prepares budgets, performance reports, and variance analysis, and provides feedback.
c. Superior and subordinate managers provide budget instructions to AIS.
d. AIS prepares special purpose reports and makes presentations.
e. The feedback reports are used to evaluate performance.

MANAGEMENT CONTROL DECISIONS USING AIS

So far we have discussed some aspects of AIS supports for management control decisions. We recognize that AIS does not fully support management control data needs, and it takes special effort to organize AIS data for management control use.

The following sections of this chapter provide examples of the use of accounting tools and data for various types of management control decisions. Because of the heavy emphasis on the functional nature of these decisions, many aspects of the information systems used in these decisions can go unnoticed.

AIS-Related Managerial Control Decisions

Managers make a wide range of planning and control decisions regarding products, personnel, production policies, marketing, research, and accounting. In many of these decision situations, accounting plays an important role. Some of these decision areas are outlined below:

Budgets and Budgetary Control: Budgets are used as planning and control tools. Budget preparation, implementation, measurement, reporting, and evaluation are management control activities that require a good accounting information system.

Capital Expenditure Decisions: Decisions to invest in long-term assets need consideration of financial and nonfinancial data. AIS provides necessary financial analysis to evaluate long-term investment decisions.

Product Decisions: Managers make different types of product decisions. Decisions for product introduction, improvement, and withdrawal rely on accounting information. The evaluation of product profitability is mostly based on an accounting analysis.

Performance Evaluation Decisions: Evaluation of performance is a very important and at the same time difficult management control task. Accounting tools and techniques that are generally used include profit plans, return on investment measures, budget reports, variance analysis, and residual income.

Transfer Pricing Decisions: In decentralized operations, goods and services are frequently transferred from one department or division to another within a company. Profit evaluation of such department requires an accounting information system to assign prices to such interdepartmental transfer of goods or services and motivate managers toward the desired corporate goals.

Cost Allocation Decisions: Accounting systems face a major problem with common or joint costs that cannot be easily assigned to a particular department and are common to all departments. An appropriate allocation method is necessary to reduce interdepartmental rivalry and conflicts and to motivate managers.

Examples of Management Controls

In this section we include two examples of management controls where AIS provides direct information input: budgets as a control tool, and divisional performance measures. Appendixes 12A and 12B present two additional illustrations of real-life applications intended to provide broader views of the use of AIS in management control.

Budgets as a Control Tool. Budget is the most widely used management control tool where AIS plays a significant role. Numerous organizational variables influence the budgetary control system. Research studies on budgets show that organizational variables such as people in the organization, production technology, size of the organization, functional areas, structure, and strategy all affect the budgetary control system of an organization.[3,4]

Figure 12–3 illustrates the budget process of an organization. It shows how four hierarchical levels are integrated through the sales and production budgets. Sales and production budgets are results of negotiations among group managers, sales, and production departments. The performance reports are aggregated hierarchically upward. Most budgetary control systems will follow this model.

Budget participation is an important aspect of the budgetary control process. It has been shown that participation by lower-level people improves budget performance. In a hierarchical system, there always exists some information asymmetry between the upper and lower levels in the organization hierarchy. Participation taps the unreported information missed by the formal accounting system.

[3] Shahid L. Ansari, "Towards an Open Systems Approach to Budgeting," *Accounting Organizations and Society,* 4, 3 (1979).

[4] See Kenneth A. Merchant, "Influences on Departmental Budgeting: An Empirical Examination of a Contingency Model," *Accounting, Organization and Society,* 9, 3/4 (1984), pp. 291–307.

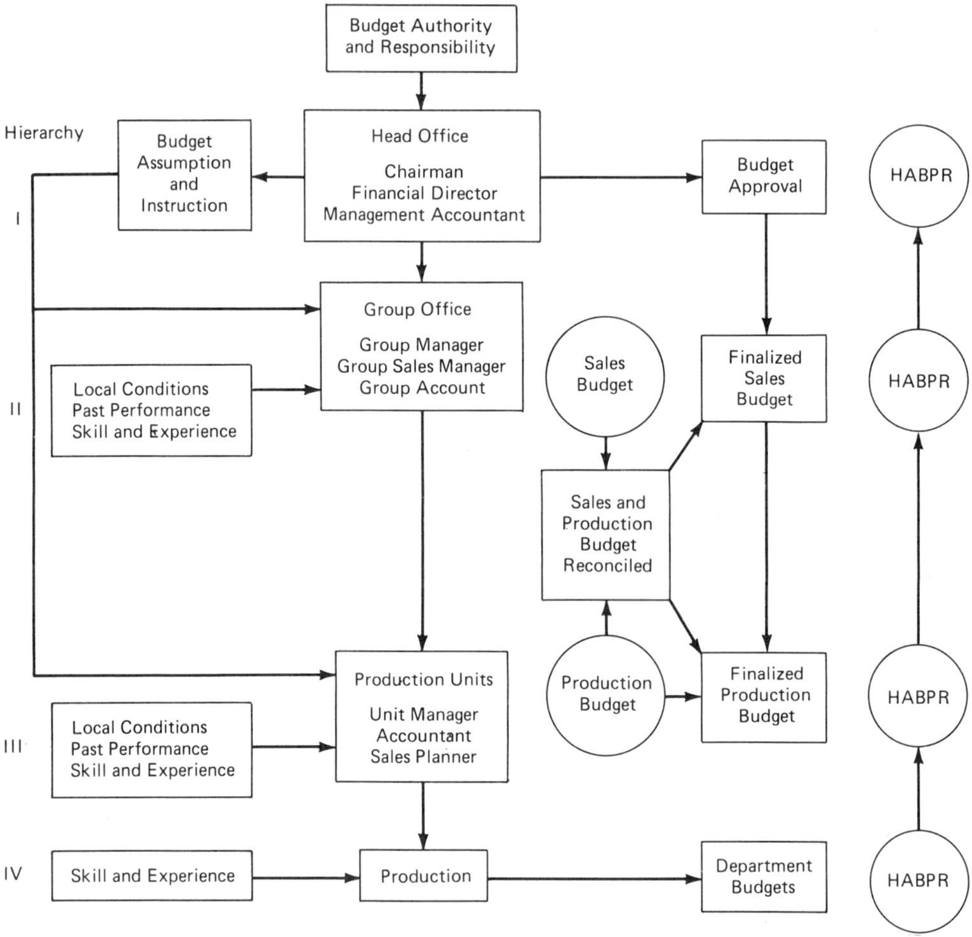

FIGURE 12–3 An Empirical Illustration of Budget Process
HABPR = Hierarchically Aggregated Budget Performance Report.

Daroca[5] cautions top management to use participation in the budget process carefully because the group process at the lower level may inhibit information instead of augmenting it. Use of accounting information for management control may encourage dysfunctional behavior that is detrimental to corporate goals. For example, divisional managers' unwillingness to invest in fixed assets may impair corporate growth and stability; budgetary control may lead to creating budget slack by departmental managers; or rigid budget use in performance evaluation may create tension in subordinates.[6]

[5] Frank P. Daroca, "Informational Influence on Group Decision Making in a Participative Budgeting Context," *Accounting, Organization and Society,* 9, 1 (1984), pp. 13–29.

[6] The following is a selection of articles that provide examples of behavioral

AIS In Divisional Performance Measures. The problems of divisional performance measures provide an intriguing and complex situation for the corporate controller and top management. The task of a corporate controller is to provide a measure of divisional performance, and the task of top management is to motivate the divisional managers toward corporate goals. There has not always been goal congruence—divisional goals and corporate goals have not always been in agreement. In order to minimize this potential danger, corporate controllers use certain criteria to establish divisional performance measures:

1. Divisional profit should not be increased by any action that reduces total company profit.
2. Each division's profit should be as independent as possible of performance efficiency and managerial decisions elsewhere in the company.
3. Each division's profit should reflect all items that are subject to any substantial degree of control by the division manager or his subordinates.[7]

Utilizing these criteria, David Solomon[8] developed a form of divisional income statement shown in Table 12–2.

The income statement shows five different types of divisional income; each focuses on certain characteristics of divisional performance, like cost variability, controllability, and assignability. The types of divisional income the report highlights are these:

1. Variable profit
2. Controllable operating profit
3. Controllable residual income
4. Net residual income before tax
5. Net residual income after tax

Return on investment (ROI) is a widely known measure of divisional performance. However, because of the multidimensional

---

consequences from the use of accounting controls: V. F. Ridgeway, "Dysfunctional Consequences of Performance Measurement," *Administrative Science Quarterly* (September 1956), pp. 240–247; A. C. Sterdy, *Budget Control and Cost Behavior* (Englewood Cliffs, N.J.: Prentice-Hall, 1960); M. Schiff and A. Y. Lewin, "The Impact of People on Budgets," *The Accounting Review* (April 1970), pp. 256–268; H. Itami, "Evaluation Measures and Goal Congruence Under Uncertainty," *Journal of Accounting Research* (Spring 1975), pp. 73–96; and A. G. Hopwood, "An Empirical Study of the Role of Accounting Data in Performance Evaluation," *Journal of Accounting Research Supplement*, (1972) pp. 156–193.

[7] See Gordon Shillinglow, *Cost Accounting: Analysis and Control* (Homewood, Ill.: Irwin, 1981), p. 688.

[8] David Solomon, *Divisional Performance: Measurement and Control* (New York: Markus Wiener, 1965), p. 82.

TABLE 12–2 A Form of Divisional Income Statement

	$	$
Sales to outside customers	xxxx	
Transfer to other divisions at market value	xxxx	
Variable charges to other divisions for transfers not priced at market value	xxxx	xxxxx
Less		
Variable cost of goods sold and transferred	xxxx	
Variable divisional expenses	xxxx	xxxxx
Variable profit		xxxxx
Add (Deduct)		
Fixed charges made to (buy) other divisions for transfers not priced at market value		xxxxx
		xxxxx
Less		
Controllable divisional overhead	xxxx	
Depreciation on controllable fixed assets	xxxx	
Property taxes and insurance on controllable fixed assets	xxxx	xxxxx
Controllable operating profit		xxxxx
Add (Deduct)		
Nonoperating gains and losses		xxxxx
		xxxxx
Less		
Interest on controllable investment		xxxxx
Controllable residual income before taxes		
Less noncontrollable divisional overhead	xxxx	
Incremental control expenses chargeable to division	xxxx	
Interest on noncontrollable investment	xxxx	xxxxx
Net residual income before taxes		xxxxx
Less taxes on income		xxxxx
Net residual income after tax		xxxxx

Source: David Solomon, *Divisional Performance: Measurement and Control* (New York: Markus Wiener, 1965), p. 82. Reprinted by permission. Copyright by Financial Executives Research Foundation, 10 Madison Ave., Morristown, N.J. 07960.

nature of divisional performance, questions have been raised about ROI as a valid measure of performance. ROI is computed as:

$$\frac{\text{net income}}{\text{assets employed}}$$

Some practitioners will show ROI as a product of the margin ratio and the turnover of assets:

$$\text{ROI} = \frac{\text{net income}}{\text{sales}} \times \frac{\text{sales}}{\text{assets}}$$

which is

$$\text{margin \%} \times \text{turnover}$$

This measure establishes a relationship among ROI, sales margin, and assets turnover. It shows how managers can influence ROI by manipulating margin percent and turnover ratio. Managers may choose to have lower margin and higher turnover or higher margin and lower turnover and still maintain the same level of ROI. Being simple and easy to understand, ROI is a commonly used divisional performance measure.

SUMMARY

In this chapter we focus on the issues emerging from accountants' new roles given current technology, and how they can participate more effectively in the management control process. Management controls include planning, measurement, reporting, and corrective actions. In the process, the data used must satisfy certain criteria in measurement: validity, sufficiency, and stability. They must also satisfy criteria in reporting: complexity, aggregation, and reporting frequency. Management control uses both internal and external data. AIS provides data support for management control through different databases. Management control uses a mix of AIS and MIS data. Data organization and manipulation for management control needs special consideration and effort beyond the usual financial and cost accounting manipulations. Accountants participate in the control process by interacting with different management levels.

AIS is used in a wide variety of management control decisions, some of which are: (1) budgets and budgetary control decisions, (2) capital expenditure decisions, (3) product decisions, (4) performance evaluation decisions, (5) transfer pricing decisions, and (6) cost allocation decisions.

The budget is a widely used management control tool. A large number of organizational variables influence the budget process. In traditional budgeting systems, budget authority and responsibility are assigned downward from the top, and reporting and responsibility are discharged upward from the bottom. In budgetary controls, two important considerations are: budget participation and dysfunctional budget behavior.

Divisional performance measurement is a challenge to the corporate controller and a headache to top management. Appropriate divisional performance measures should increase divisional income and maximize total corporate income. Controllable profit, variable profit, residual income, and ROI are some of the divisional income measures used by decentralized corporations.

REVIEW QUESTIONS, DISCUSSION QUESTIONS, AND PROBLEMS AND CASES

A. Review Questions

A12.1 Define management control. Why is it necessary?

A12.2 Describe the stages in a management control system where accounting measures are used.

A12.3 What information qualities must the AIS have to be useful for management control?

A12.4 Write some management control information characteristics and provide an example of each.

A12.5 Identify management control decisions where accounting information is likely to be used from the following list.

	Management Controls		*AIS Use*	
Decisions	*Yes*	*No*	*Yes*	*No*
(Example: Negotiating transfer price)	X		X	
1. Quality control standard				
2. Budget preparation				
3. Personnel selection				
4. Issue of materials				
5. New product development				
6. Policy statement				
7. Inventory control				
8. Budget review				
9. Purchase order processing				
10. Scheduling project employees				

A12.6 How does AIS provide data support for management control?

A12.7 Why does management control use a mix of AIS and MIS data? Is it always necessary?

A12.8 What techniques are used in the manipulation of AIS data for management control?

A12.9 Discuss the nature of accountants' participation in the management control process.

A12.10 What is budget participation? How is participation useful in budgetary control?

A12.11 Accounting information sometimes produces dysfunctional behavior. Give some examples of such behavior.

A12.12 Describe three criteria that should be followed in establishing divisional performance measures.

A12.13 What is residual income? Is it different from controllable profit?

A12.14 List different types of management control decisions where accounting information is used.

B. Discussion Questions

B12.1 Discuss the stages of a management control system. Why are they not considered adequate for effective management control?

B12.2 Management control data sources are internal and external. AIS mostly deals with internal accounting data. Would you propose to expand the AIS scope to satisfy all data needs? Provide arguments for your answer.

B12.3 Refer to Review Question A12.5 and discuss your arguments for each of your answers.

B12.4 Sometimes the usual AIS database is not adequate to provide data support to management control. Do you suggest AIS should expand to meet all data needs of management control? Support your answer with examples.

B12.5 Describe an effective way to organize AIS data support for management control.

B12.6 Why can't AIS contributions to management control be easily traced? Discuss the relevant aspects.

B12.7 Accountants increasingly face the problem of coping with people. Discuss accountants' interface with management levels in the management control process and some of the problems of coping with people.

B12.8 There is a difference of opinion about the usefulness of participation in improving budget acceptance by employees. Discuss the different views and give your conclusion.

B12.9 "Dysfunctional behaviors that are frequently reported in organizations arise because people are inherently dishonest." Do you agree? Why or why not?

B12.10 Discuss seven guidelines for effective budget systems.

C. Problems and Cases

C12.1 A company's management report provided the following information:

Sales	2,500,000
Invested capital	500,000
Return on investment	12%

Calculate, using a personal computer, (a) asset turnover, (b) margin ratio, and (c) net income.

C12.2 The following data were taken from the AIS database on three divisions of Alpha Corporation:

	Division		
	Venus	*Jupiter*	*Mars*
Sales	$15,000,000	$ 7,500,000	$90,000,000
Net income	1,000,000	800,000	1,000,000
Investment	8,000,000	50,000,000	50,000,000

Prepare a management report using appropriate ratios comparing the performances of the three divisions. (Use a personal computer.)

C12.3 Discuss the following issues with reference to the GTE case:

a. GTE uses a cost variance index and a schedule variance index in its variance reports. In what ways are these two criteria useful for management control? Do you recommend that others develop similar criteria for their variance analysis report?

b. Identify some favorable and unfavorable characteristics of GTE's Cost and Schedule Performance System.

C12.4 Discuss with reference to the GTE case whether the dynamic nature of the corporate environment has any influence on the management reporting and measurement system.

C12.5 "Our assessment of personnel is never on the basis of accounting. We do not work that way. Their performance is not measured by the amount of yarn they manage to sell . . . the salesman's environment and personal bias is important . . . my whole basis is working with people, motivating people on the basis of various factors—where accounting has never come into it."

a. Discuss the role of accounting in performance evaluation.

b. What other factors should be considered in evaluating a salesperson's performance?

C12.6 (SMA, Canada) Mr. Ringo operates a chain of retail sporting goods stores and has encountered difficulties in using his accounting data for decision making. At present, there are five stores in the chain. Each store carries the major product lines of tennis equipment, bicycles, sport clothing, shoes, guns, fishing tackle, and so on. Orders from each store are sent to the central warehouse, which does all buying and warehousing for the chain. Sales at all stores are by cash or credit card, the latter being processed centrally by a small office staff located in the central warehouse.

Once a year, the chain publishes a catalog showing all products carried in each of its stores. Prices are listed in the catalog for each product, and each store sells items at the published price. Catalogs are provided in sufficient quantities to the stores and are available to customers by mail. All mail-order business is handled directly by the warehouse.

All purchasing is done centrally by one purchasing agent, and accounts payable and payroll are handled by the central office staff. At the present time, each store deposits cash daily and forwards copies of deposit slips and credit card sales slips to the central office. The stores keep records daily (from cash register tapes) of sales by product line. At month-end, the central office prepares one income statement for the chain, with supporting schedules of sales less the average markup by product lines. Quarterly, the warehouse and all stores take physical inventory, and the cost of the goods sold figure is adjusted.

Profits have declined during the last 10 months in spite of increased sales volume. Mr. Ringo is concerned and wishes to change the accounting system so that he can obtain more relevant data necessary to determine the cause for declining profits.

You have been assigned to design a new accounting system that will provide Mr. Ringo with better performance reports for each store, as well as for the centralized warehouse operations.

a. What costs should be included in each performance report?
b. Explain whether the following costs should or should not be included in the performance reports: cost of catalog, cost of advertising, central purchasing costs, central office costs.
c. How should the profitability of central warehousing and central purchasing be measured?
d. If Mr. Ringo decides to provide performance rewards, what basis should be used to calculate bonuses for store managers?
e. What other yardsticks or control devices could be built into the system to measure performance and profitability?

C12.7 (SMA, Canada) The following information is available:

	X Division	*Y Division*
Total assets	$25,000	$125,000
Net annual earnings	5,000	18,750

Cost of capital for each division is 12 percent.

a. Using return on investment as a measure of management success, which is the more successful division? Why?
b. Using residual income as a measure of management success, which is the more successful division? Why?

C12.8 (CMA) The Justa Corporation produces and sells three products. The three products, A, B, and C, are sold in a local market and in a regional market. At the end of the first quarter of the current year, the following income statement has been prepared:

	Total	*Local*	*Regional*
Sales	$1,300,000	$1,000,000	$300,000
Cost of goods sold	1,010,000	775,000	235,000
Gross margin	$290,000	$225,000	$65,000
Selling expenses	$105,000	$60,000	$45,000
Administrative expenses	52,000	40,000	12,000
Net income	$133,000	$125,000	$8,000

Management has expressed special concern with the regional market because of the extremely poor return on sale. This market was entered a year ago because of excess capacity. It was originally believed that the return on sales would improve with time, but after a year, no noticeable improvement can be seen from the results as reported in the quarterly statement. In attempting to decide whether to eliminate the regional market, the following information has been gathered:

	Product A	*Product B*	*Product C*
Sales	$500,000	$400,000	$400,000
Variable manufacturing expenses as a percentage of sales	60%	70%	60%
Variable selling expenses as a percentage of sales	3%	2%	2%

Sales by Markets

Product	*Local*	*Regional*
A	$400,000	$100,000
B	300,000	100,000
C	300,000	100,000

All administrative expenses and fixed manufacturing expenses are common to the three products and the two markets, and are fixed for the period. Remaining selling expenses are fixed for the period and separable by market. All fixed expenses are based upon a prorated yearly amount.

a. Prepare the quarterly income statement showing contribution margins by markets.

b. Assuming there are no alternative uses for the Justa Corporation's present capacity, would you recommend dropping the regional market? Why or why not?

c. Prepare the quarterly income statement showing contribution margin by product.

d. It is believed that a new product can be ready for sale next year if the Justa Corporation decides to go ahead with continued research. The new product can be produced by simply converting equipment presently used in producing product C. This conversion will increase fixed costs by $10,000 per quarter. What must be the minimum contribution margin per quarter for the new product to make the changeover financially feasible?

SUGGESTED READINGS

ANTHONY, R., AND JOHN DEARDEN. *Management Control Systems* 4th ed. Homewood, Ill.: Richard D. Irwin, 1980.

BELL, JAN, ed. *Accounting Control Systems: A Behavioral and Technical Integration*. New York: Markus Wiener, 1983.

HOPWOOD, A. *Accounting and Human Behavior*. Englewood Cliffs, N.J.: Prentice-Hall, 1976.

HORNGREN, CHARLES T. *Cost Accounting: A Managerial Emphasis*, 5th ed. Englewood Cliffs, N.J.: Prentice-Hall, 1982.

KAPLAN, R. *Advanced Management Accounting*. Englewood Cliffs, N.J.: Prentice-Hall, 1976.

McCosh, Andrew M., Mawdudur Rahman, and Michael J. Earl. *Developing Managerial Information Systems.* London: Macmillan, 1981.

Solomon, David. *Divisional Performance: Measurement and Control.* New York: Markus Wiener, 1965.

appendix 12A
GTE's Cost and Schedule Performance System

GTE uses a management control system to control and monitor cost and performance of its contract jobs. Strict cost control and timely completion are essential in contract jobs. As in any other company, GTE's system relies on accounting information. GTE calls the system Cost and Schedule Performance Systems (C/SPS). The system has the following basic components:

1. Preparation of a task matrix
2. Preparation of a project budget
3. Preparation of a work package planning sheet

The task is monitored through three types of reports:

1. Status report
2. Budget comparison
3. Variance analysis report

The task matrix is the first step in project control. The principle of matrix organization is applied in preparing the task matrix. For example, engineering and systems design supervisors control the testing task. Once the task matrix for a project is developed, the supervisors are asked to develop project budgets for each task.

The project budget becomes the basis for preparing the Work Package Planning Sheet (WPPS), which provides the time periods, hours needed, dollar rates, and total costs for a task. It is a basic cost accounting document, and it provides data to monitor job progress.

The status report informs the supervisors and the project manager about the cost incurred to date and compares that with the budget. The cost items reported are: (1) materials, (2) labor, (3) overhead, (4) overtime premium, (5) division's general and administration costs, and (6) group general and administration costs. It shows:

1. Actual cost for work performed (ACWP)
2. Budgeted cost for work scheduled (BCWS)
3. Budgeted cost of work performed (BCWP) for the current month and year to date

The variance analysis report picks up the variances from the status report. It shows variances between BCWS, BCWP, and ACWP. Two important indexes used in the report are:

1. Cost variance index C.I. = BCWP/ACWP
2. Schedule variance index S.I. = BCWP/BCWS

The report also includes sections for (1) reasons for variances and (2) corrective actions taken. The variance analysis reports are distributed to the program manager, the task manager, and the line managers.

appendix 12B
Management Control Cycle of the Synex Corporation

Management control in the Synex Corporation is comprised of long- and short-range planning and the budgeting process.

The long-range planning involves development of a strategy for the corporation. Elements of the long-range plan are statements of objectives, industry highlights, and an appraisal of strengths and weaknesses. Factors included in the statement of objectives are: (1) market share goal, (2) growth rates for earning, (3) sales volume, (4) investment in assets, (5) return on investment, (6) margin ratio, and (7) asset turnover. Industry highlights include: (1) economic conditions, (2) competition data, (3) trends in technology, (4) risks and threats, and (5) opportunities.

The appraisal of strengths and weaknesses includes consideration of the following factors: (1) management abilities, (2) personnel skill, (3) facilities, (4) organizational structure, and (5) financial resources.

Long-range planning is a part of the strategic control that will be discussed in Chapter 13. The three sections evaluated by the Synex Corporation, (1) objectives, (2) industry highlights, and (3) strengths and weakness, were mostly judgment-based and required external and internal input.

Short-term planning comprises budgets and forecasts. Budgets at Synex include two parts: (1) The annual budget. It was the link to the five-year plan; it provided the detailed operating plan and ensured realization of the objectives. (2) The flex budgets. Flex budgets provided continuous assessment of profitability and were used as internal control tools.

Synex financial executives give special consideration to: (1) coordinating marketing and manufacturing forecasts of demands and finished goods inventory; (2) helping operating people control operating expenses; and (3) maintaining balance sheet analysis to monitor investment in assets. The flex budgets are continuously reviewed through quarterly forecasts of expenses and revenues. They are also used to achieve the "twelve-month rolling forecast." For an effective budgeting system, quarterly forecasts and twelve-month rolling forecasts provide the essential inputs.

Management reports generated by the AIS compare results against budgets and forecasts and highlight the variances. All management reports included a thorough analysis. The AIS people evaluate the techniques and data available for the analyses. Currently, data are available in manufacturing, marketing, and some service areas.

The Synex Corporation listed seven items as guidelines for an effective budget system:

1. Complete cooperation of the chief executive
2. Good organization
3. An adequate accounting system
4. Coverage of all phases of operations on a continuous basis
5. Prompt periodic reports comparing budgets and actual
6. Participation in estimates development by the line supervisors
7. Profit maximization

chapter thirteen

Strategic Decisions: DSS, AIS, and AI/ES

CHAPTER OUTLINE

INTRODUCTION

To many, AIS and strategic planning seem to be distant relations. In recent years, significant advances in hardware technology and software tools, increasing use of accounting data in managerial planning and control, and the application and expansion of corporate databases have contributed to strengthening the role of AIS in corporate strategic planning. AIS potential to contribute to strategic planning has been particularly enhanced by new developments and expansion of the use of decision support systems (DSS) and expert systems.

Organizational control through strategic planning is the task of leading the organization through a planned course to a desired future state. The decisions made at the top level to achieve the desired future state are strategic decisions. The strategic planning or strategic decision process concerns the entire organization, requires top-level initiative, needs an interface with the external environment, and focuses on a longer-term future.

Strategic planning is complex and uncertain in content and character: here the use of any information system is limited by its scope and by the nature of the problems analyzed. In this regard, the general purpose information provided by an AIS may hardly be useful. However, an AIS subsystem may be created to provide support for strategic planning needs. This chapter introduces some aspects of strategic planning and then relates aspects of strategic planning to decision support systems (DSS) and AIS. A final section introduces readers to artificial intelligence/expert systems.

STRATEGIC PLANNING: AN OVERVIEW

Strategic planning is a new subject for AIS students. The traditional contents of AIS do not include strategic planning, though AIS is an important contributor to strategic planning information. In our effort to explore the relationship between the two, we will begin by providing a brief overview of the nature and the process of strategic planning and its information needs. We will limit ourselves to those aspects that are relevant to AIS and other information processing systems.

Strategic Planning Defined

Formal strategic planning has been defined as: "The systematic identification of opportunities and threats that lie in the future environment (external and internal) which in combination with other relevant data (e.g., company strengths and weaknesses) provide a basis for a company's making better current decisions to exploit the perceived opportunities and to avoid the threats."[1]

This definition focuses on some salient features of strategic planning:

1. Strategic planning involves a system of planning and procedures formally accepted within the organization. Strategic planning also has informal aspects requiring less structure and rules and procedures.
2. Strategic planning is concerned with harnessing future opportunities and avoiding threats.
3. Strategic planning focuses on internal and external future environments, and reviews current decisions to achieve desired future outcomes.

Others define strategic planning as a process of long-range planning that affects the future of the organization: "Strategic planning is a process having to do with the formulation of long range policy type plans that change the character or direction of the organization."[2] In order to expand this definition, Anthony and Dearden use a framework for the strategic planning process which incorporates two stages: the current stage, and the future stage. The current stage comprises: (1) current outputs, (2) current goals, and (3) current resources. The future stage predicts: (1) future opportunities and threats, (2) future strategies, and (3) future resources.

A firm moves to a future state through its long-range policy plans (strategic planning), which may bring a new direction to or change the character of the firm. Appendix 13A discusses the process of interaction between the environment and the strategic planning system of a firm. Figure 13A–1, included in the same appendix, shows the role of strategic planning in linking the present and the future of the organization.

Goals and Objectives in Accounting Numbers

Strategic planning directs the firm towards its future goals. Some use the terms goals and objectives interchangeably; others use them to refer to different things.

We will use the distinction between goals and objectives as proposed by Anthony and Dearden: Goals mean broad, fairly timeless statements as to what the organization wants to achieve, and objectives refer to more specific statements of ends, the achievement of which is contemplated within a specific time period. Goals are developed in the

[1] George A. Stiener, "Formal Strategic Planning in the United States Today," *Long Range Planning,* 16, 3 (June 1983), pp. 12–17.

[2] Robert N. Anthony and John Dearden, *Management Control Systems,* 4th ed. Homewood, IL: Irwin, 1980, pp. 16–77.

strategic planning process and objectives are used in the management control process. The decisions that are taken by the organization to achieve the goals are strategic decisions. Organizational goals are expressed in quantitative and nonquantitative terms. Quantitative goals are economic goals, such as profitability and growth. Nonquantitative goals are social goals like job creation, protection of the environment, and promotion of education and culture.

Kono has made a survey of long-range planning goals of U.K., Japanese, and U.S. companies.[3] Table 13–1 shows the basic goals and productivity goals. As the table indicates, for the U.S. corporations the majority of the firms considered capital structure, product quality, rate of growth, sales, and profitability as the preferred goals. Among the basic goals, social responsibility ranked the lowest. Table 13–1 demonstrates that the dominant basic goals of companies are expressed in accounting terms—sales, assets, profits, capital structure. The performance of these goals is measured and reported through the AIS, and these are used as input to the strategic planning process.

STRATEGIC MANAGEMENT

Strategic management is a recent direction for strategic planning. Because of its origin and approach, strategic management has a definite bearing on the AIS. Strategic management addresses the issue of strategic control from strategic formulation to resource allocation through top management initiative in a coordinated way. It may be viewed as one step beyond the strategic planning process. Strategic management reduces uncertainty in corporate decisions through strategic decisions and resource allocation. Nagel has classified the components of strategic management shown in Figure 13–1.

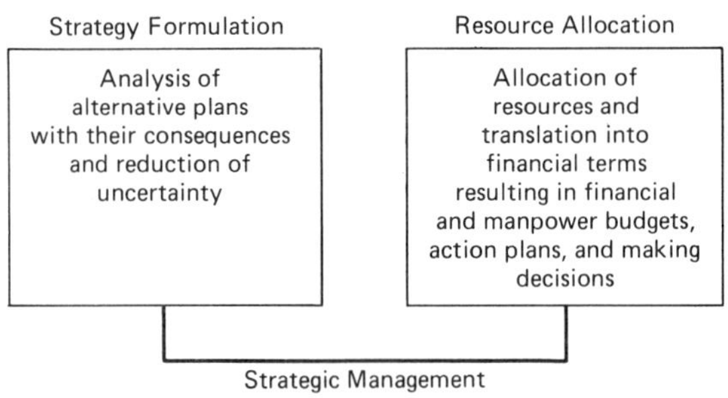

FIGURE 13–1 The Components of Strategic Management

[3] Toyohiro Kono, "Long-Range Planning of U.K. and Japanese Corporations—A Comparative Study," *Long Range Planning*, 17, 2 (April 1984), pp. 58–76.

TABLE 13–1 Goals of a Long-Range Plan
In what specific terms are the goals and policies of your long-range plans stated? (Please tick as many as necessary.)

	U.K. (%)	Japan (%)	U.S. (%)
A. Basic goals			
1. Sales	51	88*	63
2. Rate of growth (sales or profit)	59	64	65
3. Profit			
a. Amount of profit	53	87*	57
b. Profit ratio of total capital (or total assets)	59	42*	52
c. Profit ratio to equity capital	18	27	57
d. Profit ratio to sales	37	61*	44
e. Standard deviation of profit (or limit of profit in the worst case)	0	16*	9
f. Earning per share	37	18*	52
4. Market share	50	41	48
5. Capital structure	41	32	71
6. Dividend	30	43	39
7. Share price	8	2	26
8. Employee compensation	8	39*	17
9. Quality level of products	32	13*	17
10. Basic policy of growth	49	50	70
11. Basic policy of stability	14	34*	30
12. Basic policy on profit	47	51	61
13. Basic policy on social responsibility	16	19	13
B. Operational issues (productivity goals)			
1. Target value added	15	31*	4
2. Investment per employee	10	11	9
3. Target productivity of labour	37	46	13
4. Ratio of assets turnover	30	30	39
5. Policy for cost reduction	54	35*	44
6. NA	33	—	—

* indicates that the level of significance is 10 percent; comparison is between the U.K. and Japan only.

Source: Reprinted with permission from *Long Range Planning,* Vol. 17, No. 2 (April 1984), Toyohiro Kono, "Long-Range Planning of U.K. and Japanese Corporations—A Comparative Study," copyright 1984, Pergamon Press Inc.

Evolution of Strategic Management

Strategic management evolved from financial planning. At the start, the concept of planning was mainly centered around operational efficiency and thus was budget-based. Gradually it became more complex: Internal and external variables were combined, and decisions incorporating uncertainty and risk factors were evaluated. This broader look at corporate planning led the way to present-day strategic management.

Gluek[4] and others classified this background into several phases in the evolution of strategic management:

1. Basic financial planning, seeking better operational control, aiming to meet the budget.
2. Forecast-based planning—seeking more effective planning for growth and trying to predict the future.
3. Externally oriented planning—seeking increased responsiveness to markets and competition. Trying to think strategically.
4. Strategic management—seeking to manage all resources to create a competitive advantage, and trying to "create the future."

This classification emphasizes that the development of strategic management has its roots in traditional financial planning and has developed through the strategic planning process.

Strategic Planning Information: The Role of AIS

Strategic planning information consists of internal, external, historical, current, and forecasted data (Table 13–2). Internal, current, and historical data are retrieved from the functional systems; external, historical data are gathered through routine operations. Strategic data are also gathered through special surveys and market intelligence. Most of the external data are now available from commercial sources.

TABLE 13–2 Examples of Strategic Data

	Internal	*External*
Current	Interim accounting data on income	Competitor's output price and input costs
Historical	Previous period's income data	Industry performance data
Predicted	Pro forma income statement	GNP growth rates

A fully developed AIS is capable of supplying the internal financial data, as shown in this example. An AIS with a strong managerial accounting base collects most of the needed external financial data on a regular basis, through special studies or linking with external commercial databases. However, the critical feature of strategic planning information is that it is difficult to predict exactly what information is needed until the strategic problem is defined and a decision is made.

Strategic planning information covers a wide area because it seeks to answer questions on a range of variables, such as:

[4] F. W. Gluek, S. P. Kaufman, and A. S. Walleck, "Strategic Management for Competitive Advantage," *Harvard Business Review* (July–August 1980).

Product—What products?
Price—What price?
Customers—Who are the customers?
Materials—Who are the suppliers?
Labor—Is it available?
Organization—Have we enough strength?
Resources—Where are the resources?
Competition—What is the competition?
Economy—Is a recession ahead?

It should be clear that strategic planning information needs are dynamic and that no one system can completely satisfy those needs, though AIS plays a significant role.

AIS IN CORPORATE PLANNING

There is a general belief that AIS is far removed from the strategic planning system of a firm; however, on many occasions AIS is the only information system that provides internal data, takes the initiative, and helps make the decisions.

One survey[5] indicates that accountants are the most likely group to develop or use corporate planning models. In 50 percent of the cases surveyed, accountants took the initiative in the use of corporate planning models. They were followed by other departments, as follows: planning people, 26 percent; DP, or management science, 24 percent. The same survey shows a high percentage of involvement of accountants in the different phases of the development of corporate planning models:

Phases	*Accountant*	*DP*
Design and development	40%	15%
Run and operate	50%	10%
Charge	40%	20%
Support	20%	45%

It is clear that accountants really are significant contributors to strategic planning.

Most often, organizational goals are expressed in accounting terms. In such cases accounting measures of goal effectiveness require accountants to be more involved in the process. The following four examples of organizational goals and strategic decisions directly or indirectly relate to accounting measurements.

[5] John M. MacGregor, "What Users Think About Computer Models," *Long Range Planning,* 16, 5 (October 1983).

Goals	*Strategic Decisions*
Increase earning by 10%—a profit measure	Diversification into new business
Improve cash flow—cash budgeting	New credit policy
Higher customer goodwill—sales dollar	Product redesign
Social responsibility—cost efficiency	Power saving

If you examine the goals listed in Table 13–1, you will find that most of them are expressed as accounting measures. Furthermore, we have shown that accountants are among the people responsible for strategic processing in the organization. But despite its significance in strategic processing, a separate task group is rarely found as part of the AIS. AIS for strategic processing links the accounting information system with the DSS, MIS, and other control and planning information systems. This is a future direction for AIS.

DECISION SUPPORT SYSTEMS (DSS)

Decision support systems (DSS) are widely used tools for supporting strategic decision making. A DSS establishes direct links with AIS for input and data manipulations. It provides a vehicle to link AIS with the strategic planning system. Linking of AIS, DSS, and strategic planning provides effective and efficient data manipulation.

A decision support system (DSS) is defined as:

> An interactive computer based system that utilizes decision models, gives users easy and efficient access to a significant data base, provides various display possibilities and utilizes a friendly modeling language.[6]

Some consider a DSS a subset of an MIS. However, an MIS is often designed as a broad-based information support for the organization and may not utilize models. A model is an essential part of a DSS. Both DSS and MIS have data-handling capability, but the MIS may not have the modeling capability which the DSS must have. A computer-based DSS has three components: users, models, and data interfaces (Figure 13–2).

Users (decision makers) specify the model and data, which depend on their beliefs, skills, and management goals. Users determine the nature and the contents of the reports and the report media: statistical output, graphics, printout, diskette, tape, or CRT display.

[6] Robert H. Bonczek, Clyde W. Holsapple, and Andrew B. Whinston, "Future Directions for Developing Decision Support Systems," *Decision Science,* 11 (1980), pp. 616–631.

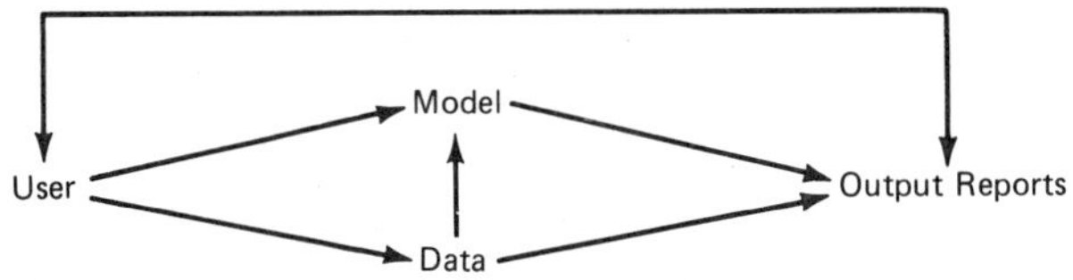

FIGURE 13–2 Computerized DSS

DSS Components

A DSS has three subsystems:

1. A language system (LS)
2. A problem processing system (PPS)
3. A knowledge system (KS)

The language system in a DSS is the computational and retrieval language that connects the user with the problem processing system. The PPS is the core of the DSS, performing the tasks of problem recognition, model formulation, information collection, and analysis (see Figure 13–3). The knowledge system comprises the database file and the body of knowledge about the problem domain. The DSS provides flexibility to the decision maker because the LS preferably is user friendly and promotes user PPS interaction. The users' general awareness of the problem is employed to manipulate PPS processes like model formulation and analysis.

A DSS brings in a lot of information manipulation capabilities to support managerial decisions. It brings together several technical tools to perform quantitative analysis, solve problems, find answers, support decisions, and generate new ideas in problem areas. The following are potential benefits from a DSS:

1. Information processing and retrieval
2. Alternative evaluation
3. Problem identification

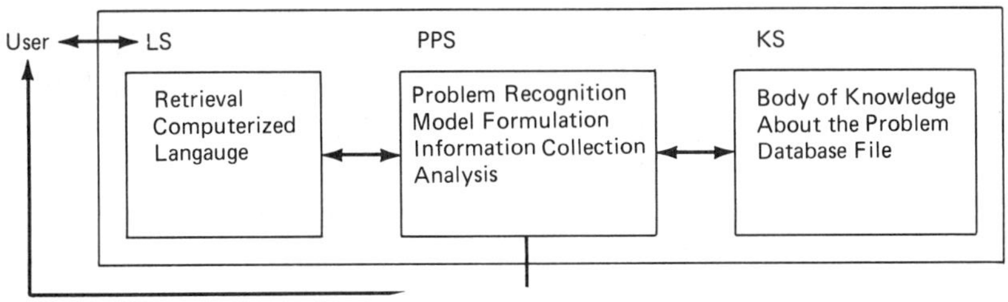

FIGURE 13–3 Generic DSS

Source: Robert H. Bonczek, Clyde W. Holsapple, and Andrew B. Whinston, "Future Directions for Developing Decision Support Systems," *Decision Sciences,* 11 (1980), p. 619. Reprinted by permission.

4. Analysis and interpretation of problems
5. Asking "what if" questions and providing sensitivity analysis
6. Multiple-step problem solving
7. Choice of output media
8. Use of mathematical models, forecasting techniques, and graphics
9. Use of accounting and financial models
10. Flexibility in report generation in format, numerical, and verbal contents

Criteria for Successful DSS Design

Sprague[7] has identified six criteria useful for successful DSS design:

1. A set of models: DSS models apply to different functional areas and managerial levels. Models support the decisions.
2. A DSS model is either stand-alone (self-contained) or interfaced (integrated) with other models.
3. DSS models extract data from the database through a language system.
4. DSS uses a command language to execute the models and direct access to the database.
5. DSS provides flexibility in modifying the procedural language and use of modules.
6. Decision makers use both models and the database.

Strategic Planning and DSS

The DSS framework applies to all managerial levels and managerial decisions. It is particularly useful in strategic processing in an organization, through its capability to support model building, sensitivity analysis, environmental scanning, use of quantitative techniques for forecasting, risk analysis, and challenges to the perceptual boundaries of decision makers.

Corporate model building is now a well accepted technique for long-range planning. The DSS supports the corporate planning model (CPM) not only through its processing system, but also by interfacing the CPM with other models that exist at functional levels. The capabilities of a DSS processing system in providing tools and techniques for data analysis and retrieval have been discussed in previous sections; some examples are included at the end of this chapter.

[7] R. H. Sprague, Jr., and H. J. Watson, "MIS Concepts—Part II," *Journal of Systems Management,* 26, 2 (1975), pp. 35–40. Also see: "A Decision Support System for Banks," *Omega,* 4, 6 (1976), pp. 157–171.

Strategic planning is among other things an innovative exercise and needs a perceptual redirection on the part of the top executive. As Hassey[8] noted:

> One of the main roles of the planning process must be to challenge the perceptual boundaries within which top management makes its strategic decisions. Many of the modern techniques are of value because by ordering information in a different way, they enable new patterns to be seen and different perceptions to be formed.

A DSS has the capability to "order information in different ways" and thus reveal new relationships in the data which may influence top management's perception and result in a strategic decision not otherwise attainable.

A DSS capable of providing a full range of support to strategic planning is sometimes called an SDSS (strategic decision support system). An SDSS supports the top executive with the models, databases, tools, and techniques that are germane to long-term planning decisions. It combines the potentials of several application packages and outside data sources with the internal database, and makes appropriate data and proper analysis available to strategic decision makers. For example, an appropriate combination of ADP's network services like Compustat with the ADR's EMPIRE may provide an SDSS. (ADP and ADR are two software vendors. An introduction to Compustat and EMPIRE is given later in this chapter.)

Distributed DSS (DDSS) supports decision makers at different locations through their own personal computers, within the available technology of micro-mainframe links. DDSS achieves data distribution and coordination through uploading/or downloading and interlinking localized systems.

From AIS to DSS and Strategic Planning Systems (SPS)

AIS, DSS, and SPS have a lot of common ground in spite of their separate domains. These domains and common grounds are presented in Table 13–3.

SPS, DSS, and AIS can be thought of as hierarchically organized where AIS is at the base, SPS at the apex, and DSS in the middle. A potential relationship between the three systems and MIS is shown as in Figure 13–4.

[8] D. E. Hassey, "Strategic Management: Lesson From Success and Failure," *Long Range Planning,* 17, 1 (February 1984), pp. 43–54.

TABLE 13–3 AIS, DSS, and SPS Domains

AIS	*DSS*	*SPS*
Accounting database	No particular database	All available data sources
Procedural language	Procedural and nonprocedural language	Uses AIS and DSS language systems
Accounting goals oriented	Decision-oriented	Uncertain or undefined goals
Uses accounting principles and techniques	Uses models and multiple quantitative techniques	Uses models
Generic reports	Decision-supporting reports	Decision-supporting reports
Realtime, on-line capability needed	Realtime, on-line capability not a must	Not necessary
Periodic and regular reports	Report, as and when needed	As and when needed
Current and long-term	Current and long-term	Long-term
Financial and accounting based	Quantitative, financial and non-financial	Quantitative and nonquantitative
The subsystems: Financial accounting Managerial accounting Cost accounting	No defined subsystems	No defined subsystem
Repetitive	Nonrepetitive	Nonrepetitive
Internal data	Internal and external	Internal and external
Operating, mid-management, and top management	Mid-management and top management	Top management
External users	No external users	No external users

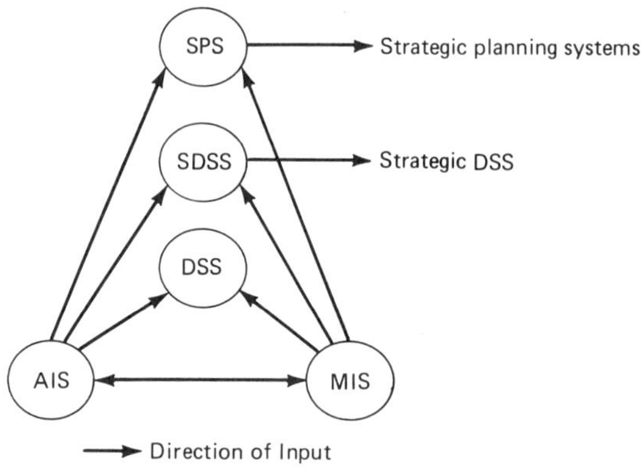

FIGURE 13–4 Potential Structural Relationships between Firm's Information and Planning Systems

DSS Software Tools

A wide range of DSS software tools is available. These tools (application packages) focus on several key areas, such as:

1. External database
2. Analytical capabilities
3. Downloading and uploading (micro-mainframe link)
4. Modeling languages

External Database. Business planning and economic forecasts rely on predicting the external environment. In the strategic planning part of this chapter we mentioned environment. Many major companies maintain comprehensive databases on external economic and industrial data. Compustat is one example of such a data source. Companies now use these commercial data sources rather than collecting their own data.

Analytical Capability. Analytical capabilities include data analysis techniques and other applications—interacting dialog, different assumptions, variable identification, modeling, regression analysis, time series, simulation, and so on.

Downloading/Uploading. Downloading/uploading is the micro-mainframe link (see Figure 13–5). This is the current trend in the development of DSS software. It supports the concept of distributed decision support systems (DDSS), where executives using their own personal computers (PC) have access to the mainframe facilities and can interact with other executives within the system. Express-mate/Express-link of Management Decision System, Inc., offers such a facility to corporate decision makers.

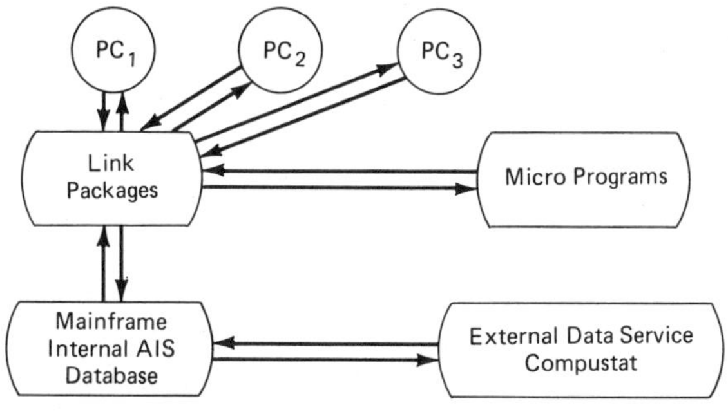

FIGURE 13–5 Micro-Main Link
PC = Personal Computer

Modeling Language. The modeling language is the language system used for DSS. Languages tend to be "English-like," with simple algebraic manipulations and notations. They are designed to be nonthreatening to the user's conceptual boundary and are called "user friendly." An example of a model created through the IFPS modeling language is included at the end of this chapter.

DSS Software Packages

In the following sections we will briefly introduce the DSS software packages of four major vendors. A list of names and products of some major software vendors appears in Appendix 13D.

Automatic Data Processing Inc. (ADP) of Ann Arbor, Michigan, in its ADP Network Services and Corporate Financial Data Bases, provides information from the income statements, balance sheets, and funds flow statements of public corporations. Here are some of the ADP databases:

Disclosure™ II—Financial and narrative data on over 9200 public companies updated weekly.

Compustat Industrial—Financial data reported annually for 6000 industrial firms and quarterly for 4500 industrial firms for up to 20 years of annual data and 10 years of quarterly data. These data are updated weekly. Compustat data sources are SEC, NASDA, company reports, Standard and Poor's, *The Wall Street Journal,* and industry sources. Compustat (R) also has databases on (1) line of business, (2) geographic, and (3) utility and telecommunication.

ADP provides business and industry statistics. ADP's data and analytical programs are helpful in projecting interest and inflation rates, spotting industry trends, identifying growth markets, evaluating pricing scenarios, evaluating capital expenditure plans, and forecasting costs and cash flows. Some of the ADP programs are:

Short-term Projection (STP)
Long-term Projection (LTP)
U.S. Economic (USECON)
Consumer Price Index (USCPI)
Producer Price Index (USPPI)

Applied Data Research's ADR/EMPIRE is a comprehensive decision support system that automates the decision-making process. The EMPIRE as a DSS provides the following analytical and modeling facilities:

1. A modeling language
2. Standard and customized reports
3. "What-if" analysis
4. Color graphics
5. Interactive forecasting capability
6. Access to corporate data

EMPIRE's application by departments is an example of the use of DSS throughout an organization:

EMPIRE Application by Departments

Department	*Applications*
Corporate planning	Economic analysis and forecasting Competitive positioning Investment analysis Financing strategies Statistical analysis Statistical planning
Marketing	Marketing and sales Strategies Alternative pricing Marketing expense forecasting
Sales	Establishment of sales quotas, sales forecasting, productivity measurement
Finance	Budgeting, pro forma projections, financing strategies, consolidations, investment analysis, capital budgeting, merger, acquisition, and divestiture analysis
Production	Production scheduling, optimizing production methods mix
Human resources	Manpower planning, regulatory compliance, recruitment planning
Data processing	Buy or lease strategy, software cost justification, user billing analysis, capacity planning

The Interactive Financial Planning System (IFPS) was developed by EXECUCOM. It offers a wide range of applications for managerial decisions and is based on a simple English-like modeling language. Some applications of IFPS: balance sheet, income statement, cash budget, operating budget, forecasting, strategic planning, project planning, real estate evaluation, risk analysis, capital budgeting, merger-acquisition analysis.

Chase Decision Systems (XSIM) provide micro-mainframe links—transfer data, computation, and report formats from the mainframe to popular micro spreadsheet packages and the reverse.

ARTIFICIAL INTELLIGENCE (AI) AND EXPERT SYSTEMS (ES)

We foresee that in future accounting systems, people will increasingly deal with DSS and with strategic planning. Another systems area that is fast developing has high application potentials in all types of complex decision making in an organization. This is the area of artificial intelligence (AI) and expert systems (ES). Applications of expert systems (ES) in accounting and auditing fields in the near future is almost a certainty.

Artificial intelligence is a higher-level use of computer technology to produce intelligent systems that can duplicate human intelligence. Expert systems are subsets of artificial intelligence. An expert system is a knowledge-based artificial intelligence. ES makes the knowledge and experience of experts available to decision makers. Data processing deals with arithmetic computation, DSS does information manipulation, and ES relies on knowledge engineering. ES is diagnostic and intuitive. ES can handle quantitative, qualitative, and symbolic data. In auditing, tax, and financial accounting, early application of ES is highly probable. ES can be based on any programming language, but LISP is the most recommended. A large number of commercially available AI/ES tools exist. One has to be selective in the choice of problems and tools for ES development and application.

What Is AI/ES?

Artificial intelligence is a higher-level use of computer resources than the usual data processing tasks or information manipulations. AI gives machines power to think like intelligent human beings in specific task situations. AI is a man-made system capable of duplicating human intelligence and requires a constellation of special purpose software tools and hardware resources. The task of working with AI is frequently referred to as *knowledge engineering,* and systems people are called *knowledge engineers.*

AI constitutes a larger area of the work of knowledge engineers and designers of "intelligent systems." An expert system is a knowledge-based artificial intelligence. It allows computers to duplicate human knowledge by capturing expert knowledge in computer programs. An ES is capable of (1) identifying facts, (2) doing backward and forward reasoning, (3) requesting additional information, (4) formulating conclusions, (5) providing recommendations, and (6) explaining reasoning.

The primary purpose of an expert system is to make available the experience and knowledge of experts in certain fields to decision makers and thus improve the quality of their decisions. ES is useful where expert knowledge is needed. There cannot be a commonsense ES; ES tasks must be beyond common sense.

Digital Corporation uses an ES named R1 (XCON) for order processing. Each order for its computer products is prepared to meet the specific needs of customers and is individually processed. Matching the customer's needs with a component mix of a large number of items is a very difficult task. Each order, in fact, is a separate product package. The use of R1 helps in carefully monitoring order processing and provides an efficient system for customization of order processing; customers get what they need, and not what the company delivers. In this business, individualized order processing would have been impossible without AI. The advantages to the corporation were not only increased customer satisfaction, but also huge cost savings, reduced errors, and increased volume.

Comparison of ES with DSS and Data Processing

Data processing deals with arithmetic computation and does not assign any meaning to data; it is mainly a clerical and transaction processing task and uses general purpose tools. DSS advances data processing to information manipulation by focusing on alternatives, restructuring data, and assigning meaning to the results achieved, but it is primarily based on arithmetic manipulation and general purpose system tools.

ES is a diagnostic system that produces synthetic knowledge and intuition, and is based on symbolic inference, not calculations. A holistic approach and ambiguity are the essence of its programs. ES systems tools are special purpose tools.

ES Applications

An ES has two components: an inference engine, and a knowledge base. An inference engine is the software configuration that manipulates knowledge provided by the knowledge base. The knowledge base captures concepts, intuition, and rules that form an expert domain in a problem area. For example, if you want an expert opinion in financial accounting, the knowledge base will include all relevant FASB statements, APB opinions on this subject, all possible examples of classifications, exceptions, and necessary footnotes. The ES will use the inference engine to ask you questions and will provide answers using this knowledge base. At the end of the interviewing, the ES will arrive at a conclusion and give a recommendation about the classification of some extraordinary item.

In general, an ES can handle quantitative, qualitative, and symbolic data. It deals with a large number of variables and with complex relationships, and flourishes in ambiguity and uncertainty. ES is now used in many specialized areas. MYCIN, used in the medical diagnosis of infectious diseases, was one of the first (1970). MYCIN acts as a consultant physician through a question and answer mode. At the end of the session, it provides diagnosis and therapy selections, and recommends drugs with dosages. It answers the questions asked by the physician about why and how the decisions were reached and provides recommendations. MYCIN optimizes the use of drugs and maximizes the overall medical benefits to patients. It is especially useful in situations of multiple symptoms where there are many possible therapy solutions requiring a diversity of drugs with possible toxic effects. MYCIN helps condense the list and select the most effective drugs for the situation.

In accounting, ES has a very high use potential, especially in the auditing, tax, and financial accounting areas. It can be used in other accounting areas too. Audit firms can use ES in capturing senior auditors' knowledge in specific audit functions, program their intuition and judgment, and make it available to junior auditors. It will revolutionize the audit programs presently used by audit firms. Some audit firms have already started using or experimenting with ES in specific areas. Coopers & Lybrand, Peat Marwick, Arthur Andersen, and Arthur Young have invested significant resources in the development of expert systems.

Arthur Young developed an expert system called Audit Smarter, Quicker (AY/ASQ) which is an integrated microcomputer-based tool. It automated all phases of audit, from planning to the preparation of financial statements. It integrated data management, graphics, word processing, and telecommunication with the DSS. The auditors now do fewer mechanical audit tasks; AY/ASQ made high-level audit techniques and judgments available to the junior auditors.

Many large businesses now use ES to make decisions in complex situations. American Express, Boeing, Ford Motor Company, Lockheed, RCA, and Texas Instruments are among the many companies presently using AI/ES technology for decision making.

AI/ES Languages

All programming languages are capable of producing results in ES. However, advanced and high-powered languages are more efficient in handling complex problem situations. FORTRAN, C, PASCAL, LISP, PROLOG, OPS, SMALLTALK, and SAIL are some of the languages used in developing ES. Languages differ from one another by their bases: FORTRAN is formula based, PROLOG is formal logic based, LISP is based on symbolic structure, and SMALLTALK is object-oriented. Generally, LISP is considered the best suited for developing ES because it is based on symbolic structure.

AI/ES does not require any special type of computer. The size of the machine needed will depend on the volume of the ES tasks. An ES can be operated on a PC or a mainframe unit.

ES Tools

An ES can be developed using commercially available systems tools. A large number of vendors market ES tools. ES tools are program packages that assist in developing knowledge-intensive programs. Generally, ES tool program packages have the capability of forward and backward chaining rules, interfacing with other languages, providing relational and object-oriented representation, and interfacing exterior data or programs, allowing users to work with concepts, ideas, and relationships and modeling questions, thoughts, and actions. Prices of the software vary, depending on the extent of the work they are designed to perform. Examples: Automated Reasoning Tool (ART)™ costs $65,000; CONTESSA, $37,500; GURU, $2,995; 1st CLASS™, $495; EXSYS, $395.

ES application software is available in many areas. In the financial area a number of commercial ES applications software are available. Example: The Financial Advisor, at $95,000; Profit Tool™, at $1,995. For a complete list of AI/ES tools, see Texas Instrument's AI Software Catalog, Fall 1986.

ES software tools, environment, people, and hardware are combined to develop a solution for an appropriate problem. A small ES system with 100 to 200 rules may take 1 to 2 months and cost between $10,000 to $40,000, whereas a large one with 2,000 to 10,000 rules may cost $1 million to $2 million and take 1 to 3 years.

ES is a fast-developing and dynamic system. One has to be very discriminating in the choice of problems and tools for ES development and applications.

SUMMARY

AIS and strategic planning have separate domains, but a lot of common ground. Advances in computer technology and software tools have contributed toward AIS use in strategic planning. Strategic planning is deciding about the future of the business by considering the opportunities and threats in the environment, and the strengths and weaknesses within the firm. Strategic planning is a way of linking the organization with the environment. The corporate environment for strategic planning includes: (1) techno-economic, (2) psycho-sociological, (3) political, and (4) multidisciplinary variables. The task of the strategic planner is to cope with a shifting and changing environment.

Strategic planning leads the firm towards its goals. Corporate goals are the long-term aims of a business. Objectives are the current short-term aims pertinent to management control. Most business goals are expressed in accounting terms. However, there are social and technical goals also.

Strategic management is the recent direction for strategic planning. Strategic management has two components: strategy formulation and resource allocation. The success of strategic management depends on: (1) the quality of management, (2) a strong planning system, (3) top management support, (4) information processing capabilities, (5) advanced conceptual awareness, and (6) the use of advanced tools and techniques.

Strategic planning among U.S. companies has improved over the last few years. Strategic planning information includes current, historical, and predicted internal and external data. A well-developed AIS is capable of supplying internal strategic planning data. AIS and accountants are very much included in the strategic planning process. AIS uses for strategic planning link accounting with other information systems within the firm.

DSS or decision support systems is an interactive computer-based system to assist managerial decision making. A DSS links the decision makers with models, data, and resources in a favorable and efficient way. A DSS has three components: (1) a language system, (2) a problem processing system, and (3) a knowledge system.

DSS may be useful in strategic planning for model building, sensitivity analysis, environmental scanning, use of analytical technique, risk analysis, and so on. A DSS capable of providing a full range of support to strategic planning is called an SDSS. AIS, DSS, and SPS (strategic planning systems) can be conceptualized in a hierarchical order: AIS at the base, DSS in the middle, and SPS at the apex.

A wide range of DSS software tools is commercially available. These tools focus on four major areas: (1) external database, (2) analytical capability, (3) downloading and uploading, and (4) modeling language.

Artificial intelligence (AI) and expert systems (ES) comprise a fast-developing area that has a high potential for accounting applications. AI involves higher-level use of computer technology. An ES is a knowledge-based artificial intelligence. An ES can handle quantitative, qualitative, and symbolic data, and can manipulate a large volume of data with complex and ambiguous relationships. Early ES applications were in medicine. Major accounting firms now have moved into the area of ES applications in accounting and auditing tasks.

REVIEW QUESTIONS, DISCUSSION QUESTIONS, AND PROBLEMS AND CASES

A. Review Questions

A13.1 How does an AIS contribute to the strategic planning system?

A13.2 What are the contributions of advances in information technology that help AIS to serve strategic planning?

A13.3 Describe the task of organizational control through strategic planning.

A13.4 Is the general purpose information provided by an AIS useful for strategic planning? Why or why not?

A13.5 Define strategic planning. What are the salient features of strategic planning?

A13.6 Strategic planning is said to have two stages. What are they? What do they include?

A13.7 What are the components of the strategic environment? (Appendix 13A.)

A13.8 What are the different types of environmental variables considered in strategic planning?

A13.9 Compare the terms *goals* and *objectives,* as defined in this chapter.

A13.10 What is an organizational goal? Can goals be quantitative and nonquantitative? Give examples.

A13.11 What is strategic management? Why is it a new direction?

A13.12 How is the strategic management capability of a firm measured?

A13.13 List the 14 factors identified as important characteristics of a good strategic planning system. (Appendix 13B.)

A13.14 What is the nature of strategic planning information?

A13.15 Illustrate the nature of strategic planning data with examples.

A13.16 Describe the capabilities of an AIS to supply strategic planning data.

A13.17 In the strategic planning process, questions are raised on a range of variables. What are these variables?

A13.18 Match the following accounting-oriented strategic goals with appropriate strategic decisions:

Accounting Oriented Goals	*Strategic Decisions*
1. Improve sales revenue of 15%	
2. Reduce credit sales by 25%	
3. Improve cash flow	
4. Higher customer satisfaction (Reduce returns)	
5. Social responsibility (Cost control)	

A13.19 Define a DSS. Is it the same as an MIS and an AIS?

A13.20 Describe the components of a DSS.

A13.21 In relation to the DSS, define: (1) a language system, (2) a knowledge system, and (3) a problem system.

A13.22 What are the potential benefits of a DSS to a user?

A13.23 List six criteria that are important in designing a good DSS.

A13.24 How does a DSS support strategic planning?

A13.25 What is a corporate planning model (CPM)? How does a DSS relate to the CPM?

A13.26 Define DDSS and SDSS. How are they different?

A13.27 List the characteristics of AIS, DSS, and SPS in tabular form.

A13.28 Develop potential relationships between SPS, SDSS, DSS, AIS, and MIS.

A13.29 What are the key areas on which DSS software tools focus?

A13.30 Review the software tools offered by Automatic Data Processing, Inc. (ADP) and provide a general description of them.

A13.31 What services are provided by the Applied Data Research (ADR) DSS?

A13.32 Give some examples of interactive financial planning (IFPS) applications.

A13.33 What is artificial intelligence? How does it operate?

A13.34 How is ES related to AI? Define ES.

A13.35 What does a knowledge engineer do?

A13.36 What is the purpose of an ES? Give the five ES capabilities outlined in this chapter.

A13.37 Distinguish between data processing, DSS, and ES.

A13.38 What are the two ES components? Define each.

A13.39 What is an inference engine? How is it related to a knowledge base?

A13.40 Give an example of ES and describe its use.

A13.41 What is the most frequently recommended AI/ES language?

A13.42 What are ES tools? Give some examples.

B. Discussion Questions

B13.1 Discuss the statement: "The strategic planning process links the future organization to the present."

B13.2 Discuss the relationship between the strategic planning process and the strategic environment component.

B13.3 Compare the similarities and the differences between the goals and objectives of an organization. Give examples.

B13.4 Discuss the nature of the long-range planning goals of U.K., Japanese and U.S. companies as shown in Table 13–1.

B13.5 How has the concept of strategic management evolved? Discuss the different stages in the evolution of strategic management.

B13.6 All characteristics of a good strategic planning system cannot be easily achieved by a firm. Why?

B13.7 It is generally believed that the AIS is far from meeting the needs of a firm's strategic planning system. Do you agree? Why or why not?

B13.8 How do accountants support strategic planning? Give your opinion of accountants' involvement in strategic planning.

B13.9 Examine Table 13–1 and list the accounting-related strategic goals. Comment on strategic decisions relating to each goal.

B13.10 Why is the DSS so widely used? Discuss the advantages and disadvantages of a DSS.

B13.11 List the potential benefits of a DSS to a user and discuss whether all these benefits can be derived by all users.

B13.12 A successful system design is always a challenging task. Discuss the usefulness of the six criteria mentioned in this chapter in designing a successful DSS.

B13.13 Discuss the concept of corporate planning models (CPM) and the role of a DSS in supporting the CPM.

B13.14 From Table 13–3, assess the potential of an AIS to incorporate strategic planning systems.

B13.15 Discuss the key areas on which DSS software tools usually focus. Which of these areas are relatively more important than others?

B13.16 Explain why AI/ES has a high potential for accounting applications.

B13.17 Compare ES with DSS and data processing. Will one replace the other? Justify your answer.

B13.18 Develop an example of an accounting problem for which ES can be used.

B13.19 Why is LISP the most frequently recommended programming language for ES?

B13.20 "AI/ES will reduce costs and increase efficiency in decision making in complex problem areas." Do you agree with this statement? Give reasons for your answer.

C. Problems and Cases

C13.1 A financial accounting system concerns itself primarily with processing accounting information for external reporting purposes within generally accepted accounting principles and standards. Management accounting processes information for managerial planning and control focused on short-term or current operations. Both of these fail to meet the strategic planning needs of top executives. There seems to be a discontinuity in the accounting information system's processing of information for top executives' long-range planning needs. Under these circumstances, outline a proposal that will link the AIS with the corporate planning system and support top executives on a regular basis.

C13.2 The concept of a decision support system (DSS) is widely used to include many activities. Some of these activities can only be classified as database operations, canned programs, or on-line data manipulations. If you are asked to develop a DSS for a medium-sized retail chain store:

- **a.** What elements of DSS will you integrate? What type of information will you provide to the managers?
- **b.** What strategic questions are the managers supposed to consider?
- **c.** Why can AIS provide information in a more cost-effective way than a separate strategic planning information system?

C13.3 Evaluate the reports and information used in the DSS illustration in Appendix 13C. Give suggestions for improvements.

C13.4 If you are familiar with a modeling language, use the DSS model given in Appendix 13C and run it with new sets of data.

SUGGESTED READINGS

ANSOFF, I. *Corporate Strategy.* New York: McGraw-Hill, 1965.

ANTHONY, ROBERT N., AND JOHN DEARDEN. *Management Control Systems,* 4th ed. Homewood, Ill.: Richard D. Irwin, 1980.

CARLSON, ERIC D. "An Approach for Designing Decision Support Systems," *Data Base* (Winter 1979), pp. 3–15.

CHANDLER, A. D. *Strategy and Structure.* New York: Anchor, 1966.

JACKSON, P. *Introduction to Expert Systems.* Reading, Mass.: Addison-Wesley, 1986.

LORANGE, P., AND R. F. VANCIL. *Strategic Planning Systems.* Englewood Cliffs, N.J.: Prentice-Hall, 1977.

MCCOSH, ANDREW M., MAWDUDUR RAHMAN, AND MICHAEL EARL. *Developing Managerial Information Systems.* London: Macmillan, 1981.

MCCOSH, A. M., AND SCOTT MORTON. *Management Decision Support Systems.* London: Macmillan, 1978.

NAGEL, ARIE. "Organizing for Strategic Management," *Long Range Planning,* 7, 5 (October 1984), pp. 71–78.

O'SHEA, T., AND MARC EISENSTADT, eds. *Artificial Intelligence: Tools, Techniques and Applications.* New York: Harper and Row, 1984.

ROTHSCHILD, WILLIAM E. *Strategic Alternatives Selection, Development and Implementation.* New York: AMACOM, 1979.

VAN HORN, M. *Understanding Expert Systems.* New York: Bantam Books, 1986.

WATKINS, PAUL. "Perceived Information Structure: Implications for Decision Support Systems Design," *Decision Science,* 13 (1982), pp. 38–59.

WILLIAMSON, M. *Artificial Intelligence for Microcomputers.* Brady, 1986.

appendix 13A
Environment and Strategic Planning

Strategic planning can be described as the task of linking with the environment. The environment is constantly changing. The impact of the shifting and changing environment on a firm's quality of performance is too pervasive to ignore. Stiener stressed that: "to cope with shifting and changing environment, the strategic planners must find new ways of exploring the shape of things to come and for analyzing strategic alternatives and at the same time must develop greater sensitivity to long term implications."[1]

[1] George A. Stiener, "Formal Strategic Planning in the United States Today," *Long Range Planning,* 16, 3 (June 1983), pp. 12–17.

In the past, the strategic environment was supposed to be restricted to the techno-economic aspect only. Companies were mainly concerned with product-market alignment. Now, the environmental reference includes a wide range of variables:[2]

1. Techno-economic
2. Psycho-sociological
3. Political
4. Multidisciplinary

Figure 13A–1 shows the environment of strategic planning in graphic form.

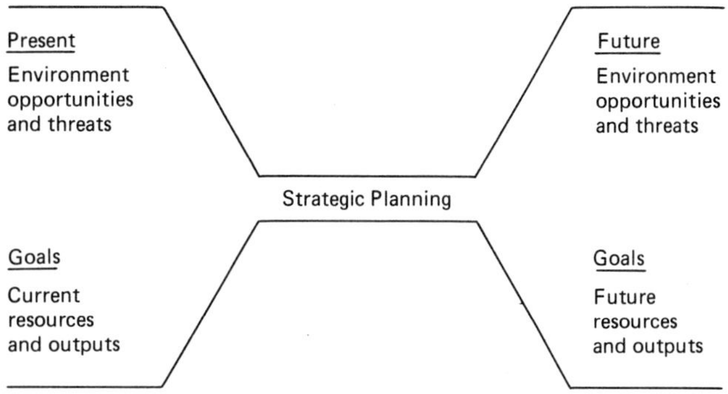

FIGURE 13A–1 The Strategic Planning Process

appendix 13B
Criteria to Evaluate Strategic Planning

Strategic management focuses on the future to answer questions like: "What has to be done to reach the stated goals?" "What are the next steps?"

The ability of the firm to achieve successful strategic management is measured through quality of management, strong planning system, top management support, information processing capabilities,

[2] Igor Ansoff, Roger D. Declerek, and Robert L. Hayes, *From Strategic Planning to Strategic Management.* (New York: Wiley, 1976).

advanced conceptual understanding, and use of tools and techniques. Stiener[1] organized these aspects into 14 characteristics of a good planning system:

1. Strategic planning interwoven into entire management process
2. CEO's (chief executive officer's) personal commitment and responsibility
3. Clear identification of purposes for strategic planning—a well-defined system
4. Balance among intuition, judgement, values, and analytical process
5. Congenial planning climate
6. Managers' conceptual skills—understanding and use of analytical tools:
   a. Strategic thinking
   b. Creative process
   c. Understanding of analytical tools
   d. Use of sophisticated quantitative models
7. Realistic appraisal of uncertainty
8. Line managers' acceptance and involvement:
   a. Top manager
   b. Middle manager
9. Focus on strategy formulation, but attention to current operation
10. Attention to effective implementation strategies
11. Linkage of capital allocation to strategic planning
12. Appropriate management reward system
13. Organizational level and influence of staff planning director
14. Simple, flexible planning system

[1] George A. Stiener, "Formal Strategic Planning in the United States Today," *Long Range Planning,* 16, 3 (June 1983), pp. 12–17.

appendix 13C
IFPS Model

```
MODEL DECISION  VERSION OF  04/01/86  14:48 -- 3 COLUMNS 36 VARIABLES
                                  1         2         3



NET OPERATING INCOME
---------------------

  SALES                       70060     73563     77241
  GROSS INCOME                66560     69888     73382
  INCOME BEFORE DEBT SER      22419      1452      8500
 NET INCOME                  -29661    -50055    -42356
PAYMENT                       56167     56167     56167
INTEREST                      52080     51508     50856
PRINCIPAL                      4087      4659      5311
BALANCE                      367913    363254    357943
 INTEREST RATE                .1400     .1400     .1400


AFTER TAX CASH FLOW
-------------------

 TAXABLE INCOME              -29661    -50055    -42356
PERIODDEPRECIATION            23250     46500     41850
BOOKVALUE                    441750    395250    353400
CUMULATIVE DEPRECIATION       23250     69750    111600

 CATEGORY                        15        15        15

 INVESTMENT                  465000         0         0
 PURCHASE YEAR                 1984      1985      1986
 TAXES                       -13051    -22024    -18636
 AFTER TAX CASH FLOW           6640     18469     18131


SALES OF BUILDING IN YEAR X
----------------------------

 SELLING PRICE               465000    511500    562650
 SELLING EXPENSE              46500     51150     56265
 NET SELLING PRICE            69187     98956    131888


TAXES ON BUILDING IF SOLD IN YEAR X
------------------------------------

 CAPITAL GAIN                -46500     -4650     41385
 CAPITAL GAIN TAX            -18600     -1860     16554


PRESENT VALUE OF AFTER-TAX CASH FLOWS AT YEAR X
-----------------------------------------------

 INVESTMENT1                  93000      4659      5311
```

```
SELLING AFTER X YEARS
---------------------
 RETURNS                        6640     18469    150019
 DISCOUNT RATE                 .1400     .1400     .1400
 NET PRESENT VALUE            -87176    -77051     20121
 INTERNAL RATE OF RETURN                           .2204
 BENEFIT COST RATIO            .0626     .2064     1.199



DATA ESTIMATES
==============
 INCOME                        70060     73563     77241
 VACANCY                        3500      3675      3859
 OPERATING EXPENSES            20891     21936     23032
 INCOME TAX RATE               .4400     .4400     .4400
 UNPAID MORTGAGE              367913    363254    357943
 CAPITAL GAIN TAX RATE         .4000     .4000     .4000
 PURCHASE PRICE               465000    465000    465000
```

```
MODEL DECISION  VERSION OF  04/07/87  15:32
10  *
20   COLUMNS 1-3
30  *
40  *NET OPERATING INCOME
50  *---------------------
60  *
70   SALES= INCOME,PREVIOUS SALES*1.05
80   GROSS INCOME=SALES-VACANCY
90   INCOME BEFORE DEBT SERVICE ='
100     GROSS INCOME - OPERATING EXPENSES - PERIODDEPRECIATION
110  NET INCOME= L90-INTEREST
120  AMORT(372000,0,INTEREST RATE,20,1,1,PAYMENT,INTEREST,PRINCIPAL,BALANCE)
130  INTEREST RATE= .14
140 *
150 *
160 *AFTER TAX CASH FLOW
170 *-------------------
180 *
190  TAXABLE INCOME= L110
200  ACRS DEPR(CATEGORY,PURCHASE YEAR, INVESTMENT,'
210             PERIODDEPRECIATION,BOOKVALUE,CUMULATIVE DEPRECIATION)
220 *
230  CATEGORY= 15
240 *
250  INVESTMENT= 465000,0
260  PURCHASE YEAR= 1984,PREVIOUS + 1
270  TAXES= L190 * INCOME TAX RATE
280  AFTER TAX CASH FLOW= L190 - L270 + PERIODDEPRECIATION
290 *
300 *
310 *SALES OF BUILDING IN YEAR X
320 *--------------------------
330 *
340  SELLING PRICE= PURCHASE PRICE,PREVIOUS SELLING PRICE * 1.10
350  SELLING EXPENSE= L340*.1
360  NET SELLING PRICE= L340 - L350 - UNPAID MORTGAGE - CAPITAL GAIN TAX
370 *
380 *
390 *TAXES ON BUILDING IF SOLD IN YEAR X
400 *-----------------------------------
410 *
420  CAPITAL GAIN= L340 - L350 - PURCHASE PRICE
430  CAPITAL GAIN TAX= L420 * CAPITAL GAIN TAX RATE
440 *
450 *
460 *PRESENT VALUE OF AFTER-TAX CASH FLOWS AT YEAR X
470 *-----------------------------------------------
480 *
490  INVESTMENT1 = 93000,PRINCIPAL
500 *--------------------
510 *SELLING AFTER X YEARS
520 *--------------------
530  RETURNS= L280 FOR 2,L280 + NET SELLING PRICE
```

```
540  DISCOUNT RATE= .14
550  NET PRESENT VALUE= NPVC(RETURNS,DISCOUNT RATE,INVESTMENT1)
560  INTERNAL RATE OF RETURN= iRR(RETURNS,INVESTMENT1)
570  BENEFIT COST RATIO= BCRATIO(RETURNS,DISCOUNT RATE,INVESTMENT1)
580 *
590 *
600 *
610 *
620 *DATA ESTIMATES
630 *=============
640  INCOME= 70060,PREVIOUS INCOME*1.05
650  VACANCY= 3500,PREVIOUS VACANCY*1.05
660  OPERATING EXPENSES= 20891,PREVIOUS OPERATING EXPENSES*1.05
670  INCOME TAX RATE= .44
680  UNPAID MORTGAGE= BALANCE
690  CAPITAL GAIN TAX RATE= .40
700  PURCHASE PRICE= 465000
END OF MODEL
```

appendix 13D

Software Vendors and Products

DSS software and data services are now provided by a large number of vendors. Some are extensive and comprehensive, and others deal with specific areas. The following list provides names, addresses, and products of some major software vendors.

Software Packages	*Vendors*
ADP Network Services	ADP Network
Datapath	
EMPIRE	
PC/EMPIRE	Applied Data Research Inc.
XSIM	Chase Decision Systems
ISIM Models	
Micro-Mainframe Link	
Horizon/370	
System W	Comshare Inc.
Micro W	
Microseek	
FCS - EPS	EPS, Inc.
Micro - FLS	
ESCA	ESCA, Inc.
Mainframe Link	
ESCA	
Decision Support System	
IFPS	Execucom System Corp.
IFPS/Dimension	
IFPS/Personal	
IFPS/Link	
Foresight	Compro Financial
Micro-Foresight	
TEICUM	
Stratagem	Integrated Planning Inc.
Stratagem (1983)	
Model	Lloyd Bush Software
Model (1983)	
Express	Management Decision Systems
Micro-Express	
Express Mate	
Gateway (1982)	SCA Products & Services Inc.

Source: Extracted from a list prepared by Nancy Clemens Croll and Jonathan Frank of Suffolk University for The Software Tools Conference. Sponsor: Professor Warren Briggs, Suffolk University.

chapter fourteen

AIS Controls

CHAPTER OUTLINE

INTRODUCTION

The problems of control in AIS relate to three aspects: information processing, reliability of financial statements, and safeguard of assets. As a result, AIS has to incorporate many control procedures to satisfy the objectives of reliability and asset safeguard, along with information processing objectives.

AIS controls consist of the systems and procedures for detection or prevention of errors and irregularities. AIS controls contain two main features: (1) the accounting aspects of control and (2) the computer aspects of control. These two sets of AIS controls influence the design, operation, maintenance, and review of an AIS.

The first part of the chapter deals with internal accounting controls, and the second part with computer systems controls.

INTERNAL ACCOUNTING CONTROLS (IAC)

Internal accounting control (IAC) consists of the routine accounting procedures set up by management to safeguard assets and ensure reliable recording of financial transactions. All internal control procedures may not be included in the AIS. Some internal control aspects are outside the AIS, such as activities of the internal audit department. The original definition of internal accounting control reads:

> Internal control comprises the plan of organization and all of the coordinate methods and measures adopted within a business to safeguard its assets, check the accuracy and reliability of its accounting data, promote operational efficiency, and encourage adherence to prescribed managerial policies. (AICPA Committee on Accounting Procedure, 1949)

This definition extends beyond the domains of accounting and finance. Thus, independent auditors subdivided internal accounting control into administrative control and accounting control. This segregation of internal accounting control suggests that both management and auditors have responsibilities for the internal control of a company. The auditors may choose to test those aspects of controls on which they plan to rely, whereas the total internal control is management's responsibility. The Foreign Corrupt Practices Act of 1977 (FCPA) made management's responsibility explicit with respect to internal control. Section 102(2) of the Act sets forth the standards that require management to: (a) make and keep books, records, and accounts, which, in reasonable detail, accurately and fairly reflect the transactions and dispositions of the assets of the issuer; and (b) devise and maintain a system of internal accounting controls sufficient to provide reasonable assurances that: (i) transactions are executed in accordance with management's general or specific authorization; (ii) transactions are recorded as necessary, (a) to permit preparation of financial statements in conformity with generally accepted accounting principles or any other criteria applicable to such statements, and (b) to maintain accountability for assets; (iii) access to assets is permitted only in accordance with management's general or specific authorization; and (iv) the recorded accountability for assets is compared with the existing assets at reasonable intervals and appropriate action is taken with respect to any differences.

Many companies have voluntarily chosen to publicly state their adherence to standards of accountability and integrity in their annual reports. The following is an excerpt from Columbia Gas System's 1986 annual report:[1]

> The accompanying consolidated financial statements and related notes have been prepared by the Corporation based on generally accepted accounting principles, and are considered by management to present fairly and consistently the Corporation's control position and results of operations subject to the outcome of the matter discussed in the accompanying Auditors' Report. The integrity and objectivity of the data in these financial statements, including estimates and judgments relating to matters not concluded by year-end, are the responsibility of management as is all other information included in the Annual Report, unless otherwise indicated.
>
> To meet its responsibilities with respect to financial information, management maintains an accounting system and related controls to reasonably assure the integrity of financial records and the protection of assets. The effectiveness of this system is enhanced by the selection and training of qualified personnel, an organizational structure that provides an appropriate division of responsibility, a strong budgetary system of control, and a comprehensive program of internal audits designed, in total, to provide reasonable assurance regarding the adequacy of internal controls and implementation of company policies and procedures. The internal audit staff is under the direction of the Vice President and General Auditor who reports directly to the Chairman of the Board.
>
> An audit committee assists the Board of Directors in its oversight role and is composed of seven directors who are not officers or employees of the Corporation. The audit committee meets periodically with the Vice President and General Auditor to review his work and to monitor the discharge of his responsibilities. The audit committee also meets periodically with the Corporation's independent public accountants, who have free access to the audit committee of the board, to discuss internal accounting controls, auditing and financial reporting matters.

Administrative Control and Accounting Control

The responsibilities for adequate internal controls rest with management, accountants, and independent auditors. The two subdivisions of

[1] Reprinted with permission from Columbia Gas System 1986 annual report, p. 36.

internal controls are administrative control and accounting control. These controls are defined in sections 320.27–.28 of SAS (Statement of Auditing Standards):

> Administrative control includes, but is not limited to, the plan of organization and the procedures and records that are concerned with the decision processes leading to management's authorization of transactions. Such authorization is a management function directly associated with the responsibility for achieving the objectives of the organization and is the starting point for establishing the accounting control of transactions. Accounting control comprises the plan of organization that is concerned with the safeguarding of assets and the reliability of financial records and consequently is designed to provide reasonable assurance that the objectives of internal accounting control are achieved.

The objectives of internal accounting control are the same as those outlined below from Sec. 102(B) of FCPA 1977.

Objectives of Internal Accounting Control (IAC)

The four broad objectives of internal accounting control are derived from Sec. 102(2) of FCPA:

1. Transactions are executed in accordance with management's authorization.
2. Transactions are recorded.
3. Access to the assets is limited.
4. There are periodic comparisons of recorded assets with the physical assets.

These objectives of internal accounting control are included to ensure asset safeguard and the reliability of financial records. The AICPA Committee on Internal Control (1977) classified these broad objectives into three major categories: (1) assets safeguard, (2) authorization, and (3) accounting. Appendix 14A reproduces a detailed list of these objectives and related controls. It is included from the Committee Report with permission.

To guide specific operations of the information system, the IAC's four broad objectives are expanded to operational objectives, from which specific control objectives are derived. The broad objectives are divided into operational objectives relating to assets safeguard and transactions recording.

For example, the broad objective of transactions recording to permit preparation of financial statements as per GAAP and maintain accountability over assets can be subdivided into several operational objectives: All transactions are recorded (1) at the correct time, (2) in the correct amount, and (3) classified, posted, and summarized. Some examples of specific control objectives and operational objectives are given below:

	Broad Objectives	*Operational Objectives*	*Specific Control Objectives*
1.	Management authorization	Established procedures are followed.	Purchase order must be signed by the manager.
2.	Transaction recording	All transactions are recorded.	Daily debit vouchers for purchases are compared with the receiving reports.
3.	Limiting access to assets	Only authorized persons are allowed to handle assets.	Inventory clerk does not make entry in the store ledger.
4.	Periodic comparison of stated and actual assets	All assets are physically counted.	Taking of physical inventory and comparing it with the inventory records.

AIS and IACS

Thus the internal accounting controls focus on the limited objectives of transaction recording and assets safeguard and of necessity deal with internal, historical, and operating data, and prevention and/or detection of errors, irregularities, and fraud. The AIS domain extends beyond these IAC objectives, as we have seen in previous chapters. We may recall that the objectives of the AIS include providing information for managerial planning and control, and are not solely restricted to the objective of preparing reliable financial statements.

Assumptions in Internal Accounting Control

The major influences on a firm's internal accounting control are external. For example, independent auditors, statements of Auditing Standards, and FCPA 1977 influence the IAC of a firm significantly. *The assumptions behind the internal control system are rigid, restrictive, and task-oriented.* Carmichael presented the following assumptions based on practice and the available literature in the subject area:[2]

1. Individuals have inherent mental, moral and physical weaknesses; therefore internal control methods and measures are necessary to achieve information processing system goals.
2. An effective internal financial system, by threatening prompt exposure, will deter an individual from committing fraud.

[2] D. R. Carmichael, "Behavioral Hypothesis of Internal Control," *Accounting Review*, 45, 2 (April 1970), pp. 235–345.

3. An individual who is functionally and structurally independent, as well as physically separated, will recognize and report irregularities which come to his attention, and also is not likely to perform discrepant actions.
4. The fear of a co-worker's rejection of an improper offer may be considered a prohibitive factor; therefore, the probability of collusion is low.
5. The plan of organization is the only determinant of power in the information processing system.
6. Actions that are not formally specified by the organization are dysfunctional for information processing goals.
7. A record system provides adequate evidence of actions such as acknowledging performance and transferring responsibility; the existence of documentary evidence implies the prior existence of concomitant actions.
8. There is no inherent conflict among the information processing goals of productivity, reliability, and safeguarding assets.

Types of Internal Accounting Control

There are three types of internal accounting controls:

1. Preventive control
2. Detective control
3. Corrective control

Preventive Controls. Control procedures designed to deter employees from committing errors or irregularities are preventive controls. When followed without deviation, carefully designed procedures are effective in preventing errors and irregularities. Separation of the recording and custodian functions for cash transactions is the most commonly used preventive control.

Detective Controls. Detective controls are used to discover errors and irregularities and draw management's attention to discrepancies. The existence of good detective controls deters employees from committing errors and irregularities. Companies have internal audit departments that check on compliance with established procedures and report the deviations to management. Bank reconciliation, periodic stock taking, and external audit act as detective controls.

Corrective Controls. Corrective controls follow the preventive and detective controls. Once the errors and irregularities are detected, corrective controls work to correct the situation, review the procedures, and remove the causes of irregularities. Detective and corrective controls are relatively less costly than preventive controls. However, they may fail to report irregularities promptly and the loss may not be recoverable, as in the case of cash embezzled by employees.

Cost-Benefit of Internal Control

In making a choice of controls, management weighs cost-benefit considerations. In other words, the costs of internal controls should not exceed the benefits expected. The cost-benefit aspects were also mentioned in the FCPA 1977. Management is

> to devise and maintain a system of internal accounting controls sufficient to provide reasonable assurance" and not absolute assurance about the asset safeguard and reliability of the financial statements.

With respect to the expected benefits of appropriate internal controls, AICPA and the SEC take similar positions:

> The benefit to be considered may often include not only quantifiable benefits, such as reduction of exposure to theft of assets, but also non-quantifiable benefits, such as, reputation of the company and its management. (*Federal Register,* May 4, 1979, p. 26704)

In general, the cost-benefit considerations include both quantitative and qualitative factors, which depend on the judgment of the management and AIS people.

Characteristics of Internal Control

The foundation of internal control rests on some essential characteristics. The Statement of Auditing Standard No. 1 (SAS) in Sec. 320 describes these essential characteristics of internal controls. The characteristics relate to transactions, functions performed, people involved, and assets safeguarded.

Recording of Transactions. Transactions should be recorded as promptly as possible. There should be elaborate procedures for recording the transactions. In order to ensure proper records, more than one employee should be involved in recording each transaction; prenumbered forms should be used and the exceptions should be investigated. Most corruption occurs at the time of recording if adequate control procedures are not strictly followed.

Segregation of Functions. In accounting transactions, manipulations involve several functions, such as recordkeeping, custodian, authorization, and operation. The functions should be segregated and performed by different people, preferably at different locations. The segregation of functions works as a deterrent to crime by collusion.

Execution of Transactions. Transactions are executed after the proper authorization and within the established procedures—goods are shipped after credit approval, with proper invoice and inventory slips. Authorization establishes responsibility, and procedures restrict variations in transaction execution.

Access to Assets. Open access to assets is at the root of many frauds. The control system should check on access to assets through control over the physical assets and document controls. Only authorized persons should have access to assets. Usually access to cash and similar assets requires the physical presence of employees.

Comparison of Physical Assets with the Records. The physical verification of assets is the test of the existence of assets. Assets should be physically verified and reconciled with the records. For example, cash securities and inventory should be compared with records.

Personnel. The effectiveness of internal control depends on the honesty and integrity of the personnel involved. The company should have explicit procedures for hiring reliable personnel, and employees should be regularly supervised and bonded.

Primary and Secondary Control Procedures

Internal control procedures may be subdivided into two groups: (1) primary control procedures, and (2) secondary control procedures.

Primary control procedures include the steps that relate to processing transactions and safeguarding assets. Examples of primary control procedures are: (1) preparing bank reconciliations, (2) a material requisition signed by an authorized person before requiring issuance of materials, and (3) requiring that approved journal vouchers only are posted to the ledger accounts.

Secondary control procedures include the environment of AIC. Company policy statements relating to controls, budgetary control, and internal audits are some of the secondary controls available.

Evaluation of Internal Controls

Internal accounting control procedures and systems are evaluated through various means. The purpose of evaluation is to assess the reliability of the controls. Independent auditors evaluate those parts of the internal controls on which they need to rely. Management has to evaluate every aspect because the whole IACS is management's responsibility.

The tools and techniques used to evaluate the IACS are:

1. Internal control questionnaires
2. Narrative memoranda
3. Procedure flowcharts
4. Control tables
5. Reliability model

Internal Control Questionnaire. The internal control questionnaire is usually administered by independent auditors to evaluate the quality of IACS. The questionnaire includes a broad range of questions relating to particular aspects of internal control. An internal control questionnaire includes questions such as these:

1. Does the company have an internal audit department?
2. Are the procedure manuals used?
3. Does management override the procedures?
4. Does the company have budgetary controls?

Narrative Memoranda. Narrative memoranda are prepared on all internal control aspects so that management and other concerned people become aware of the internal controls and their strengths and weaknesses. Narrative memoranda are time-consuming and may not always point out weaknesses; chances are that some important aspects of internal control may be overlooked.

Procedure Flowcharts. Procedure flowcharts provide graphic representation of the system and help focus attention on all aspects of the system. However, they are time-consuming and do not highlight many weaknesses in controls.

Control Tables. To overcome the weaknesses of the techniques mentioned above Loebbecke and Zuber suggested control tables to evaluate internal controls.[3] The tables relate the control procedures to specific control objectives and provide judgment on the adequacy and reliability of the control procedure. Figure 14–1 shows an example.

Reliability Model. The evaluation techniques mentioned above are judgement-based. Stratton[4] suggested the use of a reliability model to evaluate the reliability of the IACS. A reliability model is constructed by evaluating the effect of internal control weaknesses on ending dollar balances by performing sensitivity analysis. However it should be noted that the use of a reliability model is not yet a common practice.

[3] James K. Loebbecke and George R. Zuber, "Evaluating Internal Control," *The Journal of Accountancy* (February 1980), pp. 49–56.

[4] William O. Stratton, "Accounting Systems: The Reliability Approval to Internal Control Evaluation," *Decision Sciences,* 12 (1981), pp. 51–67.

Control objectives checked (✓) are those partially or fully achieved by procedures; check circled (✓) indicate those control procedures essential to meeting the objective. How many checks (✓) or circled (✓) are needed to produce a yes is dependent on the auditor's judgment.

Specific control objectives for a sales transaction

Control procedures description	All sales authorized	Sales terms authorized	Shipments invoiced	Recorded sales shipped	Sales amount correct	Sale in correct period	Sales recorded in correct amount	Sales correctly posted and summarized	Goods delivered on approved requests	Access to forms and records authorized	Details of accounts receivable maintained	Accounts receivable details agree with general ledger
Policy authorization of credit limits	(✓)	(✓)										
Specific authorization required by credit manager for extension of credit limits	(✓)	(✓)										
Use of standard order forms		✓			✓				✓			
Use of standard list of accounts to be charged, prices, discounts, terms, customer numbers		(✓)			(✓)		(✓)	(✓)	(✓)			
Independent check of order form details		(✓)			(✓)		(✓)	(✓)	(✓)			
Journal entries reviewed						✓		✓				✓
Prenumbered shipping documents (copies of sales documents) used and followed up independently for serial continuity			(✓)	(✓)		(✓)			(✓)	(✓)	(✓)	(✓)
Shipping function segregated from billing function			✓	✓					✓	✓		
Matching of sales invoices to shipping documents (packing slip signed by customer or product order validated by trucker)			(✓)	(✓)		✓			(✓)		(✓)	
Edit listing is agreed to shipping documents before files are updated			✓	✓					✓		✓	✓
Control of access to shipping area			✓	✓					✓			
Aged accounts receivable trial balance reviewed, overdue balances investigated by controller, test checked to open invoice file	✓			✓	✓			✓				✓
Review of aged unapplied payments list by controller			✓		✓			✓				
Edit listing of sales order forms agreed to detail before invoice set prepared	✓				✓		✓	✓			✓	✓
Acknowledgment copy of invoice mailed to customer				✓	✓						✓	
Programs are validated and tested periodically	✓				✓	✓	✓	✓			✓	✓
All data processing functions are segregated from other major functions	✓				✓	✓		✓		✓	✓	✓
Billing function segregated from receivables function						✓		✓		✓	✓	✓
Management review of transaction register	✓	✓					✓	✓				
Reconciliation of sales and accounts receivable posting						(✓)	(✓)	(✓)				✓
Evaluation – is the system adequately designed to achieve the control objective? (circle appropriate answer)	No (Yes)	No (Yes)	No (Yes)	No (Yes)	No (Yes)	No (Yes)	No (Yes)	No (Yes)	No (Yes)	No (Yes)	No (Yes)	No (Yes)

FIGURE 14–1 Completed Evaluation Form

Source: James K. Loebbecke and George R. Zuber, "Evaluating Internal Control," *The Journal of Accountancy* (February 1980), p. 55. Copyright © 1980 by the American Institute of Certified Public Accountants, Inc.

CONTROL IN AUTOMATED SYSTEMS

Data Processing Controls

The fundamental principles and policies in regard to internal control do not change as an organization progresses from manual accounting through batch processing accounting to interactive accounting methods. However, the procedures that are necessary and effective to ensure the adequacy of controls do change significantly. We saw in Chapter 9 that control in the AIS begins with and is integral to the software development life cycle. Constant interaction between the accounting staff and the systems development staff is required to ensure that programs do precisely what is authorized by management and that all output products meet established accounting standards. Here we consider several general principles of control as they relate to automation, and then we concentrate on the hardware, software, and procedures that are necessary to ensure that properly developed programs are used and maintained in consonance with administrative and internal accounting control policies.

Control, Data Integrity, and System Security

In an automated accounting system the issues of control, data integrity, and system security are closely intertwined. *Data integrity* refers to the requirement that all data in automated files or data bases must be accurate and up-to-date. This is clearly a prerequisite to the accounting control objective of ensuring that all financial records are reliable. In turn, data integrity can be maintained only if all transactions that affect the files are executed in accordance with management's authorization.

Computer security deals with protecting all elements of the system from physical threats, preventing unauthorized access to data and unauthorized alteration of programs, detecting any violation of the system, and recovering from any damage that might result if the system is damaged or penetrated. When we consider that many assets of an organization exist only as magnetized spots on magnetic disk or tape, the direct relationship between systems security and the accounting control objective of limiting access to assets is immediately clear.

We should note in this context that computer system security and hence accounting control can never be 100 percent effective. There are two major tradeoffs to be considered when determining how much control is desirable. First, control systems add to the cost of the information processing activities. The damage to the organization that may result from inadequate control must be balanced against the costs of increasing levels of controls. Second, control procedures necessarily make it more difficult for authorized users to access data needed for operational and managerial control. The tendency in data processing organizations has often been to sacrifice control in favor of operational efficiency. The extensive availability of on-line access to data suggests that a thorough review of this tradeoff should be conducted when evaluating internal control policies.

Control and Technology

The complexity of computer controls necessary to maintain a given level of internal control will vary with the data processing configuration of the organization.

Batch Processing Environment. In a centralized, batch processing facility we may establish a very high level of preventive control with comparative ease and little cost. Physical access can be limited to those authorized into the facility; access to data and running of programs is limited to a few designated computer operators; access to output products is controlled at a production control desk. Numerous software controls are available to ensure data integrity. An audit trail of transactions is easily maintained by keeping several generations of master files and transaction files in the tape library. This tightly controlled environment has proved inadequate to support the pace of modern business and has given way in most organizations to some degree of on-line file and interactive access.

Interactive Processing Environment. In this newer environment, control of access to data becomes vastly more difficult. There are many possible physical points of access. Programs can be executed by many personnel. Physical locks are no longer effective, and there are few focal points where controls can be applied. Output products can be generated at a large number of terminals or printers. Data processing controls in this environment must be more extensive and will be more expensive if we wish to maintain a high degree of preventive control. On the other hand, advances in technology have provided a very high degree of detective control. Modern operating systems maintain extensive logs of all transactions that are processed against the database. These logs are essential to reconstruct the database in the event of a system failure, and they provide means to trace unauthorized access to the database.

The Microcomputer Environment. The extensive decentralization of information processing resulting from the introduction of microcomputers poses a major problem for internal control. The formal controls present in the software development life cycle, the security measures that can be taken in large centralized or distributed systems, and the detective and recovery capabilities of large operating systems are all bypassed when microcomputers are operated in a stand-alone mode. If the micros are to be used in accessing or updating a centralized database, management must institute effective policies and procedures specifying the programs that are to be used and the functions that may be performed on the micros. As in the case of interactive technology, there is a positive aspect of microcomputer technology in relation to control. The use of micros by internal and external auditors has resulted in much faster analysis of accounting operations, and hence speedier identification and correction of deficiencies.

Preventive Control in the CAAIS

Preventive control encompasses those measures that prevent erroneous or unauthorized data from being processed into the database. To be effective, preventive control must ensure that (1) all authorized transactions are accurate, (2) only authorized transactions are permitted, and (3) only authorized programs are used in conducting transactions.

Controls over Accuracy of Transactions. Inadvertent data entry errors are the most common threat to data integrity. There are numerous procedural and software-based safeguards available to reduce the probability of data entry errors. Whether operating in a batch or an interactive mode, the applications software can incorporate a number of control operations.

1. *Edit Checks.* Each field can be edited to determine that it contains the correct number of characters and that the characters are those authorized for the field. For example, the "amount" field of an accounting transaction would be checked to ensure that it only contains numeric values plus, perhaps, a decimal point and a negative sign. An entry having any alphabetic data or any other special character would be rejected and an error report would be generated. The check digit technique can be used to further ensure the accuracy of numeric fields. To use this approach, the originator of the data performs some relatively simple numeric calculation involving all the digits in the data entry. This calculation results in producing a check digit which is then appended to the data value. A program that processes this data will replicate the original calculation and compare its check digit with that entered during data input. The check digit is stripped from the value and processing continues. If they do not match, there has been an error in data entry (or possibly in the original check digit calculation), and an error report will be generated. Simple check digit techniques are useful in detecting any changes in the data that might occur during data preparation or transmission. Extensions of the techique have been developed which will determine which digit in the data is in error, and in some cases even restore the original value.

2. *Reasonableness Checks.* Reasonableness checks can be performed on the fields of any record or group of records that have some necessary logical relationship among them. For example, within a single record it is possible to check that the zip code of an address is consistent with the city and the state of the address. In the case of multiple records, we can build in integrity checks so that the master accounting files will not be updated until and unless the debits and credits of a set of entries representing a business transaction are in balance.

3. *Additional Batch Processing Checks.* Some additional techniques may be employed when operating in the batch mode. Recall from Chapter 8 that batch operations may be performed in a number of ways. The significant characteristic is that transactions are grouped together in some manner and entered into the master files in a single update run. This batching of transactions provides an additional control point. All entries keyed may be verified before being accepted into the transaction file. Verification usually consists of keying the same entry twice. The only entries accepted will be those where the keystrokes of the two operations are identical. When a VDT is used in lieu of older keying hardware, a lower level of verification is sometimes used. The characters entered into the transaction file are echoed back to the VDT for visual inspection and acceptance by the operator. If the operator is satisfied that the data are correct, then the entry is accepted; otherwise, it is immediately corrected. Batch processing also employs sequence checks and batch totals. Each batch of data to be processed is assigned a sequence number. The master file will record the number of each batch as it is entered and will only process the next batch submitted if its control number is the next in sequence. Records within the batch may also be sequenced. In this case, the presence of duplicate numbers or the absence of an expected number will be signaled to the user or operator for appropriate action. Batch totals may be used in several ways. First, a manual count of the transactions in the batch can be made. This total will then be entered as part of the batch control information. During processing, the computer will keep count of the number of transactions processed and then compare this count against the control entry. A second use of batch totals is especially common in the CAAIS. Any field containing financial data can be manually totaled and in a similar procedure to that described above, compared with the totals that the computer processes. If control totals do not equal computed totals, an error message will be generated.

Controls over Authorization of Transactions. Several hardware and software controls can be implemented to limit access to programs and databases to only those personnel authorized by management.

1. *Password Control.* Perhaps the most widely used technique to limit access is *password control.* Passwords can be assigned to individual users, to departmental accounts, to databases, to files, to records, and even in some instances to fields within records. A password system simply requires an individual attempting to access the system or some component of it to know a predetermined word. Passwords can be effective if they are combined with a lockout or some other alarm system that is activated in the event that the proper password is not produced after one or two attempts. If this additional feature is not incorporated, the password is fairly easily compromised. The password system can be combined with additional safeguards that make the password valid only when entered from particular terminals or at specified time of day. These controls can be used in any combination. For example, an accounts receivable clerk can be assigned a password that will permit access to accounting files from accounting department terminals between the hours of 9:00 A.M. and 5:00 P.M. The password will be rejected and access denied if any one of these conditions is not met. In addition, the password may carry different permissions. That is, a particular user may be assigned any combination of read, write, and delete authorizations. To continue the case of the accounts receivable clerk, he may: (1) have permission to update those files supporting the accounts receivable subsidiary ledgers, to read only those files that pertain to billing and general ledger receivables accounts; (2) have no authority to delete entries; and (3) have no access at all to nonaccounting files.

2. *Procedural Controls.* Passwords may be augmented or replaced by procedures which need to be followed precisely to gain entry to various levels of software and data. Procedural controls present the user with a series of prompts which require precise, predetermined responses.

3. *Recent Developments in Access Control.* Unauthorized transactions may also be controlled by limiting access to terminals to those personnel who possess an *identification card* that contains a magnetic strip code. You are probably familiar with the use of Automatic Teller Machines (ATMs) that require you to have a magnetic strip identification card and to use a password to make cash withdrawals. Other recent access control techniques include the use of a *light pen to duplicate a signature on file* in the computer's storage, *audio voice identification,* and *terminal callback procedures*. The latter technique stores the address information in the computer's memory for each terminal. When anyone purports to be logging in from an authorized location, the communications processor is programmed to break the circuit and then recall the authorized terminal.

4. *Control over Authorization of Programs.* Controls over data accuracy prevent incorrect transactions from entering the database. Controls over authorization of transactions prevent noninformation systems specialists from improper access to data. These sets of controls are necessary but not sufficient to ensure internal control. In the automated environment, it is also essential to ensure that no unauthorized changes to programs are permitted. The control techniques applied to end user capabilities to execute programs or to access data must be applied within the information systems department to limit program changes to those which have been initiated by the accounting staff, authorized by management, and analyzed and tested prior to implementation. Internal control within automated information systems must adhere to the traditional separation of functions. In no case should the programmers responsible for program maintenance also be authorized to run the programs or to enter data into the database. The primary tools to ensure control over programs are maintenance of up-to-date documentation, a log of all authorized changes, and the activity's control logs.

SUMMARY

The problems of control in AIS relate to three aspects: information processing, reliability of financial statements, and safeguard of assets. AIS control can be divided into two parts: the accounting controls and the computer controls.

Internal accounting controls are set up by management to ensure the reliability of accounting records and safeguard the assets. All internal control procedures may not be included in the AIS. The activities of internal control extend beyond the accounting aspects. Internal control has two subdivisions: administrative controls and accounting controls. Administrative controls deal with authorization, and accounting controls deal with recording of transactions and safeguarding assets. Four broad objectives of internal control are: (1) management authorization, (2) recording of transactions, (3) limiting access to assets, and (4) periodic comparison of records with actuals. These four broad objectives are expanded to operational objectives and specific control objectives. An example of an operational objective is following the established procedures, and an example of a specific control objective is having the manager sign the purchase order.

Internal accounting control is based on certain assumptions.

These assumptions relate to: (1) moral weakness and lack of understanding in an individual, (2) independent report, (3) collusion, (4) corruption, (5) deviation from procedures, (6) documentary evidence, and (7) system capacity to expose.

There are three types of internal accounting controls: (1) preventive control, (2) detective control, and (3) corrective control. Preventive control occurs before errors and irregularities are committed, and detective control and corrective control occur after the discrepancies.

There are six characteristics of internal controls: (1) recording of transactions, (2) segregation of functions, (3) execution of transactions, (4) access to assets, (5) comparison of physical assets with the records, and (6) personnel. Accounting control procedures may be subdivided into primary and secondary controls. Primary controls relate to processing transactions and safeguard of assets, and secondary controls include the environment of IACS such as internal audits and budgetary control. Internal accounting control systems are evaluated periodically to assess the reliability of the systems. Various techniques are available: (1) internal control questionnaires, (2) narrative memoranda, (3) procedure flowcharts, (4) control tables, and (5) reliability models. Of these, the first three are the most commonly used methods of internal control evaluation.

The fundamental principles and policies in regard to control do not change with the changes in technology; however, the methods and procedures that are effective in implementing controls change considerably.

Control in the CAAIS begins with the software development life cycle. Accountants must interact with systems developers to ensure that adequate controls are built into the software. If software is to be purchased from an outside vendor, then the accountants must verify that the controls are in place and that they operate as expected.

Controls are easily implemented in a batch processing environment. The batch mode limits access to a few individuals and provides numerous check points in processing and a built-in audit trail. As we progress from batch to more flexible modes of operation, implementation of controls becomes progressively more difficult. Decentralized data entry and interactive processing permit wide access to the database. This can be controlled by a combination of hardware devices and software features, but control is often bought at the cost of ease of use—a primary concern in going to the more flexible modes.

Control over accuracy of inputs can be maintained by check digit techniques and reasonableness edits built into the program. Control over access can be maintained by password and entry procedures and by operating system features that limit access to selected terminals, to time of day, or to other characteristics selected by the users in concert with the systems security officials.

Control in the CAAIS is not complete without control over program integrity and maintenance. This depends largely on the efficient internal control procedures and the separation of functions within the information systems department.

REVIEW QUESTIONS, DISCUSSION QUESTIONS, AND PROBLEMS AND CASES

A. Review Questions

A14.1 What are the three aspects of the problems of control in AIS?

A14.2 What do AIS controls consist of?

A14.3 What is internal accounting control?

A14.4 Define internal accounting control. Who has responsibility for the internal accounting control for a firm?

A14.5 Why is the Foreign Corrupt Practices Act of 1977 (FCPA, 1977) relevant to internal accounting control?

A14.6 Describe the relevant sections of FCPA 1977 for the internal accounting control of a firm.

A14.7 How does company management respond to the FCPA 1977 with respect to internal control?

A14.8 Define administrative control and accounting control.

A14.9 Narrate the four broad objectives of internal control. Why are these four broad objectives included?

A14.10 What are the three major classifications of the broad objectives of internal control according to the AICPA committee?

A14.11 What are the operational objectives of internal control? Give examples.

A14.12 Do the AIS and the IACS represent the same thing?

A14.13 Briefly describe some common assumptions in internal accounting control.

A14.14 What are the three types of internal control? Define each of them.

A14.15 Why is cost-benefit relevant to internal control?

A14.16 Describe the characteristics of internal control in Statement of Auditing Standard No. 1, Sec. 320.

A14.17 How would you subdivide the internal control procedures?

A14.18 How is IACS evaluated? Are the independent auditors responsible for the total IACS?

A14.19 What is management's responsibility in IACS evaluation?

A14.20 Define:

- **a.** Internal control questionnaire.
- **b.** Narrative memoranda.
- **c.** Procedure flowchart.
- **d.** Control tables.
- **e.** Reliability model.

A14.21 What changes in underlying internal control policies and principles must be made when an organization automates its accounting functions?

A14.22 What two issues are closely interrelated with control in an automated AIS?

A14.23 What are two major limitations on the degree of control that is exercised in automated systems?

A14.24 What mode of computer operations provides the greatest control at the lowest cost? Why don't all accounting operations use this mode?

A14.25 What are three objectives of preventive control?

A14.26 What is the most common threat to data integrity?

A14.27 Which of these are available in both batch and interactive processing?

A14.28 What means are available to ensure that only authorized transactions are made against a database?

A14.29 Why are controls over programs essential? What control procedures are available?

B. Discussion Questions

B14.1 Discuss the important aspects of AIS controls. Why is it useful to divide AIS controls in two parts: (a) accounting aspects and (b) computer aspects?

B14.2 Review the definition of internal accounting control. Why did the independent auditors subdivide the responsibilities for internal accounting control?

B14.3 Do you think the division of control between administrative and accounting control is an efficient way to achieve better internal control? Why or why not?

B14.4 Discuss the relationships between broad objectives, operational objectives, and specific controls in IACS.

B14.5 Discuss the relationship between AIS and IACS.

B14.6 There are some common assumptions in internal accounting control. Discuss these assumptions and comment on their usefulness.

B14.7 Discuss preventive control, detective control, and corrective control. Are they equally important?

B14.8 Why is cost-benefit important in internal control? What effect does it have on the quality of the internal control system?

B14.9 Discuss the characteristics of internal accounting control systems.

B14.10 (a) How are internal accounting control systems evaluated?
(b) How does one choose a method(s) of evaluation?

B14.11 Discuss the changes in methods that are essential to controlling access to magnetically recorded assets as an organization progresses from a centralized batch mode of operations to a decentralized interactive mode.

B14.12 If control cannot be 100 percent effective in an automated environment, what criteria should be considered when establishing controls over AIS operations in general? Where would you concentrate AIS control in a retail operation? In a bank? In a hospital?

B14.13 Forward-thinking data processing authorities predict that in the future the role of the data processing department will be to maintain the security and integrity of a centralized database, and that each functional area will be responsible for developing its own applications program using microcomputers that are satellites of the database system. What control problems does this configuration pose? What policies would you recommend in this environment? How would you implement the policies?

C. Problems and Cases

C14.1 A request for purchase is initiated by the user department on a purchase requisition form. The purchasing department, after receiving the purchase requisition (PR), checks the PR for (a) authorization, (b) budget allocation, (c) correctness, and (d) store's approval. If it meets all the requirements the PR is approved; otherwise it is rejected. The rejected PR is sent back to the requesting department with the reasons for rejection. The approved PR is sent to the purchase order clerk, who selects the vendor from preapproved vendor lists, and prepares a five-part purchase order on a standard and prenumbered purchase order. The PO copies are distributed as follows: (1) Copy 1 to the vendor, (2) Copy 2 to accounting, (3) Copy 3 filed with the PR, (4) Copy 4 to the store clerk, and (5) Copy 5 to the requesting department.

Evaluate the above purchase order procedure, taking the following into consideration:

a. Does it meet any or all of these major categories of broad objectives: (1) assets safeguard, (2) authorization, and (3) accounting?

b. Identify the broad objectives, operational objectives, and specific control objectives included in the procedure.

SUGGESTED READINGS

ARTHUR ANDERSEN & CO. *A Guide to Studying and Evaluating Internal Accounting Controls*. New York: Arthur Andersen & Co., 1978.

COOK, MICHAEL J., AND THOMAS P. KELLING. "Internal Accounting Control: A Matter of Law," *The Journal of Accountancy* (January 1979), pp. 56–64.

COOPERS & LYBRAND. *Sharpening Controls: Corporate Approaches to Complying with the Foreign Corrupt Practices Act*. New York: Coopers and Lybrand, 1978.

Statement of Auditing Standards No. 1, *Codification of Auditing Standards and Procedures*. (New York: AICPA, 1973).

Statement of Auditing Standards No. 3, *Reporting on Internal Accounting Control*. New York: AICPA, 1980.

appendix 14A

Excerpts from the Report of the Special Advisory Committee on Internal Accounting Control*

THE REVENUE CYCLE

The revenue cycle covers the functions involved in receiving and accepting requests for goods or services; delivering or otherwise providing goods or services; credit granting, cash receipts, and collection activities; billing; accounting for revenues, accounts receivable, commissions, warranties, bad debts, returned goods, and other adjustments.

"Authorization" in the revenue cycle encompasses the types of products and services provided; classes of customers serviced (including related and foreign parties); distribution channels used; prices, credit, and other terms of sale; individual customer acceptance; sales-related adjustments and policies with respect thereto, such as policies on acceptance of returned goods; services furnished to customers, including warranty policies; billing and collection practices; sales compensation policies.

"Accounting" encompasses the procedures and techniques used to control the recording and classification of transactions that relate to revenue and cash receipts, deductions from revenue (for example, sales taxes, commissions, bad debts), and the distribution of such transactions to individual accounts receivable records and other subsidiary records.

"Asset Safeguarding" relates primarily to controls that safeguard cash receipts and protect important records.

Authorization Objectives

Specific Objective	*Examples of Selected Control Procedures and Techniques*
1. The types of goods and services to be provided, the manner in which they will be provided, and the	• Procedures for acceptance and approval of orders for nonstandard goods or services and for unusual delivery arrangements.

Specific Objective	*Examples of Selected Control Procedures and Techniques*
customers to which they will be provided should be properly authorized.	• Policies on export sales and sales to related parties. • Policies on customer acceptance, including policies on acceptance and approval of checks and credit cards. • Use of an approved customer list. • Assigned responsibility and established procedures for approval of customer orders (customer acceptance, credit-worthiness, prices, and other terms of sale).
2. Credit terms and limits should be properly authorized.	• Established credit policies. • Policies for investigating credit-worthiness of prospective customers. • Periodic review of credit limits.
3. The prices and other terms of sale of goods and services should be properly authorized.	• Approved sales catalogs or similar documents containing current price information and policies on matters such as discounts, sales taxes, freight, service, warranties, and returned goods. • Use of appropriate contract forms. • Procedures for approval of individually priced sales.
4. Sales-related deductions and adjustments should be properly authorized.	• Approved commission schedules. • Procedures for approval of "no charge" service invoices and services performed under a warranty. • Procedures for approval of bad debt write-offs and other credits to customer accounts, including credits given for returned goods.

Accounting Objectives

Specific Objective	*Examples of Selected Control Procedures and Techniques*
5. Deliveries of goods and services should result in	• Shipping and billing procedures that provide for the means to

Specific Objective	*Examples of Selected Control Procedures and Techniques*
preparation of accurate and timely billing forms.	account for all goods shipped or services delivered and comparisons of shipments to billings, perhaps individually or through a form of batch control. • Policies covering the types of "memo billings" that may be issued and approval procedures over such billings. • Check of quantities of goods shipped by, for example, independent counts by common carriers or double counting of shipments.
6. Sales and related transactions should be recorded at the appropriate amounts and in the appropriate period and should be properly classified in the accounts.	• Policies and procedures covering accounting routines and related approval procedures for the major functions within the revenue cycle. • A suitable chart of accounts and standard journal entries. • Written, properly communicated sales (and cost of sales) cut-off procedures and review of the cut-off. • Reconciliation of the accounts receivable subsidiary ledger to the general ledger on a regular basis. • Independent mailing of statements to customers on a monthly basis.
7. Cash receipts should be accounted for properly on a timely basis.	• Comparison of initial record of cash receipts to bank deposits and accounting entries and investigation of any unusual delays in depositing receipts.

Asset Safeguarding Objectives

Specific Objective	*Examples of Selected Control Procedures and Techniques*
8. Access to cash receipts and cash receipts records, accounts receivable records, and billing and shipping records should be	• Independent control of cash upon receipt (through, for example, lock box arrangements, cash registers, prenumbered cash receipt forms).

Specific Objective	*Examples of Selected Control Procedures and Techniques*
suitably controlled to prevent or detect within a timely period the interception of unrecorded cash receipts or the abstraction of recorded cash receipts.	• Restrictive endorsement of checks upon receipt. • Segregation of duties between access to cash receipts and keeping records of sales, customer credits, cash receipts, and accounts receivable. • Timely investigation of past due accounts.

THE EXPENDITURES CYCLE

The expenditures cycle is sudivided into purchasing, payroll, and disbursement functions.

Purchasing covers the functions involved in initiating requests for goods, other assets, and services ("goods"); obtaining information as to available vendors, prices, and other specifications; placing orders for goods; receiving and inspecting or otherwise accepting the goods delivered or provided; accounting for amounts payable to vendors, including freight-in, cash discounts, returned goods, and other adjustments. Payroll covers the functions involved in hiring employees and deciding their compensation, direct and indirect; reporting attendance and work performed; accounting for payroll costs, payroll deductions, employee benefits, and other adjustments. Disbursement covers the functions involved in preparing, signing, and issuing checks or distributing cash.

"Authorization" in the expenditures cycle encompasses the types and specifications of goods to be obtained; vendors used (including related parties); prices, specifications, credit, and other terms of purchase; the selection, hiring, termination, and promotion of employees; wages, salaries, and commission rates; types and amount of employee benefits; signing and issuance of checks; adjustments to vendor, payroll, and cash accounts, and policies with respect thereto, such as quality control policies for goods accepted, and policies for termination pay and other special employee payments.

"Accounting" encompasses the procedures and techniques used to control the recording and classification of transactions that relate to purchases, payroll, and cash disbursements, including accounts payable, purchase discounts lost, freight-in, gross payroll, payroll deductions, accruals related to such accounts, and the distribution of such transactions to the appropriate accounts, including individual payroll records.

"Asset Safeguarding" relates primarily to controls that provide reasonable assurance that payments are made only for authorized goods and authorized employees and that protect important records.

Authorization Objectives

Specific Objective	*Examples of Selected Control Procedures and Techniques*
1. The types of goods, other assets, and services to be obtained, the manner in which they are obtained, the vendors from which they are obtained, the quantities to be obtained, and the prices and other terms of sale should be properly authorized.	• Use of purchase requisitions. • Guidelines for vendor acceptability, based on considerations such as past performance, reputation, and credit standing; ability to meet delivery, quality, and service specifications; price competitiveness; legal restrictions; and policies on related party transactions. • Use of an approved vendor list based on established guidelines. • Use of priced purchase orders. • Procedures for prior review of contracts with vendors. • Established procedures for approval or purchase requisitions and purchase orders, and changes thereto, including the establishment of reasonable limitations on the approval authority of specific individuals or classes of individuals. • Assigned responsibility for effecting compliance with purchasing policies.
2. Adjustments to vendor accounts and account distributions should be property authorized.	• Use and approval of debit memos to notify vendors of goods returned to them and other adjustments to their accounts. • Assigned responsibility for approval of changes in account distribution.

Accounting Objectives

Specific Objective	*Examples of Selected Control Procedures and Techniques*
3. All goods, other assets, and services received should be	• Use of receiving reports. • Timely review of all unmatched

Specific Objective	*Examples of Selected Control Procedures and Techniques*
accounted for properly on a timely basis.	receiving reports and purchase orders. • Accounting for all issued vouchers. • Policies and procedures covering accounting routines and related approval procedures for the major purchasing functions. • Review of vendor statements for past-due items.
4. Amounts payable for goods and services received should be recorded at the appropriate amounts and in the appropriate period and should be properly classified in the accounts.	• Comparison of vendor invoices to receiving reports and purchase orders. • Clerical check of vendor invoices. • Written, properly communicated cut-off procedures and review of the cut-off. • Procedures for making appropriate financial statement accruals based on unmatched receiving reports and, where appropriate (certain other assets and services), unmatched purchase orders. • A suitable chart of accounts and standard journal entries. • Established guidelines for determining account distribution (capital vs. expense, overhead vs. administrative, etc.). • Insertion of account distribution on purchasing documents. • Reconciliation of accounts payable subsidiary ledger to the general ledger on a regular basis. • Independent follow-up of overdue items on vendor statements, payment requests, complaints, etc.

Asset Safeguarding Objectives

Specific Objective	*Examples of Selected Control Procedures and Techniques*
5. Access to purchasing, receiving, and accounts payable records should be	• Cancellation of supporting documents upon payment. • Approval of vouchers and sup-

Specific Objective	*Examples of Selected Control Procedures and Techniques*
suitably controlled to prevent or detect within a timely period duplicate or improper payments.	porting documents prior to payment. • Segregation of duties between access to cash disbursements (issuing checks or handling signed checks) and keeping purchases and accounts payable records.
6. Only authorized goods, other assets, and services should be accepted and/or paid for.	• Receiving procedures that provide an independent count of quantities received. • Comparison of specifications and quantities of goods, other assets, and services received to approved purchase orders. • Testing procedures appropriate in the circumstances for goods, other assets, and services received.

PAYROLL FUNCTIONS

Authorization Objectives

Specific Objective	*Examples of Selected Control Procedures and Techniques*
7. Employees, employee benefits, and perquisites should be properly authorized.	• Procedures for hiring and terminating employees. • Policies on vacation pay, overtime pay, sick pay, and other similar benefits. • Establishment by the board of overall policies for employee benefits and perquisites, such as company cars and use of company airplane. • Approval by the board or a committee thereof of significant individual benefits or perquisites. • Assigned responsibility for effecting compliance with company guidelines.
8. Compensation should be made at authorized rates for services rendered, and	• Assigned responsibility for approval of wages, salaries, and commission rates.

Specific Objective	*Examples of Selected Control Procedures and Techniques*
payroll deductions and adjustments to payroll-related accounts should be properly authorized.	• Assigned responsibility for approval of additions, deductions, and other changes to basic payroll information. • Maintenance of personnel files, including support for payroll deductions. • Supervisory approval of time cards or sheets. • Periodic comparison, possibly on a test basis, of rates paid to (a) individual approvals or (b) overall approvals, such as a union contract or commission policy statement. • Assigned responsibility for approval of adjustments of specific types (for example, accounting errors, termination payments, special payments).

Accounting Objectives

Specific Objective	*Examples of Selected Control Procedures and Techniques*
9. Recorded payroll should be for work actually performed.	• Policies and procedures covering accounting routines and related approval procedures for the major payroll functions. • Use of time clocks or timekeepers. • Reconciliation of payroll records to production records when employee pay is based on output. • Review of payroll register by individuals at a responsible level of management. • Comparison of actual payroll to budgeted amounts.
10. Payroll and related withholdings should be correctly computed and remitted when due.	• Reconciliation of payroll register to independent controls (such as hash totals) over source data. • Assigned responsibility for preparation of payroll tax returns.
11. Payroll costs should be recorded at the	• Review of payroll source data by supervisors.

Specific Objective	*Examples of Selected Control Procedures and Techniques*
appropriate amounts and in the appropriate period and should be properly classified in the accounts.	• Reconciliation of payroll distribution to gross pay. • Guidelines for determining account distribution (capital vs. expense, inventory vs. expense, etc.). • A suitable chart of accounts and standard journal entries. • Procedures for making appropriate financial statement

Asset Safeguarding Objectives

Specific Objective	*Examples of Selected Control Procedures and Techniques*
12. Access to personnel and payroll records should be suitably controlled to prevent or detect within a timely period duplicate or improper payments.	• Institution of physical security measures over these records. • Segregation of duties between personnel, timekeeping, and payroll preparation and distribution. • Controlled mailing of annual W-2 statements and independent follow-up on any discrepancies.
13. Payments should be made only to authorized employees.	• Periodic independent distribution of signed payroll checks, possibly on a test basis or by rotating employees. • Assigned responsibility for custody of and follow-up on unclaimed payroll checks.

DISBURSEMENT FUNCTIONS

Authorization Objectives

Specific Objective	*Examples of Selected Control Procedures and Techniques*
14. Disbursements should be made only for properly authorized expenditures.	• Formal designation of authority to sign checks, including establishment of requirements for dual signatures. • Examination by individuals authorized to sign checks of documentation, possibly on a test basis in accordance with established cri-

Specific Objective	*Examples of Selected Control Procedures and Techniques*
	teria, supporting proposed cash disbursements. • Independent mailing of signed checks. • Use of imprest bank accounts and comparison of the deposits to such accounts to expenditures. • Investigation of unusual amounts charged to "purchase discounts lost."
15. Adjustments to cash accounts should be properly authorized.	• Assigned responsibility for review of bank reconciliations and for approval of adjustments to cash accounts.

Accounting Objectives

Specific Objective	*Examples of Selected Control Procedures and Techniques*
16. Disbursements should be recorded at the appropriate amount and in the appropriate period and should be properly classified in the accounts.	• Policies and procedures covering accounting routines and related approval procedures for the major disbursement functions. • Accounting for all checks issued. • A suitable chart of accounts and standard journal entries.

Asset Safeguarding Objectives

Specific Objective	*Examples of Selected Control Procedures and Techniques*
17. Access to cash and cash disbursements records should be suitably controlled to prevent or detect within a timely period duplicate or improper payments.	• Segregation of duties between the accounts payroll and cash disbursements functions; segregation of duties within the cash disbursements function between the issuance of checks or disbursement of cash and the maintenance of cash disbursements records. • Safekeeping procedures for blank checks and facsimile signature plates. • Safekeeping procedures over the signing of checks (dual signa-

	Examples of Selected Control Procedures and Techniques
	tures, control over signing equipment and signature plates). • Reconciliation of the number of checks issued on a facsimile signature machine to the number of checks prepared. • Mutilation and retention of spoiled checks. • Independent bank reconciliations, including (a) comparison, possibly on a test basis, of paid checks with cash disbursements records and (b) examination, possibly on a test basis, of paid checks for alterations, unauthorized signatures, and unusual

THE PRODUCTION OR CONVERSION CYCLE

The production or conversion cycle covers the functions involved in production planning and control, inventory planning and control, property and deferred cost accounting, and cost accounting.

"Authorization" in the production or conversion cycle encompasses the types and quantities of goods to be manufactured or services to be provided; the methods and materials to be used; the inventory levels or service capabilities to be maintained; the scheduling of goods to be produced or services to be provided; adjustments and policies with respect thereto, such as provisions for obsolete inventory or write-downs of deferred costs; dispositions of property, scrap, and obsolete or excessive inventory.

"Accounting" encompasses the procedures and techniques used to control the recording and classification of transactions that relate to resources used, completed production, and inventory, and includes depreciation, amortization, and gain or loss on the sale or disposition of property.

"Asset Safeguarding" relates (a) to protecting the company from loss of inventory on property and (b) to protecting important records.

Authorization Objectives

Specific Objective	*Examples of Selected Control Procedures and Techniques*
1. The types and quantities of goods to be manufactured	• Preparation and review of sales forecasts.

Specific Objective	*Examples of Selected Control Procedures and Techniques*
or services to be provided, the methods and materials to be used, the inventory levels or service capabilities to be maintained, and the scheduling of goods to be produced or services to be provided should be properly authorized.	• Establishment of a production control function. • Approval of an overall production and inventory control plan, and of changes thereto. • Bills of material for goods to be produced. • Requirement for capital expenditure requests over a specified amount to include a documented cost-benefit analysis.
2. Adjustments to inventory, property, deferred costs, and cost of sales should be properly authorized.	• Policies for determining excess or obsolete inventory quantities. • Assigned responsibility for review and approval of adjustments, including adjustments to standard costs. • Periodic review of the reasonableness of lives assigned to classes of property and to deferred costs, and of the methods of depreciation and amortization.
3. Dispositions of property, scrap, and obsolete or excessive inventory should be properly authorized.	• Requirement for all movements or shipments of merchandise and assets out of the physical facility to be accompanied by appropriate documentation. • Periodic follow-up on disposition of inventory identified as obsolete or excessive.

Accounting Objectives

Specific Objective	*Examples of Selected Control Procedures and Techniques*
4. Resources used and completed production should be properly recorded on a timely basis.	• Inventory released to production based on bills of material that are used as sources for postings to inventory records. • Additional inventory transfers to production based on documents approved by a designated employee, which would include review of scrap reports. • Physical transfer of completed production on hand to a storeroom.

Specific Objective	*Examples of Selected Control Procedures and Techniques*
	• Independent check of quantities transferred to storerooms and quantities shipped. • Comparison of quantities transferred to storerooms to production reports. • Perpetual inventory records. • Periodic physical inventories or cycle counts. • Reconciliation of payroll costs to labor charged to inventory. • Investigation of significant amounts of over- and underabsorbed overhead. • Periodic physical inventory (where existence cannot be determined by other means) of property and equipment.
5. Inventory, production costs, depreciation of property, and amortization of deferred costs should be properly accumulated and classified in the accounts.	• Inventory pricing policies that are in conformity with generally accepted accounting principles. • Policies and procedures covering accounting routines and related approval procedures for the major functions within the conversion cycle, including sales or other dispositions of property. • Use of a cost system (job cost, process cost) that accumulates and allocates production costs in an appropriate manner (by cost center, department, and/or product) and that provides information adequate for pricing inventories, appropriate to the manufacturing process. • Use of standard costs with investigation of variances. • Periodic comparison of standard costs to actual costs (comparison of material costs to vendor invoices, comparison of labor rates and hours to actual rates and results of time studies, analysis of over- or underabsorbed overhead). • A suitable chart of accounts and standard journal entries.

Specific Objective	*Examples of Selected Control Procedures and Techniques*
	• Written, properly communicated cut-off procedures on transfer among inventory accounts, and review of compliance with procedures. (Purchase and sales cut-offs are covered in the expenditures and revenue cycles.) • Review of priced inventory listings for conformity with established pricing policies. • Individual records for items of property that include description, location, cost, depreciation, tax, and investment credit information. • Maintenance of appropriate records to support amortization of deferred charges. • Periodic review of appropriateness of depreciation and amortization rates.
6. All costs of sales should be recorded at the appropriate amounts and in the appropriate periods and should be properly classified in the accounts.	• Procedures that provide for the same document (e.g., a sales invoice) to serve as the source document for the recognition of revenue and the related receivable for the recognition of cost of sales and the related reduction of inventory. • Reconciliation of inventory records to the general ledger on a regular basis. • Physical inventories at the end of annual reporting periods and/or on a cycle basis.

Asset Safeguarding Objectives

Specific Objective	*Examples of Selected Control Procedures and Techniques*
7. Inventory should be protected from unauthorized use or removal.	• Physical controls (fences, restricted-access storerooms, guards, inspection of personnel, independent storeroom clerks). • Physical control procedures that vary with the individual dollar value of inventory items and with the volume of transactions.

Specific Objective	*Examples of Selected Control Procedures and Techniques*
8. Items of property should be properly controlled.	• Identification tags affixed upon acquisition. • Physical security procedures in plants and offices (fences, guards, etc.). • Periodic physical inventories of items susceptible to removal, giving due regard to the cost and lives of such items.
9. Access to inventory, property, cost, and production control records should be suitably controlled to prevent or detect within a timely period improper dispositions of inventory and property.	• Segregation of duties between those who have access to inventories and those responsible for inventory, cost, and production control records. ("Those who have access to inventories" includes those who physically receive, handle, and ship; it also includes those who prepare shipping orders or other disposal authorizations.) • Periodic physical inventories under the supervision of personnel other than those who have access to inventories. • Investigation of significant physical inventory differences by those who do not have access to inventories. • Segregation of duties between those who have custody of movable property and those who maintain the property records.

THE FINANCING CYCLE

The financing cycle covers the functions involved with the issuance and redemption of capital stock and the recording of transactions therein; the payment of dividends; the investigation and selection of appropriate forms of financing, including lease transactions; debt management, including monitoring compliance with covenants; investment management; and physical custody of securities.

"Authorization" in the financing cycle encompasses the sources, nature, and terms of equity and debt financing and any changes therein, and the nature and terms of investments, dividends, and other transactions affecting capital accounts.

"Accounting" encompasses the procedures and techniques used to control the recording and classification of those transactions.

"Asset Safeguarding" relates primarily to safekeeping procedures and segregation of duties with respect to investments, debt, and capital stock.

Authorization Objectives

Specific Objective	*Examples of Selected Control Procedures and Techniques*
1. The sources, nature, and terms associated with equity and debt financings (including lease transactions) and any adjustments or changes therein should be properly authorized.	• Approval by the board of guidelines for selection among financing alternatives based upon such factors as covenants of existing financial arrangements, rating agency considerations, existing banking relationships, internal cost of capital, and corporate financial objectives. • Approval by the board of significant financing transactions. • Assignment of approval authority for less significant financing transactions to specific members of management. • Maintenance and review of loan covenant checklists. • Preparation and review of projected cash requirements with respect to payouts relating to existing loans and equity securities. • Preparation and regular review of key financial ratios and statistics. • Legal review of all loan agreements prior to signing.
2. The nature and terms of investments, dividends, and other transactions affecting capital accounts and related adjustments should be properly authorized.	• Approval by the board of guidelines for selection among investment alternatives based upon such factors as corporate charter and bylaws, legal restrictions, required rates of return, risk, cash flow, and portfolio diversification. • Preparation and review of financial forecasts, including cash flow analyses. • Preparation and review of lease versus buy analyses.

Examples of Selected Control Procedures and Techniques

- Approval by the board of dividends, stock splits, treasury stock transactions, and significant investments.
- Assignment of approval authority for less significant investments to specific members of management.

Accounting Objectives

Specific Objective	*Examples of Selected Control Procedures and Techniques*
3. Financing, investing, and capital transactions should be promptly recorded and properly classified in the accounts.	• Policies and procedures covering accounting routines and related approval procedures for the major functions within the financing cycle. • Schedules of notes, interest payable, and commitments. • Schedules of marketable securities, including certificate numbers and tax and dividend information. • Procedures to accumulate and review financial data of investees on a regular basis. • Reconciliation of dividends paid with shares outstanding. • Reconciliation of interest accruals on debt and interest and dividends earned on investments with terms of individual notes or securities. • Comparison of recorded transactions with minutes of meetings of the board or a committee thereof. • Review of interest income and expense and cash flow analyses by reference to budgets and prior period amounts. • Procedures to account for the registration and transfer of issued shares. • Utilization of banks, brokers, independent registrars and transfer agents, and other third parties

	Examples of Selected Control Procedures and Techniques
	to account for changes in investments, changes in the company's capital stock accounts, and changes in ownership of the company's issued shares. • Prompt review of broker's advices.

Asset Safeguarding Objectives

Specific Objective	*Examples of Selected Control Procedures and Techniques*
4. Access to debt, equity, and investment records and to investment securities and capital stock records should be suitably controlled to prevent or detect within a timely period improper dispositions of investments or of funds from debt or equity transactions.	• Segregation of custody of marketable securities from accounting for marketable securities. • Use of independent safekeeping custodians. • Physical controls (safes, safe deposit boxes, etc.) • Procedures requiring two individuals to be present whenever such documents are inspected. • Maintenance of a log showing securities added to or removed from safekeeping. • Periodic comparison of securities to a schedule of marketable securities. • Segregation of duties between access to cash receipts from investments, debt, and equity, and keeping the related cash receipts records.

THE EXTERNAL FINANCIAL REPORTING CYCLE

The external financial reporting cycle covers the functions involved in preparing journal entries and posting transactions to the general ledger (to the extent such functions are not performed within other cycles); deciding the generally accepted accounting principles that the company should follow; gathering and consolidating the information required for the preparation of financial statements and other external historical financial reports, including related disclosures; preparing and reviewing the financial statements and other external reports.

"Authorization" in the external financial reporting cycle encompasses the company's accounting policies; major valuation, adjustment, and estimation decisions; and decisions with respect to the proper accounting for unusual or nonrecurring transactions or events.

"Accounting" encompasses a supervisory or review responsibility with respect to the procedures followed within other cycles as well as direct responsibility for the preparation of financial statements and reports and the accounting procedures and routines used in their preparation.

"Asset Safeguarding" relates primarily to controls that restrict access to important records and to appropriate physical safekeeping procedures.

Authorization Objectives

Specific Objective	*Examples of Selected Control Procedures and Techniques*
1. Accounting policies, including selection among alternative accounting principles, should be properly authorized.	• Written policy statements. • Written procedures manuals. • Assigned responsibility for approval of accounting policies. • Timely review of the selection of accounting principles with independent auditors.
2. Adjustments to account balances, including valuation estimates and write-offs, should be properly authorized.	• Assigned individuals to approve adjustments and write-offs. • Requirements for documentation, including supporting calculations, of adjustments and write-offs. • Assigned responsibility for independent review and approval of adjustments and write-offs.
3. Journal entries should be properly authorized.	• Use of standard journal entries. • Assigned responsibility for approval of standard and nonstandard journal entries.
4. The accounting recognition given to unusual or nonrecurring transactions and events not specifically covered in existing policy statements or procedures manuals should be properly authorized.	• Policies requiring the reporting of significant unusual or nonrecurring transactions or events to top management. • Timely review of the accounting recognition appropriate for such transactions and events with independent auditors. • Approval of the accounting treatment for such transactions or events by a senior financial officer.

Specific Objective	*Examples of Selected Control Procedures and Techniques*
5. Financial statements, including related disclosures, and other external financial reports should be prepared in conformity with management's authorization.	• Assigned responsibility for advising management of requirements of existing and new accounting rules and of the rules and regulations of appropriate regulatory bodies. • Assigned responsibility for accumulating information for disclosure. • Assigned responsibility for review of all external financial reports. • Policies and procedures governing the preparation and presentation of financial statements. • Requirement for written representations on financial statement matters from responsible employees. • Review by management and the board of directors relative to presentation and disclosure of external financial reports.

Accounting Objectives

Specific Objective	*Examples of Selected Control Procedures and Techniques*
6. Financial statements, including related disclosures, should be prepared in conformity with generally accepted accounting principles or any other criteria applicable to such statements.	• Written financial statement closing schedule with assignment of specific responsibilities, including review responsibilities. • Forms that identify for subsidiaries, branches, departments, etc., the data that is to be reported. • Overall review of the consolidated and consolidating financial statements, including comparisons to the prior year and budgeted amounts. • Reconciliation of general ledger balances to subsidiary ledgers or records. • Standard elimination, currency translation, and reclassification entries. • Procedures for an independent comparison of the financial state-

Specific Objective	*Examples of Selected Control Procedures and Techniques*
	ment working papers to source data and a comparison of elimination, currency translation, and reclassification entries to those made in prior periods. • Examinations by internal and external auditors.
7. Other external financial reports, including other information included in documents containing financial statements, should be prepared in conformity with generally accepted accounting principles or any other criteria applicable to such reports, and should be consistent with the financial statements, where applicable.	• Designation of individuals permitted to discuss financial results with individuals outside of the company. • Assigned responsibility for preparation of government and regulatory reports and for preparation procedures (similar to those in item 6, above) to the extent necessary. • Assigned responsibility for reviewing all financial information presented outside of the financial statements.

Asset Safeguarding Objectives

Specific Objective	*Examples of Selected Control Procedures and Techniques*
8. Adjustments and write-offs made to the account balances should not impair the accountability for actual amounts.	• Use of contra accounts for valuation adjustments. • Use of memorandum accounts to control adjustments such as bad debt writeoffs.
9. Access, direct and indirect, to accounting and financial records used in the preparation of external financial reports should be suitably controlled to guard against physical hazards and to prevent or detect within a timely period unauthorized entries.	• Suitable restrictions on access to work papers used in preparing financial statements. • Suitable safekeeping facilities for work papers, supporting documentation, etc., to guard against physical hazards. • Suitable records retention program. • Assigned responsibility for approval of all changes in policies and procedures covering accounting routines and related approval procedures.

Index

A

B

C

D

E

F

G

H